WARSHIP Volume VIII

Managing Editor Robert Gardiner
Editor Randal Gray
Art Editor Mark Stevens

Frontispiece
The Duke of Wellington about 1890 while
serving as a receiving ship at Portsmouth.
The design history of this ship and its part in
the development of the steam
line-of-battleship is outlined by Andrew
Lambert in this volume.
CPL

Published in the UK by
Conway Maritime Press Limited
24 Bride Lane
Fleet Street
London EC4Y 8DR

**Published and distributed in the
United States of America and Canada by**
the Naval Institute Press
Annapolis Maryland 21402

Library of Congress Catalog Card No 78-55455
UK ISBN 0 85177 354 0
USA ISBN 0-87021-983-9

Manufactured in the United Kingdom

Contents

EDITORIAL

With this issue *Warship* enters its eighth year of continuous publication which is perhaps as good a time as any for some reassessment of the magazine's aims and contents, the more so since one has inherited the daunting responsibility of editing it in the wake of the highly expert John Roberts. After five years as editor John found his other commitments too taxing; his scholarship and draughtsmanship will be sorely missed.

There is no doubt of the ever increasing validity of the subject. The unrelenting expansion of the Soviet Navy, the Falklands War, recent US Navy Caribbean and Lebanon involvements, the continuing unchronicled Gulf War, and the Royal Navy's Trident submarine programme are just a few examples of the contemporary and topical relevance of *fighting* ships. This year also marks the 70th anniversary of the 1914-18 War, a struggle whose naval aspects perhaps deserve more general interest than they get and whose very few surviving participants have a last opportunity to make their voices heard.

It will be 40 years this year since history's greatest seaborne invasion (Operation Neptune) and its largest naval battle – Leyte Gulf. Our ever lengthening perspective on World War II, which now makes the term postwar totally inadequate, does not seem to diminish either the flood of books and programmes about it or the widespread fascination for all its aspects. Yet strangely, the Korean War, which saw so many crucial maritime operations, has exerted practically no interest at all. Similarly the naval aspects of the Vietnam War, and they extended over a whole inland theatre of war (as Norman Friedman's article in this issue reminds us), get scant recognition. And since then, for the 1970s alone, Sir James Cable has tabulated over 60 incidents of gunboat diplomacy.

From these lofty thoughts it is best to descend rapidly and ask our readers in general what kind of articles they would like to see this year and beyond. It is certainly our intention to reinstate regular book reviews for we feel that we can both review individual titles at valuable length and monitor all the English-language specialist warship literature that appears. The aim in the latter category is to give full publication details and an exact count of their illustrations (something publishers do not always do) together with a brief assessment of the book's content and value. This is quite apart from the full reviews. A's and A's too should be more than occasional if readers continue to send us valuable comments. Those who lack the inclination or time to write complete articles please note!

As regards the overall balance of the journal, it is obvious that surface ships, submarines, naval aviation and warship pictorials should usually be represented in each issue. Yet mine warfare vessels, an essential, and numerous if unglamorous type, have seldom been covered save just recently. The same comment might apply to coastal and river forces. Is it necessarily true that big ships monopolise all the interest? To what extent should auxiliaries feature given the current arguable narrowing of distinctions between warship and merchantman, a theme introduced by Captain Roger Villar's article in this issue. Warship technology is a rich area for analysis: what about internal shipboard communications and ship's radio/cipher equipment? There has never been an article on the living conditions aboard warships, surely a vital factor in assessing their endurance and fighting effectiveness. What sailors think of their ships, rightly or wrongly, is equally as important as the more technical design features.

Operational history is a preference of this editor, perhaps a reflection of his technical shortcomings, but it is no good rehashing the familiar subjects unless they are given the kind of fresh comparison and deep analysis seen in the last issue's 'The Sinking of *Bismarck*'. It is ironic that warships generally see more action firing at land targets (shore bombardment either in support of landings up to 20 miles inland or the classic ship versus forts variety) than they ever do firing at their own kind yet navies rarely trained for this role before World War II. Today the Falklands and the Lebanon have again reminded us that this is *not* a secondary role. Indeed the medium calibre gun has made a comeback against the missile for this very reason. Shore bombardment is a vast subject in its own right and badly needs a history, although *Warship* can already claim to have made a start with D K Brown's Shells at Sevastopol (issue 10) and Norman Friedman's Amphibious Fire Support articles (issues 15 and 16).

Is the balance of periods, national interest, and between illustrations right in the journal? We ask these questions not out of bewilderment or even because 1984 is supposed to be compulsory for self-appraisal, but in a genuine attempt to improve a well-established journal for a worldwide readership of high intelligence and specialised knowledge from whom we would like to hear more.

Randal Gray

MERCHANT SHIPS AT WAR
The Falklands Experience

By Captain Roger Villar

Merchant ships have been used in war for centuries to support and strengthen navies. Never however have they been taken up so quickly in such a wide variety of roles as during the Falklands War of April to June 1982. Extraordinary initiatives were taken in support of the national need and much of it is as yet unsung and unpublicised. Yet there is no doubt that, without their support, the Royal Navy and the other fighting services could not have done their job and the war, brief though it was, would not have been won.

When that crisis first deepened at the end of March, the Navy had already begun the run down started by the Government's Defence White Paper 'The Way Forward' of the year before. Even without that however it would not have been strong enough to fight a major amphibious battle 8000 miles from home. Its amphibious capability had been designed for a relatively small landing in northern Norway and both major landing ships were destined for disposal with one already in reserve. There were no friendly bases nearer to the Falklands than Ascension Island nor bunkering facilities closer than Freetown. The whole structure of the Fleet had become more and more of fighting a NATO war in the North Atlantic alongside allies but not overseas alone. Even its own merchant type support in the Royal Fleet Auxiliary (RFA) was too small for the task and its specialised ships needed to be resupplied so that they, in turn, could supply and fuel the Fleet.

Yet all the plans which existed for the use of merchant ships to support the Fleet also centred on that same task in the North Atlantic. Ships had indeed been nominated not only to bring troops and supplies across the Atlantic from America in war but also to act as convoy escort oilers, as minesweepers, and in many other roles. But these latter roles were all relatively minor and close to home. Nothing existed on which to base the call up and major modification of a large number of merchant ships. They were needed not only as troopships, minesweepers and stores ships but also as assault ships, dispatch vessels, fleet repair ships, aircraft and helicopter ferries, hospital ships, tankers, water carriers, a minehunter support ship, salvage tugs, and a mooring vessel.

Thus when the Queen signed an Order in Council on Sunday 4 April 1982 authorising the requisitioning of British flag shipping, she set in train a unique and extraordinary series of events. In broad terms, the requirements for commercial shipping were thought out in the Ministry of Defence and possible ships to meet the need were then selected in conjunction with the Department of Trade from extensive records which they had kept up to date though without such an emergency in mind. The general plan of the modifications could then be worked out but survey teams had to be sent to visit the ships to confirm their suitability and to work out the further details. Ships were visited throughout Europe and one even as far afield as the Gulf of Oman. They were then chartered whenever possible. However there were a large number of occasions when charter was not possible because of an owner's existing contractual commitment and requisition had to be resorted to instead.

Subsequently ships were sailed to a fitting out port, generally in the two home Royal Dockyards of Devonport and Portsmouth, though *Uganda* was converted in Gibraltar and the minesweepers in Rosyth with some other ships being taken in hand elsewhere in limited numbers. Each presented a new problem when it came in with conversions being made at the same time as ships were being loaded, sometimes with thousands of tons of stores. Everywhere men volunteered for the work. One workman was touring HMS *Victory* with his wife on that early Sunday when he saw his workmates hard at it. He promptly handed his camera to his wife and appeared home 36 hours later. A senior Naval Constructor was celebrating his 25th wedding anniversary when he heard the news. His house became an operations room. Civilians volunteered their services as much as those already serving. It seemed that everyone throughout the nation was keen to get in and do his bit and the response and result was tremendous. Of the more than 50 merchant ships which were taken up, the average time for conversion and storing was no more than four days although some quite considerable works were completed.

STANDARD MODIFICATIONS

Virtually every ship had to have certain standard modifications. They needed additional communications gear to be able to talk to the Navy. Satellite communications

Atlantic Conveyor after conversion. As well as helicopters and
a Sea Harrier the rubber containers for aviation fuel
(AVCAT) can be seen amidships.

Crown copyright.

were also fitted widely because of the remoteness of the
Falklands and the difficulties of normal H/F radio communications. Replenishment at sea gear was installed in
virtually every ship to enable them to receive fuel and
water, and sometimes stores, from RFA ships. Many
ships needed additional fuel which could often be
achieved by converting ballast tanks although this, and
the other modifications made, often meant that the
Department of Trade had to grant exemptions from the
normal rules. Freshwater was a constantly recurring
problem, fortunately solved by installing a reverse
osmosis system already under evaluation by the Navy.
This required little but power supplies and piping to
cope with the additional men needed to operate the
communications and replenishment at sea gear as well as
the troops that might be carried. More accommodation
and galley capacity and lavatories were needed for the
naval parties and troops. The list is almost endless
though it varied widely from ship to ship.

Over and above these basic modifications, ships had

Once peace returned the normal pattern was for one or two
warships to maintain alongside the repair ship *Stena Inspector*
while remaining at short notice. The frigate HMS *Avenger* and
a Type 42 destroyer alongside.

Capt D Ede, Stena Inspector

1 MV *Norland* in Port Stanley harbour after the campaign in which she had taken 2 Para to war.

Windjammer

2 The stores ship *Avelona Star* loading in Portsmouth.

Blue Star Line Ltd

3 The 15,974-ton P & O tanker *Anco Charger* in the Falklands with a Type 42 destroyer alongside.

Radio Officer T McGrattan, Stena Seaspread

to be altered for their new functions. Many were fitted with helicopter platforms to enable troops and stores to be transferred rapidly. This was particularly necessary because of the appalling weather conditions expected in the South Atlantic winter. Small boat transfer would be impossible. Indeed enormous seas and a maximum wind speed of 105 knots were finally reported. Those helicopter decks however had to be strong enough to withstand a fully loaded helicopter crash landing. In some ships adequate strength could be found over swimming pools which had been designed to support 70 to 100 tons of water. Aluminium superstructures were however found in some passenger ships and were far from strong enough to support such heavy weights. Even the stowage of stores on *Canberra*'s superstructure caused problems. In these cases extra stiffening had to be installed which could mean going down several decks to find adequate strength. It was typical however of the way things were achieved that a Naval Constructor walked round the *Queen Elizabeth 2* deciding, on the spot, what had to be

3

cut away to provide a helicopter deck. He was followed by a workman marking it out, with another immediately behind beginning to cut.

AIRCRAFT FERRIES

The most involved work perhaps went in to the aircraft ferries. There were four of these – standard container ships which had large and relatively open decks and considerable cargo capacity below decks. Their role was to take aircraft, principally helicopters, to the scene of action rather than to operate them with the Fleet. After the first conversion, the *Atlantic Conveyor*, ships were also given a capability to maintain helicopters which was a vitally needed facility with aircraft in the Falklands flying every conceivable hour and few other maintenance facilities available. Conversion entailed stacking standard containers around the upper deck to form protective walls and also to use these where possible for such items as aviation fuel stowage and workshops. All fittings on the deck were removed, including the normal container securing points, so as to provide a flat deck for flying. *Atlantic Conveyor* had an open uncovered deck and took down 25 aircraft including both helicopters and Harrier fighters. Later ships had a light covering placed across the containers to give a sheltered hangar though there was some difficulty in making these properly weather and light proof.

Another major conversion was that of the *Uganda* to a hospital ship which was completed in 65 hours by Gibraltar Dockyard. This work included a helicopter deck for casualties, the provision of an operating theatre, and high, medium and low dependency wards as well as all the ancillaries of medical practice such as an X-ray room and a dispensary.

REPAIR SHIPS

One class of ship which both surprised and delighted the Navy was the fleet repair ships in which both *Stena Seaspread* and *Stena Inspector* were taken up. These remarkable ships, of about 6000grt, were designed for diving and surface support in offshore oil field operations. They have a steaming range of 21,000 miles and a system of propellers combined with a dynamic positioning system which allows them to hold their position to within three metres in a Force 9 gale. They were fitted with additional workshops and store rooms as well as accommodation for a large naval party and diving team of 160 to 170 on top of their normal crew. *Stena Seaspread* thus repaired and maintained 39 ships while in the Falklands as well as restoring the old whaling base at Grytviken (South Georgia) and getting the ancient generators to work again after many years of disuse.

Indeed everything about the Merchant Navy ships taken up, known as the STUFT, surprised and delighted the Navy. The *Uganda*, as a full hospital ship, with the support given by the *Canberra* with her smaller installation, the ambulance ships and shore facilities achieved wonders with a death and sickness rate that was phenomenally low – far lower than that of the Argentinians who were close to their home base. The RMS *St Helena* was outstanding as a minehunter support ship in looking after her two small charges and enabling them to carry out their work in the minimum of time with little breakdown. The 15 tankers which were taken up prior to the end of hostilities were a fundamental part of the logistic chain with, at one time, 450,000 tons of fuel on the high seas between Britain and the Falklands. The one anchor handling tug, *Wimpey Seahorse*, laid moorings in freezing conditions so cold that cast iron shackles disintegrated and crowbars broke. So it went on down to the small salvage tugs that supported the damaged ships and brought the sunken Argentine submarine *Santa Fe* to the surface.

1 RMS *St Helena* (3150grt) in her role as mother ship refuelling the 'Hunt' class minehunters *Brecon* and *Ledbury* which swept at least 11 mines after hostilities.
Curnow Shipping Ltd

2 The 1615-ton trawler *Junella*, HM Auxiliary of the 11th Minesweeping Squadron, coping with the South Atlantic
John M Davis & Associates

3 British Telecom's cable ship *Iris* sails from Devonport 29 April 1982 after modification to serve as a dispatch vessel.
British Telecom International

1

2

3

LESSONS FOR THE FUTURE

Whatever has gone before, there is no doubt that the merchant fleet has again proved its worth and the Navy has learned that its support is essential in distant water operations. There are indeed still some 20 merchant vessels supporting the Falkland Islands garrison nearly two years after the crisis. The Ro-Ro ferry *St Edmund* has already been taken into naval service. The cellular container ship *Astronomer*, used in the Falklands as a helicopter transport with maintenance facilities, has been chartered and converted to carry anti-submarine helicopters and naval stores. She will operate in support of the Fleet as an RFA rather than, as in the Falklands, in support of the land battle.

It all raises continuing questions as to whether the merchant fleet will be able to do so much in the future and whether more comprehensive preparations should be made in peacetime. There is no doubt that Britain was lucky in 1982 even down to the weather at home which remained consistently good and allowed ships to be modified and stored with the minimum of delay.

Recognition that an event such as the Falklands could occur again in the future is the first step leading to better planning. It is difficult however to proceed much beyond this. Modifications made to ships in peacetime to make them more rapidly available in war, such as improvements to endurance or freshwater making capacity or communciations, could well involve some loss of efficiency or cargo carrying capacity. Although perhaps relatively small, that could add up to something considerable over a period of world shipping recession not over yet and owners would need to be subsidised. Similarly the peacetime provision of armaments for merchant ships would be expensive. And though there are many proposals for containerised armaments and equipments which could be kept on shore and lifted on board rapidly when needed, none of these are cheap. Even the conversion of *Astronomer* referred to above requires the addition of some 73 specially fitted ISO containers to allow her to operate and maintain four anti-submarine helicopters in support of the Fleet.

The tug *Yorkshireman* assisting the larger *Salvageman* move the Argentine submarine *Santa Fe* to a safer berth in S Georgia. HMS *Endurance* is in the background.

United Towing Ltd

The hospital ship *Uganda* at work.
Windjammer

Money is the key to the problem as much as the recognition that it is necessary to prepare for similar events in the future. Luck came into many aspects of the successful retaking of the Islands as much as did the extreme dedication and initiatives of all those concerned with modifying the ships as well as of operating them. We should not rely on luck again.

NOTE

Captain Villar's forthcoming book Merchant Ships at War: The Falklands Experience *will be published by Conway Maritime Press in April 1984 at £9.50. It gives full details of the requisition, conversion and deployment of the nearly 50 merchantmen sent to the South Atlantic, being illustrated with numerous photographs not seen before including many taken by the crews at the time.*

The Chinese Battleships

By Andrzej Mach

German *Sachsen* class central citadel ironclad *Baden* on which the Chinese ships were patterned. *Baden*, last in a class of 4, was completing at Kiel just after the Chinese ships were both launched. She is seen here flying a vice-admiral's flag at the Spithead Review of 1889 with one of her boats alongside.

CPL

The Chinese Navy dates back to a period before the Royal Navy was born under the last two Henrys. However from the early part of the seventeenth century onward, while progress in Europe was rapid, Chinese naval architecture remained stationary. When Europe built their first armoured ships and steam replaced sails China still operated only a number of junks. At the time of the Second Opium War (1858) China possessed 826 junks and no steamers. The situation improved in the late 1860s when a few gunboats were bought abroad and the Foochow and Kiangnan yards began to build the first steam warships for China, but at the time of the Sino-French War (1883) about 250 junks were still in service. Moreover, the organisation of the Chinese Navy also played a part in decreasing its fighting value. The Navy was organised by provinces grouped as pairs and placed under governor-generals. Four such pairs operated naval fleets: Kwantung and Kwangsi in the far south,

Fukien and Chekiang; Kiangsi and Anhwei; and Chihli, the single province around Peking.

Small naval fleets were also operated by local authorities which were usually independent and seldom co-operated. This obsolete system had developed over a thousand years, and although reorganised a few times, prevailed until the end of the Manchu Ch'ing dynasty in 1911. Thus the Chinese Imperial Navy lacked unity of purpose, although nominally the whole fleet was under the orders of the Imperial court.

The threat from a much more united and rapidly modernising Japan began with the Formosa crisis of 1874, when a Japanese expedition was sent to occupy the island ostensibly to suppress Formosan pirates, and then came the seizure of the Liu chiu Islands. Moreover, the 1875 Japanese naval programme began with an order for three ironclads in Britain. Peking's reply in the spring of 1875 was to establish a Sea Defence Fund to be made up of one half of the 40% remissions from the maritime customs receipts. This Fund was to be divided between the northern and southern commissioners of trade and accounted for the supremacy of the fleets of the North (Peiyang) and South (Nanyang) groups of provinces, at the time under Li Hung chang and Li Tsung

Chinese battleship *Ting Yüan* rigged for her delivery voyage.
One of her torpedo boats is hoisted aboard.

CPL

hsi respectively. Li Hung chang, then commissioner of trade for the northern ports and governor general of Chihli province, had considerable influence on Chinese naval activity in the last quarter of the nineteenth century, although he personally controlled only the Peiyang Fleet. He intended to replace the old system of the provincial navies by one, centralised fleet under his command. The Fleet he planned was to possess three or four capital ships and a number of smaller units.

The first ships purchased by China using the Fund were the Rendel type gunboats. An order was placed by Li Hung chang with Sir Robert Hart, an Englishman in Chinese service as Inspector General of the Customs. Li Hung chang did not always deal with Hart, preferring to purchase through his own channels and being rather influenced by a German, Gustav Detring, the customs commissioner at Tientsin and a good advertiser of the German market.

In 1877 the Chinese minister in Europe, Liu, was invited to observe the launching ceremony of the German battleship *Sachsen* in Stettin. The Chinese delegation sent by him on 21 July 1877 visited the Baltic yard and Li Hung chang received a complete report on the German ships. He learned that the German vessels were not inferior to British ones and he moved some students to the German yard. A year later Li Fong Pao replaced Liu and became the Chinese Minister to Germany, Italy, Holland and Austria. Li Hung chang kept in close touch with him and he became Li Hung's purchasing agent. Li Fong's reports suggested ordering the ships for China in Germany.

China's favourable financial situation in 1880 caused Li Hung chang to try to realise his plans for a large Chinese fleet. He wanted to build four fast armoured ships (two for Peiyang and two for the Nanyang fleets) and ten torpedo boats. He preferred to order in Britain but British reluctance to sell China modern ships in the face of Russian objections scuppered the Chinese plans to supply the Fukien squadron with two British-built cruisers and was the main cause of the orders for capital ships going to Germany.

The official order was signed by the Chinese Imperial Government, represented by Li Fong Pao, and Stettiner Maschinenbau Actien Gesallschaft 'Vulcan' of Stettin Bredow on 4/8 January 1881 in Berlin to build two battleships (called *Panzercorvetten* = armoured corvettes in the contract) of the improved *Sachsen* class, the first to be delivered in 18 months, ten torpedo boats and a few auxiliary craft. However an unofficial order was placed a few weeks earlier when the armour and steel plates were ordered from the Dillinger Works in the Saar on 9 December 1880.

The Chinese wanted to build more battleships for the Peiyang and Nanyang fleets. On 13 September 1881 Prince Tseng Chi chai contracted in Essen with the Krupp Works for five large armoured ships (*Panzerschiffe* in the contract) and three smaller armoured ships (*Panzercorvetten* in the contract). Due to the Sea Defence Fund's depletion the large ships never materialised and none was even laid down. Of the planned smaller armoured ships only two were built and the third was replaced by a protected cruiser (= *Panzerdeckcorvette*). With three torpedo boats added in 1884 the 'Vulcan' yard had by the end of that year completed the following ships for China: two battle-ships, one protected cruiser, 13 torpedo boats, one steam yacht and one large steam dredger. The formal end in 1891 of Li Hung chang's buying programme was created by the rebuilding of the Summer Palace in Peking for which 90% of the Navy's money was diverted. The two battleships known as *Ting Yüan* and *Chen Yüan* and described below were the only battleships ever possessed by the Chinese Navy.

CONSTRUCTION AND DELIVERY

Work on the first battleship began in mid-February and she was laid down officially on 31 March 1881 in yard No 100 with the temporary name of 'Ti I T'ieh Chien' ('Number One Iron Ship') and her sister ship followed a year later in yard No 112 as 'Ti Erh T'ieh Chien' ('Number Two Iron Ship'). At noon on 28 December 1881 the first ship was launched and named *Ting Yüan* ('Eternal Peace'). The launching ceremony was attended by Li Fong Pao and General Count Leo von Caprivi, Chief of the German Admiralty. The second ship was launched at noon on 28 November 1882 and received the name *Chen Yüan* (meaning 'Striking far away'). Li Fong Pao and von Stosch, then Chief of the German Admiralty, attended the ceremony. On 2 May 1883 *Ting Yüan* under the German Captain von Nostitz ran her first trials off Swinemünde.

Baltic trials were successful and in mid-May she began the voyage to China under the German flag with a German crew of 8 officers and 240 men as well as the future Chinese captain and 8 engineers. During the voyage she held gun trials. The ship was suddenly recalled on 27 July and in mid-August returned to Stettin because of Sino-French hostilities, which began a few days later on 23 August 1883 with the French attack on Foochow. Meanwhile *Chen Yüan* had begun her first trials on 5 July. The explosion of a Krupp gun during firing practice off Swinemünde on the 19th caused critical notes on the German-built guns and ships in British papers. This provoked German newspapers to answer and many accidents to British ships were particularised. They also claimed that despite the accident the two *Yüan*s were a German success.

By the end of the year, on 1 December, the cruiser *Chi Yüan*, which had been ordered on 16 January, was launched. She was built instead of the third planned battleship. Between 29 March and 2 April 1884 *Chen Yüan* under Captain E Arnold, with Li Fong Pao and the yard's directors Haack and Wagner on board (and with assistance of the steamers *Neptun* and *Lothar Bucher*), made a trial voyage to Eckenförd in Schleswig-Hostein. Gun trials on 9 April after her return were successful, but both battleships and the recently completed cruiser had to wait in Europe until the Sino-French peace treaty was signed on 9 June 1885. By 17 June the ships were fitted with sails and fully equipped for their voyage. German crews for the three Chinese ships were enlisted by the Chinese embassy in Berlin from Hamburg for the two battleships and from Stettin for the cruiser. The squadron of Chinese ships under the German merchant flag and under the German command of A F Votz in *Ting Yüan*, Möller in *Chen Yüan* and E Arnold in *Chi Yüan* left Kiel on 3 July 1885. On 10 August the ships reached Aden, anchored at Colombo on the 29th and at the end of October they moored at Taku, where they

raised the Chinese flag and were commissioned into the Peiyang Fleet of Northern China. Chinese crews replaced the Germans, who returned on 8 November 1886 to Hamburg in the William Melbourne & Co Line's steamer *Huntingdon*.

A few Germans, such as Kapitan Möller, remained in the Chinese service joining many other foreigners in the Chinese Navy. An 1890 list mentions 2 Germans and 3 Englishmen in each of the battleships. Some of the foreigners took part in the Yalu battle. They were Major von Hannecken, Tyler, Nichols (gunnery Lieutenant killed) and Albrecht (chief engineer) in *Ting Yüan*; US Cdr McGiffen and Heckmann (gunnery Lieutenant) in *Chen Yüan*.

DESIGN

The Chinese battleships broadly resembled the contemporary *Sachsen* class of four German central citadel ironclads, built for coast defence (*Ausfallcorvetten*). The *Sachsen*s had been designed by the Ship construction division (*Konstructionsamt*) of the *Reichsmarineamt* in the years 1872 to 1874. The *Reichsmarineamt* gave permission for the Vulcan yard to use the *Sachsen* design. The hull construction and body lines were almost identical to the *Sachsen*'s while the most important differences between the German and Chinese ships were as follows:

(1) *Sachsen*'s main armament consisted of four 260mm (10.2in) pieces in a central barbette and two mounted in a pear-shaped barbette forward. This was replaced by four 305mm (12in) guns grouped by pairs en echelon forward of midships. This layout resembled the one used on the completed Italian and British citadel ships, but each Chinese ship had her guns in one, common barbette, not in turrets.

(2) Four funnels, between the fore and aft barbettes, arranged in pairs, (which caused the *Sachsen*s to be nicknamed 'Cement Works') were replaced by two funnels aft of the barbette.

(3) Engine power was increased from 560ihp to 600ihp, with 3-cylinder single expansion engines being replaced by compound versions.

(4) Steel was used for hull construction in place of wrought iron.

(5) Armour of up to 406mm (almost 16in) arranged in two layers was replaced by one layer of 355mm (almost 14in) armour.

(6) Three torpedo tubes were fitted. The *Sachsen* class were built without torpedo tubes and received their 3-350mm (14in) tubes apiece only from 1886.

GENERAL ARRANGEMENT

The general arrangement was that of a central citadel system. A fighting hull was formed by a rectangular armoured castle covering engine and boiler rooms and attached to this was a completely submerged hull of ordinary form with a ram and a bow, with two screws and a submerged rudder and helm. Fore and aft unarmoured superstructures were added to give her a good performance in a seaway and contributed substantially to stability. A conning tower was placed in the barbette between the main guns.

Ting Yüan in a home port.

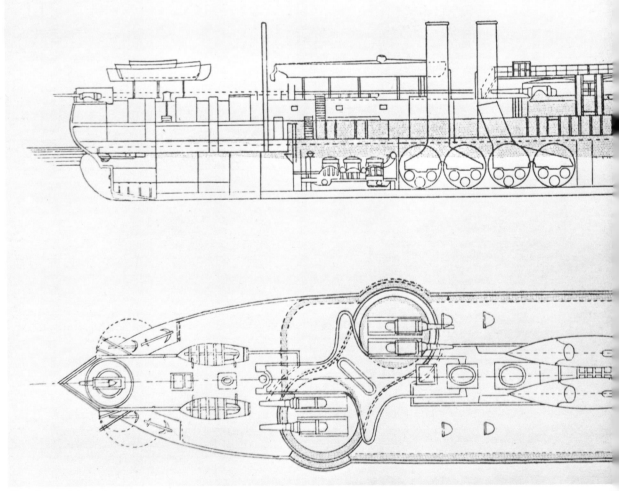

Elevation and deck plan.

HULL

The ships were built of steel of which 2400 tons were supplied by Dillinger Works, who already produced armour plates. In the steel hull the cellular system was adopted, as in the *Sachsen* class and similar to that used by Sir Edward Reed in the British battleships starting from the 1865 *Bellerophon*. The double bottom extended from the central girder to the lower deck. There were six longitudinal girders on each side, the sixth giving support to the armour and backing. Besides the central girder, the fourth and sixth side girders were made watertight. They formed with a number of bulkheads, cofferdams, etc about 200 watertight compartments below the tweendeck of which 24 at the sides aft of the citadel were filled with cork. Above the tweendeck the hull was subdivided into another 23 watertight compartments fitted with watertight doors in the bulkheads. Space between the tweendeck and the armoured deck was divided by cork bulkheads into a number of places where coal and stores were stowed. The 3m long ram was placed 3.5m below water. The main difference between the two ships was thickness of

Fred T Jane's drawing of *Chen Yüan* in close action at the Battle of the Yalu, 17 September 1894.

underwater plates, caused by the reduction of costs in *Ting Yüan*, which cost RM 6,200,000 as against RM 6,297,500, the price of the *Chen Yüan*.

MACHINERY

Two shafts fitted with two four-blade bronze screws of 5m diameter were powered by two sets of horizontal trunk 3-cylinder compound engines manufactured by Vulcan. The machinery was designed to provide 6000ihp for 14.5 knots. Eight cylindrical boilers with a working pressure of 5 atmospheres were grouped by fours in two boiler rooms with one funnel serving each. These two boiler rooms were arranged within one watertight compartment. The shafts and the boiler plates were produced by the Krupp Works. For the voyage to China the ships were brig rigged with three sails on the foremast. The rigging was removed when they reached China.

On trials *Ting Yüan* developed 6200ihp with a mean of 14.457 knots at 64rpm and her sister ship made 7200ihp with a mean speed of 15.384 knots. During trials they turned in a radius of 300 yards at a speed of 12.5 knots. The maximum stowage of 1000 tons of coal (700 tons normal) rendered possible a range of 4500nm at 10 knots. Their designed coal consumption was 60 tons per day.

AUXILIARY MACHINERY

Electricity was produced by three dynamos giving an output of 70kW, which supplied a rig of 62 volts lighting 240 lamps and two searchlights, one of 8000 candle power and the second of 2000 candles fitted on masts. Steering could be hydraulic or hand driven. The hydraulic steering gear was placed in a shaft tunnel below the armoured deck and the handgear was placed in the aft superstructure.

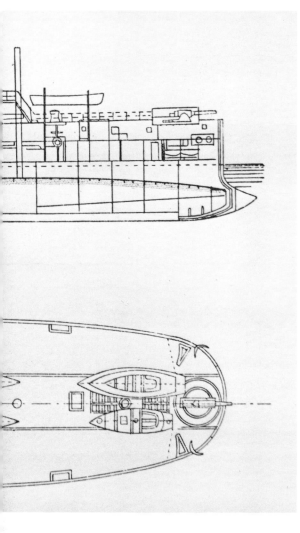

ARMOUR PROTECTION

Armour weighing 1461 tons was delivered by the Dillinger Works on the Saar, which had taken up armour manufacture in 1876. The armour plates used on the Chinese battleships were of the compound type used for the first time on HMS *Inflexible* in 1876. Those produced by the Dillinger Works were one third steel (face) and two thirds iron (back).

The armour protection consisted of the central citadel amidships with the conning tower and the main gun barbette and the armoured deck. The central citadel 42m long (137ft 10in), rising 2.336m (7ft 8in) above the waterline, was formed by narrow belt and lateral bulkheads. The belt 355m (almost 14in) thick backed by 355mm teak was extended to 0.6m (almost 2ft) below water, thence tapering from 305mm (12in) to 206mm (8.1in) at the lower edge, 1.5m (4ft 11in) below the waterline. The 355mm thick lateral bulkheads of the citadel joined the 75mm (3in) armoured deck at a depth of 0.6m. The armoured deck extended from the ram to the rudder head.

The barbette covering the main guns and the conning tower between was made of 304mm thick armour. The main guns were protected by thin 25mm shields which were mistaken for turrets. The conning tower was plated with 203mm (8in) armour. The turrets for the 150mm (5.9in) guns were of 75mm steel armour and had 25mm shields.

ARMAMENT

The main armament comprised of four 305mm (12in) Krupp breech-loading 25-calibre pieces mounted by pairs en echelon in a common barbette, the starboard pair forward. The guns' arrangement was identical in both ships, although some sources (probably affected by *Jane's Fighting Ships'* suggestion) erroneously reported that the *Ting Yüan* gun positions were reversed. The heavy guns were transported from Essen to Swinemünde on a special iron coach built by Krupp Works. The transport took four days. The 305mm guns were mounted on a hydraulic or hand driven turntable with hydraulic braking. Each gun was supplied with 50 projectiles. The secondary armament was formed by two 150mm Krupp breech-loading guns in turrets, one in the stern and one in the bow. Six Hotchkiss 37mm revolver guns were placed on the superstructure as well as two on a fighting mast. Each ship was also fitted with two 75mm (100kg) boat guns. Shortly before delivery the ships were fitted with some additional guns: two 75mm pieces and two 47mm Hotchkiss.

Two fixed torpedo tubes were fitted above water forward of the citadel in the tweendeck, one on each side. The third torpedo tube was fitted in the stern above water, 21 torpedoes of 380mm diameter and 4.25m (14ft) long were carried for them. The torpedo tubes and torpedoes were produced by Schwartzkopf Works, Berlin. This factory, whose torpedoes were made of phosphor bronze to avoid corrosion, had become since 1880 the single supplier of torpedoes to China because of the Chinese wish to standardise. German instructors were in the new torpedo school at Canton.

Shot holes in *Chen Yüan* after the Battle of the Yalu.

ATTACHED TORPEDO BOATS

Four of the ten torpedo boats originally ordered (designed as vedette boats attached to the battleships) had the following particulars:

Displacement 15.705 tons
Dimensions 19.7m (64ft 8in) oa/ 19.2m (63ft) bp
× 2.62m (8ft 7in)
max / 2.52m (8ft 3in) wl × 1.55m (5ft 1in)
depth × 1.07m (3ft 6in) draught
Material Steel
Machinery one set compound engine;
200iph = 15kts
(15.5 on trials); one steel boiler
of locomotive type; one three-blade
bronze screw
Armament two 380mm (14in) torpedo tubes fitted
in bows.

These four boats were built by Vulcan in the following order.

Yard number	Laid down	Launched	Completed
121	1882	1883	Feb 1883
122	1882	1883	Apr 1883
127	1883	1883	Apr 1884
128	1883	1883	Jun 1884

The former two were fitted on *Ting Yüan* and were named after the ship with the suffix 'first' and 'second'. The latter pair were so designated for *Chen Yüan*. They were stowed on skids 2m above the superstructure. Four steam-powered davits were fitted on each ship to handle the torpedo boats. The ships were also equipped with two large boats each placed abaft the mainmast and

TABLE 1: GUN ARMAMENT

	MAIN GUNS	SECONDARY GUNS
Mark	30.5cm (12in)	15cm (5.9in)
Calibre	305mm (12in)	149.1mm
Length of bore	25 cal	35 cal
Weight of gun	32,000kg (31½ tons)	4770kg (4¾ tons)
Shell weight	329kg (725lb)	51kg (112lb)
Muzzle velocity	500m/s (1640fps)	530m/s (1738fps)
Muzzle energy	4192mt	730mt
Firing rate	3 rds in 10 min	1 rpm
Year of construction	1880	1880

raised by hydraulically operated derricks on the mainmast.

TABLE 2: COMPARATIVE SHIP DATA

	SACHSEN (Design)	TING YÜAN (Design)	(both ships) Steel	CHIN YEN (IJN service)
Material	Iron			
Displacement	7280t	7144t		7200t
	7400	7500		7670
Length (bp)	91.0m/298ft 7in		91.0m	
Beam	18.3m/60ft		18.3m	
Draught	6.0m/19ft 8in		6.1m (fore)/20ft	
Depth	8.2m/26ft 11in		8.336m/27ft 4in	
Tonnage	3500grt		3200grt	
Machinery	5600ihp		6000ihp	
Speed	14.0kts		14.5kts	
Armour: citadel	406mm/16in		355mm/14in	
barbette	254mm/10in		304mm/12in	
deck	75mm/3in		75mm/3in	
CT	140mm/5½in		203mm/8in	
Gun armament	6 × 260mm/22 (18t)		4 × 305mm/25 (32t)	
	6 × 87mm/24	2 × 150mm/35		4 × 152mm/40
	8 × 37mm	8 × 37mm		8 × 47mm
	-	2 × 75mm		2 × 57mm
Torpedo tubes	3 (fitted 1886)		3	
Coal	420/700t		650/1000t	
Radius at 10kts	1940nm		4500nm	
Complement	317	363		350
Cost	RM 8.3 million		RM 6.2 million	

UNDER THE DRAGON'S FLAG

Shortly after the delivery in 1886 both battleships accompanied by two cruisers were sent to Korea, where the British were in occupation of Port Hamilton. Then on 1 August 1886 the four warships entered the Japanese port of Nagasaki on a courtesy visit. In 1888 the Peiyang Fleet was reorganised. Its command was vested in Admiral Ting Ju ch'ang, aided by the post captains Lin T'ai tseng and Li Pu ch'an (*Chen Yüan* and *Ting Yüan* respectively). Training in the fleet was given to a British captain, William H Lang, commissioned by Li Hung chang as admiral. Lang made great efforts to establish discipline and efficiency on the Chinese ships, which deteriorated after his removal. The Fleet was divided into seven functional squadrons. The seagoing ships were put into three 'wings' of three ships each, with the battleships *Ting Yüan* and *Chen Yüan* respectively in the right and left wings. Other squadrons had support tasks. This arrangement was a reflection of British influence and showed strategic sophistication, and could be seen in the early stages of the Yalu battle. Besides two battleships the fleet actually possessed seven cruisers, six Rendel gunboats, six torpedo boats (excluding the battleships' attached boats) and a few transport and training vessels. Two ships were added later, the cruiser *Ping Yüan* in 1889 and torpedo boat *Fu Lung* in 1890. On 15 July 1891 a squadron, consisting of six Peiyang Fleet ships, visited Yokohama, hardly with casual interest as it coincided with the growing tension between the two countries over Korea. Both battleships excited much attention in Japanese naval circles. One of the Chinese cruisers, *Ping Yüan*, entered Kure to be repaired at the navy yard. According to Togo, then commander of the Kure naval base, the crew lacked discipline, the guns were not clean, and were furthermore festooned with laundry. Togo was not impressed with a Navy that treated its weapons in such a fashion.

The probable cause of such crew behaviour was that Admiral Ting Ju ch'ang was not a professional naval man, but an ex-Anhwei Army cavalry officer, one of Li Hung chang's 'own', and he was furthermore the first to admit it. From Yokohama the ships went to Shanghai and in the same year took part in large North-South manoeuvres.

In early 1894, shortly before the Sino-Japanese War, Admiral Ting Ju ch'ang asked Li Hung Chang for an increase in the armament of the six best Peiyang ships, excluding the two battleships, with a total of 21 Krupp 120mm QF guns at a cost of 613,000 taels (about £100,000). Due to lack of money this plan was reduced to only 12 guns, six for each battleship. The cost, including shells and charges, fell dramatically to about 35,400 taels (about £5750). The Board of Revenue also rejected this plan because the money was needed for the Empress Dowager's Diamond Jubilee (1835 to 1895).

SINO-JAPANESE WAR

Sino-Japanese rivalry in Korea caused the war, which Japan declared on 1 August 1894, although the naval action began a few days before on 25 July off Asan, where the Japanese attacked a Chinese squadron. Only the cruiser *Chi Yüan* escaped from the battle. During the action her fore gun shield was struck by a shot, killing a number of the gun's crew. Other shots caused fire on board. As the result of this experience the Chinese removed all superfluous wooden equipment, spars and boats from the ships, excluding one six-oar boat for each ship. Wooden sea ladders were replaced, if it was possible by rope ladders, etc. From the battleships the thin steel shields to the main guns were also landed. Shields to fore and aft 150mm guns were left to protect the gunners from the blast when the main guns fired. Shells for secondary guns were laid in the unarmoured superstructure, where sand bagging 4ft high and 3ft thick was formed. The barbettes were overlaid by coal bagging. Two extra 47mm 5-barrelled Hotchkiss guns were also fitted on each battleship.

Till the beginning of September the Peiyang Fleet, strengthened by a few ships transferred shortly before the war from other fleets, was used for the defence of the Chinese coast, when the situation in Korea caused Li Hung Chang to send a large convoy under Ting's protection to the Yalu river. On 14 September 1894 six steamers with 4000 soldiers left Taku. They met with the Peiyang ships in Talien Bay. On the 16th the Chinese began landing and a day later the Japanese fleet, consisting of 12 ships under Vice-Admiral Count Yuko Ito, attacked them. Ito's fleet was superior in tonnage, speed, leadership, crew discipline and in QF guns. The two battleships were the only Chinese advantage, but their slow-firing weapons and their arrangement were obsolete against the Japanese quick firers.

Ting Yüan, during the battle flagship of Admiral Ting with his adviser Major von Hannecken, and her sister ship were the prime targets for the Japanese, but their heavy guns and armour stopped the attackers. The two battleships fired 197 shots from 305mm and 167 from 150mm. At the end of the battle the Chinese lacked shells, so they were shooting charges. Of the Chinese shots only 10 of 305mm reached targets, including 4 charges. *Ting Yüan* hit and caused fire on Ito's flagship, the French-built protected cruiser *Matsushima*, which lost 28 killed and 68 wounded men. Also the auxiliary cruiser *Saikio Maru* was heavily damaged by *Ting Yüan*'s shot, but the day belonged to the Japanese QF guns. Five Chinese ships were sunk or destroyed.

Ting Yüan herself suffered about 160 hits, being four times on fire and left the battle in flames. Her casualties were 17 killed and 38 wounded. *Chen Yüan* was hit by about 220 shells being eight times on fire and suffered 13 killed and 28 wounded. *Chen Yüan* had been down 3ft by the head and was said to be almost in a sinking condition. Both battleships' superstructures were heavily damaged, but the two ships were still in a fighting condition with their big guns. It seems that if they had been armed with the QFs Ting had requested they would have inflicted a great deal more damage.

When darkness fell the battle was over. Ito barred the way to Wei Hai Wei, but what survived of the Chinese fleet went to Port Arthur. After repairs China still had seven ships that could fight. When the Japanese forces landed on the Liaotung peninsula and advanced toward the fortress, Ting's fleet was ordered to get out from Port Arthur to Wei Hai Wei. Japanese laxity meant that the Chinese fleet crossed the Gulf of Chihli without incident. Unfortunately *Chen Yüan* was severely damaged through striking a reef when entering Wei Hai Wei with the sad result that her Captain Lin T'ai tseng committed suicide and the second-in-command Yang Yung replaced him.

By the end of November the Chinese had 13 ships (including two battleships), 12 torpedo boats and a number of merchantmen. They also made attempts to buy new ships. In Wei Hai Wei the fleet was waiting for the enemy. On 20 January 1895 the Third Japanese Army of 26,000 men on 50 transports landed SE of Wei Hai Wei with the Chinese blockaded in harbour by the Japanese squadron. The Chinese fleet was kept at anchor and to eliminate it the Japanese decided to attack using a torpedo boat flotilla at night. The first attempt on the night of 30/31 January was unsuccessful, but the second attack on 4/5 February succeeded. Ten Japanese torpedo boats entered the base through the gaps in the barring booms made during the preceding night. *Ting Yüan* was hit by the torpedoes of *TB 9* and as her watertight doors were not in order she had to be beached on 6 February with only her deck above water and abandoned save as a fort.

During numerous attacks the Japanese seized the Chinese forts along Wei Hai Wei harbour and began bombarding the Chinese ships from their positions. They demolished the formerly beached *Ting Yüan* and heavily damaged *Chen Yüan*, which was sunk in shallow water on 9 February. The Chinese torpedo boat flotilla, including three of the battleships' attached torpedo boats, had to be beached under Japanese fire when attempting to run the blockade on 7 February. Admiral Ting received an order from the Imperial Court that none of his ships should fall into enemy hands; on the other hand he knew that scuttling the ships would be followed by reprisals from the victors, so he decided to commit suicide on 11 February. He was followed by the two battleship captains and the fortress commanders. A day later Wei Hai Wei surrendered.

IN JAPANESE HANDS

The Japanese flag was hoisted on the grounded *Chen Yüan* on 17 February 1895. Refloated, she was towed by *Saikio Maru* to Port Arthur, entering the harbour on 27 February. On 16 March 1895 she was placed on the Japanese Navy list as *Chin Yen*, becoming the first Japanese battleship. In Port Arthur she was docked from 4 April to 1 June, refitted and partially reconstructed by the Japanese. They put shields back on the main guns. The Krupp 15cm guns were replaced by Armstrong 6in, fore gun in a turret and the aft on a pedestal mount protected by a shield. Two single identical guns were added on sponsons one to each side, abreast the main mast. A number of small guns were also fitted. On 4 June her machinery was tested, on 25 June the boilers fired. After positive trials off Port Arthur on 3 July, she was sent via Nagasaki next day to Yokosuka, which she entered on 28 July. On 21 March 1898 she

Chin Yüan as the Japanese *Chin Yen* in or before 1904.

was rerated as a second class battleship and on 11 December 1905 as a first class coast defence ship.

During the Russo-Japanese War she belonged to the 5th Force of the Third Fleet, consisting of *Matsushima*, *Hashidate*, *Itsushima*, *Chin Yen* and *Yaeyama*. She took part in the first attack on Port Arthur on 9 February 1904, in the seventh attack on 21 March and in the ninth combined attack on 23 June, then in the severe Battle of Yellow Sea on 10 August 1904, and in the famous Tsushima battle on 27 May 1905 (see *Warship* Nos 5 & 6). From February to September 1904 she was also on blockade duty and escorting transports. Moreover before that war, together with other Japanese ships, she had joined the international force against the Boxer Rebellion in 1900. After the Russo-Japanese War she was used for towing and escorting ex-Russian warships refloated at Port Arthur, namely *Hizen* (ex-*Retvizan*), *Suvo* (ex-*Pobeda*), *Aso* (ex-*Bajan*) and *Tsugaru* (ex-*Pallada*).

On 1 May 1908 she was designated as 'Unyou Jyutsu Renshu kan' (It means 'general navigation training ship'). Removed from the list on 1 April 1911, she was used as a target ship for battleship *Kurama*'s 20cm guns and after 24 November for various other shell and torpedo tests. She was sold on 6 April 1912 and scrapped at Yokohama, according to S Fukui records, but probably in 1914 or later she was towed to Kobe and her material was used for two merchantmen. Her conning tower and other items were landed at Kobe. The conning tower was burnt out in a World War II air attack, but one of her anchors still exists in Okayama Prefecture near Kobe. Some more parts of *Chin Yen* exist in theMunaka Shrine in Kyushu.

Her sister ship *Ting Yüan* had been refloated in 1897 by a Japanese civilian, formerly Kagawa Prefecture Governor. A memorial house to her was built at Fukuoka Kyushu using her equipment, disused articles, fixtures, etc. This house still exists administered by Dazai Fu Tenmagu Shrine. *Chen Yüan*'s attached vedette boat No 2 was captured aboard her and on 15 October 1895 commissioned as IJN *TB 28*. During trials she made only 10.5 knots at 90ihp. She was removed from the list on 14 May 1901.

CONCLUSION

One hundred years ago a German yard built the largest warships ever possessed by China, although Chinese history claims that in 1406 eunuch Cheng Ho, who was ordered to take an expedition through the Western Ocean, built 62 large ships each 44 chang long and 18 wide (ie 528ft × 216ft). Unfortunately we do not know anything more about these unusual floating boxes, so the Vulcan built battleships seem to be the only capital ships of Chinese modern history.

Ting Yüan and *Chen Yüan* were also the biggest warships completed for export in Germany, due to the fact that the Greek dreadnought *Salamis* was never completed, but they were sometimes erroneously reported as the first warships built in Germany for any foreign navy. They were in fact preceded by a number of ships built for Russia, beginning with three oared gunboats built by Klawitter yard in 1848.

The two battleships, considering the circumstances under which their service took place, were valuable ships, although not well handled in Chinese hands. During the Yalu battle the armour of these ships did excellent service, and the unarmoured ends preserved the stability better than would be expected, judging from the criticism to which this type had been subject. Li Hung's plans to use them as prototypes for home-built ships never materialised due to fiscal problems. China planned to build battleships in a 1896 naval programme, but the Boxer Rebellion collapsed it, and a large 1909 naval programme was never realised because of the fall of the Ch'ing dynasty in 1911.

REMARKS

1. In 1880 the Chinese authorities probably ordered one British-built double turret steel ironclad from Mitchell & Co, on the Tyne. She was to have had a speed of 16 knots, the machinery to be built by Hawthorn of Newcastle. But the order was rejected for the political reasons described.

2. The names of both ships need some more explanations. The meaning of *Yüan* (遠) is a territory away from the capital city, eventually foreign, the hieroglyph *Tin* (定) means 'to establish', 'to make peace' and so on, the hieroglyph *Chen* (鎮) means 'rule', 'to support', etc, so the names of the Chinese ships cannot be simply translated into European languages, and in the text I have given only approximate meanings. Moreover we must remember that the Japanese did not change the names of the captured Chinese ships, but only gave them the Japanese reading of the Chinese names. In this article I have used the common English transcription for the Chinese names, but the Chinese since 1 January 1979 have in use the official transcription called 'pinyin'. According to it the names of the Chinese battleships are '*chèn yuǎn*' for *Chen Yuan* and '*dìng yuǎn*' for *Ting Yüan*.

Chin Yüan now the Japanese *Chin Yen* while drydocked in Port Arthur 4 April – 1 June 1895.

HMS UNICORN:
The Development of a Design 1937-39

By D K Brown

During the Italian invasion and conquest of Ethiopia in 1935-36 the Royal Navy learnt much concerning sustained operations from aircraft carriers. Planning allowed for the following aircraft operating hours:

maximum flying hours per month	60
per fortnight	42
per week	30

In a month this could lead to 20% crashed or damaged beyond repair and 10% requiring substantial repair.

Repair and the bigger maintenance tasks could not be carried out in hangars of an operational carrier without seriously obstructing the work of flying. In consequence, it was decided in 1937 to design an aircraft maintenance ship that would support the new fleet carriers coming into service.

The new ship was to be similar to the Queen Bee tender then planned. (Queen Bee was a radio controlled aircraft, based on the Tiger Moth, used as an AA gunnery target.) The maintenance ship was to have a landing-on deck, workshops for 32 aircraft, and a speed of 20 knots. Machinery could be steam or perhaps diesel. Other requirements were an accelerator; a lift; 2 cranes; 2in armour on the flight deck; 4 twin 4in AA guns and 2 8-barrel pompoms.

By early in 1938 the role of the new ship had been further refined. She was to service three *Illustrious* class fleet carriers, each carrying 33 aircraft. The maintenance carrier was to carry 42 aircraft erected but with wings folded and to be able to repair another 8 aircraft with wings unfolded. The requirement to act as a Queen Bee tender was dropped. The sea-going speed was to be 13½ knots with an endurance of 4,000 miles at that speed. An unusual requirement was that for shallow draught (18ft) so that she could use areas of harbours unsuitable for other big ships.

Two big aircraft lighters were to be carried, lifted on board by crane. The hangar was to be protected against 250lb bombs and divided by fire curtains. Torpedo protection against 440lb warheads was specified. Aircraft fuel stowage for 40,000 gallons was to be provided and a Link trainer installed. The armament was increased to 8 4.5in guns.

The design team, under H H Palmer RCNC, came up with their first proposal in February 1938. At this stage a 'design' consists of a very rough estimate of dimensions and particulars so that a first order of cost can be obtained. Design A had the following particulars:

Length	555ft (wl), 610ft (oa)
Beam	88ft
Draught	17ft 6in (20ft 6in deep)
Depth	79ft
Standard Displacement	13,820 tons
Speed	20,000shp = 20 knots
Armour	2in armour deck

Weight (tons)	
Hull	8920
Protection	1464
Machinery	1790
Armament	324
Air Equipment	544
General Equipment	781
	13,823

The ship was costed at £2,172,000 (Vote 8) and her weapons at £37,000 (Vote 9). The metacentric height was 5ft (light) and 6.2ft (deep). Of her aircraft 8 with spread wings could be carried in the upper hangar, 21 with folded wings in the lower hangar and the remaining 13 in a deck park. It would seem that *Argus* was used as the type ship for weight estimating.

A preliminary design, such as this, stimulates the imagination for better and for worse and a considerable number of variants were proposed and studied. The idea of converting *Eagle* or *Hermes* to a maintenance ship was floated and rapidly abandoned when it was found that they could only hold 3 aircraft spread and 8 folded. The effect of increasing speed to 24 knots was estimated as an increase of 700 tons. Briefly, a much larger ship was considered, 755ft length (oa) and 18,350 tons but retaining 13½ knot speed. This would have cost £2.9 million.

Much discussion took place on the number of repair staff needed. It was agreed that a typical repair job would take 6 days with three shifts of 6 men in each. By now Palmer had two Assistant Constructors on

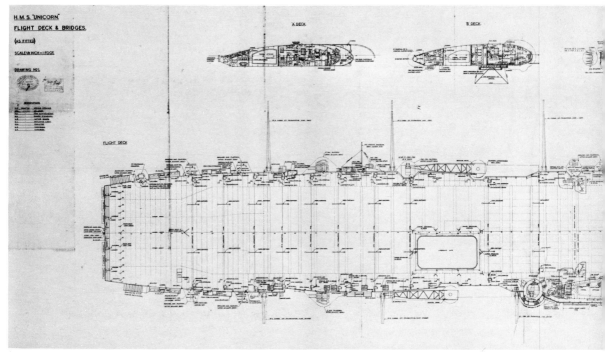

HMS *Unicorn*, flight deck and bridges as fitted 1943.
NMM

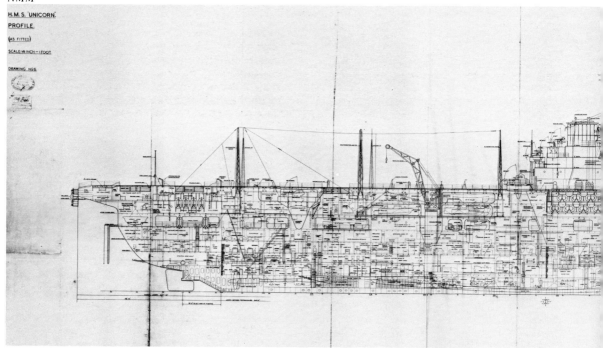

Unicorn, sketch of rig August 1942.
NMM

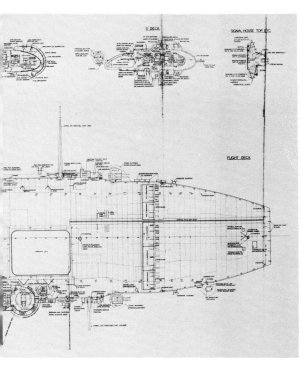

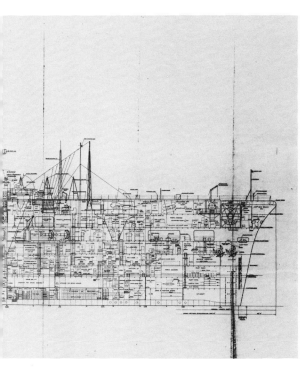

calculations and 10 draughtsmen. They produced a series of variants described in the table below:

TABLE 1: UNICORN DESIGN VARIANTS

	D	C	C[1]
Length (oa, ft)	550	615	640
Displacement (tons)	11,000	14,000	14,800
Shaft horse power	20,000	40,000	40,000
Speed, deep (knots)	20.75	24	24
Guns	8-4.5in	8-4in	8-4in
Aircraft (spread)	7	7	7
(folded)	20	20	20
(boxed)	6	21	21
Cost (£ million)	2.2	2.5	2.625

All had the following protection: Magazines (3-4in NC sides, 2in ends, 2in crown); Flight deck (2in); Bridge (⅜in-½in). There were two lifts, both 46ft long, the forward being 22ft wide and the aft 24ft. Each had a 46 second working cycle when carrying a 14,000lb aircraft. The lift platform was 1* NC (Nickel Cement) steel.

Towards the end of 1938 there was some discussion on which category of the various naval treaties this ship would fall within. It was said that she was NOT primarily designed or adapted for carrying and operating aircraft and hence was an auxiliary. If she was neither an auxiliary nor an aircraft carrier she would automatically be classified as a battleship with a minimum displacement of 17,500 tons! The Controller advocated being open and frank with the other treaty powers but in November 1938 they were informed that she was an auxiliary even though she would look like an aircraft carrier.

The next idea was to use her as an MTB depot ship as well but her high freeboard and lack of heavy lifting gear were seen to make her unsuitable. The requirement to act as a Queen Bee was restated and two rangefinders (each £744) and a plot were added. The Fifth Sea Lord redefined her three functions as supply and repair of aircraft, being a small operational carrier and acting as a WT base ship.

In the meantime, the designers were looking at some of the technical problems of this unusual ship. The combination of high freeboard and shallow draught was likely to make her difficult to handle in windy conditions and a detailed comparision of rudder size was made with other ships.

TABLE 2: BRITISH CARRIER RUDDER SIZES

Ship	Rudder area (sq ft)	Immersed profile area (sq ft)	Above water area (sq ft)	B/A	C/A
	A	B	C		
Hermes	198	12,700	17,000	64	86
Courageous	229	21,500	44,000	94	192
Ark Royal	260	19,800	40,700	76	157
Unicorn	230	12,650	31,000	55	135

The DNC, Sir Stanley Goodall, was also concerned that the great depth of the ship would cause the centre of

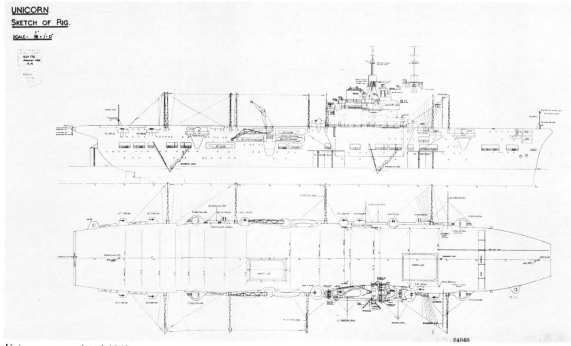

Unicorn as completed 1943.
NMM

gravity to be high which, combined with the small draught, would give poor stability at large angles of heel. He was reassured by the following figures:

Condition	Max Righting Lever (GX) ft	Angle at which max GZ occurs
Deep	4.8	35°
Standard	2.8	35°

The rearmament programme was building up and design staff were scarce. The Deputy DNC, Boyland, had a series of meetings with section heads eventually agreeing the allocation for the sketch design of *Unicorn*, though some were only part-time on this ship.

By November 1938 the design was approaching the final configuration:

Standard displacement	14,800 tons
Length (bp)	545ft
Beam	90ft
Speed	24kts
Aircraft (upper hangar, spread)	7
(lower hangar, folded)	20
(dismantled)	14-15

Detailed strength calculations with this ship on a wave of height equal to 1/20 of the length of the ship showed that stresses were low, due to the depth of the hull.

TABLE 3: STRESSES (tons/sq in)

Position	Hogging		Sagging	
	Keel	Flight Deck	Keel	Flight Deck
For'd lift	2.34	3.24	1.51	1.75
Amidships	2.65	2.59	2.2	1.71
Aft lift	2.68	3.47	1.8	1.74

Unicorn probably with Eastern Fleet in the Indian Ocean 1944. Hellcat fighters lead a line up including Barracuda torpedo bombers and a Corsair.

The metacentric height was now 5ft in the standard condition and 7.5ft in the deep.

The argument was then re-opened as to whether she was an auxiliary or an aircraft carrier. A detailed paper was produced to justify her as an auxiliary under the various clauses of the London Naval Treaty of 1936. It argued she did not mount guns over 6.1in or more than 8 guns of over 3in, that she was not equipped to fire torpedoes. She only had deck armour protection allowed to auxiliaries and her speed was below 28 knots. Even more straining credibility was the statement that she was not primarily designed to operate aircraft. Finally she was not to carry more than 2 accelerators. Soon afterwards the signs of approaching war brought a sense of reality and she was redefined as an aircraft carrier.

The upper hangar was mainly used as a workshop and was 324ft × 65ft × 16½ft. The lower hangar was 360ft × 62ft × 16½ft high to underside of beams. Six arrester wires were fitted and a BH111 catapult. The aircraft complement as an operational carrier was variously stated as between 20 and 30. The total hangar area, allowing for obstructions, was nearly 40,000 sq ft, much the same as that of the fleet carrier *Indomitable*. The lifts were nearer the centre of the hangar than in the fleet carriers with their operating pillars causing obstruction. During World War II, *Unicorn* operated 20 fixed wing Seafire II fighters but could carry 69 of the folding wing Seafire III.

Unicorn had stowage for 36,500 gallons of petrol and 1800 gallons of paraffin. The ship's machinery plant was based closely on destroyer practice. She had 4 boilers giving steam to 2 turbines of 20,000hp each. Fuel stowage for 3000 tons gave her an endurance of 7000 miles at $13\frac{1}{2}$ knots in the worst condition – deep displacement, tropical waters, six months out of dock. Her 8 4in guns had 3816 rounds while the pompoms had 1200 rounds per barrel. Deck protection, of 2in NC, was limited to a length of 378ft over the full width of the flight deck. The lift platforms were still 1in NC. The magazine had 2in crowns and 4-$4\frac{1}{2}$in sides.

Changes were still being demanded as, for example, in February 1939 it was proposed and rejected to alter the main armament to 8 4.5in guns. Prolonged discussion took place over the pompom armament and it was finally decided to fit 4 4-barrel mountings. The cost of 3 8-barrel and 4 4-barrel were compared:

	3 × 8	*4 × 4*
Mountings	£37,500	£30,000
Guns	£23,500	£15,600
Ammunition	£99,000	£64,000

Only one aircraft lighter could be stowed, under the stern.

By March 1939 the design was being developed by Harland & Wolff, the chosen builder and there was considerable concern when their machinery weight of

Entering Kure naval base, Japan, during the Korean War. Her deck cargo includes a DUKW and Firefly fighters. She had taken out 100 spare FAA aircraft to Singapore in late 1949.

1285 tons exceeded the design figure by 75 tons. The propeller was designed by the DNC department in association with the Admiralty Experiment Works at Haslar. Each propeller had to develop 90 tons of thrust at full speed when working at 180rpm. The dimensions selected were 15ft diameter, 17ft 9in pitch and an area of 85.6 cubic ft.

The final ship design figures were:
Displacement (tons) 14,750 standard, 20,300 deep
Dimensions (ft) 646 (oa) × 90 × 25 deep
Flight deck (ft) 646 × 80 clear
Design complement 976 (up to 1200 in wartime)
These corresponded to the following cost breakdown:

TABLE 4: UNIT COSTS

Dockyard items, labour & materials	£ 22,000
Machinery, mains and auxiliary	£ 735,000
Hull	£1,502,000
Boats	£ 10,000
Armour	£ 162,000
Gun mountings	£ 90,000
Torpedo and mine equipment	£ 10,000
	£2,531,000
Guns	£ 37,000
Ammunition	£ 124,000
	£2,692,000

Unicorn was laid down at Belfast on 29 June 1939 but her completion was not given high priority and she was not launched until 20 November 1941, completing on 12 March 1943. She was soon employed operationally in support of the Salerno landings in Italy but after that returned to her true role as a maintenance or ferry carrier, first in the Indian Ocean and then the Pacific. She served as a troopship and even did 4in gun shore bombardment in the Korean War before being broken up in 1959. *Unicorn* successfully met her stated requirements but these roles were over complex. No repeats were planned and the light fleet carriers of 1942 were a simpler concept.

Unicorn astern of the battlecruiser *Renown*'s final
decommissioning at Plymouth on 2 June 1948. The carrier was
in reserve but reactivated the following summer for Far East
service.

WARSHIP PICTORIAL

The Sinking of the Königsberg 1940

By Pierre Hervieux

Among German naval forces involved in the 1940 occupation of Norway, Operation 'Weserübung', was Group 3 under the command of Rear Admiral Schmundt, which was sent to the harbour of Bergen. This group was composed of the sister light cruisers *Köln* and *Königsberg*, the torpedo boats *Leopard* and *Wolf*, the gunnery training ship *Bremse*, the E-boat tender *Carl Peters*, the E-boats *S 19, S 21, S 22, S 23* and *S 24*, the auxiliary ships *Schiff 9* and *Schiff 18*.

On the morning of 9 April 1940 they steamed into Bergen Fjord and engaged Norwegian shore batteries. Resistance was brief and the town was quickly occupied. *Königsberg*, was damaged by a 6in shell hit just above her waterline, was moored to the Skoltegrund Mole for repairs, being unfit for sea, and her position was soon transmitted to Britain by Norwegian Resistance workers. *Bremse* had also been slightly damaged by the shore batteries. At 6pm, on the same day, while all important ships of Group 3 were still in Bergen's harbour, 12 Wellingtons and 12 Hampdens of the Royal Air Force attacked them, but with no result. *Köln* and the two torpedo boats put to sea at 8pm that night for the return journey, but the activity of the Home Fleet caused Rear Admiral Schmundt to postpone the break-back. The cruiser therefore laid low for the night in a fjord south of Bergen. She weighed again the following afternoon, the 10th, and arrived home safely.

On the evening of the 9th, 800 and 803 Squadrons of the Fleet Air Arm, based on land in the Orkneys, were detailed for a bombing attack on the *Königsberg* and at 5am the following morning 16 Blackburn Skua dive-bomber crews boarded their aircraft. Seven Skuas from 800 Squadron were led by their commander, Major R T Partridge RM, while nine from 803 were led by their CO, Lt W P Lucy RN. Each loaded with a single 500lb SAP bomb, the 16 Skuas struggled off RNAS Hatston's inadequate runway into a murky dawn. After some two hours they made landfall dead opposite to Bergen. Climbing to 8000ft, Lucy put the Skuas into line astern formation and peeled out of the sun to attack. At 4000ft

German flak opened up, but the first real warning *Königsberg*'s crew received was Lucy's 500lb bomb exploding close to the cruiser's stern, lifing her out of the water and battering her against the mole. Soon afterwards the following Skuas' bombs scored 3 direct hits on the 6650-ton light cruiser. *Königsberg* was set on fire, later she capsized and sank. Jinking along the fjord on their run-out from the now murderous flak, 3 Skuas suffered real damage, one crew (Lt Smeeton and Midshipman Watkinson) were last seen heading up the fjord and were never seen again. At 9.45am, with fuel tanks almost dry, the remaining 15 Skuas touched down at Hatston. [In 1943 the wreck of *Königsberg* was refloated and dry-docked. On 22 September 1944 it capsized, was abandoned and broken up.]

This was the first sinking of a major warship by dive-bombing (unless one counts the Japanese sinking of the US gunboat *Panay* in 1937), and it was one of the greatest ironies of all that much of the potential of the dive-bomber as a ship-sinking weapon was demonstrated in such a way to the Germans by the British themselves, by the Royal Navy in fact. On the previous day, the *Luftwaffe* also got its 'premiere' when German planes, probably Junkers Ju 88 semi dive-bombers, off Stavanger in Norway too, sank HMS *Gurkha*, the first British destroyer ever to be sunk by air attack. The sinking of the *Königsberg* gave proof of the superiority of this method of aerial attack over the high-level bombing which had up until then failed so obviously when mounted by Wellingtons or Heinkels.

The British appeared blind to their success and soon afterwards the Skua squadrons were disbanded, but Germany, with the most powerful dive-bomber force in the world, took note. *Königsberg* was to be avenged many times over in the years that followed; as late in the war as 6 October 1943 Junkers Ju 87s dive-bombed and sank 3 modern Soviet destroyers, off the Crimean coast, so dismaying Stalin that after this masterstroke, he forbade the employment of surface ships from destroyer upwards without his permission!

Königsberg in 1938 and carrying a Heinkel He 60c seaplane. She was lead ship of the 3 'K' class German light cruisers, the first to have triple gun turrets and turbine/diesel machinery.

Drüppel

Königsberg moored at the Skoltegrund Mole (Bergen) and burning. This sequence of photographs was taken by Norwegians in Bergen.

ECP Armées

Listing to port and about to capsize. Severe damage to the hull is visible above the Junkers Ju 52/3mW floatplane's rudder.

ECP Armées

A close up of the burning cruiser with her crew abandoning ship.

ECP Armées

A midships view of the burning ship, seaplane still aboard, and casualty evacuation in progress.

ECP Armées

Königsberg lower by the bows.
ECP Armées

A close up of the capsized cruiser showing her rudder and
starboard propeller.

ECP Armées

Königsberg having just capsized.
ECP Armées

Blackburn Skuas from *Ark Royal* in formation before World War II. Ironically the Fleet Air Arm fighter/dive bomber (and first monoplane) scored its greatest success while land based. Skua endurance was only $4\frac{1}{2}$ hrs at 125-143kts with a ceiling of 19,100ft. Armament consisted of 5 × .303 machine guns and single 500lb bomb.

Popperfoto

British Naval Guns 1880-1945 No 12

By N J M Campbell

6in BL Mk XII For many years this was one of the standard naval guns. It was of wire wound construction with tapered inner A tube, A tube, full length jacket, breech ring and breech bush which screwed into the A tube. The usual Welin screw breech block was used with hand worked 'pure couple' mechanism. Mk XII was to indicate guns without an inner A tube but none appear to have been made. Mk XIIA referred to guns with a modified chamber which had a parallel front end, and Mk XIIB to guns with this modified chamber and with the bore reduced to 5.985in as the clearance between projectile and bore was considered to be too great. Where possible it was preferred not to mix XIIB guns with XII and XIIA. Altogether 463 guns were made for the Navy and none for the Army, though many were

transferred in World War II for emergency coast defence batteries.

Ships with Mk XII and its variants comprised the *Queen Elizabeth* and *Royal Sovereign* battleship classes, light cruisers from the *Birmingham* class to the *Emerald* and *Enterprise* and also the rearmed *Effingham*, World War I monitors *Abercrombie*, *Raglan*, *Sir T Picton*, *M29 – 33* and in World War II the gunboats *Aphis*, *Cockchafer* and *Scarab* as rearmed, many AMCs and some liners. It was also mounted in the monitor *Terror* and the cruiser *Frobisher* for experiments and training and 3 guns were sent to the 1919 Caspian Force in the Russian Civil War. Shells were 4crh except that 6crh were provided in World War II for *Aphis*, the AMC *Canton* and possibly *Alcantara* and *Monowai*. Super-

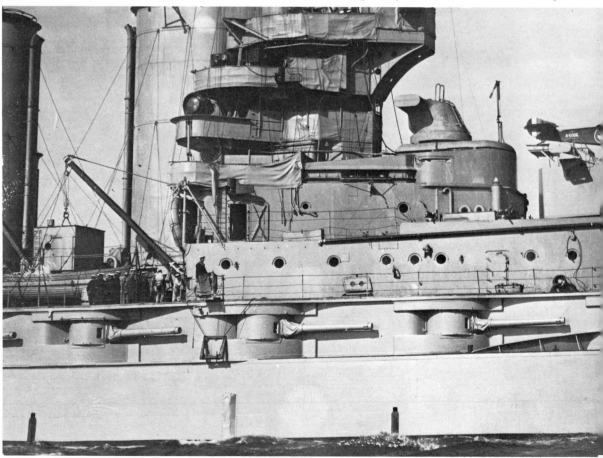

charges were only issued to *Aphis* and *Canton*.

There were several different mountings:

Mark	Elevation	Ships and notes
PVII	15° in some later 20°	*Birmingham* class
PVII*	15° in some later 20°	*Arethusa* to *Centaur* classes, differed in thinner shield
PIX	14° in some later 17½°	Battleships, monitors, also *Cleopatra*, *Champion* for a time.
PXIII	30°	*Adelaide*, had heavy shield
PXIII*	30°	*Caledon*, *Cardiff* classes, *Effingham*
PXIII**	30°	*Cairo* class
CPXIV	30°	*Danae*, *Emerald* classes
XVI	40°	*Diomede*, one gun in weatherproof shield
XVII	40°	*Enterprise*, one twin turret

The Caspian Force guns were in PIX, and in the World War II *Scarab* had CPXIV, *Aphis* and *Cockchafer* PXIII*, the latter PIX previously. AMCs mostly had PVII* with some PVII, XIII, PXIII**, CPXIV, and coast defence batteries PVII, PVII*, PIX, or if MNBDO, PXIII*, PXIII**.

6in BL Mk XIII An Elswick design with inner A tube, A tube and breech piece joined by a securing collar, wire, B tube, jacket, breech ring and breech bush. Reserve guns

were built like Mk XII but with B tube and jacket instead of a full length jacket. It was introduced in the battleship *Agincourt* (1913) and was later in *Aphis* and *Ladybird* for a time, as well as in World War II emergency coast defence batteries. Altogether 24 guns were made. The PXI mountings originally allowed 13° elevation, later increased to 15° or 20°. Shells were 4crh.

6in BL Mk XIV and SV These were respectively the R and L guns in the twin turrets of the World War I monitors *Humber*, *Mersey* and *Severn* though only the first carried them for long. They were of typical Vickers wire construction with cannelured rings at the forward inner A/A tube shoulders, though the 2 reserve guns which were not used, had tapered inner A tubes. In all 4 of each mark were made. The twin turrets which had no mark assigned to them, allowed 15° elevation and shells were 4crh.

6in BL Mk XVI Another Vickers design with cannelured rings but differing in that it was wire wound for only part of the length, the B tube being directly over the A, forward of the jacket. The reserve guns which did not go to sea, differed in having a tapered inner A tube. It was mounted in the 1913 battleship *Erin* only, apart from some in World War II emergency coast defence batteries. Mk XVI had the highest muzzle velocity of any British service 6in without supercharges, and 19 guns were made in all. Shells were 4crh and the PX mountings allowed 15° elevation.

6in BL Mk XVII An Elswick design originally ordered by Chile and mounted in the battleships *Canada* and *Eagle*. Construction was similar to that of Mk XII but Elswick sliding hinge mechanism was fitted, with the fore part of the breech block conical. A total of 29 guns were made. Shell were 4crh and mountings were PXII in *Canada* and PXII* in *Eagle* with respectively 15° and 20° elevation.

6in BL Mk XVIII Another Elswick design and originally 5.87in for the 1914 Norwegian coast defence ships *Björgvin* and *Nidaros* taken over as the monitors *Glatton* and *Gorgon*. Construction was similar to that of Mk XVII but the long jacket was replaced by a B tube and shorter jacket. Production totalled 10 guns, shells were 4crh and the single turret mountings which allowed 20° elevation, were known as Mk IV.

6in QF Mk IV A 45 calibre Bethlehem gun of which 12 were bought from stock, 8 going to World War I defences at Scapa and 4 to DAMS. Full details no longer exist but the guns had screw breeches and fired separate ammunition with 4crh 100lb shells and MV 2600fs. The mountings allowed 15° elevation.

6in BL Mk XIX A World War I heavy field gun designed by Vickers and of only 35 calibre bore length. Up to 11 November 1918, 310 were delivered to the Army and it was still in service in World War II though its MV of 2420fs made it obsolescent when compared to equivalent US or German guns.

A magnificent view of the starboard casemated 6in Mk XII PIX battery in the battleship *Queen Elizabeth* c1917. The aircraft is a Sopwith 1½ Strutter.

CPL

PARTICULARS OF 6in GUNS

	6in (5.985in) BL Mk XIIB	6in BL Mk XIII	6in BL Mk XIV, XV
Weight inc BM (tons)	6.8875	8.777	8.094
Length oa (in)	279.728	310.425	309.728
Length bore (cals)	45.11	50.0	50.0
Chamber (cu in)	1770	1550	1650
Chamber length (in)	40.81	31.683	32.98
Projectile (lb)	100	100	100
Charge (lb/type)	27.81 SC122	24.44 SC140	28.63 MD26
	27.13 MD19	24.63 MD26	
Supercharge	34.25 SC150		
Muzzle Velocity (fs)	2807	2770	2900
Supercharge	3070		
Range (yds)	15,660/20°	13,475/15°	14,130/15°
	18,750/30°		
	20,620/40°		
Supercharge (6crh)	20,020/20°		
	23,770/30°		

	6in BL Mk XVI	6in BL Mk XVII	6in BL Mk XVIII
Weight inc BM (tons)	8.144	8.716	8.733
Length oa (in)	310.07	310.425	303.925
Length bore (cals)	50.0	50.0	48.92
Chamber (cu in)	1910	1650	1650
Chamber length (in)	44.433	33.75	33.75
Projectile (lb)	100	100	100
Charge (lb/type)	32.91 SC150	28.13 SC140	28.63 MD26
	32.31 MD26	28.63 MD26	
Muzzle Velocity (fs)	3000	2905	2874
Range (yds)	14,640/15°	16,190/20°	16,020/20°

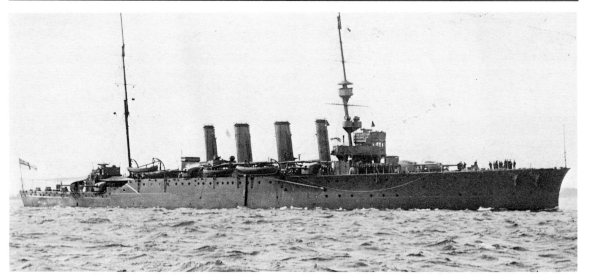

The light cruiser *Birmingham* with her beam 6in Mk XII PVII trained to starboard.

Popperfoto

6in BL Mk XX This was to be built like Mk XII, Mk XX* having no inner A tube, but with a shorter and lower volume chamber in an attempt to cure oval wear to which Mk XII was prone. A total of 37 guns were ordered in October 1917 but cancelled as trials showed loss of accuracy, and the only Mk XX was converted back to Mk XII.

6in BL Mk XXI This was originally ordered by Chile for coast defence and as completed was virtually Mk XVII but with a longer chamber, and B tube and jacket instead of full length jacket. It is believed that 16 guns were made of which 10 were taken over by the Army for coast defence using the low velocity Mk VII charge which took over 300fs off the potential MV, though it is thought that in World War II the heavy charge for Mk VII was issued. [**Note:** *A breech-view photograph of the 6in Mk XII PXII was prematurely published in Warship 28.*]

RN 77ft ELCO PT Boats

By Al Ross II

PT 65 and a sister at Melville, Rhode Island, USA 1943. The RN Elcos would have appeared like this had they been completed for the USN. The two after torpedo tubes have been replaced by depth charges on these two boats, a fairly common modification.

PT Boat Museum

MTB 315 at Alexandria. A somewhat blurred photo, but the single .50 calibre machine guns are clearly visible forward, as is the single 21in tube and the Vickers Mk V turret. She still has USN style pennant numbers and overall light grey scheme.

H Tong

MTB 315 was one of ten 77ft Elco PT boats transferred to the Royal Navy early in 1942. Originally part of the *PT 45-68* production batch, these ten boats were renumbered *BPT 1-10* (British PT) and were modified according to RN specifications, the major changes being:

1 The two twin .50 calibre machine gun turrets abaft the cockpit were replaced by a single Vickers Mk V .303in machine gun turret on the centreline.
2 Two single .50 calibre machine guns were fitted on tripods just forward of the wheelhouse.
3 The four trainable 21in Mk 18 torpedo tubes were replaced by two fixed 21in RN pattern tubes.
4 A hinged armoured plate was fitted to the aft end of the cockpit.

During February and March 1942, these ten boats (*MTB 307-316*) were assigned to the 15th MTB Flotilla (Lt D Jermain RN) at Alexandria, where they operated with 10th MTB Flotilla (*MTB 259-268*, 70ft Elco boats). Between August 1942 and April 1945, the 15th MTB engaged Axis forces in North Africa and the Aegean, losing six of their boats to enemy action. Four of these losses occurred during the disastrous commando attack on Tobruk on 14 September 1942. MTBs *308, 310* and *312* being lost to aircraft while *MTB 314* was damaged and captured. *MTB 314* was subsequently repaired, rearmed, and operated with the Germans until she was lost to Allied air attack herself in 1943. *MTB 311* was mined and sunk off Bone, North Africa on 2 May 1943 and *MTB 316* was sunk by the Italian cruiser *Scipione Africano* in the Straits of Messina on 17 July 1943. The remaining four boats were returned to the US Navy in October 1945 for disposal.

1 *MTB 263*, one of the 70ft Elcos of the 10th MTB Flotilla. The family resemblance to the 77ft boats is unmistakable.

PT Boat Museum

2 *MTB 307, 315*, and two US-built Vospers, possibly at Malta. While the image quality is poor, it does show that the boats of the 15th MTB Flotilla were repainted at least once. Although the boats were delivered in an overall light grey scheme (possibly 507-C) with USN style white, shadowed pennant numbers, this shot shows them in the more common RN scheme of white and light blue/grey (G45 or B55) with dark numbers.

H Tong

3 Officers of 15th MTB Flotilla (and possibly some from 28th MTB Flotilla) standing in front of a 77ft Elco MTB. The Vickers Mk V turret is clearly visible above the heads of the men to the far left.

PT Boat Museum

1

2

3

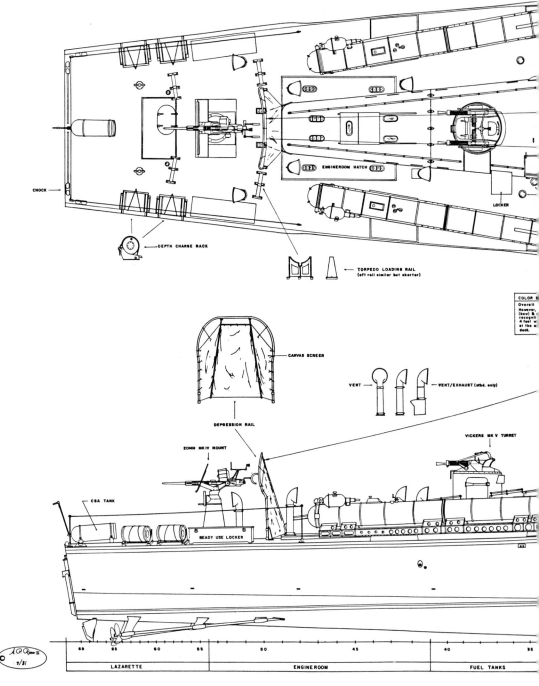

The subject of this drawing, *MTB 315*, participated in a series of operations between August 1942 and December 1943 that resulted in the destruction of at least four ships, several landing craft, an F lighter, and damage to an Italian cruiser. Returned to the USN in October 1945, *MTB 315* was subsequently transferred to the Italian Navy in 1947, being reclassified as *GIS 0020* and based at Taranto. Her ultimate fate is not known to the author.

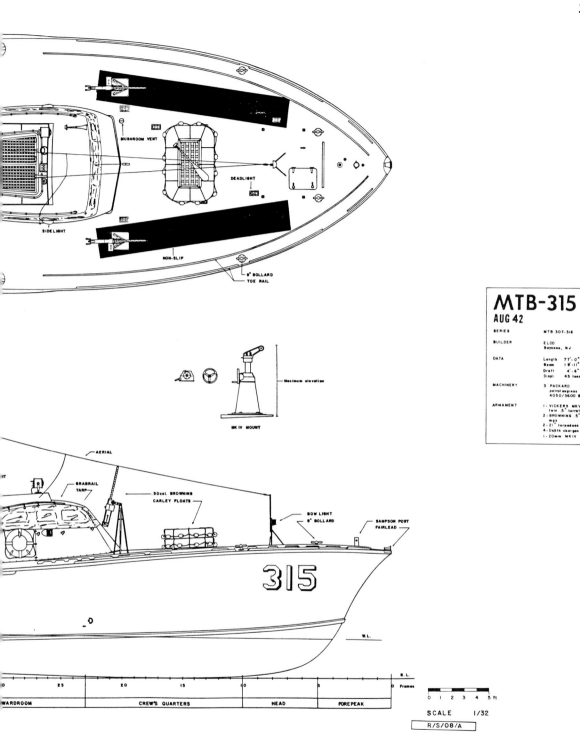

MUSHROOM VENT

DEADLIGHT

SIDELIGHT

NON-SLIP

9" BOLLARD
TOE RAIL

Maximum elevation

MK IV MOUNT

MTB-315
AUG 42

SERIES	MTB 307-316
BUILDER	ELCO Bayonne, NJ
DATA	Length 77'-0" Beam 19'-11" Draft 4'-6" Displ 45 tons
MACHINERY	3 PACKARD petrol engines 4050/3600 BHP
ARMAMENT	1- VICKERS MKV twin .5" turret 2- BROWNING .5" mgs 2- 21" torpedoes 4- Depth charges 1- 20mm MKIV

AERIAL

GRABRAIL
TARP

50cal BROWNING
CARLEY FLOATS

BOW LIGHT
9" BOLLARD

SAMPSON POST
FAIRLEAD

315

W.L.

B.L.

25   20   15   10   5   0 Frames

WARDROOM   CREW'S QUARTERS   HEAD   FOREPEAK

0 1 2 3 4 5 ft

SCALE   1/32

R/S/08/A

'BROWNWATER NAVY'
US Small Craft in Vietnam

By Norman Friedman

Historically, the United States Navy has always emphasised large ships and bluewater operation. When, from time to time and especially during the American Civil War, it has found itself fighting a coastal or riverine war, new 'brownwater' fleets have generally been extemporised. Vietnam is the most recent example, requiring the construction of an entirely new generation of small craft. Hundreds were built, and most of them were left in Southeast Asia when the United States withdrew. Only a very few remain in US service, although recently there have been attempts to develop a successor generation.

Relatively little of the history of these craft has been compiled. This article is an attempt to summarise the existing record so as to place the several types of Vietnam-era small craft in perspective. No design histories have been found, but it was possible to assemble something approaching a consistent account of the rise of the brownwater fleet employed in Vietnam, and of the operations it carried out.

Virtually all US coastal craft, including PT boats, were discarded in the first decade after World War II. The main exceptions were amphibious craft, such as the LCVP, LCPL, MSL (minesweeping launch) and LCM(6), which were carried aboard ocean-going ships en route to landings. They became the basis for the new brownwater fleet, since they were the only naval small craft in production when the Vietnamese emergency began. Similarly, the armament of the brownwater navy had to be extemporised, largely from Army weapons: 40mm and 20mm machine cannon, many of them electrically fed, and 0.50 and 0.30 calibre machine guns. There were many proposals for recoilless rifles (considered too dangerous) and also for missiles, such as Redeye (not ready in time).

One other weapon was introduced: the 81mm mortar. Mortars had never really been popular aboard ship, because they had such a small bursting area that they could rarely be expected to hit moving targets. But tests around 1961 showed that the mortar was uniquely valuable as an illuminating device for close-range night warfare. Since its muzzle blast could not be seen, it could not be taken as a point of aim. Yet it could project a relatively heavy illuminating round, and it was also the most powerful weapon a small boat could carry.

The American reversion to coastal operations began late in the 1950s as military advisers aboard began to ask

for a counter to the increasing tide of Soviet-built fast attack craft. About 1959 the US Ship Characteristics Board began to ponder designs for a US equivalent, primarily for export, and a few years later there was a competition for a hydrofoil gunboat, which led to the construction of the *Tucumcari* and *Flagstaff*. At about the same time, the US began to export military versions of the very successful Coast Guard 95ft coastal cutter, for a combination of river patrol and coastal security. The fast attack craft ultimately evolved into the big *Asheville*, described in *Warship* 21.

Meanwhile, the United States was approaching combat in South Vietnam. Inshore warfare there took several forms; naval forces operated both along rivers and along the coast. The US strategy was to deny the Vietcong shipments of arms by coastal craft (Operation Market Time, Task Force 115); to keep the Mekong channel to Saigon open (Operation Game Warden, Task Force 116); and to seek out and destroy Vietcong main and local units in the Mekong Delta (the riverine force, Task Force 117). In addition, riverine forces fought in the north near Hue during and after the Tet Offensive in 1968, as Task Force Clearwater. Finally, there was a small harbour defence force (Operation Stable Door, under Task Force 115).

When he took over as Commander of US Naval Forces, Vietnam in September 1968, Rear Admiral Elmo R Zumwalt (who later became CNO) ordered an offensive to seize control of the Rung Sat Special Zone, through which ran the channel to Saigon. He also tried to reorganise so as to accelerate Vietnamisation. Operation 'Sea Lords' added a river patrol along the Cambodian border to the existing Market Time blockade (Task Force 194). It combined Swift and PBR patrol boats as well as existing river assault units.

As in other aspects of the Vietnamese War, to some extent US tactics were patterned on those developed by the French during 1946-54. For example, the latter devised Naval Assault Divisions (DNA, or Dinassaut), which were developed further by the South Vietnamese themselves from 1954 onwards. By 1960 the Vietnamese Navy operated six River Assault Groups (RAGs), patterned on the DNA, each consisting of about 20 boats: monitors, command and control boats, French-built STCAN/FOM (patrol/minesweeping boats), armed LCVPs, and LCM(6) for troop lift. The monitor and command boats were conversions of the

Monitor *M-112-1* in the Mang Shit Canal, Mekong Delta June 1968.
USN

ubiquitous World War II LCM(6). In addition, the French and Vietnamese used the US-built LSSL gunboat, which was the only type for which the US riverine force had no direct equivalent. Unlike the DNA, the early RAGs had no integral Army troops, and were subordinate to a district Army commander, who tended to use it primarily for logistics.

RIVER CRAFT PROPOSALS 1961-62

Given the DNA/RAG precedent, the earliest US ideas for assistance were extensions of the existing riverine force. An ad hoc Navy group was formed late in 1961 to develop appropriate small craft. By March 1962 it had identified three categories:

Shallow water operations Swimmer support craft, carrying up to 6 men, had already been used successfully in Vietnam. There were also air-transportable 3-man craft, and there was a need for a 15-man troop-carrying utility boat.

Logistics/transport A variety of beaching craft were available, but they could not achieve the desired speed of 15 knots, nor could they meet the draft limit of 3ft 6in. The group therefore suggested a new riverine LCVP, which it christened RCVP. The configuration would roughly match that of the existing LCVP, although the 36ft length restriction on that boat, due to transport davit dimensions, could be relaxed to about 40ft. Construction would be of welded steel rather than wood or plastic, and the ramp height greatly reduced, as there was no need to drive through surf. Twin screws (compared to a single screw in the LCVP) would be protected

by tunnels in a W-shaped hull. There would be no armour as such, 1in plate would be enough to stop rifle bullets at short range, but twin engines, compartmentation, and all-steel construction would all contribute a measure of survivability. Such a craft might be armed with two 0.50 and two 0.30 calibre machine guns, as well as miscellaneous hand-held weapons, such as flamethrowers and Redeye missiles. It could even carry an 81mm mortar. The designers hoped that it could be built by the Saigon Navy Yard.

Patrol This was typified by the existing LCP(L) Mark 4, a personnel boat adapted as a gunboat. A Riverine Patrol Craft, or RPC, similar in design to the RCVP, would be better. Its hull would be roughly similar to that of the RCVP, but it would have no ramp. The same standard LCVP engines would be used, since they were in the existing Military Assistance Program. Armament would consist of a 20mm cannon forward, a 0.50 calibre machine gun aft, and two 0.30 calibre machine guns on either side abaft the pilothouse. The non-gunner crew members would be a helmsman and an engineer or relief coxwain or commander, and weight would be allowed for up to 18 troops. Cost was estimated at $25,000 on a production basis, compared with $30,000 for the existing plastic LCVP.

The ad hoc group could also see a need for an offshore patrol boat, but felt that the converted Coast Guard cutter/gunboat(PGM) was an adequate interim solution. It seemed underarmed, but that could be solved if all ASW capability was deleted. Clearly the faster type, then slowly evolving towards the *Asheville*, would be more satisfactory as part of a longer-term programme. It was also possible to imagine a requirement for something intermediate between RPC and PGM, and the ad hoc group proposed the Norwegian *Nasty*, which would

A PBR on Mekong patrol February 1968.
USN

River firepower from a PCF or 'Swift' during an Operation 'Sea Lords' raid, R Cua Lon, 11 November 1968. Weapons include an M79 66mm rocket launcher and the combined .50 cal machine gun/81mm mortar mount.

USN

soon be bought as the PTF. Both the PGM and the PTF could not go close inshore because of their excessive draft.

This was a prophetic study. The US 'brownwater' navy, as it developed during the Vietnam War, included both a river patrol boat (ultimately the PBR, or 'plastic') and a close inshore patrol boat (the Swift, or PCF), as well as a variety of river personnel carriers and one type *not* predicted, the river monitor. Of the craft proposed in 1962, only the RPC was actually built in the form intended. At least in concept, it appears to have been based partly on an existing French design, the STCAN, and it was probably influenced by a Thai Navy proposal sent to the US Navy at this time. However, it was very much a US design, and appears to have been the only major American design failure of its time. The RPC had excessive draft, and performed poorly in weed-clogged water. It was, therefore, cancelled after 36 had been completed in 1965. Of this total, 26 were transferred to South Vietnam in 1965, and six more to Thailand. The others were retained as minesweepers.

The other categories were filled by improvisation, drawing on both the US civilian market and on the existing range of Navy small craft, largely amphibious. The only fresh design was the ASPB, the river 'monitor' or 'destroyer'.

ORGANISATION 1966
American advisers went to South Vietnam in 1962, and the US riverine force was patterned on the RAGs. Reportedly at least six studies from 1961 onwards had called for the formation of a river force to fight the Vietcong in the Mekong Delta, and this requirement became more urgent as the Vietnamese government proved less and less effective in 1964-65. The US Military Advisory Command proposed the formation of a brigade-size Mobile Afloat Force, and detailed plans were completed by March 1966 and approved by Secretary of Defense Robert S McNamara in July. River Assault Flotilla One (TF 117) consisted of River Assault Squadrons 9 and 11 (TG Groups 117.1 and 117.2), each consisting of two River Assault Divisions (91, 92, 111, and 112, respectively).

As originally planned, each Assault Squadron was to consist of 34 converted LCM(6) and 16 newly-designed ASPBs, the latter being the only fresh design employed by the brownwater navy. The LCM hulls were to be converted into 26 armoured troop carriers (ATC), 5 monitors, 2 Command and Control Boats (CCB), and one refueler. In addition, the 9th Infantry Division, which was the attached Army force, provided 105mm howitzers on barges which the Force could tow. All 68 converted LCMs were on hand by June 1967 which gives some idea of the speed with which such craft could be procured in this emergency. By September 1968 TF 117 operated 103 ATC, 17 monitors, 6 CCBs, 4 refuelers, and 31 ASPB.

River Support Squadron Seven (TG 117.3) provided support, with 2 (later 4) self-propelled barracks ships (APB), 2 repair ships (ARL), 2 support ships (LST 1156 class), 2 heavy salvage craft (LHC), 2 light salvage craft (LLC), 2 tug boats (YTB), and 2 harbour clearance teams. The barracks ships *Benewah* and *Colleton* were recommissioned for Vietnam service on 28 January 1967, followed by *Mercer* and *Nueces* in 1968; all decommissioned in 1969-71 as US forces disengaged. *Benewah* was modified for flotilla/brigade command and control; *Colleton* was adapted for the river assault squadron commander and battalion commander, and at the end of 1967 she was provided with hospital facilities. In Vietnam, their complement of 12 officers and 186 enlisted men was supplemented by 900 troops and boat crews; armament was two 3in/50, 2 quadruple 40mm, 8 0.50 calibre and 10 0.30 calibre machine guns. For repair and maintenance the Riverine Force had the converted LST *Askari* (ARL 30), which had been decommissioned since World War II. The supporting LST 1156 class ship was chosen for her size, to provide sufficient storage space without excessive draft. She carried a 10-day supply of ammunition and emergency rations, as well as the brigade helicopter detachment, four H-23s. A second LST shuttled from Vung Tau to the mobile riverine base weekly.

RIVER MONITORS AND ASSAULT BOATS
The first monitors were converted from LCM(6) (landing craft) hulls, which formed the basis for many of the river craft. Typical armament was a 40mm gun, a 20mm, 2 0.50 machine guns, and 81mm mortar (or 2 M10-8 flamethrowers). Later units (Mk V) were built as such from the keel up. They used the same hull as the CCB command boats, with a twin 20mm bow turret, an 81mm mortar in a well, and a smaller turret on the superstructure for a 0.30 machine gun. Total armament included 4 0.30s. Some had a 105mm howitzer in place of the bow turret and mortar well. Both types were armoured against shaped-charge rockets with characteristic venetian blind-like armour slats. There was also a ZIPPO flamethrower conversion, intended to attack waterside bunkers. Numbers built are not available, but all survivors were transferred to the Vietnamese Navy in 1973. They included at least 22 converted LCM(6) (transferred 1964-67) and 42 purpose-built monitors.

The ASPB (Assault Support Patrol Boat) was the only craft specially designed for the river war, described as the destroyer and minesweeper of that specialised fleet. Built by the Gunderson Brothers Engineering Corporation of Seattle, it had a steel hull with an aluminium superstructure. It was equipped with a chain drag to counter command mines, and armed with a 20mm cannon, a twin 0.50 calibre machine gun, 2 Mk 18 grenade launchers, and 81mm mortar. ASPBs generally led riverine operations, sweeping ahead of the assault formation; they were also used as escorts, patrol craft, and counter-ambush craft. One unusual feature was the underwater exhaust system, adopted for silencing. The ASPB was built in two marks in 1967-68, both with welded steel hull, and capable of about 14 knots (compared with 16 as designed). The ASPB hull was also used for minesweeping (as the MSR) and for CCB duties. At least 84 ASPB were transferred to the South Vietnamese Navy.

Monitor *M-91-2* underway 9 May 1967 at close to the full speed of 8.5kts. The star marked turret is the 40mm gun with the 81mm mortar well between it and the main turret cluster of broadside cal .50s and a stern 20mm.

USN

Troops were generally carried in converted LCM(6)s, ATCs (Armoured Troop Carriers), each carrying a platoon of about 40 men. Some (ATC-H) were protected against mortar fire by hard steel plating overhead, fashioned into a helicopter pad. They were employed as battalion first aid stations. In addition, until the arrival of the specially-designed ASPB, the ATCs were the minesweepers of the Riverine Force. Each was armed with a 20mm cannon, 2 0.50 calibre machine guns, and 2 Mk 18 grenade launchers. Postwar, a new mini-ATC was developed, primarily for Special Forces operation, with an alluminium hull and ceramic radar, quiet engines (for 28 knots), shallow draft (1ft), and space for up to 7 pintle-mounted weapons. Unlike the ATC, they are not covered against plunging fire. In effect, they are fast craft for clandestine raids rather than plodding troop carriers. As of 1981, a total of 18 had been delivered, one powered by gas turbines.

For command and control, the riverine navy had CCBs, converted from LCM(6)s, and similar to the monitors except that a command module replaced the 81mm mortar of the latter; it was inserted between the after superstructure and the covered gun position in the bow. The latter could accomodate one 20mm or 40mm gun, and there were typically several 0.30 and 0.50 calibre machine guns.

RIVER OPERATIONS

The River Patrol Force (TF 116) was intended to secure the channel to Saigon, in Operation Game Warden. It tried to deny the Vietcong free passage down or across the rivers of the Mekong Delta by the ubiquitous sampan, to disrupt the enemy tax collection system along the rivers, and to help destroy the enemy infrastructure completely. Its primary weapon was the 'plastic' or PBR, the direct successor of the first US riverine craft in Vietnam, four 36ft LCPL-4 which operated from the Saigon Navy Yard in 1965, fighting the Vietcong cross-channel traffic in the Rung Sat Special Zone, through which ran the Long Tau shipping channel to Saigon. They were also intended to test the concept of waterborne interdiction patrols, which would complement Market Time (coastal operations). At this time the LCPL, designed as a small landing craft, was the only available suitable American craft: the US Navy had no craft designed for riverine warfare. The river patrol command, TF 116, was formally established in December 1965, to carry out Operation Game Warden.

The successor RPC having proven a failure, representatives of the major US commands met at Saigon in September 1965, to decide on a next-generation boat. They believed that about 120 patrol craft were urgently needed for work in the Delta and in the Rung Sat Special Zone. The Bureau of Ships was ordered to procure a new type, then designated PCR, in September. It asked for bids for a 25 to 30 knot craft, with a draft of only 18in when stopped (and 9 when cruising). A contract for 120 was awarded to United Boatbuilders of Bellingham, Washington, on 29 November, calling for delivery by the following April. The first boats arrived in Vietnam on 22 March 1966.

This new PBR, or 'plastic', was based on a 31ft plastic pleasure boat. It was much faster than the LCPL and had a much shallower draft than the RPC. The PBR had a plastic-foam lined fibreglass hull, and was propelled and steered by water jets, for an extremely shallow draft (3ft compared with 4ft for a Swift). A typical battery consisted of a twin 0.50 machine gun forward, a single 0.30 calibre machine gun aft, and an infantry-type 40mm

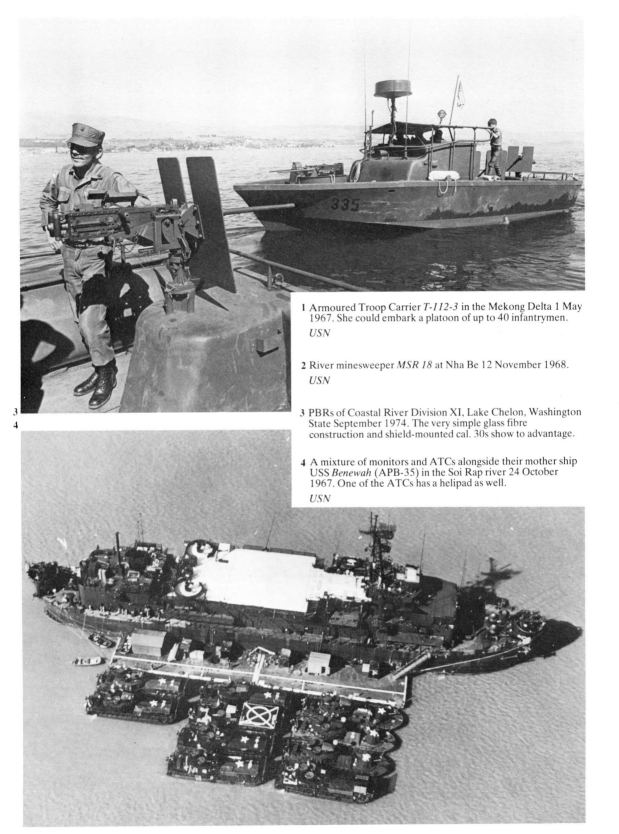

1 Armoured Troop Carrier *T-112-3* in the Mekong Delta 1 May 1967. She could embark a platoon of up to 40 infantrymen.
USN

2 River minesweeper *MSR 18* at Nha Be 12 November 1968.
USN

3 PBRs of Coastal River Division XI, Lake Chelon, Washington State September 1974. The very simple glass fibre construction and shield-mounted cal. 30s show to advantage.

4 A mixture of monitors and ATCs alongside their mother ship USS *Benewah* (APB-35) in the Soi Rap river 24 October 1967. One of the ATCs has a helipad as well.
USN

grenade launcher. The somewhat larger Mark II typically had 3 0.50s (one twin and one single) and a 60mm mortar; it had more powerful engines and enlarged mufflers. A total of 160 Mark I were built by United Boat Builders, Bellingham, Washington between December 1965 and April 1966. More than 500 were built in all, through 1973, the great majority being transferred to South Vietnam.

As originally conceived in 1965, TF 116 would consist of 120 PBRs, supported by 20 LCPL, 4 LSDs (as tenders and repair ships), 4 LSTs, and 8 UH-1B helicopters. In theory the LST and LSD, anchored off a major river mouth, could support 30 PBR and two helicopters. Reportedly World War II LSTs had been considered for this function as early as 1962. The first such tender was the *Jennings County* (LST 846), which served from May 1966 onwards. Others were *Harnett County* (LST 821), *Hunterdon County* (LST 838), and *Garrett County* (LST 786). Alterations included enlargement of the cargo hatch, installation of a 10-ton crane to lift out the patrol boats, and removal of a 50ft square section of main deck for installation of a helicopter deck. Ship communications were enlarged into a PBR command centre, and stowage for JP-5 fuel and 2.75in rockets installed. In addition, special barges were built to operate as mobile PBR bases, providing berthing and messing for crews, as well as command and control and support for the boats. The major problem was weather, which could be rough off a river mouth. In July 1966, for example, River Patrol Section 512 reported that it could operate only about half the time. PBR support therefore gradually moved up the rivers into calmer water.

By September 1968 TF 116 had 197 PBRs, out of an authorised strength of 250; by October, there were 220. They were organised in groups of ten, and many were retained in the United States for training.

COASTAL OPERATIONS
The coastal blockade force developed in parallel. As early as December 1961 US ocean minesweepers joined Vietnamese barrier patrols near the North-South border. They did not actually stop suspicious junk traffic, but vectored Vietnamese ships. Similar patrols, by US destroyer escorts, in the Gulf of Thailand began in February 1962. Few arms carriers were intercepted, and the patrols ended later in the year. From a tactical point of view, however, they were precursors of the large Market Time coastal operation. That began in 1965, as the Vietcong armed for what they expected would be the decisive phase of their insurgency.

After a North Vietnamese coastal ship was forced to beach in Vung Ho Bay, South Vietnam, in February 1965, over 100 tons of munitions was found aboard, and the blockade (Operation Market Time) was set up, with coastal surveillance centres at Da Nang, Qui Nhon, Nha Trang, Vung Tau and An Thoi; TF 71 was established as the Vietnamese Patrol Force. In August, responsibility shifted from the US Seventh Fleet to a specially-formed TF 115 (Coastal Surveillance Force). Market Time operated against two distinct sets of targets, coastal junks (which could lose themselves among about 50,000

PBR of River Patrol Force 116 approaching 25kts on the Saigon river November 1967. Note the low-mounted calibre .50s in the bows.

USN

civil craft) and trawlers or larger craft which had to operate further out to sea. Task Force 115 originally consisted of 7 former radar picket destroyer escorts, 2 ocean minesweepers, 2 (then 3) LSTs (to provide radar coverage of the entrances to the Mekong River), 17 82ft Coast Guard cutters, and patrol aircraft (both Marlins

and Neptunes). The surveillance area was divided into nine patrol zones, each controlled by a destroyer escort or minesweeper; the 82-footers were used for barrier patrols along both the North-South border and along the Vietnamese-Cambodian border in the South.

An entirely new type, the 'Swift', was introduced for inshore patrol. It was adapted from a standard commercial boat used to support oil drilling rigs in the Gulf of Mexico. All were built by Sewart Seacraft of Berwick, Louisiana, beginning in 1965, although procurement continued through FY72. The first 104 were Mark I, the remainder (of about 200 built), Mark II, with less sheer, a broken deck line, and the pilothouse set more astern. A typical armament was a twin 0.50 calibre machine gun above the pilothouse, with a combination 81mm mortar/0.50 calibre mount aft. PCF denoted Patrol Craft, Fast, a typical rated speed being 28 knots.

American 'Swifts' and Vietnamese junks patrolled inshore, under the radar control of the offshore craft. Late in September 1965, Market Time was reviewed,

Inshore Undersea Warfare 51, a large personnel landing craft (LCPL), inspects a Vietnamese sampan for contraband or infiltrators 13 September 1967.

USN

and various US commanders decided to increase the allotted forces, from 9 to 14 offshore patrol ships, from 17 to 26 Coast Guard craft, from 45 to 84 'Swifts'. A fourth LST was added, and patrol plane coverage doubled. The same conference recommended the formation of a river patrol force, of 120 craft operating from LST tenders, their patrols extending about 25 miles upriver. It became Game Warden (see above).

Market Time tactics employed aircraft and large ships to vector the small craft to intercept potential targets. The boats were kept in port awaiting interception calls, so as to reduce the maintenance they required. In 1969, while considering proposed production of hydrofoil gunboats, the Bureau of Ships argued that none of the existing craft (which then included PTFs and *Asheville*s as well as 'Swifts') could maintain sufficient speed to intercept in rough water. It was estimated that sea state three would be equalled or exceeded on 9-12 days of a typical month, and cloud cover would be frequent enough to preclude air surveillance. As a result, it appeared that the small craft could intercept their targets only one day in five. The Bureau argued at the

A varied array of landing craft beside their repair ship USS *Askari* (ARL-30) May 1967.

USN

US hovercraft No 1 in the My Tho river, Mekong Delta December 1967. Despite their high technology glamour the 6 used were not conspicuously successful from May 1966 and 3 were transferred to the Coast Guard in October 1969.

USN

time that the only solution was a boat capable of very high speed in rough water, a hydrofoil.

Other US small craft were also employed in Market Time: the *Asheville*s, also used in the riverine war, the hydrofoil *Tucumcari*, employed briefly and experimentally, and ocean minesweepers, which kept station offshore. The Coast Guard sent 26 82ft vessels (A and B types) to serve in Vietnam, armed with four 0.50 calibre machine guns and one combination 0.50 gun/81mm mortar. They were replaced in Coast Guard service by new boats numbered 82345 through 82370.

The Patrol Boat (PB) was developed postwar as a successor to the Swift. Two Mark I were completed by Sewart Seacraft in 1972 and delivered in 1973. They have one twin and four single gun positions for 20mm or 0.50 calibre guns. An alternative Mark III design by Peterson Shipbuilders of Sturgeon Bay, Wisconsin, won in competition with Mark I and is being procured, in 1983, for inshore warfare. Like the Swift, it is adapted from a Gulf of Mexico support boat. The pilothouse is offset to starboard to provide maximum deck space, and the nominal armament of four 0.50 machine guns can be reinforced by heavier weapons on the main deck. For

example, in 1981 the Norwegian Penguin III anti-ship missile was evaluated for them; it proved too heavy.

The riverine force ultimately operated a wide variety of craft, the largest being the 225ft *Asheville* class motor gunboat. There were also three Bell SK-5 hovercraft (licence-built British SRN.5 type), which the Navy classed as PACV, Patrol Air Cushion Vehicles. They were relatively unsuccessful, reportedly because they could not climb steep canal banks, and were transferred to the Coast Guard in October 1969. Three others were operated by the US Army.

In 1983 small numbers of PCFs and PBRs remain in service with the Naval Reserve, to preserve a core of riverine and coastal warfare expertise. There is also a project for a new coastal boat, tentatively designated PCM, which is to replace the existing PBR. Alternatives under consideration include surface effect craft as well as conventional displacement hulls; it is not clear to what extent truly amphibious operations are contemplated.

NOTE

Two articles in the US Naval Institute's *Naval Review* were particularly useful for the preparation of this one: 'River Patrol Relearned', by Cdr S A Swarztrauber, and 'The Naval War in Vietnam 1950 – 1970', by Cdr R L Schreadly (1971). Other information has been taken from official (unpublished) sources.

WARSHIP WINGS

No 8 Sopwith Pup

By Roger Chesneau

It is generally accepted that the Sopwith Pup was the first practicable carrier-borne aircraft. Although by the time the Pup was taken to sea in early 1917 aircraft had been operating successfully from warships for nearly four years (since the 1913 Naval Manoeuvres in fact, which saw the adapted cruiser *Hermes* pioneer the concept of shipboard air reconnaissance) the machines employed had been by and large seaplanes, which although capable of taking off directly from flying-off platforms using trolley assistance, could not land back on board again.

The Pup was a wheeled aircraft. First flown in February 1916, it immediately caught the attention of both the Royal Flying Corps and the Royal Naval Air Service owing to its magnificent handling qualities, reliability, high performance and excellent all-round view for the pilot. Significantly, it could also be landed at an approach speed of around 25mph IAS. It was the latest in a series of first class designs from Thomas Sopwith

such as the Tabloid, Schneider and 1½-Strutter, and reputedly originated from a chalk sketch scribbled on the company's workshop floor. It had already earned for itself a reputation over the Western Front as a highly successful scout/fighter when it was selected to replace Sopwith Baby seaplanes as a shipborne anti-Zeppelin interceptor. The problem with the seaplanes had been that their floats imposed severe weight and drag penalties. They prevented the aircraft from meeting the high-flying airships effectively. Recovery was more certain, but flotation gear in the form of inflatable air bags fitted to the undercarriage of landplanes should ensure that the pilot at least would survive a Pup's ditching.

Trials with the Pup were conducted aboard the seaplane carrier *Manxman*, and the persistence of Flt Cdr F J Rutland proved that the aircraft was even more adaptable to shipboard operations than had been imagined. By rigging tail trestle equipment at the start of the take-off run in order to raise the fuselage to its flying attitude, he was able to demonstrate the practicability of launching Pups from platforms as short as 20ft, a feat which led to the Sopwith fighter being embarked not only aboard seaplane carriers but also on forecastle ramps of cruisers (*Yarmouth* was the first such) and on flying-off platforms built atop the main turrets of battleships and battlecruisers (which could be turned into the wind for maximum effectiveness). The value of cruiser-borne interceptors was demonstrated in startling fashion even while experiments were being conducted, for on 21 August 1917 Flt Sub-Lt B A Smart rose from *Yarmouth*'s bow ramp and promptly shot down Zeppelin *L23*.

Less than three weeks earlier, on 2 August, the Pup had achieved another 'first', when Sqn Cdr E H Dunning performed the first-ever successful landing of a production military aircraft on board a carrier. Despite this achievement and its justly celebrated memory, the effect was to demonstrate how *impractical* such manoeuvres were, since they were accomplished only by dint of superb courage and unique airmanship. Dunning's death as a result of a subsequent attempt to repeat the landing (made on the forward flight deck having negotiated the swirling eddies set up by *Furious'* superstructure) served to accelerate the production of a flush-deck aircraft carrier. An interim solution seemed to be a landing-on platform aft to complement the forward flying-off deck: *Furious* was so fitted, but the air currents set up while the ship was under way proved almost as big a handicap to this system. Experiments with Pups fitted with skids in place of their wheels were hardly more successful, even when used in conjunction with longitudinal arresting wires fitted to the landing deck.

The Pup's work as an experimental carrier-borne aircraft continued after World War I, particularly in respect of landing trials. For example, the aircraft was used to test various pieces of arresting equipment,

A Sopwith Pup takes off from the forecastle ramp of the light cruiser HMS *Yarmouth*, 1917.
IWM

Sqn Cdr E H Dunning makes the first ever deck landing on a ship underway in a Sopwith Pup, literally arrested by manpower aboard the carrier HMS *Furious* 2 August 1917. Special attached straps just saved the Pup before it went over the side.

Roger Chesneau

including grooved wheels fitted beneath the lower mainplanes, rudimentary arrestor hooks fitted to the tailskids, and, perhaps most bizarre of all, a contraption above the aircraft's wing centre-section which would theoretically engage a high-rigged wire and bring the machine to a halt in that manner. Most of this experimental work was conducted at the Experimental Construction Depot on the Isle of Grain, and it continued until at least 1922, when the advent of flush-deck carriers rendered the more outlandish trials superfluous.

SOPWITH PUP SPECIFICATION

Overall length	19ft 3¾in
Span	26ft 6in
Max height	9ft 5in
Wing area	254 sq ft
Engine	(Typical) 1 × Le Rhone 9C rotary engine, 80hp
Max speed	111mph at sea level
Combat radius	About 120nm
Weight	785lb empty; 1225lb loaded
Weapons	1-0.303in Lewis machine-gun, 8 Le Prieur rockets

A Semi-submersible attack craft of the Imperial Japanese Army

By Hans Lengerer

One of the most interesting and curious craft the Tenth Military Experimental Station at Murotsu, Honshu, an Army establishment, investigated during World War II was the semi-submersible attack craft designed to run almost submerged in order to avoid detection. In September 1944 the Station began studies for a small craft capable of making concealed approaches very close to enemy vessels and attacking these vessels with torpedoes or explosives.

On 7 May 1945 the Station delivered Report No 17-45 on the mixed wood-iron construction that could be used either to launch torpedoes or as a suicide boat to the Army Ordnance Administration HQ. Up to this time three types had been tested out of which the second, named *Shisei kan sen kōgekitei* (*Shisei* = Experimental, Trial, *kan* = half, *sen* = submerged, *kogeki* = attack, *tei* = boat) was foreseen for mass production.

The research began in the middle of 1944, the design started, as already mentioned, in September and was completed in December of the same year. One experimental boat was built at Ujina Shipbuilding Co at Hiroshima and the boat was tested at Shikoku on 27 December. The experimental boat had a displacement of 5 tons, was 7m long and had a diameter of 1.2m. She was driven by a 60hp diesel motor that gave a speed of 8 knots. The complement consisted of one man only. The armament was either 2 simple torpedoes or 2 250kg depth charges. The almost submerged condition was taken in during running only.

Based on experience with the first experimental boat, named type T 1, another type, the already mentioned *Shisei kan sen kōgekitei*, was derived. The mass production design began in January 1945 and one month later construction started at Maeda Shipbuilding Co in Osaka. During the next month large parts of the builder's plant were burnt by US air attacks and Ujina Shipbuilding Co again built trial boat No 2. She was completed in the first ten days of April 1945 and tested on the 13th. Official tests were conducted from 22-29 April 1945 at Komouva Island. She displaced 6t, measured 10m long with a diameter of 1.5m. She drew 1.2m above the water and 1.5m below. Her top speed was 8kts to carry 2 torpedoes and 2 men into action.

Because it was this type that was intended for mass production the technical description will deal with it

whilst the drawings show *Go shiki kan sen kōgekitei* (*Go* = 5, *shiki* = type) that was only slightly different from *Shisei kan sen kōgekitei*. Only one Type 5 experimental boat was built by Maeda Shipbuilding Co and a ten hour test run was carried out at Osaka Bay during 21-27 March 1945.

TECHNICAL DESCRIPTION

The *Shisei* semi-submersible attack craft consisted of the hull, engine section, armament, accessories, and spare parts. Figure 1 is a rough overall plan of the boat.

Hull and fittings consisted of the shell, steering mechanism, hoisting gear, mooring gear, towing gear, ventilation system, and observation ports.

Shell was divided into three sections (Fig 2). The central section was made of steel while the forward and aft sections were made of wood. The steel section was a watertight cylinder consisting of outer plate, reinforcing ribs, inner plate, forward and aft bulkheads. The forward and aft bulkheads were removable. There was an engine mount on the inner deck, a small conning tower and a manhole on the top.

The wooden section were made up of the outer plates, reinforcing ribs, inner plates, longitudinal stringers and were of simple, non-watertight construction. The steel and wooden sections were coupled with bolts (Fig 3).

Steering mechanism By turning the steering wheel mounted on the steel section, the rudder at the stern was controlled by action of the control cables. The control cables passed through the conning tower to the outside (Fig 4). An unusual feature was the rudder that was a cylinder made of steel plates, framed in place by the rudder post and enveloped the propeller, thereby protecting it. Control cables were fastened to both sides of the forward edge of the rudder (Figs 5, 6). The Japanese reported that this rudder was very effective.

Hoisting, mooring and towing gear There were four hoisting rings on the top side of the steel section, one mooring fitting on both forward and aft wooden sections, and one towing fitting on both the steel and forward wooden sections (Figs 7, 8, 9).

Ventilation system This consisted of the intake pipe, water trap, and exhaust pipe. The air drawn in through the intake was separated at the trap from any salt water that might come in simultaneously and circulated

FIG 1 ELEVATION AND PLAN

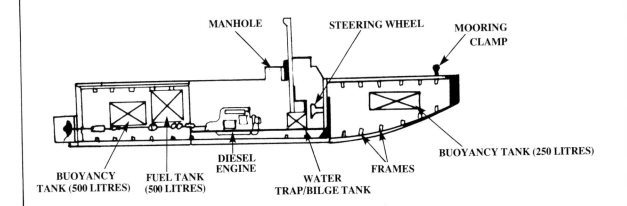

MANHOLE   STEERING WHEEL   MOORING CLAMP

BUOYANCY TANK (250 LITRES)

DIESEL ENGINE   FRAMES

BUOYANCY TANK (500 LITRES)   FUEL TANK (500 LITRES)   WATER TRAP/BILGE TANK

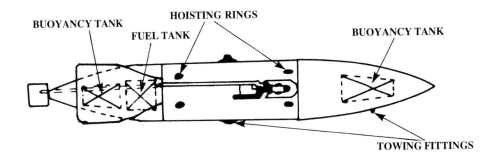

BUOYANCY TANK   HOISTING RINGS   BUOYANCY TANK

FUEL TANK

TOWING FITTINGS

FIG 2 ASSEMBLY SECTIONS OF THE SUBMARINE

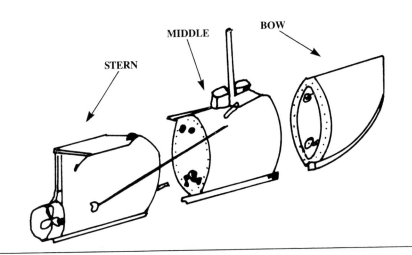

STERN   MIDDLE   BOW

FIG 3 STEEL AND WOODEN SECTION BOLTS

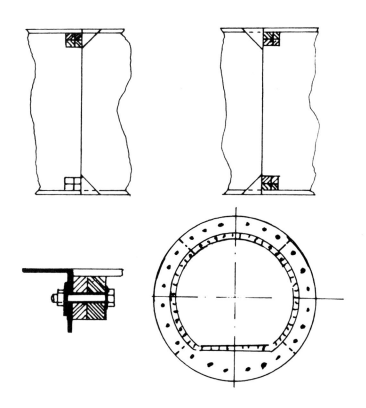

FIG 4 STEERING MECHANISM

**CONTROL CABLES WERE FASTENED TO BOTH SIDES
OF THE FORWARD EDGE OF THE RUDDER**

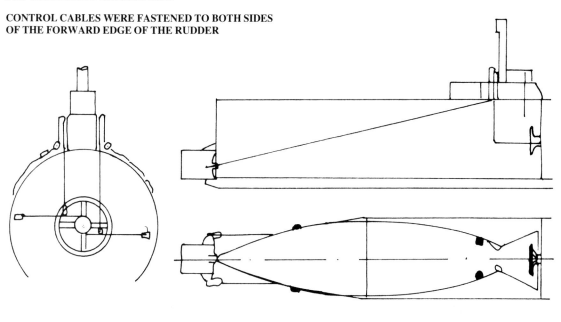

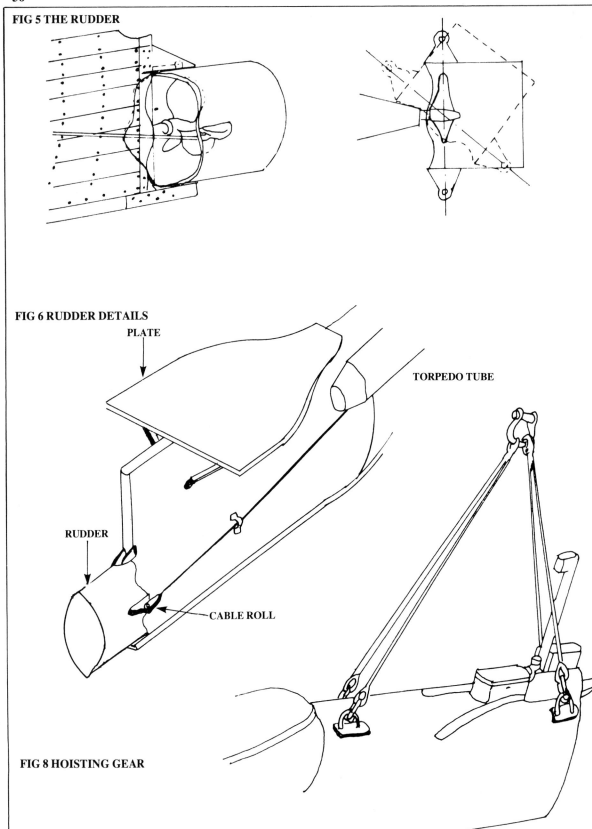

FIG 5 THE RUDDER

FIG 6 RUDDER DETAILS

PLATE

TORPEDO TUBE

RUDDER

CABLE ROLL

FIG 8 HOISTING GEAR

FIG 7 GENERAL DISTRIBUTION OF HOISTING, MOORING AND LOWERING GEAR

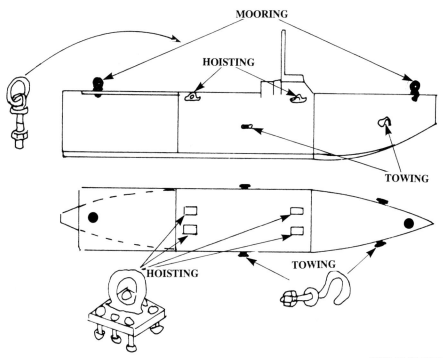

MOORING

HOISTING

TOWING

HOISTING

TOWING

FIG 10 VENTILATION SYSTEM

FIG 9 TOWING GEAR

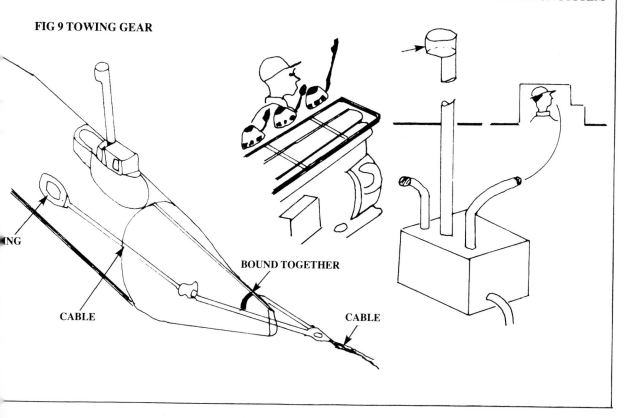

NG

CABLE

BOUND TOGETHER

CABLE

FIG 11 OBSERVATION PORTS AND SECTION

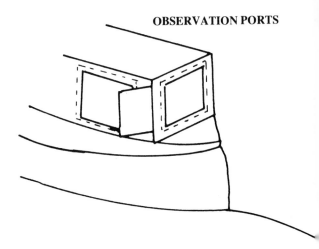

OBSERVATION PORTS

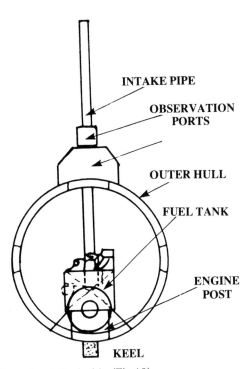

INTAKE PIPE

OBSERVATION PORTS

OUTER HULL

FUEL TANK

ENGINE POST

KEEL

throughout the inside (Fig 10).

Observation ports were placed on both sides and front of the conning tower (Fig 11).

Engine section comprised a main power unit, propeller shaft assembly, various tubes and tanks, and electrical equipment.

Main power unit was a 60hp diesel engine with an electric starter motor and charging generator as accessories (Fig 12).

Propeller shaft assembly consisted of the propeller shaft, shaft bearing, stern tube and propeller. The propeller shaft was broken into three sections by a universal coupling and shaft coupling. The shaft was held in place by the watertight bearing in the aft bulkhead of the steel section (Figs 13 and 14).

Tubes and piping comprised fuel lines, coolant lines, air exhaust pipes, and water exhaust pipes (Fig 15).

Tanks included the four tanks given as follows plus necessary tubes, pumps, valves, and cocks.

Buoyancy tank	250 litres	Forward wooden section
Buoyancy tank	350 litres	Aft wooden section
Fuel tank	500 litres	Aft wooden section
Water trap	150 litres	Steel section.

Filling or exhausting the buoyancy tanks with salt water, determined semi-submerged or normal afloat attitudes (Figs 15, 16).

Electrical equipment included power sources, electric lights, and distribution lines. The power source came from four batteries (6V, 140-ampere-hour). Lighting was provided by two portable electric lights. All this

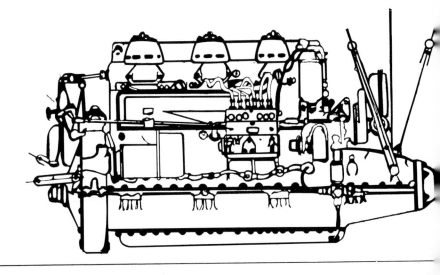

FIG 12 60 HP DIESEL ENGINE

FIG 13 PROPELLER SHAFT ASSEMBLY

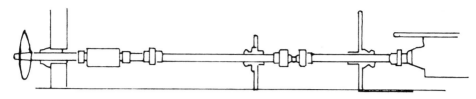

FIG 16 FILLING OR EXHAUSTING THE BUOYANCY TANKS DETERMINED THE TRIM

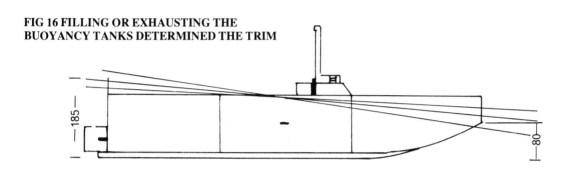

185

80

FIG 17 TORPEDO (ROCKET TYPE)

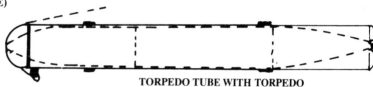

TORPEDO TUBE WITH TORPEDO

EXPLOSIVE

BUOYANCY CHAMBERS

ROCKET

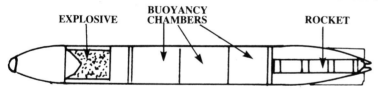

FIG 14 WATERTIGHT BEARING (AFT BULKHEAD BULKHEAD OF STEEL SECTION)

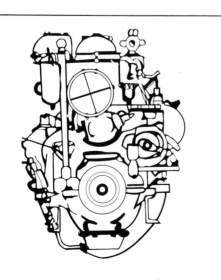

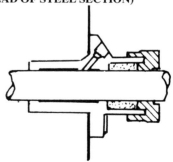

equipment was located within the steel section.
Armament One torpedo, either an explosive-propelled, simple type (Fig 17) or a 45cm (16in) electric-propelled type (Fig 18), was placed on either gunwale (Fig 19) or approximately one metric ton of explosive was placed in the forward wooden section.

FIG 15 TUBES, PIPES AND TANKS

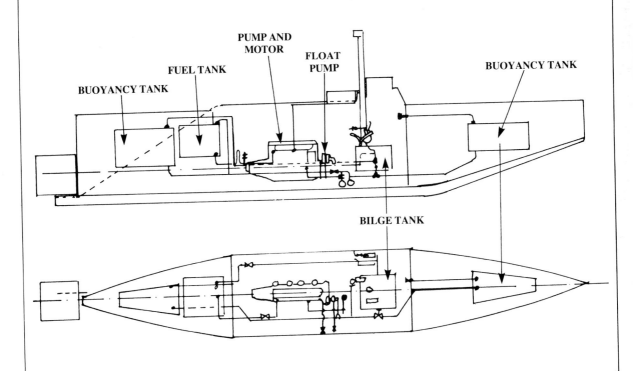

BUOYANCY TANK

FUEL TANK

PUMP AND MOTOR

FLOAT PUMP

BUOYANCY TANK

BILGE TANK

FIG 18 TORPEDO (ELECTRIC)

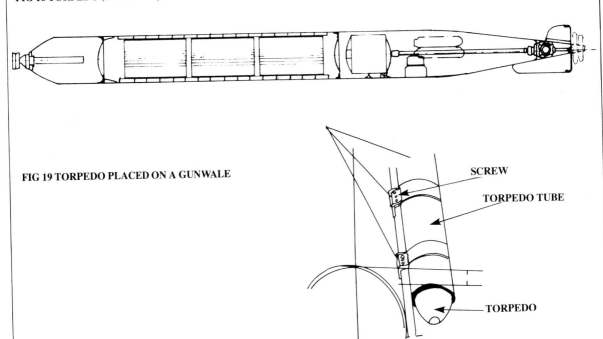

FIG 19 TORPEDO PLACED ON A GUNWALE

SCREW

TORPEDO TUBE

TORPEDO

LESSER KNOWN WARSHIPS OF THE KRIEGSMARINE
Marine Artillerie Leichter (MAL)

By M J Whitley

The advance of the German armies into Russia, particularly towards the oil fields of the Caspian Sea in 1942, led to the *Kriegsmarine* having to plan the construction of some form of warship which could reach these waters so distant from the borders of the Reich. Furthermore, there was not only the Caspian Sea to be considered, but also en route to it, the Sea of Azov and, in the Army Group North sector, the large lakes of Peipus and Ladoga over which it might also be necessary to exercise some limited form of sea power. The constraints on any design of such a craft were considerable, bearing in mind the distances over which they would have to be transported, the size limitations caused by the confined waters in which they would operate and the local facilities, which might be available for docking, maintenance etc.

Employment on the lakes of the Northern sector presented somewhat less of a problem than did the Caspian Sea, which was much farther afield. Given the small size of the vessels in question, the geographical situation and the *Kriegsmarine*'s lack of command of the sea, there was in fact only one means of getting them into their operational area – by rail from Germany. The decision had already been taken to build these craft in Germany and not sub-contract the work to local yards as was done with the *MFP*s (ferry barges) and *KFK*s (armed trawlers). It was, in any case, doubtful if there would be any building facilities available in occupied Russia. The obvious solution was to produce a pre-fabricated design that could be dismantled readily for transport by rail.

The initial design, of which 12 units were to be constructed by Krupp at Rheinhausen in 1942, was designated *MAL* Type I and intended for use on the Sea of Azov and Caspian Sea. It was a very simple and essentially crude design, consisting of a number of pontoons bolted together to produce a broad-beamed, flatbottomed, shallow draft landing craft type of limited sea-worthiness. Each pontoon section of about 18 tons could be accommodated on a single railway wagon, with further wagons carrying the engines and other ships fittings. The main armament, which was bolted directly to the tank deck, was to consist of two 8.8cm (3.5in) guns in single mountings. Two 2cm single guns provided light flak protection. About three lorries could be accomodated in addition or, if the 8.8cm guns were landed, five or six lorries could be carried.

DEPLOYMENT AND OPERATIONS

Of the first 12 ships, *MAL 1 - 4* and *MAL 8 - 11* were intended initially for the Black Sea and Sea of Azov where they were to form the 3rd Artillery Landing Flotilla. *MAL 5* and *MAL 12* were allocated to the Aegean, while *MALs* 6 and 7 were to go to the Tyrrhenian coast of Italy.

The ships allocated to form the 3rd Flotilla began to arrive in the Black Sea about April 1943 and from May were based in Sevastopol. The Flotilla was divided into two groups of which *MAL 1 - 4* formed the first, while *MALs 8 - 11* formed group 2 (Oberleutnant zur See Hell). With the securing of the Straits of Kerch and the capture of Rostov by the First *Panzer* Army, the flotilla moved into the Sea of Azov, where it operated for the remainder of its existence, supplying the armies along the littoral and defending the *MFP* convoys from attacks by the AMGBs of the Soviet Azov Flotilla. The flotilla operated between Taganrog, Berdyansk, Mariupol, Genichesk, Kerch and Sevastopol, between June and October 1943. The main opposition was from the air but the greatest hazards were mines laid in these shallow waters, which, although they did not count any *MALs* among their victims, a number of *MFBs* were so lost. Some surface actions occurred, principally one on 18 August 1943, when *MALs 1* and *2* engaged a force of AMGBs, claiming two sunk.

Even in the confined waters of the Sea of Azov, adverse weather conditions were experienced and the primitive *MALs* showed some shortcomings. They were lightly constructed and in relatively mild sea conditions (2-3) it was found that seas coming on deck penetrated the seals on the upper hatches to the pontoons, which rapidly filled with water. This problem was exacerbated by the scuppers being too small and not draining the decks quickly enough. After such a passage to Sevastopol in May 1943, it was seriously considered that the pontoon sections should be welded together permanently. These defects made conditions aboard miserable bearing in mind these early types were not fitted with mess decks for the crews. Furthermore, the freshwater stowage was found to be inadequate, necessitating the installation of extra tanks and there was serious danger to the crew and vessel from the fact that no training stops were fitted to the armament. Navigational equipment was spartan and, as a result of air attacks, shields were fitted to the 8.8cm guns.

This extra load reduced the already low freeboard of the craft and, together with the square, blunt bows and flat bottom, made for very poor handling and sea-keeping ability. Thus it was the sea which claimed the first loss, when *MAL 8* was lost in the Sea of Azov through stress of weather on 1 September 1943. By the beginning of the following month, *MAL 2* and *MAL 4* had been withdrawn to Sevastopol for refits and repair, leaving *MAL 1, 2, 9, 10* and *11* remaining in the Sea of Azov at Genichesk. The German armies had by now over-reached themselves in their drive to the Caspian Sea and did not possess the strength to reach their final objective. Thus, in October, the Kuban Bridgehead was evacuated in Operation Brunhild to Sevastopol and the Crimea with as many craft as possible being withdrawn

Probably a Type I *MAL*, as used in the Sea of Azov. The low freeboard and simple construction is evident from this photograph. This early vessel carried two single 2cm guns on the deckhouse for air defence.

J Meister collection

from the Sea of Azov, while the Germans still controlled the Kerch Straits. However, weather conditions were at this time poor and the chances of the *MALs, MFPs* and other slow craft in Genichesk getting out in time were slim. On 28 October, the Admiral Commanding Black Sea, Vice-Admiral Kieseritzky passed orders over the telephone to the flotilla instructing them to land ships companies and such light guns as was possible, then scuttle the flotilla in the port. At 0500 the following day, the five *MALs* (*1, 3, 9, 10* and *11*), together with some *MFPs* and the patrol vessels *RM2* and *RM3* were anchored in three lines off the harbour, then sent to the bottom with a 250kg bomb in each. All the crews were then evacuated back to the Crimea by road.

The flotilla was reformed on 6 March 1944 composed of *MFPs* while *MAL 2* and *MAL 4*, the only survivors, were dismantled at Sevastopol and sent by rail to the Rumanian port of Constanza, where they remained until the final German withdrawal from the Black Sea. Their subsequent fate is unclear and they were probably scuttled off Constanza in late August as that port was evacuated.

Neither Danube Flotilla records nor the report of Rear-Admiral Zieb's retreat up the Danube in August 1944 makes any further mention of these two craft, so it would appear a fair assumption that both were scuttled as stated. *MAL 9* was scuttled in the Sea of Azov and not as given in Gröner. It was *AT 913* which was sunk with *F 316* by Rumanian monitors on 27 August.

To follow the story of the other Type I craft we now go to the Aegean Sea, where *MAL 5* and *MAL 12* had been railed to Piraeus to join the *Kustenschutz* Flotilla 'Attika'. Both units commissioned at Piraeus on 12 August 1943 and formed part of the 'VP' (or patrol boat) group of the flotilla. Supporting and supplying the Aegean islands, the two craft served until the German withdrawal from the area towards the end of the war. *MAL 5* was last recorded in Piraeus on 31 March 1944 and her subsequent fate is unknown. *MAL 12* survived hostilities and was among the haul of minor vessels captured by the Royal Navy in the Leros/Kalimnos/Kos area in 1945. Her subsequent fate is not recorded.

Of the remaining Type I craft to be discussed, *MALs 6* and *7* were dispatched by rail to Pola at the head of the Adriatic where they were assembled and commissioned on 14 May 1943 for service with the 2nd Landing Flotilla in the Tyrrhenian Sea. Both craft made the long sea journey down the length of the Adriatic and around the toe of Italy to Taranto without incident. *MAL 6* joined the second group of the flotilla while *MAL 7* joined the 3rd. Both then operated in the Naples/Catania/Vibo Valentia area. On 22 March 1944 they were transferred to the 10th Landing Flotilla for service in the Adriatic.

ADRIATIC OPERATIONS

After rail transport back to Trieste, where they arrived on 28 April 1944, both recommissioned on 23 May for the first group of the flotilla under Leutnant zur See Emmel. In the Adriatic, both craft, by now fitted additionally with a 2cm vierling, carried out supply and escort missions along the Dalmatian coast. Here the opposition was fierce in the form of MTBs and MGBs of the Royal Navy's (and RCN's) 56th, 57th and 61st Flotillas, which operated continuously against German convoy traffic as the Dalmatian coast was evacuated.

By October 1944 German forces were evacuating the Dalmatian area under intense pressure from the Partisans. On 9 October, both *MAL 6* and *MAL 7* were in Dubrovnik where *MAL 6* was experiencing engine problems, but on the 17th, both were in action against Partisan forces in Ombla Bay. In the course of this engagement, *MAL 6* suffered a barrel burst in one of her 8.8cm guns. The following day, the Naval Commandant (South Dalmatia) signalled the commander (10th Landing Flotilla) that he intended to sail an evacuation convoy consisting of both *MALs* and a number of I boats from Slano on the evening of the 20th bound north-wards. However, the engine problems aboard *MAL 6* still remained, despite emergency temporary repairs to the port motor, so that she was only capable of 3kts and that for only a short distance. Added to the fact that half her armament was out of action, this put an unacceptable burden on the evacuation convoy with the result that it was decided to leave the craft behind. *MAL 6* was scuttled at 0700 on 19 October at Doli and her crew transferred to units of the 3rd E-boat Flotilla for evacuation. The *MAL* Group commander, Ob Lt z S Müller, took over command of the remaining I boats, *I 10, 46, 15* and *68*, with the intention of sailing them northwards, but in the event, this proved impossible and these boats too were scuttled, whereupon Müller and the remaining boat crews joined up with Naval Shore forces and managed to fight their way through Partisan lines back to German-held territory. After heavy fighting, the small band managed to rejoin 10th Flotilla on the 24th.

Meanwhile, *MAL 7* together with the sea-worthy *I* boats, *I 07, 12, 34, 65, 74, 96* and *114* sailed from Slano at dusk on the 20th under the command of Ob Lt z S Ritter, to attempt to reach Trieste. The first leg was from the Island of Sipan to Ploca at the slow speed of 5kts. The attempt was however, doomed, none of the craft reached their destination, for the whole convoy was annihilated by Allied coastal forces farther north along the Dalmatian coast.

MODIFICATIONS

The experience gained with the Type I design led to a modified design, Type Ia, which introduced features rectifying the obvious shortcomings of the earlier craft. These principally involved the incorporation of living quarters for the crew and a better design of wheelhouse on a slightly greater displacement hull, part of which increase was due to an increase in bunkerage from 6000 to 6360 litres of diesel fuel. The individual pontoon sections were also strengthened. Main propulsion remained two 130hp 6-cylinder Deutz F6M lorry engines. AA armament was increased to one 3.7cm SKC/30 and one vierling 2cm/38. Guns crews for the flak armament were drawn from the after 8.8cm when air attack threatened. However, many units received no more than two 2cm guns plus two 15mm MG 34 machine guns. It had been intended to rearm all Type Ia craft with the more powerful 8.8cm KM 41 in flak LM 41 or the anti-tank 7.5cm PAK 40M in LM 43 or 39/43 or 10.5cm on SKC/32 in MPLC/32ge mountings, but by

July 1944, the Naval staff reported that this would not be possible in the foreseeable future, due to shortages in supply.

Ship's company consisted of one officer or petty officer in command, coxswain, ERA, bosun, 16 gunners, rangefinder, cook, ordnance mechanic, two radio operators, one signalman and four stokers, a total of 30.

LAKE PEIPUS FLOTILLA

A series of 24 ships (*MAL 13-36*) were planned and ordered from Krupp on 12 March 1943. All these were intended for service on Lake Peipus in Estonia, but only 12 reached the 1350 square mile lake before the Soviet offensive drove Army Group North from its shores in August 1944. Once again, dismantled craft were railed up from Germany, this time to Dorpat, where on the Embach river, they were assembled for service. The first two to reach Dorpat, *MALs 13* and *15*, commissioned there on the morning of 23 May 1944 as part of the 4th Artillery Landing Flotilla under the command of Korvetten Kapitan Wassmuth.

The flotilla had been formed exactly a week earlier. It was Wassmuth (then Kpt Lt) who had formed the 3rd Flotilla in the Black Sea the previous year. Also attached to the flotilla were the other light forces then operating on the lake. These consisted of two patrol boat groups both 21 units, No 1 (*V111 - 115, V121 - 125, V131 - 135, V141 - 146*) and No 2 (*V212 - 215, V221 - 225, V231 - 235, V241 - 246*). The KS boats (*Kleine Schnellboote*) *KS 1, 2, 9, 10, 12, 16, 25* and *26* and KM (*Kleine Minenleger*) minelayer boats *KM 4, 5, 19, 22-29*, also served with this flotilla. As the *MALs* reached the lake, they were formed into groups, initially two: Ob Lt z S Leithof's 1st (*MAL 13, 15, 17*) and Ob Lt z S Brandt's 2nd (*MAL 14, 16*). Later, numbers *19, 21* and *23* joined the Leithof group with *18, 20, 22* and *24* going to Brandt's.

In the summer of 1944 the advancing Soviet forces once again reached the lake and formed a lake flotilla from 23rd and 25th Independent River Craft Brigades. The German forces patrolled the lake, shelled enemy position on the eastern shore and occasionally engaged Soviet patrol craft. However, it was aircraft which caused the brunt of losses, the first of which was *MAL 19*, bombed, beached and burnt out at Mustevee on 19 July. *MAL 15* and *17* were damaged, then further damaged and destroyed by fire the following day. Air attacks continued with *MAL 13* being bombed and sunk off the Ranna-Pungerge river on the 27th. The next day, *MAL 15* was severely damaged for the third time by aircraft. Salvage proved impossible apart from one of two pontoons.

A good view of the Finnish *M32*, ex-*MAL 32*, on Lake Ladoga in the summer of 1944. The low freeboard and wide beam are quite plain. This Type Ia craft shows the glazed wheelhouse in lieu of the open position of the earlier type. On the foredeck are the two U-boat pattern 8.8cm guns with ammunition stowage between. The flak outfit is now increased to a quadruple 2cm vierling on the deckhouse with a 3.7cm single below and abaft of it.

J Meister collection

On 1 August, the remaining 8 ships formed four groups:

1st (Ob Lt z S Brandt)	*MAL 18, 22*
2nd (Ob Lt z S Schlotel)	*MAL 20, 24*
3rd (Ob Lt z S Bellstadt)	*MAL 14, 23, 16*
4th (Ob Lt z S Leithof)	*MAL 21*

However, *MAL 16*, lying under camouflage on the Embach river was bombed by six JL2 aircraft on the 2nd. Her magazine exploded and she was quickly burned out.

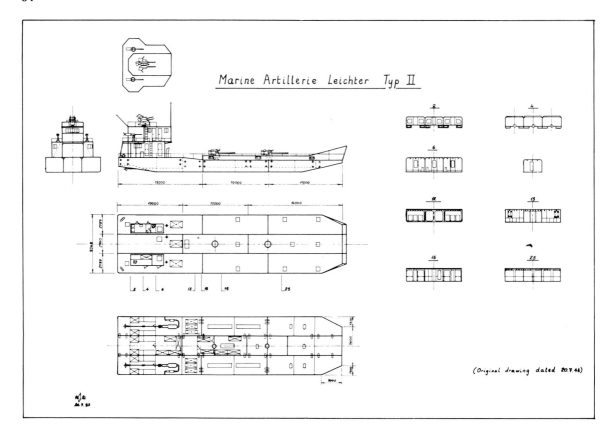

Marine Artillerie Leichter Typ II

(Original drawing dated 20.7.43)

Air raids also damaged *MAL 22, 23* and *24* (1-8 August). The numbers were once again reduced when *MAL 22* went aground off Marapalu 3nm south of Praaga in the early hours of the 16th and was declared a total loss the following day. Then on the 17th, *MAL 20* near Lunza bridge on the Embach river was sunk by air attack.

By August 1944 the Red Army was threatening German forces around Lake Peipus and by the end of that month, the position had become critical. Admiral Commanding (Eastern Baltic) informed his Army counterparts on the 24th that 4th Flotilla intended to station two *MALs* in support of the bridgehead off Praaga, one similarly employed at Kavastu, some 15km east of Dorpat and one in support of the army at Kastre. The following day, the last four KM boats were withdrawn to Reval, their light armament and high fuel consumption rendering them useless for further service on the lake. At Reval they were attached to 31st Minesweeping Flotilla. There were now few craft left on Lake Peipus for eight KS boats had previously been sent up to Narva Bay and the Army now intended to withdraw all their *Pioneerlandunsboote*. In the face of heavy Soviet attacks, Dorpat had to be evacuated on the 25th, with the current flotilla commander, K Kpt Kahle, being killed in the withdrawal. On 30 August *MAL 18* and *24* were bombed and shot up at Ranna-Pungerge and a day later *MAL 23* suffered a similar fate at Mustevee.

Reduced now to only two vessels, *MAL 14* and *21*, the flotilla continued to engage the Soviet forces until, on 19 September, the two craft shot off the last 900 rounds of 8.8cm ammunition, before scuttling themselves.

The original intention to send all this group of *MALs* to the lake was thwarted by the Soviet advances. This became obvious by mid-1944, for already *MAL 25* and

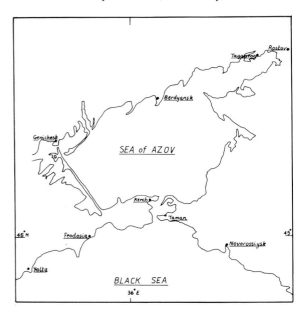

26 had been diverted for service with the *Ausbildungsabteilung* (Amsterdam) of 1st Landing Training Division. It came into action after the allied invasion, when on 9 November 1944, *MAL 25* was sunk in action with army artillery at Moerdyk in South Holland. *MAL 26* was presumably lost in the area about the same time too.

Four more ships, *MALs 27, 28, 29* and *30*, had been earmarked for use on the Danube, of which more later, but another four, *MALs 31, 32, 33* and *34*, were already in transit to Dorpat when it was realised that they would probably not arrive in time. The Finns were at this time negotiating to buy gunboats for Lake Ladoga, where strong Soviet forces had opposed a weak German/Finnish/(and earlier) Italian flotilla. In June 1944 therefore, these four MALs were sold to the Finns. Also scheduled for transfer were *AFP 18, 19, 21, 22, 23, 26, 27, 33* and *38* but these gun ferries fall outside this account. The first two, *MALs 31* and *32*, left Dorpat each on a train of 9 wagons with pontoons, two with ships fittings and two with other equipment in the evening of the 5 July, arriving in Reval on the 7th. Travelling with them were their crews and a Finnish liaison officer. In Reval, they were loaded aboard the ss *Drechtdjk* the following day. Arriving in Helsinki. they were transhipped once more and put on the railway. Travelling via Viborg, the trains reached the assembly point, Lahdenpokja, on the NW corner of Lake Lagoda on 11

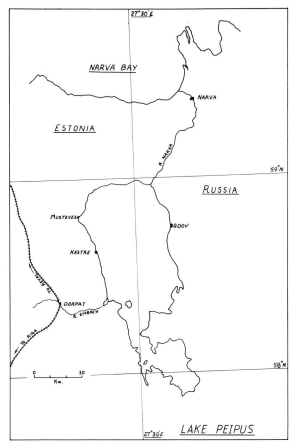

July. *MAL 33* and part of *MAL 34* arrived here on the 19th but the latter's engines were left behind in Reval. *MAL 31* and *32* were running engine trials by the 22nd which was the day the Soviet armies reached the 1940 Finnish frontier beside the lake. Their operational service was brief, for the Finns pulled out of the war on 2 September and all four craft fell into Soviet hands at the armistice.

DANUBE FLOTILLA

To return now to those units diverted to the Danube Flotilla, *MAL 28* and *MAL 30* arrived in Vienna in November 1944. The composition of the Danube Flotilla was established on 1 December as 4 *MALs* (*27, 28, 29, 30*); 2 *AFP* (*AF 916, 917*); 7 escort *MFPs*; 4 *Sperrbrecher MFP* (mine destructors); and *Schiffe 192*.

A second series of Danube barrage breakers was also planned. Four of the new *Marine Nachschub Leichter* (*MNL*) or supply lighters were to be so converted as soon as they were available (*MNL 1, 2, 11* and *12*).

It would appear that only *MAL 28* and *30* saw active service on the river as German forces retreated up it back into Austria from the Black Sea. Under the command of Lt z S Kuhk and supported by the depot ship *Weichsel* (132-ton steam tug), the two craft performed numerous escort and fire support operations on the middle and upper reaches of the Danube during the last month of 1944 and January 1945. The deteriorating situation on the river demanded increased fire support for the armies on its shores and to this end, both *MAL 28* and *30* were earmarked for conversion to monitors. Also, the four MNLs referred to above were to be converted to monitors and not CAM *sperrbrechers* as originally intended. However, on 8 January, the conversion of these four was cancelled as was their transfer to the Danube because *OKM* considered that the reduction in the sphere of operations of the flotilla no longer warranted their despatch there.

MAL 28 and *30* were ordered to winter at Vienna in January 1945 with *MFP 139, 170, 307, 909, 1028, 1033* and *1041*, the first three of which were also to be converted to gun-carriers, By the new year, *MAL 29* and *27* had also arrived in Vienna but by early February, both had been so badly damaged by air raids that they later sank. The original pair entered the 'Gute Hoffnungshutte' yard at Vienna-Freudenau on 24 January for conversion to monitors with a planned completion date of 10 March 1945. The armament of the planned conversion was to consist of 2 - 8.8cm SKC/35, 1 - 3.7cm; 1 - 2cm vierling; 4 - 8.6cm RAG; and 2 - Mg 151. Also to be fitted was 20mm side armour and 16-17mm bridge protection. The subsequent fate of these two units is not known but since the Red Army was at the gates of Vienna by the beginning of April, it is probable that this conversion was never completed and that both vessels were either scuttled, or captured by the Soviets.

TYPE II

The third series of craft, designated Type II, resulted in a much larger design, with displacement increased by 47% to produce a much more seaworthy craft. It remained a

TABLE 1: CLASS TECHNICAL DETAILS

	Type I	Ia	II
Displacement	140 tons	146 tons	185/177 tons
Length	112ft 2in (34.2m)	112ft 6in (34.3m)	116ft 6in (35.5m)
Beam	25ft 11in (7.7m)	25ft 11in (7.72m)	28ft 3in (8.6m)
Draft	2ft 10in (.89m)	2ft 9in (.83m)	2ft 4in/3ft 7in (.72/1.1m)
Machinery	2×Deutz F6M	2×Deutz F6M	2×Deutz SA6M
Horse Power	260 = 8.5kts	260 = 8.5kts	250 = 6.5kts
Bunkers	1320 gal	1400 gal	1400 gal
Radius of action	790nm at 8.5kts		900nm at 6.5kts
Armament	2 × 8.8cm SKC/35 in ULC35		
	2 × 2cm C/38		
	Type Ia in addition 1 × 3.7cm SKC/30		
	and some with vierling		
	Type II : 2 × 10.5cm SKC/32 in MPL C/32 ge		
	or 2× 8.8cm KM 41 in FLAK LM41		
	or 2 × 7.5cm PAK 40 in LM43 or 39/43		
	2 × 3.7cm FLAK LM42 in LM42		
	1 × 2cm vierling 38/43U		
	4 × 8.6cm RAG		
Payload	80t	80t	120t = 240m
			160 men as ferry
			90 men for day
Crew	21	28	28

Two *MALs* interned at Deggendorf in the Bayrischer Wald on the Danube between Regensberg and Passau, May or later 1945. These two ships are probably *MALs 28* and *30*. The provision of shields for the main armament would be essential for close quarters river engagement.

J Meister collection

sectional, portable design but with the pontoon sections increased to 20.3 tonnes each. A series of 84 units (*MAL 37 - 120*) was planned for deployment in the Adriatic and Aegean seas, to be completed at a rate of eight per month from October 1944. All were to be constructed by Krupp at Rheinhausen. *MAL 37 - 48* were ordered on 7 April 1943, *MAL 49 - 72* on 5 June and the rest on 3 March 1944. It is probable that construction never went beyond *MAL 47*. The main armament was to consist of two 10.5cm SK/C32 together with two 3.7cm SKC/30 guns in single mountings ULC/39. In addition, one 2cm vierling in 38/43u mounting was also carried. It was intended that the flak outfit would be altered to two 3.7cm 43M, one 2cm DL44 twin and two Mg 151 as and when these guns became available. This also applied to the fitting of 4 8.6cm RAG.

It would appear that units up to *MAL 45* were to be deployed either on Lake Peipus or retained in home waters after the loss of German control over that theatre. Seven further units, *MALs 46, 47, 50, 51, 54, 55* and *58* were allocated to the Adriatic while *MALs 48, 49, 52, 53, 56, 57* and *59* were appointed to the Aegean. None of these ever reached their intended theatre of operations. The deployment of higher numbers was apparently not discussed.

MAL 37 was destroyed during an RAF air raid on Sassnitz in the night of 6/7 March 1945, while *MALs 38, 43, 44, 45, 46,* and *47* are believed to have survived the war. *MAL 38* and *47* are, however, the only ones to appear on the Tripartite Commission's list of captured enemy ships. It is possible, however, that others survived in Soviet controlled areas but were never declared to the Commission by the Russians. Further incomplete units are reported to have been utilised as postwar harbour auxiliaries.

TABLE 2: MAIN GUN ARMAMENT

8.8cm SKC/35

Calibre	88mm (3.5in)
Muzzle velocity	700m/s (2296fps)
Shell weight	9kg (19lb 13oz)
Shell length	397mm (16⅛in)
Filling weight	1.365kg (3lb)
Weight of round/length	13.1kg (28lb 13oz)
Length of round	75cm (29½in)
Max horizontal range	11,950m (13,068yds, 6.4nm)
Max vertical range	
Barrel calibre/length	45cal/398.5cm (13ft)
Liner calibre/length	42.4cal/373.1cm (12ft 3in)
Constructional gas pressure	2400kg/cm
Elevation/depression	+30°/−10°
Training arc	no limit
Weight of barrel plus breech	776kg (1710lb)
Weight of cradle and brakes	280kg (617lb)
Weight of mounting	1180kg (2601lb)
Weight of complete gun	2425kg (5346lb, 2.3 tons)

Another view of Deggendorf with, in the lefthand edge, the outboard craft of the previous photograph. She appears to have the starboard *vierling* and single 3.7cm aft. The remainder of the vessels are the surrendered remnants of the Danube Flotilla – a motley collection of MFPs, armed steamers and other river craft.

J Meister collection

TABLE 3: CLASS LIST

No	Commissioning Date	Fate
1	3.43	Scuttled Genitchesk 29.10.43
2	3.34	Probably scuttled Constanza, listed missing from 28.8.44
3	3.43	As *MAL 1*
4	3.43	Probably scuttled Constanze 8.44
5	12.8.43	Lost or scuttled Aegean 1945
6	14.5.43	Scuttled Doli, Yugoslavia 19.10.44
7	14.5.43	Probably sunk by RN MTBs N of Dubrovnik 20.10.44
8	4.43	Weather loss Sea of Azov 1.9.43
9	5.43	As *MAL 1*
10	5.43	As *MAL 1*
11	5.43	As *MAL 1*
12	12.8.43	Surrendered Leros/Kos/Kalimnos area 5.45
13	23.5.44	Sunk after bomb damage, Ranna Pungerge 27.7.44
14	31.5.44	Scuttled L Peipus off R Embach mouth 19.9.44
15	23.5.44	Bombed, beached & burned out, Mustevee 20.7.44. Towed to Dorpat but not repaired
16	31.5.44	Bombed, Embach river 2.8.44 Wreck blown up 19.9.44
17	7.6.44	As *MAL 15*. Raised 11.8.44 and abandoned.
18	20.6.44	Sunk by air attack, Mustevee 30.8.44
19	20.6.44	Bombed, burned & burned out, Mustevee 19.7.44
20	20.6.44	Bombed & sunk, R Embach 17.8.44
21	25.6.44	Scuttled L Peipus off R Embach mouth 19.9.44
22	3.7.44	Grounded Marapalu, 16.8.44. Total loss 17.8.44
23	3.7.44	Sunk after bomb damage, Mustevee 31.8.44
24	14.7.44	Sunk by air attack, Mustevee 30.8.44
25		Sunk by army gunfire, Moerdyk, Holland 9.11.44
26		Probably lost in Holland 1944
27		Sunk by air attack, Vienna 2.45
28		Scuttled or captured in Vienna 5.45
29	27.10.44	Bombed & sunk, Vienna 2.45
30	22.11.44	Scuttled or captured in Vienna 5.45
31		Sold to Finland 7.44. Captured by USSR 9.44
32		As *MAL 31*
33		As *MAL 31*
34		As *MAL 31*
35		?
36		?
37		Sunk by RAF at Sassnitz 6/7.3.45
38		To USSR 1946
39		
40		
41	10.44	
42	10.44	
43	10.44	Salvage lighter at Duisberg 3.48, US Army 12.50
44	10.44	Capsized in tow of *Fairplay XII*, Hubergatt 18.3.48
45		To USSR 24.1.46
46		As *MAL 44*
47		To USSR 16.3.46

A's & A's

POL III From Frank Abelsen, Grålum, Norway
'German Torpedo Boats at war – The *Möwe & Wolf* classes' by Pierre Hervieux, published in *Warship* 25, is not correct in saying that the Norwegian patrol boat *Pol III* was *sunk* by the German torpedo boat *Albatros*. The facts are as follows:

Pol III, a converted 214-ton whaler, was built in 1926 for the whalecatcher company Polaris A/S in Larviko. The whaler was requisitioned by the Royal Norwegian Navy in September 1939 and converted into a patrol boat. She was armed with one 76mm gun, probably made by Krupp.

On the night of 8-9 April 1940 *Pol III* was a guardship in the first sea defence district, Oslofjord Guard Division and was on patrol outside the Faerden Lighthouse in Oslofjord. The German forces were observed at 2300. Captain Welding-Olsen immediately signalled the Admiralty about the German warships and fired a warning shot. *Pol III* tried to get nearer to check their nationality, but was then involved in a collision with *Albatros* in the dark. *Albatros* was holed in the port side amidships. The German ship opened fire immediately with machine guns and Welding-Olsen was badly wounded. *Pol III* answered the fire with her slow-firing 76mm gun. One or two shots were fired before the ship was abandoned. She was by this time on fire from hits by *Albatros*. The lifeboat with the crew capsized and they were picked up by *Albatros*, but Welding-Olsen was drowned; the first Norwegian to die in the war with Germany.

The German ships continued up Oslofjord and the burning *Pol III* drifted off into the night. The burnt-out wreck was observed by the Norwegian patrol boat *Farm* on the morning of 9 April and towed to Tønsberg by the patrol boat *Skudd II*. The wreck was later taken over by the Germans and towed to Oslo to be repaired. She was renamed *Samoa* and entered the *Hafenschultz Flotilla Oslo* as *No 05*. Later the ex-whaler was transferred to the *61th Vorposten Flotilla* as *V-6105* and later again transferred to the 65th Flotilla as *V-6501*.

After the German surrender in May 1945 the boat was taken over by the German Minesweeping Administration. In 1947 she was bought by Skipsvedlikehold A/S, Oslo, renamed *Pol III* and sold to Midtgaard & Lodoen, Maaløy. She was again sold in 1949 to Johan E Hareide A/S, Hareid, converted into a fishing vessel and renamed *Johan E* with registration number M-16-HD. In 1978 she was sold to K/S Helgelandsføring A/S & Co, Ørnes and renamed *Odd Oscar*. In July 1982 she was auctioned to A/S Nordfisk Trading, Bodø and renamed *Fisktrans*. And so the first Norwegian warship to engage German forces in World War II is still afloat today!

POPULARITY OF CERTAIN WARSHIPS From Alan S Mallett, Cottishall, Norfolk
The editorial in *Warship* 27 seems to me to be the victim of some rather muddled thinking. If I understand it correctly John Roberts is trying to argue that the loss of a major warship is a material contribution to her popularity. He then goes on to admit that this rule does not apply to all, citing *Barham* and the three old carriers in support of this secondary argument. He does not, however, seem to draw the logical conclusion from these two standpoints.

The evidence, certainly so far as major warships are concerned, would appear to be that it is the loss and not the ship herself which is the factor under study. The article cites the loss of *Hood*, *Ark Royal*, and *Prince of Wales* and *Repulse*. The popularity of the first was largely based, as John Roberts recognises, on her great pre-war popularity as the largest and fastest, and most beautiful of the capital ships and also her connections with the then Prince of Wales' tours of the Empire. Her loss added to the legend, because of the shock and also of the political importance of that loss. The same political effects apply to the losses of *Prince of Wales* and *Repulse* and also that of *Royal Oak*. It is significant that there was less public shock or misgiving at the losses of the carriers and *Barham* and they have had no great interest. That of *Ark Royal* has received attention, partly because it was not inevitable and partly because of her political importance to both sides.

I would suggest that the popularity of *Prince of Wales* lay in part in her being involved in the Atlantic Charter meeting, and that of *Kelly* in her career and distinguished first commanding officer.

We seems to come to the point that whilst the loss of a ship under unusually controversial circumstances does attract interest it does not follow that that loss is more than a small factor in that ship's popularity and therefore it may be more accurate to regard the interest in such ships in this light. I think such books as the biographies of *Warspite*, *Kelly*, *Ark Royal* and *Renown* bear this out and the loss of two of these ships is incidental in that their recognition stems from their careers and successes.

IRONCLAD OR PREDREADNOUGHT?

From Ralph I Cook, Maidenhead, Berks

Karl Lautenschlager's series on *Majestic* class pre-dreadnoughts (*Warship* 25 and 26) is based on a concept of the type which is, in my opinion, incorrect. I would define these ships thus:

1 Provision of at least four heavy guns, effective against 16in compound (about 11-12in Krupp) armour at 3000yds.
2. A broadside of four or more QF guns of 5in calibre or more.
3 a) Protection of hull-vitals (stability, machinery, magazines) and main armament against the heavy guns of an enemy. (Employing vertical armour and deck protection).
   b) Protection of lower deck side and secondary guns against secondary guns of an enemy.
4 Guns well distributed to reduce effects of local damage.
5 Ability to fight main and secondary armament in a seaway.

My main objection is to his fire-control and '7000yds range' criteria, also to his comments concerning the protection of the lower deck side against heavy guns.

The turn of the century preoccupation was with QF guns of about 6in calibre. It was the provision of these guns in large numbers, with protection against such weapons, that really distinguished predreadnoughts from their predecessors and successors. Scott, Simmons and their 'Gunnery Revolution' of the early 1900s concentrated on accuracy and rate of fire at moderate ranges. The new techniques were geared primarily to the effective use of small and medium size guns, even at this date. Only after about 1903 did 'long range fire' begin to feature.

Karl Lautenschlager confuses what ships were capable of with what they were designed to do. True, the *Majestic*s were better able to cope with fire at 7000yds than their predecessors, but once such ranges became accepted as being probable in war, dreadnoughts were developed. Indeed, some later predreadnoughts, with their complex mixture of 12in and 8in and 6in guns, were less able to control their fire at these ranges than were earlier ships fitted with the new sights and rangefinders (which were easily retro-fitted).

Incidentally, I am not sure that the old 13.5in gun – with lower velocity but much heavier shells – would have been that much inferior to the 12in Mk VIII even at 6000-7000yds.

As for protection, the *Royal Sovereign*s and all subsequent predreadnoughts were designed to exclude 6in (later also 8in) projectiles from the lower deck side, not 12in. Mr Lautenschlager does not deny this. Usually, the idea was to explode heavy shells before they could damage the protective deck, employing moderate armour backed by coal bunkers. True, given actual conditions at sea, the lower side armour of some of the later ships may have resisted heavy shells at 7000yds – but expected battle range was 3000yds.

I think too much attention is paid to the lower deck side amidships. Interestingly, a most dangerous place for a ship to be holed is close to the waterline forward – this almost cetainly caused the loss of both *Osliabia* and *Alexander* at Tsushima. The *Majestic*s were very vulnerable here – *Illustrious* was holed by a picket boat in Malta harbour!

For all the above reasons I rank the *Royal Sovereign* class as the first predreadnoughts, along with the French *Brennus*. I reject out of hand the suggestion that the *Royal Sovereign*s 'followed similar French designs by several years and had the same deficiencies in their scheme of protection'. Karl Lautenschlager presumably refers here to the *Marceau* class and their contemporaries. These ships had no lower deck side armour at all and open, unprotected batteries of (initially) slow-firing guns. They were obsolete before *Royal Sovereign* was laid down.

If more war experience with modern ships had been available it is probable that the predreadnought design – concept as I have defined it above would have been proved untenable. The 'hail of fire' would have expedited the fitting of optical sights and forced ranges well beyond 3000yds. A range of 7000yds eventually became practical but it effectively excluded the 6in guns which were so significant a feature of predreadnought designs. At such ranges the *Majestic* and the later predreadnoughts were only marginally superior to their immediate predecessors and not very effective in absolute terms – that is why the dreadnought was built.

M CLASS From Lt Cdr M R Brady RN, Cosham, Hants

Please explain to readers the apparent contradiction in my *Warship* 27 'A & A' on the 'M' Class submarines. What appears as one letter was complied from two – one written before I had the chance to consult Technical History No 21, the second to correct my initial erroneous statement that the 12in gun could not be left loaded while the boat was submerged, nor fired by remote control from inside the boat. The trial report stated that the first was possible, and the time of 25 seconds from periscope depth to firing could only have been achieved with a loaded gun fired by remote control. The phase which occurs later – 'I do not believe that the gun could be fired by remote control' – must have been left in by mistake. My fault, in not consulting all available sources before writing. (*Also an editing error, Ed*.)

I stick to my belief that the practice of leaving the gun loaded while submerged would have caused trouble in service, notwithstanding the trial which proved that to be possible. However, the war service of the class was very limited, so we shall never know whether my belief is justified.

BOOK REVIEWS

US AIRCRAFT CARRIERS:

An Illustrated Design History by Norman Friedman
Plans by A D Baker III
Published by US Naval Institute/Arms & Armour
Press, July 1983
427pp, 300 illustrations ISBN 0 85368 576 2 £27.50
This is a big book, with 427 pages, each 11in × 8¼in, with
a large number of photographs both of ships and of
models (including ship model tank tests) of designs
which were not built. Baker's numerous line drawings
add much to understanding. It is also, perhaps, Norman
Friedman's best book yet, containing an immense
amount of information assembled in a most enjoyable
style.

The arrangement is largely chronological after a brief
introduction on the role of the carrier in the USN,
summarising the author's *Carrier Air Power* (Conway).
After a few hesitations, there was a steady development
to the *Essex* class, probably the finest class of fighting
ships ever built. The only omission in the book is a full
discussion on the resistance of these ships to wartime
damage.

The contribution of the carrier to victory in World
War II is so great that it is easy to forget that 1945 is not
even the halfway point in the life of the aircraft carrier.
Friedman's informed account of the arguments over the
size and cost of postwar carriers is fascinating. The
debate between the 'best' ships and cheaper ships which
can be built in greater numbers is one which can have no
absolute solution. It is interesting to note that the
Forrestal design, produced in rather a hurry, 30 years
ago has proved so successful. The amount of data on
nuclear powered ships is particularly remarkable.

The book includes the amphibious assault carriers and
the paddle wheelers *Wolverine* and *Sable*. There is a
rather brief section on equipment – catapults, arrester
gear, etc and some 30 pages of tabulated data. Mistakes
are very few but I do dislike Sir Stanley Goodall RCNC
being described as Director of Naval Communication
(Construction)!

D K Brown

OTHER BOOKS RECEIVED

Cruisers of the World 1873-1981, compiled by Michael
Burgess (Burgess Media Services Ltd, Wellington, NZ,
June 1983) 128pp, 135 photographs, index, $NZ11.45.
ISBN 0-908641-30-3. A BMS Pictorial History in their
small format but glossy paperback warship series. This
devotes a page and photograph to 121 cruisers or cruiser
classes (sister ships *not* named) in 18 navies from HMS
Shah to the Soviet nuclear-powered *Kirov*. Very brief
notes supplement basic data in metric and imperial.

*Assault from the Sea: Essays on the History of
Amphibious Warfare*, edited by Lt Col Merrill L Bartlett

USMC(Ret) (Naval Institute Press, Annapolis
Maryland, October 1983) 453pp, 15 maps, 32 paintings
or photographs, bibliography, index, £18.95 plus £1.45
p & p from Arms & Armour Press. ISBN
0-87021-088-2. A massive compilation of 51, mainly US
and British periodical articles (some Soviet ones translated) in chronological order from 490 BC to 1982 with
a look ahead as well. This is a fascinating treasure trove
on its subject though the maps, unlike the bibliography,
are a token effort.

Guide to the Soviet Navy, Third Edition, Norman Polmar
(Naval Institute Press, Annapolis, Maryland, October
1983) 465pp, 413 photographs and drawings, £27.95
plus £1.45 p & p from Arms & Armour Press. ISBN
0-87021-239-7. The exhaustive reference work worthy
of its subject down to colour plates of flags and rank
insignia. The cut-off date seems to be May 1983 just
before the maiden voyage of *Novorossiysk*.

Naval Engineering: Present and Future (Mechanical
Engineering Publications of Bury St Edmunds,
September 1983) £32 (£41.50 overseas). Proceedings of
a conference organised by the Institution of Mechanical
Engineers to mark the RCNC centenary.

Complete contents: Postwar developments in naval
ship machinery; A new look at steam propulsion for
warships; Surface warship propulsion – what causes
change; RN experience with marine gas turbines during
the Falklands campaign; High speed diesel engines for
naval applications; Warship propulsion electronic
machinery controls – present and future; Computer-
aided design of diesel engine driven systems for acceptable torsional vibration characteristics; Load transfer
systems: prediction of performance in a seaway;
Accurate motion compensation using an active
hydropneumatic system; A development in nuclear
submarine atmosphere control systems; Feed water
pumps the heart of the matter; Naval desalination;
Future naval gear design; The application of transmission error measurement to the reduction of airborne
and structure-borne noise in gearing transmission
systems; Fluid couplings for naval manoeuvring trans-
missions; The design of mechanical seals for high and
variable pressures; Nuclear submarine machinery
upkeep data systems; Materials for naval machinery
systems; Fire hazards associated with warship hydraulic
equipment; Diesel fuel for the RN – present and future.

Air War South Atlantic, Jeffrey Ethell and Alfred Price
(Sidgwick & Jackson, October 1983) 260pp, 72 photographs, 12 appendices, index, £9.95. ISBN
0-283-99035-X. About the 40th English publication
(there has even been a novel) on the Falklands War but a
worthwhile contribution with pilot interviews from both
sides, detailed lists of aircraft losses, and aviation orders
of battle. The narrative runs day by day.

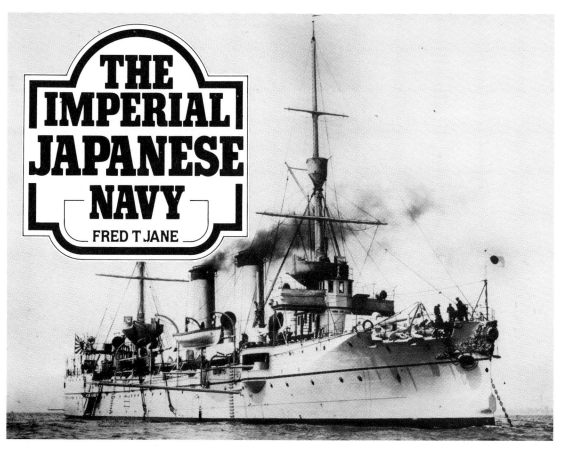
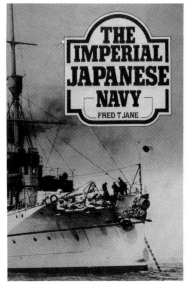

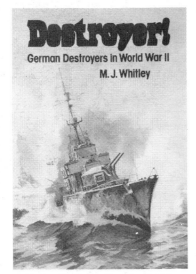

EDITORIAL

This issue ranges from the US Navy's turn of the century *Arkansas* class monitors to the current dominance of the gas turbine in the technology of surface warship propulsion. It profiles two of the fastest, most powerful yet shortlived conventional destroyers ever built, *Mogador* and *Volta*, largely eclipsed by their smaller but better known *Fantasque* class predecessors (most of whom survived) and sets them alongside the numerous and mass-produced Japanese 'Kaibokan' escorts of the same era. It is fascinating to learn that the Imperial Japanese Navy or rather Mitsubishi Industries decided that this lowest priority ship should nevertheless be built to the highest standards. This policy of quality before quantity meant that the bloated seaborne Japanese Empire of 1942-43, even if her naval planners had paid the slightest attention to the ASW, could never have deployed in time the sheer numbers of convoy escorts (with trained ASW crews) needed to save her merchant shipping from massacre by the US submarine force in the Pacific.

What a contrast with the Atlantic at the same juncture where the Allied shipyards on both sides of the Atlantic were pouring out hundreds of cheap and far from ideal anti-submarine hulls to counteract the more concentrated threat of Hitler's U-boat arm. As Norman Friedman feelingly remarks in his article on US SSK ASW submarines, this was 'the last great ASW war', the experience of which guided the US Navy's ASW plans during the Cold War. It is incredible to read now that their 1948 prediction of the Soviet underwater threat in about 1960 was the little matter of 2000 submarines for which the West's most effective counter was going to be the construction of 970 hunter-killer boats.

We may take some comfort from this illustration of the fact that the worst case does not always arise. Furthermore the very same geographical constraints on Russian submarine deployment apply in 1984 just as surely as they did in 1948. What changed the equation was the naval revolution wrought by nuclear power. It is perhaps ironical that in the middle of all the fashionable concern with East-West nuclear *warheads* the atom in its largely forgotten role of underwater propulsion has immeasurably sustained the cause of deterrence and peace.

Just as on land the West can never hope, nor has it ever planned, to match the Warsaw Pact division, tank for tank, gun for gun or missile for missile so at sea it can be argued that the nuclear-powered submarine has, in both its missile-carrying and hunter-killer guises, saved the West from the crippling financial and perhaps politically impossible burden of furnishing the requisite non-nuclear naval forces. Nuclear submarines are expensive but they offer unmatchable endurance and mobility for a very small expenditure of manpower which is kept largely out of sight (of land) and mind.

It is the nuclear dimension above all that colours the fact that in terms of this fast diminishing twentieth century we are as far in time from the Battle of Leyte Gulf as its participants were from the Battle of Tsushima. This issue of *Warship* has a salutary assessment of the constant effect of wind and weather on the surface warship but the acknowledged if easily forgotten dreadnoughts of our time operate beneath the waves, their vulnerabilities seldom exposed to the world at large. They exert a silent dominance that has persisted now for more than two decades. Only five nations operate vessels of this type and in eloquent contrast with all the other outpourings of the arms trade these are not weapons for sale.

The continuing fuss in some quarters over the sinking of the Argentine cruiser *General Belgrano*, one is tempted to say, is partly a reflection of the *nuclear* submarine's awesome capabilities. The fact that a World War II ship was sunk with World War II torpedoes was of far less importance than it was done by a nuclear submarine which had stalked her prey for more than 30 hours. It was not even the first successful submarine torpedo attack since 1945 (that can be credited to the Pakistan/French built *Daphne*-class diesel boat *Hangor* which sank the Indian frigate *Khukri* with heavy loss of life in the Arabian Sea on 9 December 1971) but that brief British use of a weapon with latent power has had a lasting psychological impact on friend and foe alike.

The argument for nuclear submarines is very much a closed one involving as it does the most secret technical details of all in a sphere that is remoter to the layman than outer space. But the emphasis of Sir John Nott's 1981 White Paper 'The Way Ahead' on an ASW partnership of hunter-killer nuclear submarine and maritime patrol aircraft may only have been an extreme statement of what is already the daily reality of NATO deterrence. As such, however desirable more surface ships of all kinds would be for in and out of area tasks, the central strategic balance rests on the quality of a handful of high speed underwater ASW and missile platforms manned by specialist submariners.

Randal Gray

The Gas Turbine at Sea

by John M Maber

MGB 2009 on trials in Stokes Bay (Solent) during which she exceeded 34 knots. Engined with the Metropolitan-Vickers Gatric, the first gas turbine to see service at sea.
Popperfoto

The marine gas turbine is accepted today as a compact propulsion plant of proven reliability suited to the needs of medium and high powered warship installations either in a multiple unit configuration or in association with the diesel engine. Compared with conventional steam turbine machinery burning oil fuel, the modern aircraft-derived gas turbine reduces engine room manning and requires less onboard maintenance. It is also easier to replace with a new unit when a major overhaul is due.

RESEARCH BEFORE 1914

The idea of burning fuel in a gas generator and using the resultant combustion gases to drive a turbine wheel is by no means a recent concept and indeed numerous, although generally impractical, proposals were made in the course of the nineteenth century. In the event, it is probable that attention was first given to the development of a practical self-contained internal combustion turbine towards the end of the century by a German engineer, Dr Stolze, who in 1900 actually constructed and was able to demonstrate a working unit. Some six years later M Rene Armengaud converted a de Laval impulse steam turbine to operate on compressed air

mixed with metered quantities of petroleum vapour, the mixture being fired continuously by means of an incandescent platinum wire igniter. The useful output was about 30hp.

Inevitably, the designer came up against the problem of high gas temperature which was to prevent any substantial advance in practical gas turbine design until the 1940s when the needs of war engendered significant developments in the field of metallurgy. In Armengaud's machine combustion took place at about 1800° C and the combustion chamber was lined with carborundum (silicon carbide), a crystalline refractory material, but steam generated in a steam coil sited within this chamber mixed with the gaseous combustion products to bring the turbine inlet temperature down to about 400° C (762° F).

In addition to Armengaud's work in France, a sizeable effort was devoted to gas turbine development in Germany where in 1910 Holzwarth designed and built at the Thyssen works in Mulheim, with the help of Korting Brothers and the Brown-Boveri company, a vertical 1000hp constant volume internal combustion turbine directly coupled to a direct current generator mounted above the unit. In lieu of the continuous ignition principle of the Armengaud turbine, ignition in the Holzwarth machine was achieved through a spark generated by a high tension magneto. The hot gases produced passed to a two-stage Curtis impulse turbine and steam generated by otherwise waste exhaust heat was used to drive the turbo-compressor that supplied the combustion air. In fact, however, this 'waste' heat represented a major part of the theoretical output of the machine and in practice the useful power amounted to something like 160bhp only!

The gas turbine's potential as a possible marine propulsion unit was discussed, with particular reference to the Holzwarth design, in an article in *The Naval Annual* for 1913, but development work in Germany came to a halt following the outbreak of war in 1914. Trials were resumed in 1918, however, in the wake of interest shown by the Prussian State Railway administration and in the following year an order was placed for a 500hp traction unit coupled to a direct current generator. At about the same time renewed consideration was given to using an internal combustion turbine for marine propulsion and in December 1920 a Holzwarth unit arranged for mechanical transmission via reduction gearing was delivered for trials.

Like modern gas generators this marine unit had a number of equally spaced combustion chambers, in this case six, arranged around a horizontal shaft but as in earlier Holzwarth designs the centrifugal air compressor was driven by a steam turbine utilising the exhaust gas heat for steam generation. The design of a 500kw marine internal combustion turbine of this configuration was discussed and illustrated in *The Motor Ship* for May 1922 but at best the machine was regarded only as an uncertain rival for the well-proven geared steam turbine.

HMS *Grey Goose*, a former steam gunboat re-engined in 1952-54 with a pair of Rolls Royce RM60 turbines.
MoD

BRITISH DEVELOPMENT 1938-48

As matters turned out, the Holzwarth design's complexity, with its inefficient steam driven compressor and doubts about its material reliability in view of the high temperatures involved, militated against further practical marine gas turbine development for another 20 years. Between the wars, however, the Parsons Marine Steam Turbine Company in England, among others, did devote considerable effort to the development of an axial flow compressor and in 1938 this company built an experimental gas turbine incorporating an engine-driven compressor of axial flow design thus opening the way ahead for the later development of a compact self-contained gas generator.

Elsewhere the gas turbine was under development as an aircraft jet engine and in 1941 Frank Whittle (later Sir Frank Whittle) produced his first successful aero-engine prototype. In the meantime, research work continued on what was essentially an internal combustion version of the marine steam turbine since advantages were seen in its basic simplicity compared with the diesel engine and in the fact that it could be run on a wide range of fuels. Compared with the aircraft gas turbine, such machines were heavy and comparatively slow running although in fact this was not considered to be any great drawback. It was expected that engine life would equate to ship life, far exceeding an aircraft engine's and would require little onboard maintenance.

Apart from marine gas turbine design work stemming from a steam ancestry, with which Metropolitan-Vickers Ltd of Manchester were primarily associated, the Admiralty had not been slow in developing a propulsion unit based upon Sir Frank Whittle's pioneering work. The naval staff requirement was in fact twofold: first there was a demand for a compact high-powered, short

HMS *Bold Pathfinder* (MTB 5720), one of a pair of
experimental prototype fast patrol boats engined with
Metropolitan-Vickers G2 gas turbines in a 4-shaft CODAG
arrangement.
Author's collection

design. A successful series of trials followed, extending
over three years, and this engine, the first gas turbine in
service at sea, is now preserved in the Science Museum,
London.

RN 'BOLD' CLASS 1950s TRIALS

Towards the end of 1948 a further contract was placed
with Metropolitan-Vickers for the development of a
larger marine engine based upon the Beryl aircraft turbine. Four gas turbines of this type, known as the G2,
were built for installation as boost units to run in parallel
with ex-German Mercedes Benz MB 518 diesel engines
at high speeds in a four-shaft arrangement for a pair of
prototype fast patrol boats to be named *Bold Pathfinder*
and *Bold Pioneer*. Built respectively by Vospers of Portsmouth and J Samuel White of Cowes, these two craft
were intended to assess the relative merits of round bilge
and hard chine construction. The 2500hp diesel engines,
which were direct reversing and thus used for manoeuvring, drove the inner shafts while the gas turbines drove
the outer shafts. No clutches were provided and the wing
shafts with the power turbine rotors were trailed at
cruising or manoeuvring speeds.

life engine (of aircraft derived design) for high speed
coastal craft; second, in the longer term, there was a
need for a boost plant for the surface warship which
spends the greater part of its operational time at sea at
cruising or lower speeds. Thus, in 1943 a contract was
placed, again with Metropolitan-Vickers Ltd, to develop
a propulsion gas turbine based on Whittle's F2 aircraft
jet engine. The marine engine required the addition of
an output power turbine in the jet pipe and was to burn
diesel oil rather than the kerosene (paraffin) burned in
the aircraft application. Shore trials were completed in
1946 in the wake of the solution to a number of design
problems and in the following year an engine of this
type, known by this time as the Gatric, was installed in
place of the centre-line Packard Merlin piston engine
(aviation fuel) in *MGB 2009*, a three-shaft 115-ton wartime built motor gunboat of Camper & Nicholson

Sea trials with HMS *Bold Pioneer* started late in 1951 but many teething troubles were encountered although much was learned and the G2 engine added considerably to the sum total of practical marine gas turbine propulsion. In particular, there were no air intake filters and the gas generator suffered from the build up of salt deposits on the compressor blading such that, in other than low sea states, water washing was necessary at intervals of about 20 minutes. *Bold Pathfinder* followed in 1953. After these trials a G2 Mk II engine was developed which, although never fitted in any vessel for the Royal Navy, was purchased by the US Navy and installed in a PT boat for trials. A later, more robust, G4 development was similarly overtaken by events in so far as the RN was concerned but did go to sea in the 197-ton Italian motor gunboats *Lampo* and *Baleno* completed in 1963-65.

COSAG 1950s AND 1960s

In the development of an engine for larger warships, early work centred on a turbine designed and built by the English Electric Co at Rugby. This 6500bhp EL60A turbine was intended to replace one of the steam sets in the twin screw turbo-electric frigate *Hotham*, a US-built vessel of the 'Captains' class selected in view of the comparative ease with which the power turbine drive could be matched to the electric transmission. In the event, manufacturing difficulties delayed development and it was not until late in 1951 that the gas turbine set was delivered for shore trials. By this time it was already becoming apparent that there was little future for an

HMS *Exmouth*, the world's first all gas turbine major warship in which a Perseus/Olympus COGOG arrangement replaced the original steam plant.

Author's collection

engine of this type based on steam turbine practice for main propulsion duty and plans for *Hotham*'s conversion were abandoned.

This was not to say, however, that no future was seen for the long life steam turbine derived boost unit and design work, which continued at Metropolitan-Vickers (subsequently part of AEI Ltd), in association with the Admiralty, resulted eventually in the development of the G6. This 7500bhp gas turbine was for installation as part of the combined steam and gas turbine (COSAG) propulsion packages in the Type 81 'Tribal' class frigates and the Seaslug-armed guided missile destroyers of the 'County' class that entered service during the early 1960s. In both classes the gearing was arranged so that the gas turbine drive could not only boost the steam plant for full speed, ahead only, but also could be employed, independently, for manoeurvring ahead and astern thus permitting a quick getaway of the ship from cold. Once again limited teething troubles were experienced, but the plant proved itself and pointed the way to the future although in fact the G6 was to be the last of the heavy, comparatively slow-running and low-powered marine gas turbines derived from the steam age. Franco Tosi built G6 turbines in a twin-screw combined diesel and gas (CODAG) arrangement were chosen also in the 1960s for the ageing Italian destroyer *San Giorgio* (ex-*Pompeo Magno*), launched in 1941 but completely rebuilt in 1963-65 as a cadet training ship, and for the 2689-ton frigates *Alpino* and *Carabiniere* completed in 1968.

BRITISH ALL-GAS TURBINE PROPULSION

In the meantime, Messrs Rolls Royce, in association with the Admiralty, had developed for fast attack craft a lightweight if complex engine designated the RM60

HMS *Devonshire*, the first of the COSAG engined 'County' class destroyers. Completed in 1962, she was equipped with four AEI G6 boost turbines, each of 7500bhp.

Author's collection

which although not aircraft derived did owe its origins to aero-engine design expertise. Following extensive shore trials two of these units, rated at 5400bhp, were installed in the former steam gunboat *Grey Goose* (ex-*SGB 9*), the first warship in any navy to be powered entirely by gas turbines. HMS *Grey Goose* ran successfully for some four years (1952-55) building up an impressive total of engine running hours although very expensive in fuel. In the event, however, development of the sophisticated RM60 was abandoned in favour of the naval Proteus turbine developed by Bristol Aero Engines for fast craft.

The Bristol Proteus first ran in January 1947 and consideration for its development as a marine engine followed in 1954 when Vosper of Portsmouth was given a contract to undertake a design study for a new class of fast patrol boats (FPB). Various engine combinations and arrangements were investigated but eventually the choice fell on a three-shaft configuration with three Proteus gas turbines each rated at 3500bhp. Orders for two boats, to be known as the 'Brave' class, went to Vospers in March 1956, but subsequent reappraisal of the Royal Navy's role within NATO led to the effective abandonment of Britain's coastal forces although in fact when the end came in 1957 it was agreed that the two 'Braves' should be completed for use in a training role.

One of the greatest success stories to date in the marine gas turbine field has been this development of the Bristol (Rolls Royce from 1967) Proteus. Its debut at sea came in the FPB *Brave Borderer* during 1958. A compact engine, it had been designed to power propeller-driven aircraft and thus incorporated a power turbine at the outset. No great modification was required other than some change of materials and redesign of the fuel system to enable the engine to run on diesel oil. The 'Braves' were followed by a series of similar Proteus-engined hard chine hulled craft for the Danish, Malaysian, Brunei, Libyan and West German navies. The Swedish 'Spica' class MTBs, too, employed a similar machinery configuration. Proteus has also been fitted in a variety of British, US and Italian-designed hovercraft and hydrofoils. Two Proteus turbines, uprated to 4250bhp, were fitted as cruise engines in the converted Type 14 frigate HMS *Exmouth* as the Royal Navy's, and indeed the world's, first operational all gas turbine major warship which recommissioned for service in June 1968.

The high speed plant in the *Exmouth* COGOG (combined gas or gas) conversion comprised a single Bristol Siddley (later Rolls Royce) Olympus TM1A module. Although rated at 22,500bhp it could not be used at its full output because the existing hull design restricted the maximum to 15,000shp. Similar engines have been fitted, however, in a number of frigates of commercial design built for the Brazilian, Iranian, Malaysian and Thai navies by the Vosper-Thornycroft, Vickers and

Yarrow companies, and also as the boost plant in the COSAG-engined guided missile destroyer HMS *Bristol*. The Olympus TM1A gas generator was derived from the aircraft turbojet employed in the supersonic transport Concorde redesigned to burn diesel fuel instead of kerosene and exhausting into a single-stage power turbine of robust 'ship life' design to drive the gearbox input shaft.

Marine gas turbine progress was not confined to Britain of course and during the 1950s, in both the United States and France, successful units were developed to the trial installation stage, of both the turbine and an opposed piston gas generator type. Elsewhere in Europe the Brown-Boveri company of Mannheim, again active in the gas turbine field, developed on behalf of the Federal German *Bundesmarine* a 12,000bhp gas turbine for the 2750-ton twin screw CODAG *Köln* class frigates, the first of which commissioned for service in April 1961. At about the same time the first units of the 1150-ton CODAG-engined 'Petya I' class escort vessels joined the Soviet Fleet. In these triple screw craft the centre shaft is driven by a pair of 3000bhp diesel engines while the wing shafts, which are trailed at crusing speeds up to 16-18 knots, are driven by 15,000bhp gas turbines.

The development of such plant in the United States for active fleet duty lagged somewhat behind that achieved for the European navies. Not until August 1966 did the first CODAG-powered patrol gunboats of the US Navy's *Asheville* class commission for service. These 245-ton (full load) twin screw craft were engined with a pair of 875bhp Cummins diesels and a single aircraft-derived General Electric LM1500 gas turbine of 14,000shp.

It must be borne in mind of course that marine gas turbine operating cycle and its environmental conditions are vastly different from those applying to the aircraft engine. The marine unit must be capable of running continuously at near full power day after day, while the problems of salt and water ingestion necessitate careful design of the air intake system. Additionally there is the problem of waste heat disposal which in the equivalent steam plant is transferred to the condenser circulating water and is thus conveniently discharged into the sea. In a marine gas turbine plant the hot exhaust goes from the power turbine pass via the uptakes to atmosphere necessitating attention to design detail to keep the gases clear of the ship's structure and the employment of high cost alloy steels for the uptake system. In early commerical marine installations, attempts were made to utilise the waste heat but the heat exhanger weight and size, necessarily sited high in the ship, destroyed any advantage that might have been gained while its very presence in the exhaust path resulted in a significant reduction in engine output.

COGOG TODAY

HMS *Bristol*, the last steam driven (COSAG) warship for the Royal Navy, entered service a decade ago and, in her wake, the present generation of missile armed destroyers (Type 42) and frigates (Type 22), together with the older Type 21 frigates, is engined with the uprated

HMS *Birmingham*, a Seadart armed Type 42 destroyer (on contractor's 1976 sea trials) fitted with the two-shaft Tyne/Olympus package.
MoD

Starboard side of the gearbox of the Metropolitan-Vickers Gatric gas turbine that can now be seen in the Science Museum, London.

Popperfoto

(28,000bhp) Olympus TM3B gas turbine for high speed and a naval Rolls Royce Tyne (4250bhp), the RM1A, for the low speed range in a twin-shaft COGOG arrangement with controllable pitch propellers. In all these vessels the layout of the machinery spaces has been designed for ease of engine exchange when major overhauls become due thus to minimise ship downtime and, in turn, to ensure maximum availability. Both these engines were successfully changed at sea by repair ships in the aftermath of the Falklands War. A similar Olympus/Tyne COGOG configuration is employed in contemporary Dutch destroyers and frigates, respectively of the *Tromp* and *Kortenaer* classes. Two further Type 42 destroyers, for the Argentine Navy, were delivered in 1976/81, one built at Barrow and the other built locally in the Rio Santiago Navy Yard, in addition to which Olympus and Tyne propulsion modules have been supplied for four 2900-ton twin screw COGOG destroyers (*Almirante Brown* class) built for that same navy by Blohm & Voss at Hamburg. In the case of the 19,500-ton *Invincible* class VSTOL carriers (CVS) a twin-shaft arrangement with four Olympus TM3B driving fixed pitch propellers is employed.

The Soviet Navy, too, following experience gained with the 'Petya' classes, adopted gas turbine propulsion extensively, initially for the new generation destroyers/frigates of the 1960s and 1970s such as the 'Kashin' and 'Krivak' classes and, more recently, for the heavily armed cruisers of the 9800-ton 'Kara' class (4 engines driving 2 shafts). The latter's successor class, the 'Krasinas', beginning with *Slava* in mid-1983, are similarly equipped.

As mentioned above, the United States lagged behind

in marine gas turbine development and not until 1970 did the US Navy place an order with Litton Industries for a class of 7800-ton missile armed destroyers engined on two shafts with four General Electric LM2500 turbines, each of about 20,000bhp. The gas generator is derived from the TF39 turbofan aircraft engine and, as in the case of the Royal Navy, this type of plant has been adopted because of its compact design, reduced operator and onboard maintenance demands compared with the equivalent steam plant, rapid cold start capability and the ease of unit exchange. The lead ship of the class, USS *Spruance*, first commissioned in September 1975 and the delivery of 31 vessels has now been completed. Two General Electric units of the same type power the smaller frigates of the *Oliver Hazard Perry* class, although in this case reliance on a single shaft COGAG arrangement with two large engines to cope with the total power range would appear to lack the flexibility of the Royal Navy's Olympus/Tyne system.

In the late 1960s, during the course of development of the Olympus/Tyne propulsion package, a need was seen for an engine of medium output, since at other than the upper sector of its power range the Olympus is relatively inefficient. This requirement stemmed from the advent of sonars capable of being employed effectively at greater speeds than hitherto. In 1972 the Ministry of Defence placed a feasibility study contract with Rolls Royce for a naval version of the well-proven Spey turbofan engine. The most powerful engine in the Spey range, the TF41, was chosen for this exercise and in 1977 a development contract followed for the design and construction of a 12.5 megawatt (16,750bhp) unit, known by this time as the SM1A. The gas generator is of twin spool design with the low pressure and high pressure compressors independently driven by their own two-stage turbines. They are thus able to run at their optimum speeds having a much improved fuel economy compared with that possible in the earlier generation of engines. The module incorporates a two-stage power turbine of 'ship life' design.

Development of what has the makings of a very successful unit preceded any committment to a specific ship, but the Spey SM1A is now to be fitted, together with an uprated Tyne, the 5340bhp RM1C, in the Batch 3 Type 22 frigate and as a boost unit in association with a diesel-electric cruise drive for the Type 23 quiet running frigate, details of which were announced late in 1983. In the meantime a twin-screw Spey SM1A/Olympus TM3B COGOG propulsion plant has been specified by the Japanese Maritime Self Defence Force for three 4500-ton destroyers, the first of which was launched by Mitsubishi at Nagasaki in May 1983.

Today the majority of warships in the destroyer and frigate categories are gas turbine powered, either by a COGOG or COGAG (combined gas turbine and gas turbine) plant, or by employing diesel cruise engines with gas turbines for higher speeds in a CODOG configuration, or alternatively with a boost turbine in a CODAG arrangement. Much the largest gas turbine engined warships are the 19,800-ton *Invincible* class VSTOL carriers, but the US Navy is currently building a series of 8910-ton missile armed cruisers, known as the

HMS *Ardent* in June 1977, a Tyne/Olympus COGOG engined Type 21 frigate. She was lost during the Falklands War.
Author's collection

Ticonderoga class, engined on two shafts like the *Spruance* class with four General Electric LM2500 turbines. Meanwhile the Italian Navy has specified the same engine fit, manufactured under licence by Fiat, for the 13,250-ton light aircraft carrier *Giuseppe Garibaldi* now under construction by Italcantieri at Monfalcone.

The Royal Navy apart, Rolls Royce aircraft derived gas turbines are installed as propulsion engines in the

HMS *Battleaxe*, a Tyne/Olympus engined Type 22 frigate. Note the massive gas turbine uptakes.
Author's collection

warships of no fewer than 19 navies. And if one takes into consideration the fit of other makes of engine, including General Electric of USA, Pratt & Witney (USA), GE-Fiat (Italy) and those of Russian origin, it is clear that the gas turbine is today's preferred powerplant for fast warships. The gas turbine does present problems for the naval architect, however, in that it does not like the ingestion of salt laden spray while the fact that all the waste heat is exhausted to atmosphere makes necessary very large uptakes. Again, the radiated heat itself presents an attractive target for heat-seeking missiles. Against this must be set the advantages enumerated at the beginning of this article and it is likely that the gas turbine powerplant will continue to be favoured for fast, medium-sized craft of the destroyer/frigate classes for the foreseeable future.

WARSHIP WINGS

No.9 Sea Harrier

by Roger Chesneau

While it is stretching things to claim that the remarkable Harrier family of aircraft has revolutionised fixed-wing naval aviation, it cannot be denied that its development has had a significant impact on the ability of navies to project carrier-based air power. The explosive growth in carrier aircraft size and weight during the postwar years, dictated by ever-increasing speeds, range, carrying capability and electronics complexity, has left the United States and, probably, the Soviet Union as the only nations able, or perhaps willing, to afford the vast and expensive ships necessary to operate a comprehensive range of types. However, by addressing such questions as take-off distance, and obviating the need for catapults and, indeed, arrester gear, V/STOL (Vertical/Short Take-Off and Landing) aircraft strike deeply at several major factors contributing to the size and cost of modern fleet carriers.

It is not proposed here to recount the Harrier development story nor to relate the events of the spring and early summer of 1982, when the aircraft, confounding its not inconsiderable numbers of critics, proved itself during the 45 combat days of the Falklands War as a highly effective air defence, strike and reconnaissance fighter; these topics have been covered in depth by numerous publications already. Rather, we might attempt to outline some aspects of the Harrier's versatility and its impact on parent ships.

V/STOL AND THE FLIGHT DECK

Theoretically, V/STOL requires a platform only a little more generous in overall dimensions than those of the aircraft itself, but in practice VTO (Vertical Take-Off) imposes several limitations on the machine's performance. For example, lift is provided exclusively by the thrust of the powerplant, thus placing weight restrictions (generally affecting the variables, ie armament payload and/or fuel) on the airframe; as a result, range or offensive capability (or both) are penalised. Moreover, VTO is inherently a fuel-thirsty manoeuvre. At a different level, little safety margin is available to a pilot engaged in VTO in the event of crisis, such as engine failure.

Hence STO (Short Take-Off) rather than VTO is the rule for Harrier operations at sea, although landings are generally conducted in the vertical mode, at least in the Royal Navy. STO is of course enhanced via the well-known 'ski-jump' technique (invented by Lt-Cdr D R Taylor in 1978), which conveniently tackles the problems mentioned above by giving the departing aircraft a semi-ballistic trajectory and allowing the wings to generate lift, as they do in conventional take-off rolls. Ski-jump STO gives the Sea Harrier 2000lb more payload than ordinary STO. In fact, a further benefit is that short rolling take-offs via ski-jumps actually increase the tempo of the flight-deck cycle, a typical operating figure being one machine every 15-20 seconds. It is no exaggeration to say that the ski-jump device alone made possible the Harrier operations in the South Atlantic.

Although V/STOL has immense benefits with regard to take-off roll and renders superfluous the elaborate launching and recovery equipment necessary to operate conventional aircraft, ship impact in other respects is modified less significantly. Thus V/STOL confers few advantages insofar as stowage, hangar or flight deck, is concerned, other than in the sense that airframe weight,

Eight Sea Harriers of No 809 Squadron in formation 1982. This squadron was reformed between April and December for the Falklands War.

British Aerospace

Underside view of Sea Harrire ZA174, showing the
arrangement of the jet nozzels and the large twin Aden 30mm
gun pods beneath the fuselage. The doppler panel below the
nose is clearly evident.

British Aerospace

A Sea Harrier lifts off from RNAS Yeovilton's land-based training ski-jump, 1980. The aircraft is finished in the original colour scheme of Extra Dark Sea Grey and White and is carrying Sea Eagle ASMs on the inboard pylons.
British Aerospace

and hence size, is limited by the thrust available from the preferred powerplant and consequently smaller aircraft occupy a relatively smaller space. But, static aircraft do, after all, consume a fixed volume, and such considerations as magazine and aviation fuel capacity are more intimately related to the number of machines in the air group, the fuel consumption and the range of those aircraft, and the number of operational flights each is expected to undertake, rather than to the method by which they leave or arrive on board the carrier. Onboard limitations can, however, partly be alleviated by the versatility of an airframe. If an air group comprises what is essentially a single aircraft type, fewer spares and weapons of less varieties will be needed, and the maintenance, in the form of both manpower and facilities, will take up less space on board than in a ship operating several types of aircraft. Furthermore, equipment such as lifts presumably makes fewer demands on designers if a wide variety of aircraft types does not need to be handled.

The Sea Harrier operates as a fighter, reconnaissance and strike aircraft (hence 'FRS') and its multi-role capability, decried by many as requiring too much of a compromise in aircraft design, has in this instance proven remarkably successful. It is worth remembering too that for the last 10 days of the Falklands War Sea Harriers and RAF Harriers operated from the improvised 285-year 'Sid's Strip' at Port San Carlos with an almost fourfold improvement in time on patrol. Such flexible

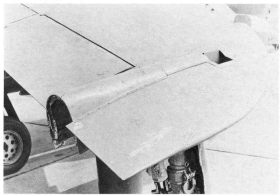

Close-up of the starboard wingtip, showing the RCV (Reaction Control Valve) duct, used for manoeuvring at very low speeds. Similar valves are fitted to the nose and tail of the aircraft. Note the lash-down lug on the outrigger wheel leg.
Linewrights Ltd

operation from a temporary land base is obviously not possible for conventional naval aircraft.

SCADS

The attraction of V/STOL in requiring only relatively basic flight deck facilities in order to operate modern, high-performance aircraft, has led to a large number of studies for austere carriers, many taking the form of readily convertible merchant ships. One current project, encouraged by the success of extemporary aircraft ferries deployed to the South Atlantic in 1982, is SCADS (Shipborne Containerised Air Defence System). Proposed by British Aerospace, it envisages a container ship fitted with a flight deck terminating in a ski-jump, plus a

Refuelling an 899 Sqn Sea Harrier, RNAS Yeovilton, August 1983. This and the preceding photograph are representative of a very large selection of Sea Harrier close-up views included in *Aeroguide 3: Sea Harrier*, recently published by Linewrights Ltd at £2.95.

Linewrights Ltd

Seawolf SAM system and a basic electronics (including ECM) suite. The air group would comprise six Sea Harriers plus a couple of Sea King AEW helicopters, accommodation and control facilities being provided during rapid conversion by means of standard containers already fitted out for the purpose. British Aerospace foresee a valuable role for SCADS particularly as a convoy protection vessel, with a viable anti-air and anti-surface component in the form of her aircraft. Doubtless an ASW role could also be conferred on the ship, given the appropriate equipment. The analogy with World War II escort carriers, and in particular with CAM/MAC-ships, is obvious.

SKYHOOK

More radical is a proposal to deploy and retrieve Sea Harrier aircraft by means of the Skyhook space-stabilised cranes. A ship so fitted would be able to 'catch' a hovering aircraft and either hold it for refuelling or bring it aboard for rearming, maintenance or stowage within a small hangar. The principle involved is the acquisition by the pilot of a 10 cubic ft 'box' wherein the crane, stabilised to cope with seas up to State 6, can locate by sensor a pick-up point on top of the aircraft's fuselage, following which the pilot could shut down.

SEA HARRIER FRS Mk I SPECIFICATION

Overall length	47ft 7in
Span	25ft 3in
Max height	12ft 2in
Wing area	201.1sq ft
Engine	One Rolls-Royce Pegasus 104 vectored-thrust turbofan, 21,500lb static thrust
Max speed	Probably in excess of 640kts
Combat radius	(Surface strike, no external fuel) 210nm
Weight	26,200lb max take-off; 16,900lb design VL
Weapons	(Typical air defence mode) 2 × 30mm Aden cannon, 2 × AIM-9L AAMs, 2 × 190gal drop tanks. Twin Sidewinders can be accommodated on each outboard pylon, and for the strike role 3 × 1000lb bombs, or 68mm SNEB rocket pods or ASMs (Martel, Harpoon, Sea Eagle) can be carried

Deployment uses the reverse procedure, the Harrier's unique hovering capabilities being utilised to stabilise the aircraft prior to uncoupling and departure. British Aerospace estimate that ships displacing as little as 3000 tons would be able to operate such a system, aircraft launch occupying about one minute and recovery twice that.

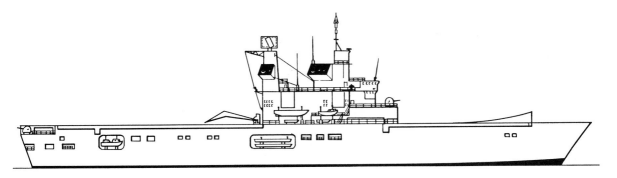

Vickers Shipbuilding drawing (issued July 1981) of a possible low-cost 'Sea Harrier Carrier' with ski-jump.
Vickers

Skyhook trials have included holding a Sea Harrier on station with a fixed reference point (in this instance a 50ft high fire ladder), using a basic parallax sight. Note that the aircraft demonstrating the concept here is an Indian Navy machine.
British Aerospace

Whether these schemes come to fruition is a matter of doubt; despite the Sea Harrier's proven success, there seems to be some reluctance on the part of navies to introduce them. Perhaps they are waiting for the emergence of Sea Harrier's *supersonic* successor – the radically different P1216 being developed by British Aerospace and McDonnell Douglas in the USA. However, recent reports of the Indian Navy increasing its Sea Harrier order from 8 to 20 aircraft and of the Italians seriously contemplating the purchase of a number of machines for deployment aboard their new carrier *Garibaldi* are perhaps the start of renewed interest. One thing is evident: the naval V/STOL story has only just begun.

TECHNICAL NOTE
It's rough out there

by D K Brown RCNC

The sea is rarely smooth, often rough and sometimes very rough indeed. The influence of bad weather on maritime operations is much greater today than in the past. Until the wars of the French Revolution it was common for the fleets to stay in harbour during the winter months, a practice finally stopped by Lord St Vincent when enforcing a continuous blockade of French ports throughout the year. Even so, the weather did not have a dominating effect on naval operations since its effects were the same on both fleets. If the battleships of one fleet, sail or steam, were slowed down or otherwise affected by the weather the Admiral could be confident that his opponent was experiencing similar problems.

Modern maritime operations involve submarines and aircraft as well as surface ships and, though all these vehicles are affected by the weather, they are affected in different ways and at different times. The effectiveness of one category may be seriously impaired while its enemy retains 100% capability. This article will look at how weather is measured and how often it occurs in different parts of the ocean. A later article will expand on the effect of weather in the surface ship and how the naval architect designs a ship to minimise such effects.

The earliest system of measurement was introduced in the 1830s by Rear-Admiral Sir Francis Beaufort, the Hydrographer. He related the strength of the wind to the amount of sail that could be carried and, with some changes, his scale is still in use. It is important to note that the Beaufort Number relates only to wind speed and does not directly say anything about wave height. Note that the current definition in terms of wind speed is slightly different from the original.

Wind blowing over the surface of the sea will generate waves but it takes some considerable time and distance before the wave heights reach their maximum. The stronger the wind, the greater the fetch needed before the highest waves appear. For example, in a Force 7, at least 108 miles are needed for waves to be fully developed. In consequence, the earlier European naval wars, with fighting in the North Sea, English Channel and Mediterranean, were rarely exposed to fully developed seas. The shallow waters in many of these areas does, however, lead to very steep waves.

Since World War II, wave height has been described in terms of sea state, a number which relates to the observed height. The wave height is taken as the average of the one third highest waves in a confused sea. Comparison between observation and measurement shows that this definition – significant wave height – agrees quite well with the subjective view of an experienced observer. Use of a scale related to wave height alone is inadequate since it gives no timescale. Length of wave, closely related to the square of the period, is important as a small boat, for instance would not feel bad in a 2 metre sea and a period of 15 seconds but the same height with a period of 5 seconds would seem very nasty.

Table 2 shows sea state, significant wave height, the number of days a year on which these wave heights are likely in the North Atlantic and the wind speed (Beaufort Number) that would produce these waves in the open ocean.

Wind and sea states vary considerably from one part of the ocean to another. Table 3 shows the percentage occurrence of various sea states over the whole of the Atlantic and for the whole North Sea area both over the year and in winter. In addition, data is included from two weather ships, *India*, well off Northern Scotland (19°W 59°N) and *Famita* off Norway (3°E 57°30'N).

What does all this mean in ability to fight? As the sea gets rough, men get tired and sometimes sea sick, their capability to make a correct judgement diminishes and even simple physical tasks take much longer. It becomes increasingly difficult to land and handle a helicopter, the efficiency of weapons and sensors (particularly sonars) is degraded. Details are closely guarded secrets but the following broad indications have been released.

Helicopter operations the limiting conditions are: average roll less than 5°, vertical velocity of deck due to pitch and heave less than 2 metres a second and half that for transverse velocity.

In general for a 110m (361ft) frigate up to Sea State 4 there is little or no effect on fighting efficiency. At Sea State 5 (31% of the year) the ship will be rolling 3° either way, if stabilised, pitching 1½° and heave through 1 metre. Speed is reduced to about 24 knots. Every job takes longer, the motion is seen as inconvenient and some sensors are affected. Replenishment is possible but difficult.

In Sea State 6 (21% of the year) the ship is rolling 4°, pitching 2° and heaving 1.5 metres. Speed will be 20 knots. Up to a third of the crew will be sick and all are

TABLE 1: FROM FINCHAM MASTING 1840

Beaufort Number	Description	Pressure (lb/in²)	Wind Speed (knots)	Sails		Today Revised Wind Speed (knots)
11-12	Hurricane		60-100			over 56
	Storm		45-50			
10	Heavy Gale	7.35/9	40	Close reef main topsls, storm stay sail or closed reefed main topsl only		48-55
9	Strong Gale	5/7	34	Reefed courses, close reef main topsl Take in main in rough seas		41-47
8	Fresh Gale	4/5	28	Close reefed topsls. Reefed courses Take in spanker and jib		34-40
7	Moderate Gale	2.5/3.5	23	2-3 reef topsl		28-33
6	Strong Breeze	1.5/2.3	15-20	Single reef topsl and topgallants In heavy seas 2 reef & take in topgallant		22-27
5	Fresh Breeze	.6/1.3	14	Royals & flying jib in. In heavy seas 2 reef topsail	Plain sail. Jibs, fore & main course driver, 3 topsails 3 topgallants	17-21
4	Moderate Breeze	.4/.45	13	All sail		11-16
3	Gentle Breeze	.2/.3	8	All sail		7-10
2	Light Breeze	.1/.14	5	All sail		4-6
1	Light Airs	0-0.05		All sail		1-3

TABLE 2: NORTH ATLANTIC SEA STATES

Sea State	Wave Height (metres)	No of days per year N Atlantic	Fully developed sea		Notes
			Beaufort	Wind Speed (knots)	
0-2	0-0.5		0-3	0-10	Calm
		55			
3	0.5-1.25		4	11-16	Large wavelets. Crests beginning to break
4	1.25-2.5	153	5	17-21	Small waves becoming larger, numerous whitecaps
5	2.5-4	99	6	22-27	Moderate waves. Many whitecaps, some spray
6	4-6	40	7-9	28-47	Larger waves forming whitecaps everywhere. More spray
7 & over	over 6	18	10 & over	over 48	Sea heaps up, white foam blown in streaks

TABLE 3: SEA STATE AS A PERCENTAGE OF THE YEAR

Sea State	N Atlantic		*India*		North Sea		
	All Year	Winter	All Year	Winter	All Year	Winter	*Famita* (winter)
0-3	15	9	8	2	36	27	11
4	42	34	31	3	44	43	33
5	27	32	31	27	15	20	33
6	11	17	21	48	5	8	15
7 & over	5	8	9	20	2	2	5

fatigued. Sleep is difficult as is helicopter operation. Many weapon systems are degraded.

Sea State 7 (9% of the year) the ship is ineffective as a fighting unit. She will roll about 10°, pitch 2½° or more and heave at least 2 metres. At best, the speed will be reduced to 10 knots.

Particularly in Northern waters the loss of efficiency is serious. The notes above show slight loss of efficiency 31% of the year, appreciable loss over 21%, and total ineffectiveness for 9%. A later article will show how the naval architect designs new ships to minimise the effects of bad weather.

US ASW SSK Submarines

by Norman Friedman

It is so common, now, to read that submarines are the only effective counters to other submarines that one might reasonably wonder why that was not so during the last great ASW war, 1939-1945, or just how this truth came to be understood. In its time, the concept of submarines as ASW platforms was quite radical, and submarine services, such as that of the United States, adopted it only relatively slowly and with considerable reluctance. The catalyst was the 1944 shock of the German Type XXI U-boat, which the Western navies expected the Soviets to duplicate rapidly and in great numbers after 1945. So poorly did existing ASW systems perform against the Type XXI that both major Western navies were quite willing to adopt radical expedients. The ASW submarine or, in American terms, the SSK, was one of several.

The problem was that a very fast submarine could evade existing surface ship sonars almost at will. Operating at high frequency, the latter were limited to ranges between 1500 and 3000 yards and there was little hope that enough sonar-equipped escorts could be provided to ring a convoy with solid coverage. As in World War II, then, much would have to depend on catching submarines once they revealed themselves by attacking. However, a Type XXI was so fast that, submerged, it could often outrun existing escorts. Hence the pressure to build fast escorts postwar, or to convert destroyers as an interim solution: the existing slow frigates and corvettes just could not expect to cope.

PRECEDENTS FROM 1914-18 AND 1939-45

Given the probable failure of convoy tactics, the best solution was somehow to deal with the submarine before it could reach its patrol area. Possible solutions included mining Soviet waters, and attacking Soviet submarine bases. The other possibility was to intercept transiting submarines. This was not a new idea. During World War I, faced with the apparent failure of most ASW measures, the Admiralty assigned British submarines to patrol both German transit routes and U-boat patrol areas, reasoning that submerged submarines could ambush surfaced U-boats. This idea was rational because, to make good any considerable distance, a submarine had to proceed on the surface. British submarines did again patrol German waters during World War II, but a much greater proportion of U-boats were sunk by convoy escorts and by aircraft, the latter often directed on the basis of long-range locators such as HF/DF, and actually locating surfaced submarines by means of radar.

Aircraft were, at least theoretically, far more efficient than surface ships or submarines because they were much faster, and therefore could be employed in more limited numbers. But they were ineffective against submerged submarines because they had no long-range detector that could penetrate the surface of the water. Thus the advent of the Type XXI, which would almost always operate submerged, was a disaster for the Allies: their most effective ASW systems were negated.

BARRIER STRATEGIES

The only compensation was that, in order to reach its operating area, a submarine had to snorkel, and snorkelling was quite noisy. Although existing surface ship sonars were not well suited to passive operation, it was soon discovered that suitably silenced submarines could detect snorkellers at appreciable ranges. Hence the concept of the SSK: a submarine equipped with a large passive sonar and homing torpedoes, and placed athwart the probable transit route of enemy submarines. The number of SSKs depended upon the effective engagement range: the longer the range of sensor and torpedoes, the fewer might be needed to maintain a barrier of a given length. As first formulated, the SSK strategy was to station submarines very close to Soviet bases, so that relatively few submarines would be able to slip by. However, more modern concepts entail the use of relatively long-range systems, and that in turn permits a small number of more expensive SSKs to patrol a much longer barrier line. Hence the current NATO concept of the Greenland-Iceland-United Kingdom Gap (GIUK) barrier, to protect vital shipping in the North Atlantic.

In practice, there was no expectation that a submarine barrier would be leak-proof. However, even a relatively leaky barrier could whittle down the Soviet submarine force quite rapidly, because each submarine would have to pass through the barrier both at the beginning and at the end of each patrol. For example, imagine a barrier capable of killing only 20 per cent of the submarines trying to penetrate it. That would amount to a net probability of 36 per cent that any submarine would be sunk either before or after its patrol, not counting other ASW measures. The average submarine would survive only two such patrols.

From 1947 onwards, US scientists experimented with carefully-silenced submarines listening at very low frequencies; they discovered the convergence zone effect, by means of which sounds can be detected at extreme ranges (in typical conditions, at multiples of about 35 miles). At the same time, the US Navy, which before and during World War II had concentrated on high-frequency acoustics, began to experiment with the low-frequency equipment developed by the German Navy. One system in particular excited interest: GHG, an array of passive sonars. It became the US BQR-4, the basis of the SSK programme.

US 1948 ASW PLANS

The FY48 Program included a specialised anti-submarine submarine (SSK), which would lie in wait on enemy transit routes, listening for snorkellers and for surface transits. The new technology of acoustic torpedoes would provide the weapon. At this time it was assumed that a submarine would have to snorkel virtually continuously to make good any considerable distance as it transitted towards its patrol area. It was clear from the first that very large numbers of such ASW submarines would be needed. In 1948 American ASW planners expected a short-term Soviet fleet of 356 modern submarines, and a long-term threat of 2000.

USS K1, lead boat of the SSK class, on 8 November 1951 two days before her official completion by Electric Boat. She had been laid down on 1 July 1949 and launched on 2 March 1951. Her most important feature is the massive BQR-4 passive sonar dome in the bows. She was renamed *Barracuda* in December 1955 and withdrawn from the SSK role in 1959 to become training boat *T1* until reclassification as an attack boat on 1 August 1972. She was stricken in 1973 long after her two younger sisters.
US Navy

On these bases they were able to calculate production requirements for the special submarines; three boats were needed to keep one on station in the forward areas. They would operate near Soviet bases, and also in barrier formations in the open sea. Others, whose numbers were not calculated, might form barriers around convoy routes, or work with hunter-killer teams. Two different strategies are evident. Against the immediate 356-submarine threat, the ASW submarines would operate well inshore, near the Soviet bases:

	On station	Total
North Cape-Cherry Island-Spitzbergen	56	168
Petropavlovsk (Soviet Far East base)	6	18
North End Sakhalin (Sea of Okhotsk)	6	18
La Perouse Strait (Japan/Sakhalin)	7	21
Tsgaru Strait (Hokkaido/Honshu, Japan)	2	6
Training		19
Total	77	250

Against the longer-term threat, however, they would form barriers much farther out to sea. The reasoning of the time is not clear, but there may have been an assumption that Soviet ASW would be much more effective by the time the 2000-boat fleet materialised, perhaps about 1960. Presumably the numbers were all predicated on

an assumed 20,000-yard range against a snorkeller:

Greenland-Iceland-Scotland	124	372
NE Pacific Coast Kamchatka Peninsula	10	30
Wales-Spain	86	258
Petropavlovsk	6	18
Kuriles	30	90
Tsugaru	2	6
Kyushu-China	42	126
Training		70
Total	210	970

Note the need to seal the southern exit of the English Channel in the 2000-submarine case. Presumably it was expected that minefields in the Baltic would seal in the Baltic Fleet in either case. By this time a snorkelling submarine had been detected out to first convergence zone, 35 miles, and there were claims that 'any submarine which exceeds cavitation speed becomes noisy and would be detected. They give up quiet operations when they exceed 6 knots . . .'

Modern sonars are much more effective. Although the breakdown of US submarine functions by number is classified, clearly the number required to fill the GIUK Gap barrier cannot much exceed ten. There are only about 90 attack submarines altogether, some of which are rated as 'second line' and thus probably excluded from so demanding an assignment. Each carrier battle group is to have one or two, which suggests a total of about ten submarines so occupied in peacetime at any one time (or 30 so dedicated, given the usual ratio); others would surely be assigned to convoys, to the Pacific, even to SSBN escort duty. In that case the ratio of early ASW submarines to current-type attack submarines is probably about ten to one, for the same barrier. That is probably not far from the ratio of sonar ranges, which suggests that current types expect to detect targets at about two or three convergence zones (say up to 210,000 yards or 100 miles), although attacks will occur at much shorter ranges. Another way to look at these figures is to suggest that any very severe reduction in US passive sonar range would effectively destroy the barrier strategy, since impossible numbers would be required.

SSK DESIGN

In 1948 the proposed solution was a boat so simple that it could be mass produced, even by builders not familiar with submarine practice in wartime. It was not a fast submarine, but it is included here because it was directly inspired by the advent of the Type XXI. The major simplification was to trade submarine performance (hence size) for *torpedo* performance. Much slower than attack submarines, at 8.5 knots submerged (one-hour rate; 6 knots when snorkelling), the very quiet SSK would not have to close its targets. Instead, it would

detect them passively at 20,000 yards or more, and attack with fast homing torpedoes.

The design was adapted to mass production and operation in several ways. First, it was limited to a diving depth of 400ft, where the new attack submarines were intended for 700ft. Given its low submerged speed, there was no need to be able to rig in the bow planes. The carefully silenced diesel engine was 'packaged' for unit replacement at a forward base, and the engine room was to be unmanned, to reduce crew size. A contemporary Navy account suggests that silencing was expected to be

USS *K3* off Mare Island (N of San Francisco) on her completion day by that yard (11 February 1952). She was laid down on 17 March 1950 and launched on 21 June 1951. Above her BQR-4 bow sonar is the BQS-3 'single ping' active sonar installation. She was renamed *Bonita* in December 1955 and ceased her SSK role in 1959 after 1958 service as a nuclear test target (superficial damage), serving as attack boat SS 552 until stricken in April 1965 along with *Bass* (ex-*K2*). *US Navy*

easier for a small, low-powered diesel; the original design showed a single screw.

The SSK did follow attack submarine design standards in having no conning tower in its sail; instead a command and information centre was combined with the control room. It also resembled the larger submarines in having a passive sonar in a chin position. Mission requirements included provision for underwater anchoring on a picket station and paired fathometers, one on the keel and one atop the hull, tiltable for under-ice operation.

As in many other warship design projects, size kept creeping upward. In the case of the SSK, the original 480-ton hull could not fit enough batteries to allow for sufficient loiter time. It turned out that even passive electronic equipment was a sufficient drain on battery charge to require much more capacity. And by the time the SSK was ordered it had grown to 750 tons, with two propellers in place of the original one, and four rather than two torpedo tubes. It was also limited to production by specialised yards. In the event just three were completed between November 1951 and February 1952.

The huge BQR-4 passive sonar, $20 \times 10 \times 10$ ft, was expected to have sufficient bearing descrimination to permit the submarine to close a target. Design sketches show it wrapped around the SSK sail, but it was actually installed in the bow, presumably for better isolation from engine and propeller noise. This installation was typical of later American ASW submarine practice. The higher-frequency BQR-2 (the sole sonar of the original design, adapted from the German *Balkon*), was a 3ft high circular array of vertical line hydrophones, 5ft in diameter, in a keel dome. With a claimed bearing accuracy of 1/10 of a degree, it would be used for fire control (attack). A hydrophone could be suspended clear of the hull for very long range (but non-directional) listening, and there was also a modified World War II JT passive sonar (BQR-3) intended as a back-up for the newer sets. Although space and weight were reserved for the possible installation of an active sonar, none was ever fitted.

Performance was spectacular: off Bermuda in 1952, the prototype, *K1*, detected a snorkeller at 30 miles, and tracked it for five hours. Even so, no mass production was ordered. Even though it was too large for true mass

production, in service the SS proved too small to withstand the rough conditions of its projected wartime operating area.

The only other source of large numbers of submarines was the numerous survivors of the war-built attack submarine fleet. An SSK conversion programme was one of several parallel ASW initiatives: the others were the projected mass conversion of *Fletcher* class destroyers (to DDE, 18 were completed before the programme was dropped) and the ASW conversion of existing light carriers (CVL). In each case, new construction was considered preferable, but it was inconceivable, given the sheer size of the newly-completed wartime fleet. In the case of the SSK, the conversion programme was conceived as a parallel source of submarines rather than as a replacement, since the problems of the original design were not evident until well after the conversions were underway. Although only seven boats were actually converted (the prototype, *Grouper*, in the FY50 Program, and six others under the FY52 Program, all before the original SSK had been completed), the design of the contemporary attack submarine conversion (the 'Guppy') was arranged to facilitate later SSK conversion. Moreover, other submarines were converted to a 'fleet snorkel' configuration which itself was designed for relatively easy conversion to 'Guppy' status.

The first of the conversions, *Grouper* (SSK 214), had her BQR-4 array wrapped around the front of her sail, but later boats had their BQR-4s in their bows, displacing two of the six forward torpedo tubes. Although ultra-quiet operation had originally been needed, the Bureau of Ships was able to modify these submarines to the point where they could listen while running equipment such as air conditioners, which, according to an official account of the period, 'improved habitability and also reduced electronic maintenance problems'.

SSK EXERCISES

By the mid-1950s, then, the SSK concept was well understood and well accepted. It had, moreover, been proven operationally. A February 1954 exercise SW of Iceland illustrates SSK tactics and performance. The new *K1* operated against the converted fleet submarine *Cavalla*, for a total of 36 runs. *K1* achieved an average detection range of 28 miles (11 runs); *Cavalla* was limited to an average of 13 miles (25 runs). In 26 cases one submarine or the other was able to get into attack position, and 21 attacks were judged successful. By this time the big BQR-4 was being used for attack as well as search and track; it was credited with half-degree accuracy at firing range. *K1* used the new technique of estimating range by plotting target motion as she manoeuvred, but she was limited by errors due to an insufficiently stable gyro; she could not adequately measure her own motion.

One run began at a range of 60 miles, the target submarine *Cavella* running for 2 hours on batteries at noncavitating speed (4.5 knots), alternating with 1 hour snorkelling at 6 knots, while zigzagging (short legs superimposed on longer ones to make target motion analysis difficult). She was essentially undetectable while on batteries. Even so, contact was made at 38 miles, and 6 hours and 35 minutes later the ambushing *K1* was in attack position, 1200 yards off the target's beam. This remarkable performance was attributed to the effectiveness of the self-noise reduction programme and to the range of the BQR-4 array sonar, about ten times that of the wartime JT. By 1955 it was being credited with 10-50 miles.

The great defect of the SSK was its limited speed: it could detect a target much farther away than it could attack. Several solutions were tried. The SSK could relay data to a destroyer by underwater telephone, which had a range of 8-11 miles but also disclosed the submarine's position. Alternatively it could vector in a carrier- or land-based attack airplane. Patrol plane-SSK operations were quite common in the 1950s; reportedly the Atlantic Fleet war plan included an SSK-air barrier off Argentia (Newfoundland) barring Soviet submarines from the US East Coast, as late as 1962. This concept survives in some forms of 'direct support' of battle groups. Finally, the submarine itself could be provided with a much longer-range weapon, which became Subroc, the underwater-launched ballistic ASW missile, with a nuclear depth bomb warhead. Subroc was generally employed in combination with a more effective sonar, the spherical BQQ-2, in nuclear submarines, but it was conceived in the SSK era.

THE NUCLEAR SSK

By 1955 it was clear that the next stage was a nuclear SSK with a new and more powerful sonar. By this time the nuclear reactor designers had obtained sufficient experience to propose a range of powerplants, including a small one, of about 2500shp, which might be used to power a very small submarine. In January 1955, for example, a Bureau of Ships study of future warship designs included a 900-ton SSKN powered by a 1500shp engine, its bow filled with sonars, and the torpedo tubes abaft it, angled outwards. This must have been the origin of the USS *Tullibee*.

There were two problems. First, SSKs had to be small and cheap. Nuclear endurance on station could reduce the numerical requirements drastically, particularly if the barrier could achieve its results very early in a war, before the boats had to be relieved on station. Although all nuclear powerplants were expensive, clearly a small SSKN would be more economical than a large one. The other problem was more difficult: noise. The first nuclear submarines were extremely noisy. Partly this was due to the use of geared turbines with their inherent whine. Partly, too, however, it was a consequence of the nature of the nuclear reactor itself, which required constant pumping of coolant. In the SSKN design, gearing noise was eliminated by shifting to turbo-electric propulsion, which, if inherently quieter, was also a larger consumer of internal space. The pump problem may have been more tractable at lower power levels.

Unfortunately, just as in the case of the original SSK, the SSKN grew uncontrollably, to displace about 2300 tons (with 2500shp). It did introduce the new sonar replacement for BQR-4, the BQQ-1 (later BQQ-2) that

USS *K3* in April 1954 when she and *K2* were based at Pearl Harbor. The class displaced 765 tons standard (1160 tons submerged), measured 196ft 1in oa × 24ft 7in × 14ft 5in and carried a crew of 37 with 4 × 21in torpedo tubes (2 bow and 2 stern). Twin GM diesels gave a surface speed of 13 knots and 8.5 knots submerged (1050shp).
US Navy

included a massive spherical transducer occupying the bow. It was the submarine equivalent of the surface ships' SQS-26, and ranges as great as 50 miles were claimed for it. Although the nuclear submarine *Thresher* of 1960 was not fitted to fire it, her sonar was later linked with a new type of underwater weapon, the Subroc ballistic missile, fired from underwater at a submarine target. In theory, Subroc was the ideal SSK barrier weapon, since it could engage targets at the ranges the new sonar made possible. In practice, Subroc is less than ideal because it is a nuclear weapon, subject to the very strong political and policy constraints of such systems. Its successor, SOW, will probably be a non-nuclear version, armed with the new Mark 50 Advanced Light Weight Torpedo (Barracuda).

For FY58 the issue was whether or not to build a new SSKN based on *Tullibee*. For some years the US Navy had been pursuing two parallel courses, the specialist SSK and the general-purpose attack submarine.

Although the latter could carry ASW torpedoes, it was much more a lineal descendant of past attack submarines, which were primarily means of dealing with surface ships. This orientation appears not to have been questioned, even though the Soviet surface fleet of the day was a minor problem compared to the threat of Soviet submarines.

The key decision was that, in future, there would be only one type of submarine, aside from such clearly specialist types as missile and radar picket craft. *All* submarines would have SSK capability; similarly, all would be capable of attacking surface ships. In practice, with the anti-ship role no longer opposed to the ASW role, ASW came to predominate, to such an extent that it is now the principal role, and indeed the justification, of the nuclear attack submarine force. However, current nuclear attack submarines are so much more mobile than their SSK ancestors that the barrier may not be the best way to use them; in that sense the SSK concept may be on its way out.

From a physical point of view, this particular compromise was reflected in the two major design features of the new *Thresher* (now, with the loss of the prototype, *Permit*) class. One was high (but now silenced) power, the attribute of the attack submarine. Turbo-electric

USS Bream (SS 243), off Oahu 29 January 1962, was a more
conventional fleet boat/SSK with an enlarged bow housing the
BQR-4 passive sonar. The small dome above it carried a
BQS-3 active set. Another active sonar is in the smaller dome
farther aft.
US Navy

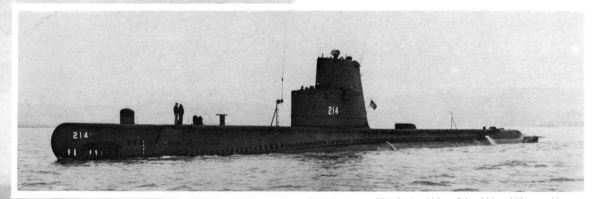

USS *Grouper* (SSK 214) of Mare Island Naval Shipyard in June 1951. She was the first of seven fleet submarines to be converted to the SSK role. Her BQR-4 sonar was wrapped around the front of the bridge fairweather. Although at first glance she appears to be a conventional 'Guppy', the men on her bridge are some distance away from its front edge and, unlike a 'Guppy', it has no upper level windows.
US Navy

drive was considered, but it was rejected because of the design delay entailed. Instead, the geared drive of the most recent attack class was retained, but the engines and gearing were mounted on a raft, sound-isolated from the hull of the submarine. This made for a materially larger submarine. The other major feature was the big bow sonar of *Tullibee*, combined, as in that boat, with torpedo tubes located abaft the bow, and angled outward. These two features, high (but relatively quiet) speed and a big bow sonar, have characterised both subsequent US attack submarine designs, the *Sturgeon* (launched 1963-71) and the *Permit* (launched 1961-66). In that sense the SSK idea had triumphed.

During the 1960s, Admiral Hyman G Rickover tried to revive the distinction between the fast attack submarine and the slower, but much quieter, barrier submarine, proposing that the United States build two parallel nuclear classes: the *Los Angeles* for attack and some development of the *Glenard P Lipscomb* or *Narwhal* for the barrier mission. Economics made this impossible. However, this time the decision went against the specialist barrier submarine, because the faster *Los Angeles*, which was almost as quiet, could carry out a new type of ASW mission, the direct support of fast carrier groups. At the same time she was quiet enough for barrier work.

From time to time the submarine, with its superior sonar performance, was proposed as the primary antisubmarine vehicle. For example, in February 1962, Rear Admiral Ralph K James, who was then Chief of the Bureau of Ships, suggested that in future surface ASW ships should be confined to use in shallow water and in protecting convoys that might also be threatened by air attack.

NOTE
Much of this article has been adapted from Norman Friedman's forthcoming book *Submarine Design and Development* to be published in May 1984 by Conway Maritime Press at £15.

Was there a Serbian Navy?

by René Greger

Maybe readers will smile when reading this title as none of them will have ever met any mention of a Serbian Navy in the naval literature issued before or during World War I. But they would smile too soon. It is fact that there was neither a Serbian regular navy or river flotilla but there were ships flying the Serbian ensign (red, blue and white stripes with the Serbian eagle in the middle) both on the Danube and in the Adriatic and Aegean Seas during 1914-18.

When World War I broke out in July 1914 Serbia did not have any seacoast, but the frontier between old rivals, the Austro-Hungarian Empire and the young and small Serbian kingdom, was formed by three great rivers; the Drina in the west, the Danube and the Sava in the north.

Austria-Hungary had a very strong river flotilla including numerous auxiliaries. Its monitors armed with 120mm (4.7in) guns could influence operations on the whole front excluding the wild Drina. On the other hand very poor Serbia could not afford to spend money building river warships of a similar type, quite apart from the fact that she lacked the trained sailors to man them. The first river transport organisation in Serbia (*Srpsko Brodarsko Drustvo*) was only established in 1890. At that time there was just one river vessel in the country – the passenger steamer *Deligrad* owned by the government from 1862. Serbia therefore asked her allies for help and received it.

At the end of August 1914 a group of 106 Russian seamen appeared on the Sava river and installed there the first torpedo battery and laid 12 mines. British and French groups followed soon, bringing torpedoes and naval guns. While the Russians concentrated on minelaying and had great success with it sinking the Austrian monitor *Temes*, the British expedition led by Vice-Admiral Troubridge tried to use torpedoes against the aggressive monitors. The torpedo batteries installed on the land had no success but a British picket boat caused the Austrians some trouble. This large steam boat under the command of Lieutenant-Commander Kerr was armed with torpedo launching apparatus (if not tubes?) and attacked the Austrian monitors anchored at Zemun on the evening of 22 April 1915. Two years later, the British Prize Court made a declaration that the commander, officers and crew were entitled to prize money amounting to £514 for the destruction of the Austrian monitor *Koros* in the Danube. In fact the Austrian vessel was not hit and the following attack on 17 May against an Austrian patrol boat also failed. Both attacks made by the British boat, operating (according to some unconfirmed sources) under the Serbian flag,

were the only river operations undertaken from the Serbian side.

The Russian 'Special Expedition' sent no combat boats to the front, but tried to protect the convoys of supply ships sent from Russia to Serbia up the Danube. The most important stretch – the Iron Gates – was to be defended by the armed Russian steamer *Tiraspol* and two motor gunboats originally used on the Amur, against possible raids. This never happened. Not known is the existence of a Serbian ship, manned by the Army, which took part in the defence of Russian convoys coming to the small Serbian port of Prahovo. Armed with a machine gun, the tug *Stig* was to protect the supply ships against Austrian aircraft. When Bulgaria attacked Serbia in October 1915 all ships on the Serbian bank had to be scuttled or tried to reach the Rumanian port of Corabia. *Stig* was scuttled.

The tug *Stig* manned by the Serbian Army on the Danube in 1915.
Author's collection

The torpedo boat *Srbija* in the Gulf of Salonika 1916-18.
Author's collection

Several weeks later the defeated Serbian Army reached the Adriatic coast of Albania after a long and distressful retreat. About 140,000 remaining Serbian soldiers were evacuated by Allied ships from Durazzo and Valona to Corfu by the end of March 1916. On that Greek island the tired Serbs were placed in many camps and communication between them was difficult. At first some Greek private boats were hired, but the Army Command and Serbian Government wanted a vessel of their own. Besides this the Prince Regent (later King Alexander I) had had a bad experience, not having any boat or vessel under his own command, during the final phase of the Serbian retreat in Albania at the end of January. On the morning of 21 January he came from evacuated Scutari to the small port of Medua and wished to be transported as soon as possible to Valona. There were two small Italian destroyers in the harbour, waiting for the old Montenegrin King Nicholas I who left his defeated small kingdom with his whole court. Personal relations between Alexander and his old uncle Nicholas were far from good, especially after the bombing attempt organised against Nicholas by Alexander's family. Alexander had to wait until Nicholas' entourage came and, after a brief public conversation with his uncle, he was informed by the Italian commander that he

The torpedo boat *Srbija* at Salonika in 1918. Her crew are in French Navy uniform and her funnel bands represent Serbia's national colours in the red, blue and white ensign at the stern.
Author's collection

would be transported to Valona via Brindisi after Nicholas and his court had left the ships in that Italian harbour. The enraged Alexander refused that proposal, mounted a horse and left Medua with his retinue for Durazzo by land, Alexander never forgot this incident and wished to have a vessel under the Serbian flag.

Fortunately an old Greek former torpedo boat, named *Paxo* (or *Paxoi*?) was discovered in the main harbour of Corfu and bought for 50,000 drachmas (about £2000 at that time). The vessel received the name *Srbija* (according to another serious source the name was *Velika Srbija* ie The Great Serbia). Not many of her technical details could be found in later Yugoslav documents except the length 23.1m (75ft 9in), beam 4m (13ft 1in) and a speed of 16 knots. She was probably one of four French-built small torpedo boats, bought in 1880 for the Greek Navy and deleted from the list in 1910. According to standard naval yearbooks they had the length of 22m (72ft 2in) and beam of 3.96m (13ft). Their crew was 12 men the same number as the Serbs who could be met in the ship in 1918.

The rested and reorganised Serbian Army was transported to the Salonika Front in May 1916 and the small *Srbija* had to follow. Her inexperienced crew did not dare risk the passage on their own and so the vessel was towed by a French destroyer to Patras. Perhaps a diplomatic incident between Italy and Serbia also influenced this solution. Italy protested against the use of the 'unknown and internationally not allowed' Serbian flag at sea. Only after the Serbian Government promised that the vessel would not be armed, did Italy cease to protest. Italy's fear that Yugoslav warships would appear in *mare nostrum* (ie the Adriatic) was just as acute as between the wars.

Srbija served under the Serbian flag in the Gulf of Salonika up to November 1918 and later as one of the first vessels under the new Yugoslav flag in Boka Kotorska during the early 1920s. She was never armed in spite of her official Yugoslav classification as '*torpiljer*' (torpedo boat) and she was scrapped in 1928.

THE LAST SUPER DESTROYERS?
Mogador & Kléber Classes

by Robert Dumas

The *Mogador* class destroyers were the ultimate evolution of their type in France. By virtue of their dimensions and their armament these two ships were the biggest conventional destroyers ever built; indeed they could have been classified as light cruisers like the Italian 'Capitani Romani' class (see *Warship* 7 and 8). They were an enlargement of the *Fantasque* class, the French designers aiming to increase their offensive power by installing twin-pseudo turrets (fully enclosed gunhouses) with 5.5in (138.6mm) guns.

Mogador was built under the 1932 budget and *Volta* under that of 1934.

BUILDING

Mogador, named after the Moroccan seaport, was built at Lorient Dockyard, *Volta*, named after the West African river, by Ateliers et Chantiers de Bretagne at Nantes.

	Laid down	Launched	In service
Mogador	28.12.34	9.6.37	10.8.38
Volta	24.12.34	20.8.37	21.3.39

Mogador at Le Havre, 12 November 1938, three months after her completion. A twin 13.2mm Model 1929 machine gun mounting can be seen below the bridge.

Author's collection

Mogador at the same juncture. Super destroyers obviously had no new means of drying laundry!
Author's collection

Their main armament was not ready when they entered service and their proving trials continued afterwards.

CHARACTERISTICS

Displacement	2884 tons standard, 3500-3600 tons normal, 4018 tons full load
Length overall	137.5m/451ft 2in
Length between perpendiculars	131m/429ft 9in
Beam (maximum)	12.67m/41ft 7in
Beam (waterline)	12.56m/41ft 2in
Draught	3.65-4.57m/12-15ft
Main armament	8 × 5.5in/45 Model 1934 guns in 4 twin mounts (30° elevation)
Anti-aircraft armament	2 × 37mm CAD Model 1933 guns 4 × 13.2mm Model 1929 Hotchkiss machine guns in twin mounts

Note: I have found that 8mm Hotchkiss Model 1916 machine guns were mounted in *Volta*, a twin mount and one single on the after deckhouse (on the centreline of the ship) and two singles in the bridge wings. It was intended eventually to carry 40 mines (Breguet 500kg/1100lb type).

Ammunition	1440 rounds of 5.5in plus 85 starshell 2480 rounds of 37mm
Torpedo tubes	10 × 550mm/21.7in in two triple and two twin mounts
Rangefinders	2 × 5m/16ft 5in (one for the main director, one for the foretop) 1 × 4m/13ft 1in Type A for the after director 2 × 1m/39in for the anti-aircraft guns (one for the forward 13.2mm machine gun platform and one abaft the after director)
Searchlights	2 × 75cm (port and starboard of the after funnel) 2 × 45cm/17.7in (port and starboard of the main director)

Mogador from astern at the same time. Her name has yet to be painted on in the regular fashion on the quarter not far from the stern depth charge chutes (24 440lb DCs was the normal large destroyer armament).

Author's collection

Boats	2 × 7m/23ft motor launches (port and starboard of the forward funnel) 2 × 7m/23ft motor pinnacles (abaft the forward funnel) 1 × 5m/16ft dinghy between the pinnaces 1 × 3m/9ft pram stowed in the dinghy 1 × 7m/23ft whaler on derricks to starboard 1 × 7m/23ft rowing cutter on derricks to port
Machinery	4 Indret vertical small-tube boilers with superheating 4 collectors and 2 superheaters of air Boiler pressure 35kg/sq cm Superheater temperature 385° C 2-shaft Rateau-Bretagne geared steam turbines of 92,000shp and 105,000shp
Speed	39 knots
Trials	*Mogador* over 8 hours: at 3512 tons, 104,925shp = 41.274 knots in 9th hour: at 3098 tons, 118,320shp = 43.45 knots *Volta* over 8 hours: at 3168 tons,? = 42.09 knots in 9th hour: at 3105 tons,? = 43.78 knots
Oil	310 tons normal load, 710 tons maximum
Range	4000 miles at 18 knots 3000 miles at 20 knots
Crew	251 peacetime (15 officers, 41 petty officers, 195 ratings) 264 wartime (15 officres, 249 ratings) 284 flagship

MODIFICATIONS

Both ships had a cap fitted to the forward funnel, probably at the end of 1938. A steel bulwark was built round the 13.2mm machine gun platform (early 1940).

In *Mogador* the searchlight was plated (spring 1940). During the major repairs following the damage she sustained at Mers el Kebir it was decided to alter her armament. Number 3 turret was removed and Number 4 was raised. The anti-aircraft armament was increased by six 37mm Model 1933 guns in twin mounts on the after deckhouse. It is likely that *Volta*'s armament would also have been augmented. (The photographs of the scuttled

1

2

3

1 *Mogador* moored at Brest in December 1939 after one of the Allied searches for *Scharnhorst* and *Gneisenau*. She was repainted in the superstructure light grey early in the New Year.

ECPA/Author's collection

2 *Volta* steams off Toulon early in 1941 after her AA armament had been increased. The battlecruiser *Strasbourg* can just be seen above her stern.

Author's collection

3 *Mogador* at the end of 1940 showing her amputated stern caused by a direct hit from a British 15in shell at Mers et Kebir 3 July 1940. She had begun to sink by the stern on fire but the main engine bulkheads stood firm enabling her to be towed and beached out of harm's way. She still contributed AA fire on 6 July when *Dunkerque* was cripped by *Ark Royal*'s Swordfish.

Author's collection

Mogador do not show any guns still on the after deckhouse.) The number of oil fuel bunkers was increased.

In *Volta* the foretop rangefinder was given a steel roof (end 1940). Two 13.2mm CAS Browning machine guns were installed on small platforms on either side of Number 3 turret (early 1941). At the end of 1941 or beginning of 1942 the Hotchkiss machine guns were removed from the platform forward of the bridge. They were replaced by two 25mm Hotchkiss guns. Finally two 13.2mm CAS Browning guns were installed on new platforms to port and starboard of the navigation bridge. The 37mm gun shields were strengthened as was the Type A rangefinder tower. The searchlight tower was closed in as in *Mogador*. Finally extra ammunition lockers were fitted for the 37mm mounting on the forward platform and lifejacket holders fixed to stanchions on the navigation bridge.

COLOUR SCHEME AND MARKINGS
Both ships had dark grey hulls from the end of 1939 to the beginning of 1940 with a light grey superstructure. The latter colour was extended to the whole of both ships for the rest of their existence.

Until 21 March 1939 *Mogador* and *Volta* carried the hull numbers 4 and 5 respectively. From that date they were changed to X61 and X62 in white, becoming brick red from April 1940. Both ships carried a blue band on

108

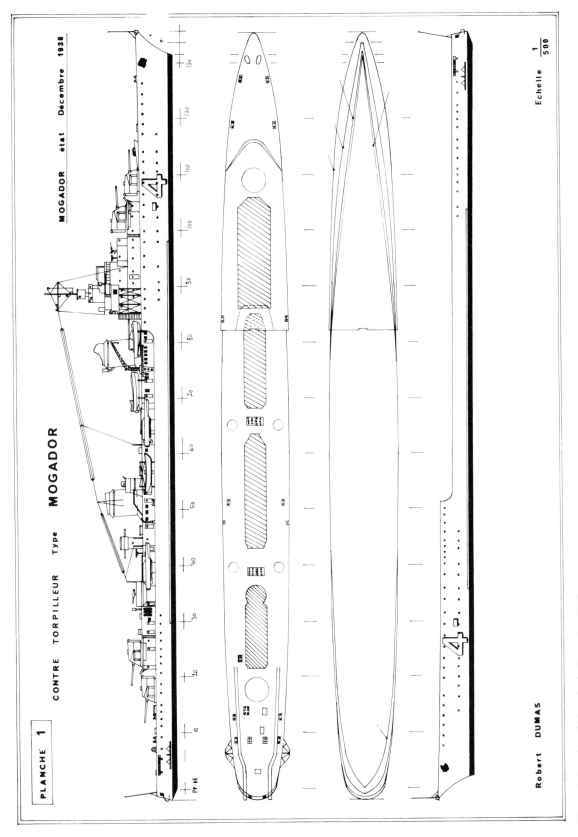

PLANCHE 1   CONTRE TORPILLEUR   Type   MOGADOR

MOGADOR   état   Decembre 1938

Echelle $\frac{1}{500}$

Robert DUMAS

Plan and elevation of *Mogador* in December 1938 as completed.

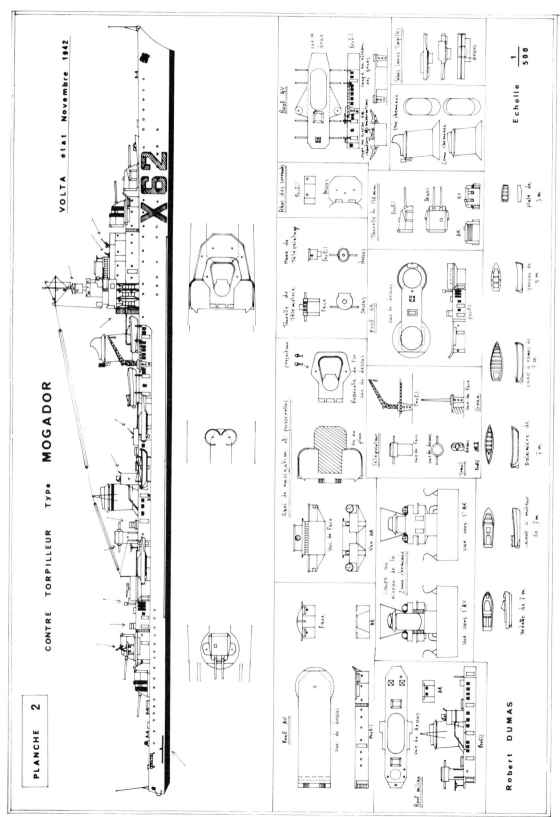

Elevation and superstructure details of *Volta* in her final guise, November 1942.
Robert Dumas

Mogador scuttled and disarmed at Toulon November 1942.
On her starboard side is the smaller and older *Guépard* class
destroyer *Valmy*, one of 5 destroyers of that class to share
their bigger consorts' fate. *Valmy* was refloated by the Italians
and served as their *FR24* until scuttled again at Genoa.

Author's collection

the second funnel, the sign of the 6th Destroyer Division
they belonged to. They had national Tricolour markings
on the sides of Numbers 2 and 3 turrets (2 and 4 for *Volta*
from the beginning of 1941).

OPERATIONAL HISTORY

From their entry into service *Mogador* and *Volta* formed
the 6th Destroyer Division in the 2nd Light Squadron.
This was part of the elite 1st Squadron of the Atlantic
Fleet at Brest whose major ships were the battlecruisers
Dunkerque and *Strasbourg* together with the cruisers
Georges Leygues, *Montcalm* and *Gloire*.

The two destroyers escorted many British convoys
bound for France during September and October 1939.
From that date *Volta* underwent repairs at Brest. In
November *Mogador* accompanied *Dunkerque* and HMS
Hood in the hunt for *Scharnhorst* and *Gneisenau* and
then escorted the Allied battlecruisers in the Atlantic
approaches.

Both ships were with the Atlantic Fleet at Mers el
Kebir (Oran) when it was attacked by Admiral Sir James

Somerville's Force H on the evening of 3 July 1940. A
British 15in shell hit *Mogador*, leading the six destroyers
present ahead of *Strasbourg*'s breakout, in the stern and
set off her depth charges, killing 38 of her crew. *Volta*
escaped the tragic massacre with the four other destroyers and *Strasbourg* which they escorted towards
Toulon where they arrived next day. *Volta*'s screening
efforts included the long-range firing of torpedoes at
Hood.

Mogador was put into a floating dock at Oran for
temporary repairs. She left Mers el Kebir for Toulon in
November 1940 under tow from the ocean tug
Laborieux. Final repairs were made at Toulon.

Both destroyers were scuttled at Toulon among the
60-odd warships so denied the Axis on 27 November
1942. Though refloated by the Italians in mid-1943
neither was fit to be used and both wrecks were scrapped.

CONCLUSION

Mogador and *Volta* were the final stage in French destroyer construction. Like their immediate predecessors,
the *Fantasque* class, they were given the heaviest possible main armament and the most powerful machinery to
achieve extremely high speed. The French naval staff
wanted to use them as raiding ships against enemy forces
and coasts, but war experience revealed certain defects.

The 5.5in main armament was fragile and complicated. It was often in a damaged state that seriously restricted the rate of fire (normally 6rpm). The anti-aircraft armament was very limited and indeed French warships in general had inadequate air defence. This defect was partially remedied by adding 25mm and 13.2mm guns to *Volta*.

The French Navy was equally backward in anti-submarine warfare, lacking the Royal Navy's Asdic and powerful depth charge throwers. The latter weapon in French service was not very efficient.

Their radius of action was limited by insufficient oil fuel bunkers. That should not have been allowed in what were intended to be ocean escorts.

On the credit side their very solid construction should be mentioned. At Mers el Kebir *Mogador* survived a direct hit from a capital ship that exploded her depth charges as well. High speed was another asset as demonstrated by *Volta*'s escape from the carnage. This virtue had already been seen in three of the *Fantasque* class making a 35-knot sortie into and out of the Skaggerak during the Norwegian Campaign, surviving heavy air attack. *Mogador* and *Volta* had also previously showed their seaworthiness in the North Atlantic.

PROJECTED KLÉBER CLASS
To complete this study it is necessary to recall that France planned a modified and slightly larger *Mogador* class, the *Kléber*. Four destroyers were authorised, all

Volta scuttled at Toulon November 1942.
Author's collection

named after some of the Revolution's most dashing generals. *Kléber*, *Marceau* and *Desaix* came under the 1938 budget (vote of 2 May) and *Hoche* under that year's supplementary budget.

CHARACTERISTICS

Displacement	3750 tons normal, 4180 tons full load
Length overall	as *Mogador* class
Beam (maximum)	13.8/42ft 7in
Beam (waterline)	12.97m/42ft 7in
Draught	3.7m/12ft 2in forward, 4.65m/15ft 3in aft
Main armament	8 × 5.5in/45 Model 1934 guns in 4 twin mounts (35° elevation)
Anti-aircraft armament	4 × 4in/100mm Model 1930 guns in twin unpowered mounts able to elevate 80° 8 × 13.2mm Hotchkiss machine guns in four twin mounts
Torpedo tubes	6 × 550m/21.7in in two triple mounts
Oil	850 tons
Range	3600 miles at 20 knots
Other characteristics	as *Mogador* class

The Third Republic's last warship building programme, decreed on 1 April 1940, included six more super destroyers and it is almost certain that they would have been similar to the *Kléber* class. The names of two have been given as *Bruix* and *Bayard*.

Volta in the Toulon area early in 1941.
Author's collection

BUILDERS
Kléber Ateliers et Chantiers de France at Dunkirk
Marceau Atliers et Chantiers de France at Nantes
Desaix Ateliers et Chantiers de France at Dunkirk
Hoche   Arsenal de Lorient
None of these ships had been laid down by the time of the armistice of June 1940. If France had not been conquered by Germany they would have entered service about 1943-44.

Volta again in the Toulon area with her 1942 increased AA armament.
Author's collection

CONCLUSION
The *Kléber* class had important improvements in air defence, anti-submarine equipment and range (20 per cent more) over the *Mogador* class. And war experience would certainly have enhanced these additions. But these magnificent intended ships fell victim to that same war though it is interesting to note that their characteristics served as the point of departure for the *Surcouf* class cruiser escorts laid down from 1951 and still serving in the French Fleet.

ARKANSAS Class Monitors

by Frances J Allen

According to an article published in the *Scientific American* of December 1901; the *Arkansas* class of monitor was a direct result of 'panic legislation' itself caused by the Spanish-American War. The monitor was seen as solely a 'harbor defense vessel, and would be practically useless . . . in naval operations on the high seas'.[1]

In truth, however, the monitors that were acquired by the US Navy between the years 1898 and 1903, ten in all, were considered by many to be well suited to harbour defence and coastal protection. The notion that this was

Sketch plan of US *Arkansas* class monitor, prepared by the Bureau of Construction and Repair, Navy Department.
US Naval Museum, Washington DC

the correct and proper strategy for a Navy with ambitions to world power was also a contributing factor to the purchase of these ships described as a 'wallowing curiosity'.[2]

Five out of the ten monitors were 'holdovers from the Old Navy, twenty years in the building and constructed with iron hulls instead of steel'.[2] These were *Puritan* and four ships of the *Amphitrite* class. These new, yet ancient, warships had been started by the deceptive accounting procedure of using money earmarked for repairing Civil War monitors of the same names, to lay down new construction. The actual building of the vessels took an inordinately long time. This was a time of stagnation for America's armed forces and the Navy budget was no exception 'although considerable sums of

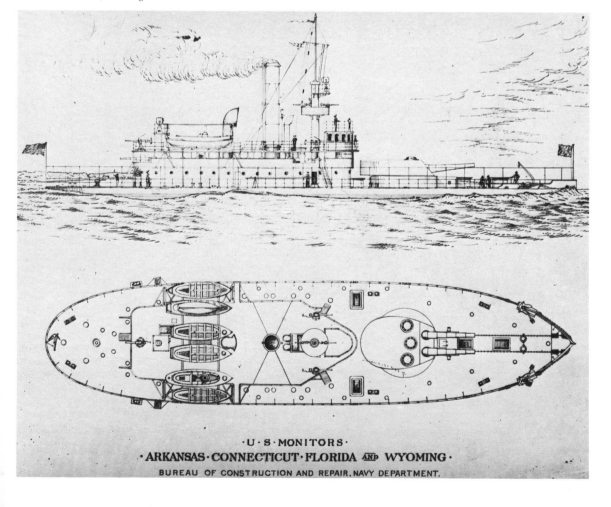

· U · S · MONITORS ·
· ARKANSAS · CONNECTICUT · FLORIDA ᴀɴᴅ WYOMING ·
BUREAU OF CONSTRUCTION AND REPAIR. NAVY DEPARTMENT.

USS *Arkansas* (BM7) 1906.
Library of Congress

money were dribbled into them under some cloudy constructual dealings'.[2]

With all of the dealings and long building schedules there was at least one benefit that was to be passed along to the later construction 'in 1887 armor requirements for them . . . four (monitors) were combined into a single order large enough to include United States industry to build the necessary steel forging and rolling facilities'.[2] This policy would result in some delays in the armour, but the Navy Department accepted this to be free of its dependency on foreign supplies.

It was by an act of 4 May 1898 that Congress appropriated the money for four monitors of a modern design. While the Navy was authorised to build double turreted monitors, they opted for a single turret design because of the limited available funds. The ships were to be of 3200-ton displacement and mount 12in rifle guns in fully balanced turrets, modern boilers and much electrically powered auxiliary machinery.

The new monitors were to be given state names just as battleships were. In 1908-9 these names would be exchanged for the names of cities in the state after which they were originally named.

Although these vessels were obsolete before they were even authorised, they did manage to render 'some contributions to naval progress . . . in 1908 the *Florida* . . . was employed as an experimental target in the Chesapeake Bay to determine the effects of modern large caliber projectiles and torpedoes on contemporary armour and hull construction. In another major experiment, the following year (1909), the West Coast

Monitor, *Cheyenne* (ex-*Wyoming*) was converted into the US Navy's first successful fuel oil-burning warship'.[2]

The single turreted monitors of the *Arkansas* class soldiered on into World War I and beyond. They were even used as submarine tenders 'although their low freeboard was about the only feature making them suitable for such a duty, *circa* 1913'.[2] Service was rendered by these ships as station ships, receiving and gunnery training vessels, militia and target ships.

The first decade of the twentieth century saw the use of *Arkansas, Florida, Nevada, Puritan* and *Terror* as Academy drill ships at the US Naval Academy, Annapolis, Maryland. During the 1920s all were sold as scrap except USS *Cheyenne*. This ship's 'modern engineering plant kept her on active Navy list until 1937 as a Naval reserve drill ship'.[2]

As the first of her class USS *Arkansas* is representative. She was built by Newport News Ship Building and Dry Dock Company from plans furnished by the Navy Department with the details to be worked out by the contractor. The price of $860,000 (about £172,000 at that period) was agreed upon minus boats, anchors, chains, armour and guns.

GENERAL ARRANGEMENT

'The hull was constructed of milled steel with transverse frames 3ft apart, special frames being worked in where necessary. The stem and stern posts are cast steel . . . the armour sits on a shelf and is 8in thick at midship and tapers to 4in thick forward and aft at waterline.'[3]

The ordnance authorised for *Arkansas* consisted of two 40-calibre 12in rifle guns in a balanced turret with traverse through 150° on each side; four 50-calibre 4in Mk 7 rapid firing rifles at corners of the superstructure; three 6pdr semi-automatic, four 1pdr Maxim-

USS *Florida* (BM9), *Arkansas* (BM7) and *Nevada* (BM8)
underway *c* 1905.
US Naval Museum

USS *Florida* (BM9).
National Archives, Washington DC

1
2

3

1 USS *Tallahasee* (BM9) anchored in Hampton Roads on 10
December 1916, a few months before America's entry into
World War I. Alongside the monitor submarine tender are
two submarines *K-6* (SS37) and *K-5* (SS36).
US Naval Museum

2 USS *Arkansas* (BM7) coming down the Kenebech River to
Bath, Maine.
US Naval Museum

3 USS *Arkansas* being launched at the Newport News
Shipbuilding and Dry Dock Company, Newport News,
Virginia, on 10 November 1900.
US Naval Museum

118

1 USS *Cheyenne* (BM10) in drydock at the Philadelphia Navy
Yard in December 1919.
US Naval Museum

2 USS *Florida* (BM9) fitting out at the Crescent Shipyard,
Elizabethport, New Jersey in 1901-2.
US Naval Museum

3 USS *Florida* (BM9).
US Naval Museum

2

3

USS *Wyoming* (BM10) off Mare Island Navy Yard, San Francisco, February 1903.

US Naval Museum

USS *Wyoming* (BM10) making 12.4 knots during her trials off San Francisco, California, in October 1902.

US Naval Museum

Nordenfeldt machine guns, a 1pdr rapid firing gun and two 6mm Colt automatics.

She carried four 28ft boats; a steam cutter, launch, whaleboat, and gig whaleboat. There were two 26ft cutters and an 18ft dinghy.

There were a total of eight ventilating systems on board and these were supplied by 11 fans, two powered by steam while the others were electric. Two fans for the forward system were in the dynamo room. They drew their air 'from ventilators in the hammock nettings and discharge through ducts leading forward on either side of the turret to all compartments forward of and including the dynamo room'.[3]

Two fans were also provided for the after system, one per shaft alley that fed all of the compartments on the berth deck abaft of the engine room. There was in addition to these a system for the steering engine room, a 70in fan and one No 5 Monogram fan in a main-deck system, two 70in fans for the engine room, a gravity system in the coal-bunkers, two steam fans in the after part of the boiler room for forced draft and finally the air spaces around the magazines were fed by the other fan systems.

The electrical plant was on the berth deck abaft the turret and forward of the firemen's wash room. For its day the system was well provided for, the engines and dynamos were supplied by General Electric Co. There were four dynamos of 32kw each. The main switchboard, the searchlight switchboard and the air compressor were located in the dynamo room. The turret was

trained by two 35hp motors and elevated by a pair of 3½hp units. The ammunition hoists were all electrically operated: two 3¾hp motors for the 4in ammunition hoist; two 12in hoists powered by a 20hp motor each; and the 3 and 6pdr ammunition hoist of 3¾hp each.

There were two searchlights using 50 volts and 70 amperes; eight 5-candlepower incandescent lamps; 249 of 15-candlepower; 10 32-candlepower with a total of 4344 candlepower.

Arkansas was provided with three sets of engines. The steering engine was manufactured by Williamson Bros Co of Philadelphia, and was capable of putting the helm amidships to hard-to-starboard in 13 seconds by use of a worm-and-screw-gear working the tiller. The Hyde Windless Co of Bath, Maine, built the anchor engines. This engine in official trials 'took in two anchors, weighing 5480lb starboard and 5130lb port with 114 fathoms of chain out at the rate of 6 fathoms per minute'.[3]

Placed abreast and in one watertight compartment were the main engines. These were three cylinder, triple expansion direct-acting. These engines were fed from four Thornycroft type, Daring pattern boilers, placed in

USS *Wyoming* (BM10); waves breaking over the ship's bow during her trials off San Francisco, California, in October 1902.

US Naval Museum

USS *Wyoming* (BM10) building at the Union Iron Works, San
Francisco, California.
National Archives

USS *Wyoming* (BM10) showing her pre-1909 white
paintwork and bow scroll decoration to advantage.

USS *Wyoming* (BM10) moored in West Coast waters before 1909.
US Naval Museum

one watertight compartment with the fire room running athwartships. 'Each boiler has one steam drum, three water drums and two furnaces...The boilers were designed to carry a working steam pressure of 250lb.'[3]

This power train commanded twin screws of a modified Griffiths design. They were made of a manganese bronze compound. They were three bladed, adjustable pitch, right handed on starboard and left handed on the port side. The hubs were spherical, cut off at the ends.

'The standardization trials were made on the Barren Island course in the Chesapeake Bay, and the speed trials were run off Cape Henry in free route in the open sea. The bottom was clean and the vessel was in good condition. The coal was the New River, Collins Mine, hand picker. The draught during the trial was forward, 12ft 5¾in; aft, 12ft 9in; 12ft 7³/₁₆in.

The speed trials took place Tuesday, 7 August 1902 off Cape Henry, and the following data was taken. The run lasted two hours and the data was taken at half-hour intervals from 12.05 to 1.35pm.'[3]

REFERENCES
1 'Special Navy Issue-Development of the United States Navy Since the Spanish War,' *Scientific American* LXXXV (1901) pp373-90.
2 John D Alden, *American Steel Navy* (Naval Institute Press, Annapolis, Maryland, 1972).
3 Lt C K Mallory, USN, 'Description and Trials of US Monitor *Arkansas*' *Naval Engineers Journal* pp1172-85 (Vol 14 1902).

TABLE 1: GENERAL CHARACTERISTICS

Displacement	3200t (normal)
Length	252ft
Beam	50ft (max)
Draught	12ft 6in (mean)
Armament	2 × 12in/40 BL
	4 × 4in/50 QF
Armour	11in-5in (side)
	10in-9in (turrets) 7½in (CT)
Machinery	twin-screw vertical triple-expansion
Coal	350t
Speed	12.03kts; 1739ihp (*Arkansas*)
Complement	13 officers; 135 enlisted men

TABLE 2: SHIPS' HISTORIES (OUTLINE FORM)

USS *Arkansas*	Monitor No 7
Built	by Newport News Ship Building and Dry Dock, Co, Newport News, Virginia
Authorised	4 May 1898
Laid down	14 November 1899
Launched	10 November 1900
Commissioned	28 October 1902
Renamed *Ozark*	2 March 1909
Sold	26 January 1922
USS *Nevada*	Monitor No 8
Built	by Bath Iron Works, Bath, Maine
Authorised	4 May 1898
Renamed	from *Connecticut* during construction
Laid down	17 April 1899
Launched	24 November 1900
Commissioned	5 March 1903
Renamed *Tonapah*	2 March 1909
Sold	26 January 1922
USS *Florida*	Monitor No 9
Built	by Lewis Nixon, Elizabethport, New Jersey
Authorised	4 May 1898
Laid down	23 January 1899
Launched	30 November 1901
Commissioned	18 June 1903
Renamed *Tallahassee*	20 June 1908
Sold	25 July 1922
USS *Wyoming*	Monitor No 10
Built	by Union Iron Works, San Francisco, California
Authorised	4 May 1898
Laid down	11 April 1899
Launched	8 September 1900
Commissioned	8 December 1902
Renamed *Cheyenne*	1 January 1909
	Served as a Naval Reserve training ship 1920-1926
	Unclassified IX-4.
Stricken	25 January 1937
Sold	20 April 1939

Japanese 'Kaibokan' Escorts Part I

by Hans Lengerer

The term *Kaibokan* was introduced into the Imperial Japanese Navy by the Navy Ministry's communique No 34, dated 21 March 1898, which concerned the classification of major warships (*Gunkan*) and torpedo boats (*Suraitei*) (*Kantei ryubetsu*).[1] This term did not relate to a new type of ship; instead the new classification was to include the old cruisers and battleships whose fighting power was no longer up to the demands of the front line battlefleet, although still adequate for defensive service around the coasts of the home country. The new desig-

nation was an ideal reflection of their role, since the literal translation of *Kaibokan* is 'coastal defence ship'.

But the Japanese Navy did not possess armoured vessels of the coastal battleship type that had been specifically designed for coast defence duties by various navies up until the beginning of the twentieth century. This article does not, however, deal with these reclassified ships; instead it covers the vessels built under the name *Kaibokan*, principally as escorts. These ships were designed from the start as a new type of warship with

entirely different duties from earlier ships of that designation.

The idea of building these coast defence ships dates back to the period after the 1930 London Treaty. The Japanese Navy wanted to construct small coastal guard-ships under the name of *Kaibokan* (*Engan Keibikan*), intended for fishery protection and security tasks in the northerly Kurile islands, in order to circumvent the restricting regulations of this treaty. The Kuriles were in Japanese hands from 1875 to 1945 under the name Chishima. As a result of the strained financial situation, the plan could not be put into practice, as the funds had to be used for the building of higher priority ships. It was not until the Third Navy Armaments Extension Programme of 1937 that approval was granted for the construction of four ships under the designation *Kaibokan*. In further building programmes the Imperial Japanese Navy projected 364 ships, of which 167 had actually been completed by the end of the war. Together with the ships of the *Shimushu* class, a total of 171 ships were completed; 7 of them were commissioned by the Second

Disarmament Office (with approval of the American authorities) after the end of the war to carry out repatriation duties; in the case of 17 vessels, construction was stopped either early in 1945 or on 17 August 1945. The remaining 173 ships were cancelled. With a completed total of 171 ships, and 17 more laid down, the *Kaibokan* achieved the highest number of any one Japanese warship type constructed during the war. (They were only overtaken in the final phase of the war by a few special attack weapons and motor torpedo boats.)

The coastal defence ships were officially divided into Type A (*Ko*), C (*Hei*) and D (*Tei*), subdivided into the following classes: *Shimushu*, *Etorofu*, *Mikura* and *Ukuru* of Type A; *No 1* of Type C and *No 2* of Type D. However, if the ships are considered according to the changes made in their design, armament and equipment as a result of the many amendments, and in some cases complete redesigning, of the construction plans, then it seems more logical to divide them into the types to which they were allotted during initial planning. The *Shimushu* class is an exception here.

The result is the following arrangement:

Type A (*Ko*)	*Shimushu* class, *Etorufu* class
Type B (*Otsu*)	*Mikura* class
Modified Type B (*Kai Otsu*)	*Ukuru* class
Type C (*Hei*)	*No 1* class
Type D (*Tei*)	*No 2* class

The *Shimushu* class did not really belong to any type; it was conceived as the prototype of a new category of ship, but was in fact allotted to Type A, as were Types B and B Modified, and retained this classification. The only ships designed as Type A were the *Etorofu* class.[2]

Initially the coast defence ships were designed as multi-purpose vessels, with escort duties being regarded as only third priority. In the case of the *Etorofu* class, however, the design was altered to make convoy protection the most important role. Nevertheless in real terms convoy escort did not become the overriding requirement until the *Mikura* class, and if strict standards are applied, not until the *Ukuru* class. The desire for design simplicity, which had already led to the redesign of the *Etorofu* to *Ukuru* classes, had a decisive influence on later vessels. Prefabricated methods of mass production were regarded as necessary and this meant that the C and D Types were designed from the outset as cheap, single-purpose convoy escorts.

It should be remembered that although British corvettes and sloops were engaged in a life-or-death struggle with German U-boats in the Atlantic at this time, the Japanese Navy had virtually no comparable vessels. Even when Dönitz's early 1942 Operation *Paukenschlag* ('Drumbeat') against US East Coast shipping underlined the vulnerability of unescorted merchant ships, Japanese naval leaders gave no consideration for their own supply lines. The doctrine of the

The Kaibokan *Shimushu* (Type A) on trials in the Inland Sea June 1940 only 6 months after being launched by Mitsui.

TABLE 1: BUILDING PROGRAMMES IN WHICH KAIBOKAN WERE BUILT

Building programme	Building number	Type	Class	Planned	Built	Completed postwar	Building stopped	Stricken
Third Naval Armament Extension Programme of 1937 (budget for the financial year 1937)	9-12		*Shimushu*	4	4			
Fifth Naval Armament Extension Programme of 1942 (proposal for the financial year 1942)	750-793	Mod Class (*Kai Gata*)	*Shimushu*	4				4
Urgent war building programme for 1941 (budget for the financial years 1942 and 1943)	310-319 321, 323, 325, 330	A (*Ko Gata*)	*Etorofu*	14	14			
	320, 322, 324 326-329, 334	(*Otsu Gata*)	*Mikura*	8	8			
	331-333, 335-339	Mod B (*Kai Otsu Gata*)	*Ukuru*	8	8			
Modified Fifth Naval Armament Extension Extension Programme of 1942 (Special war budget of 1943)	5251-5284	Mod B (*Kai Otsu Gata*)	*Ukuru*	34	12		4	18
War Programme 1943-44 (Special war budget 1944-45)	4701-4721	Mod B (*Kai Otsu Gata*)	*Ukuru*	21	9			12
	2401-2532	C (*Hei Gata*)	No 1	132	53	3	9	67
	2701-2843	D (*Tei Gata*)	No 2	143	63	4	4	72
Totals				368	171	7	17	173

Notes

1 In the case of the *Mikura* and *Ukuru* classes, the type is that obtained at the time of initial planning.

2 The 'Planned' column only shows the ships included in a building programme. According to Fukui's *Japanese Naval Vessels at the End of the War* pages 71, 73, 75 there were further ships projected, as follows:

Ukuru class : approx 78 ships
No 1 class : approx 168 ships
No 2 class : approx 57 ships

The total number of ships planned (368) and of ships projected (approx 303) amounts to about 671.

The number of projected ships should be considered as unreliable, as the author has no further documentary evidence to confirm these figures.

decisive surface action, for which they constantly prepared, resulted in the neglect of all defensive tasks. This made a realistic assessment of the situation impossible, and the chance to take measures in good time against the US submarine menace was lost.

When the sinking of Japanese merchant ships by American submarines began to rise steadily, and the tanker losses en route from the vital South East Asian oil fields became critical, the countermeasures came too late. Priorities for anti-submarine vessels rose gradually from third in 1943 to first late in 1944, but even then the rate of production was inadequate. However, lack of numbers cannot entirely explain their low success rate against US submarines. Certainly the standard of Japanese sonar equipment and anti-submarine weapons was inferior to Allied equivalents, but the main reason was inadequate training. New ships were rushed into service without a proper work-up period, and whereas American submarines had had over two years to perfect their tactics, Japanese anti-submarine techniques had been almost entirely neglected. Furthermore towards the end of the war most Japanese escorts operated in areas where the US Navy had total mastery of the skies, or at least air superiority. In the circumstances, the failure of the Japanese anti-submarine forces, and the *Kaibokan* in particular, seems no more than inevitable.

TECHNICAL DESCRIPTION OF TYPE A, SHIMUSHU CLASS

The conditions of the London Treaty of 22 April 1930 imposed a total destroyer tonnage of 105,500 tons standard displacement on Japan (article 16). On 30 September 1930 Japan possessed 56 first class destroyers (totalling 75,125 tons) and 48 second class destroyers totalling 35,070 tons, ie a total of 104 ships with an aggregate displacement of 110,195 tons standard. Hence the construction of new destroyers was only possible if obsolete ships were replaced. However, article 8 paragraph (b) allowed the signatory powers to build surface vessels with a standard displacement of between 600 and 2000 tons, provided that they carried no guns larger than 155mm calibre, no more than 4 guns over 76mm calibre, no torpedo armament, and not more than 20 knots maximum speed. In consequence, Japan planned to build coast defence ships as a new type of vessel, to fill the space left by the urgently required destroyers. They were to have absolutely nothing in common with the ships earlier categorised as *Kaibokan*, and could be built in unlimited numbers in accordance with article 8 (b).

This is the reason why, in the first draft of the First Naval Armaments Extension Programme (*Dai ichi ji kaigun gunbi hoju keikaku*), which envisaged the construction of 117 warships of all types in two groups, four *Kaibokan* of 1200 tons standard displacement were included. The modified programme, reduced to 76 ships, contained the same number of *Kaibokan*, but with displacement reduced to 900 tons. Building costs were estimated at 9,380,000 Yen (a matter of £938,000 in precise contemporary terms), or 2,347,000 Yen (£234,700) per ship. Naval Minister Baron Kiyotane Abo proposed an alternative programme in secret document No 943, dated 7 October 1930, addressed to Prime Minister Yuko Hamaguchi; this was a reduced programme containing 59 ships, among them one coastal defence ship of 900 tons standard displacement, costing 2,100,000 Yen. But when the building programme was finally approved during the 59th session of parliament (26 December 1930 – 28 March 1931), under the abbreviated designation of First Programme (*Maru ichi keikaku*), it only included 39 ships: the coast defence ships had fallen prey to the finance minister's red pencil.

The first draft of the Second Naval Armaments Extension Programme (*Dai ni ji Kaigun gunbi joju keikaku*) again included four *Kaibokan* of 1200 tons standard displacement. The strategic/technical requirements were detailed in the appendix to secret document No 199 from the Admiralty staff, dated 14 June 1933. Speed was to be 20 knots, range more than 5000 miles at 14 knots. Four 127mm (5.1in) guns were the main armament, along with the required number of machine cannon, depth charges and depth charge throwers. When the programme was finally accepted during the 65th session of parliament (26 December 1933 - 26 March 1934) the fate of the first programme was repeated. The building programme, now known under the abbreviated title of Second Programme (*Maru ni keikaku*) contained only 48 ships instead of the proposed 88, and among that number were no coast defence ships.

After the renouncement of the Washington disarmament Treaty and the withdrawal of the Japanese delegation from the Second London Disarmament Conference, Japan became free of all treaty restrictions as of 1 January 1937. The reformulation of the national defence policy on 3 June 1936 was followed by the acceptance of the Third Naval Armament Extension Programme on 31 March 1937, during the 70th session of parliament (26 December 1936 - 31 March 1937). In this programme – the most extensive Japanese construction programme since the Washington Treaty of 6 February 1922 – the building of the four coastal defence ships, demanded since 1930, finally came about. Under the title of 'warships Nos 9-12' the third programme (*Maru san Keikaku*) covered the construction of four coastal defence ships. A total of 12,240,000 Yen (£1,224,000), or 3,060,000 Yen (£306,000) per ship and 2550 Yen (£255) per ton of displacement was the projected cost. In 1941 the budget was raised by just over 5% due to inflation, and the actual costs amounted to 12,866,112 Yen, or 3,216,529 Yen per ship/2680 Yen per ton of displacement.

A standard displacement of 1200 tons was stated on the budget. In fact the ships displaced only 860 tons, as a proportion of the funds was used for building the super battleships *Yamato* and *Musashi*. A further change was the replacement of the four 127mm AA guns in two twin mounts, required by the Naval General Staff, by three 120mm (4.7in) low angle guns. Speed was only 20 knots, while a range of 5000 miles at a speed of 16 knots was specified.

Except for the special duty warships (*Tokumukantei*), this was the first time that a major warship type was designed by a private yard. The basic plans were drawn up by Mitsubishi Heavy Industries warship design division. This design office had only been founded shortly before, to assist the Navy design department if it was overloaded or to draw up its own independent plan if foreign warship contracts were in prospect. Mitsubishi were granted the design contract because the Navy's design office was fully occupied with planning the great ships of the Third Programme (among them the super battleships *Yamato* and *Musashi* and the carriers *Shokaku* and *Zuikaku*). In any case the design of a ship destined for defensive tasks was considered unimportant.

One specification of the contract was that the ships should be suitable for use in the North Pacific as well as the South Seas and therefore had to be fitted out accordingly. The ships' principal role was as guardships (*Keibikan*) for patrol and fisheries protection in the Kuriles, so that the destroyers (*Kuchikukan*) hitherto entrusted with these duties could be released; the destroyers were not suited to this function and were urgently required to fulfil their real purpose. The secondary role was considered to be their use for minesweeping duties, and in third place came their use as escort ships for convoys (*Sendan goeikan*); a task which later became their principal purpose. Their final duty included anti-submarine and anti-aircraft work. As with gunboats, these ships were also intended for use during periods of diplomatic tension. For this reason they were to be built in such a way that they gave the appearance of strong, battleworthy ships.

Although the Navy design office wanted a simple design, the experienced team at Mitsubishi worked out a very thorough, but complex design. The complicated structure and equipment made prefabrication impossible, and extended building times considerably. Although the design was far removed from a simple, fast and easy-to-build ship, it was accepted under the basic planning number E 15, principally because of the Navy's low priority for these ships. In this way a design drawn up to suit one set of duties became the prototype for a vessel which had to carry out other escort duties. The initial misplacing of priorities, combined with the insistence on retaining an unsuitable design, had its inevitable effect later; it was an important factor in the failure of Japanese anti-submarine warfare.

GENERAL ARRANGEMENT

At the planning stage the rough seas and the cold climate of the North Pacific (Kuriles) were given special consideration, and great emphasis was placed on good stability – even with an ice-covered superstructure, which would raise the centre of gravity – along with structural strength and good insulation. The required stability was

Shumushu in a peaceful anchorage early on in the Pacific War. Her 10ft draught is being used to good advantage. The US Office of Navy Intelligence thought she was part of an 8-ship minelayer class but then reclassified her as a patrol frigate.
Author's collection

achieved by favourable weight distribution and construction methods, which resulted in a low centre of gravity and a large metacentric height (the hull weight as a proportion of the whole was 38% of the trials displacement). The inclusion of a forecastle deck ensured adequate freeboard, which provided relatively good seaworthiness (reserve buoyancy) and stability at large angles of heel; the relatively large draught also helped in these respects. The second requirement was met by making the hull plating 12mm ($\frac{1}{2}$in) thick at the waterline, running from the bow to about half the length for protection against drifting ice and thin sheet ice), by the use of a full-length double floor up to the level of the lower deck, narrow frame compartments, and by the fitting of mainhull members of appropriate strength for the enormous stresses encountered in the North Pacific. The third main requirement was approached by fitting a powerful steam heating system, by providing for insulation and by designing the superstructure to allow movement from forward to aft inside the ship in poor weather and with iced-up deck and superstructure. The two auxiliary boilers, used to drive the heating and auxiliary machines, fed steam tubes that were used to melt the ice from the anchor chains and to keep the windows of the bridge ice-free. For the ships' use in warmer zones there was adequate ventilation, and even a small air-conditioning system.

With an overall length of 78m (255ft 11in) and maximum beam of 9.1m (29ft 10in) the ships displaced 860 tons standard. The machinery consisted of 2 Model 10 No 22 diesel engines (*22 go 10 gata*), of 4500bhp (3310kW) with twin shafts, giving the ships a maximum speed of 19.7 knots at 520rpm. The use of diesel engines made it possible to achieve a considerable range of 8000 miles at 16 knots with 220 tons of fuel.

These and the following classes had a forecastle deck

TABLE 2: KAIBOKAN BUILDERS

YARD	Shimushu (A–A)	Etorofu (A–B)	Mikura (mod B)	Ukuru	No 1 (C)	No 2 (D)	Ukuru (postwar)	No 1 (postwar)	No 2 (postwar)	TOTAL
Fujinagata (Osaka)						3			1	4
Harima (Aioi)						10				10
Hitachi										
Mukojima (Mukajima)									(3)	(3)
Sakurajima (Osaka)		4	3	9			(2)			16 (2)
Ishikawajima (Tokyo)						4			1 (1)	5 (1)
Kawasaki										
Kobe Shipbuilders						5				5
Senshu (Tanagawa)						4			2	6
Kyowa (Kobe)								(3)		(3)
Maizuru DY					3					3
Sasebo DY	1			4						5
Yokosuka DY						6				6
Mitsubishi					10			(2)		10 (2)
Kobe										
Nagasaki						31				31
Mitsui Shipbuilders										
Tamano	2	4		5						11
Naniwa Dock (Osaka)					3					3
Nihonkai Dock Industry (Toyama)					6			(2)		6 (2)
Niigata Iron Works					4			(1)		4 (1)
Nippon Steel Tube Co										
Tsumi (Yokohama)	1	2	5	4	27			3 (1)		42 (1)
Uraga Dock										
Uraga (Yokosuka)		4		7			(2)			11 (2)
TOTALS	4	14	8	29	53	63	(4)	3 (9)	4 (4)	171 +
			177					7 + (17)	7 + (17)	

TABLE 3: ANNUAL KAIBOKAN DELIVERIES

Class	1940	1941	1942	1943	1944	1945	Total
Shimushu	3	1					4
Etorofu				13	1		14
Mikura			2	6			8
Ukuru					14	15	29
No 1					36	17	53
No 2					44	19	63
Totals	3	1		15	101	51	171

with a curved hancing piece. In the case of the *Shimushu* class, the length of the forecastle (or superstructure) deck was about 23m (75ft 6in). It had a slight sheer and at the deck step the odd angular shape also characteristic of *Hatsutaka* class minelayers and also contemporary destroyer classes (*Fubuki*, *Hatsuhara*, *Kagero* and so on). The bow shape was also typical of Japanese ships of this period, curved into a gentle 'S' shape with a large overhang at the stem. There was a short gap between the deck step and the superstructure that extended to the after part of the ship. This allowed internal movement fore and aft, thus reducing the danger for the crew of working on the exposed and sometimes frozen upper deck.

The forward end of the bridge was enclosed but the bridge windows allowed all-round visibility. The open platform above it was dominated by an enclosed 3m (39in) rangefinder with an 8cm (3.1in) binocular sight forward. The rear, open part of the bridge extended almost as far aft as the tripod foremast. A lookout position was fitted at the upper end of the supporting legs, which were raised aft. The topmast also carried yards for signal halliards, wind direction indicator, anemometer, signal lamps and so on. Two forward-raking yards carrying the radio aerials, completed the top-hamper. Between the tripod mast and a platform carrying a 75cm (30in) searchlight was the radio direction finder. Abaft the searchlight platform came the funnel, which was raked aft. The upper part was reduced in cross-section above the level of the searchlight, in order to increase the illumination arc aft. The galley funnel, angled forward at the top, ran along the after side of the funnel and finished just above the latter. The shorter, tripod mainmast was raked strongly backwards and was somewhat farther distant. The tripod foremast's vertical arrangement and the yards' forward rake allowed longer radio aerials, since the mainmast's yards were again forked aft, in similar fashion to those of the *Yamato* class battleships. The engine room ventilators were located abreast the foremast.

ARMAMENT

The main armament consisted of three 12cm/45 (4.7in) low angle guns of the Year 3 type (*3 nendo shiki*) introduced into the Japanese Navy in 1914; they had an elevation of only 33° in the Type G mounting. These were the same weapons as were mounted, for example,

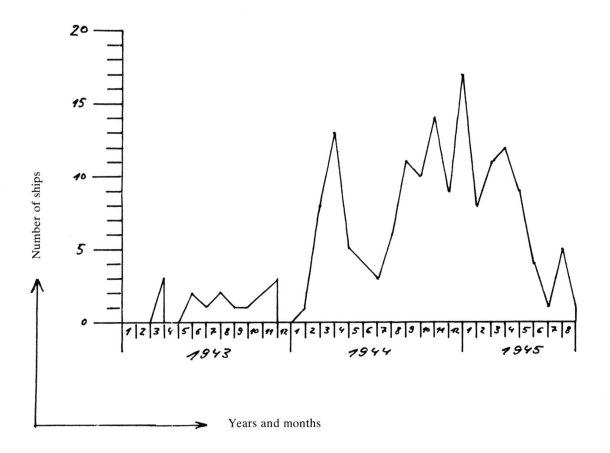

Number of ships

Years and months

on the *Mutsuki* class old destroyers. They were disposed on the centreline, with one forward of the bridge, and two aft (one on the superstructure deck). Careful consideration was given to the effects of blast, and all three were given wide arcs of fire.

Four 25mm automatic guns were provided for anti-aircraft defence, in two twin mounts on platforms to port and starboard of the bridge at the superstructure deck level. A practice gun was fitted abaft the after 12cm mount, along with a Model 94 (1934)[3] depth-charge thrower and a Model 3 loading frame. Three depth-charge launchers were mounted on each side of the quarterdeck right aft, and 18 Model 95 depth charges were carried.[4] The installation of hydrophones and sonar equipment was planned, but this class was completed without them. Minesweeping gear was carried abreast the superstructure 12cm gun platform, and a cutter and a motor boat, both 6m (19ft) long, were slung in swivelling davits each side of the funnel.

REDESIGNATION AND REARMAMENT 1942-44
Until 1 July 1942 the coast defence ships were classified as major warships (*Gunkan*). On this date the *Kaibokan* were removed from the list of *Gunkan* by secret order

No 1186, and the type was reintroduced as minor warships (*Kantei*) coming next after the submarines (*Sensuikan*).[5] The official communication No 192 (for naval circles only), also dated 1 July 1942, altered the classification from *Gunkan* to *Kaibokan*. The old armoured cruisers (*Junyokan*), *Yakumo*, *Iwate*, *Izumu*, at this time still classified as *Kaibokan*, were reclassified as first class cruisers (*Itto Junyokan*); their contemporaries *Asama*, *Azuma*, *Kasuga* were reclassified as special duty warships (*Tokumukan*).

Designating the *Shimushu* class as *Kaibokan* required them to be treated as major warships. The Imperial crest, the chrysanthemum, was fitted at the bow; it was made of wood, had a diameter of 450mm (16in) and was gilded. The captain's quarters consisted of an audience room and a sleeping cabin, as on the larger gunboats. In the audience room (to starboard, at the forward gun position) hung the portrait of the Emperor and Empress. The captain, despite the small displacement of his ship, was a Commander or a Captain*, simply because of the ship's classification. Nevertheless, when a destroyer was met, no salute was fired, although she would be commanded by a Lieutenant Commander or at best a Commander. Putting *Shimushu* in the ship's classification list as a 'Mini-Kaibokan' when her principal duty was to protect whaling ships, had in fact led to some disquiet, as the other coastal defence ships were large; especially as her displacement had been stated incorrectly in the list as 8600 tons.

The thorough design resulted in a ship with a satisfactory performance, although the design was certainly too complex, and 90,000 man-days of 8.5 hours each were required for hull construction alone. The long building time was the greatest problem, and it was only from the *Ukuku* class onward that good results were obtained. The *Shimushu* is a good example of how the Japanese dictum 'quality before quantity' could have most unfortunate results in practice.

After the outbreak of war all four ships of the *Shimushu* class were sent to the North Pacific. In 1942 a Model 93 sonar unit (1933)[6] was installed, and the number of depth charges was doubled (to 36). One year later this was increased again (to 60). The depth-charge launchers on either side of the stern were removed and replaced by launching rails. At the same time the fitting of Type 22 radar also began, the aerials being fitted on the foremast, which was modified accordingly, and fitted with a platform. From autumn 1944 the ships were fitted with a Type 13 radar set, whose fixed aerial was mounted on the mainmast.

After the Battle of the Philippine Sea (18-22 June 1944) extensive augmentation of anti-aircraft weapons was carried out on all Japanese ships. The *Shimushu* class carried 15 25mm machine guns in five triple mounts after this refit. The twin mounts were replaced by triples, and two further triples were installed on platforms between the funnel and mainmast on either side of the superstructure deck. A further AA bandstand for the fifth triple was fitted at the extreme end of the forecastle. In addition the bridge was extended forward and an 80mm (3.1in) Army mortar was installed there.

Shimushu was hit by a torpedo from the US submarine *Haddo* in the western half of Manila Bay on 25 November 1944, and her bow blown off. During the repair the simplified bow form of that period was fitted, so at the end of the war the ship had a straight stem. The *Schimushu* class numbered four ships, of which one was sunk during the war.

As a result of the satisfactory performance of these ships, and the urgent need for escort ships, the plans were altered only slightly to build the *Etorofu* class.

To be continued

TABLE 4: SHIMUSHU CLASS TECHNICAL DETAILS

Basic planning number	E15
Number built	9
Standard displacement	860 tons
Trial displacement	1020 tons
Length between perpendiculars	72.5m/237ft 11in
Waterline length	76.2m/250ft
Overall length	77.7m/255ft
Waterline beam	9.1m/29ft 10in
Side height	5.3m/17ft 5in
Average draught	3.05m/10ft
Machinery	2 No 22 type 10 diesels (4500bhp)
Speed	19.7kts
No of propellers and rpm	2 × 520rpm
Fuel	220 tons
Range	8000nm/16kts
Armament	3 × 12cm/45
	4 × 25mm
	18 Mod 95 depth charges
	Mod 94 thrower
	Mod 3 loading frame
Additional armament	11 × 25mm
	8cm army mortar
Sensors	Type 13 radar
	Type 22 radar
	Sonar
Crew	
(according to budget)	147

NOTES

1 Below the category of cruisers (*Junyokan*) three different classes of coastal defence ships were registered as follows: first class ships of more than 7000 tons, second class of between 7000 tons and 3500 tons, and third class of under 3500 tons normal displacement. As early as 28 August 1912 there was a change to a two-class division, with the first class over 7000 tons and the second below. In this connection it is worth mentioning that before the term *Kaibokan* was introduced, the 'three ships of the finest landscapes', the protected cruisers *Itsukushima*, *Matsushima* and *Hashidate* were designated as coastal defence ships during the Sino-Japanese War of 1894-95

2 These data are based on table 2 ('Naval building programmes in the Sino-Japanese conflict until the Second World War') in Shizuo Fukui's book *The Japanese Warships (Nihon no gunkan)*, and in the text of the book on page 146. Other designations are not accurate, as Fukui, writing of the *Etorofu* type, writes 'this ship, classified as Class A, began . . .'. This state-

TABLE 5: SHIMUSHU CLASS OUTLINE

Running no	Building no	Name	Builder	Laid down	Launched	Completed
1	9	*Shimushu*	Mitsui, Tamano	29.11.38	13.12.39	30. 6.40
2	10	*Kunashiri*	Tsurumi	1. 3.39	6. 5.40	3.10.40
3	11	*Hachijo*	Sasebo DY	3. 8.39	10. 4.40	31. 3.41
4	12	*Ishigaki*	Mitsui, Tamano	15. 8.39	14. 9.40	15. 2.41

Notes
1 Repatriation, laid up Maizuru. To USSR 5.7.47 as *Nachhodka*.
2 Repatriation, wrecked off Omaezaki 4.6.46. Hull above surface, BU Japan.
3 Out of action at Maizuru 15.8.45, BU 5.4.48 by Ino, Maizuru.
4 Sunk 31.5.44 US Submarine *Herring* (70nm W of Matsuwa island - Kuriles)

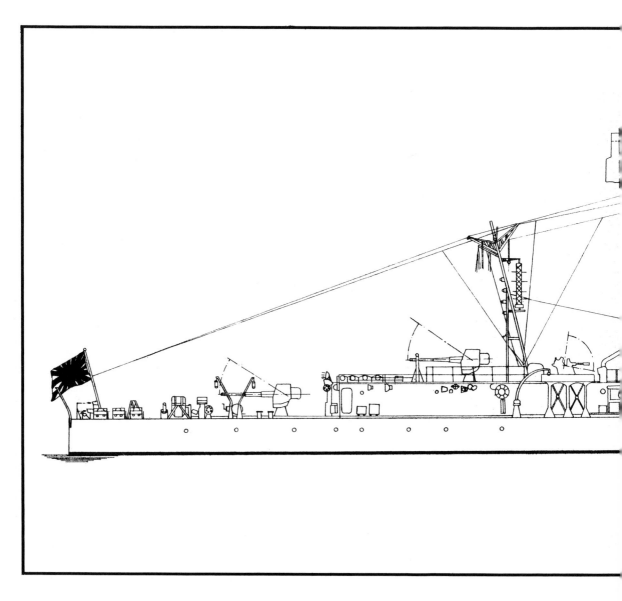

Sketch 1 Type A, *Shimushu* class; *Shimushu* after receiving a
strengthened A A armament, less minesweeping equipment
and with the bow of the Type C, which she received after being
torpedoed in the Philippines on 25 November 1944.
Small sketch, right Original form of the bow on *Shimushu*.
Small sketch, left Section through the funnel of the *Shimushu*
class. *Shimushu* was fitted with the funnel of the *Etorofu* class
during the repair.

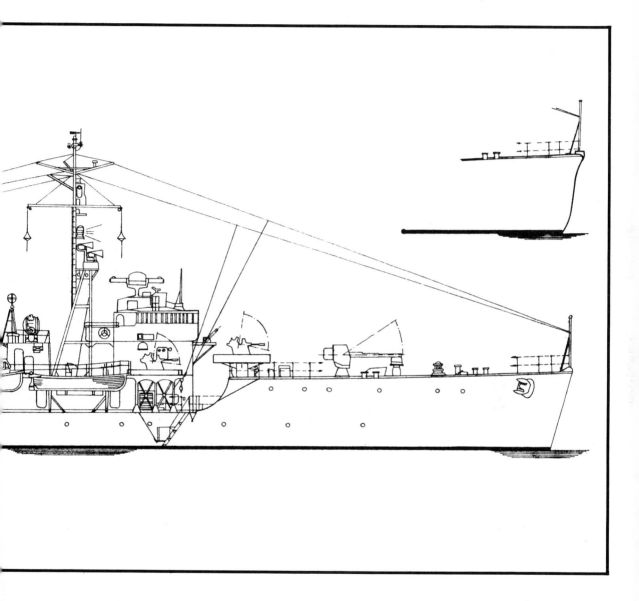

Note: With the exception of the *Etorofu* class the Type No 2,
the sketches in this series are based on photographs of the
coastal defence ships published to date. As most of these have
been taken at an oblique angle, which is not exactly ideal for
measurements, the draughtsman/artist has been forced to
estimate dimensions. This is especially true of the small
sketches.

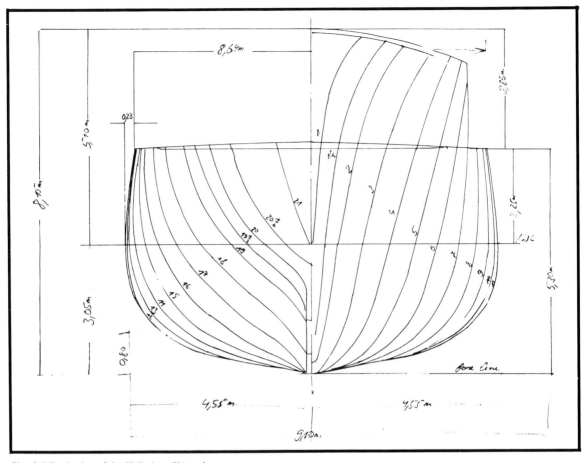

Sketch 2 Body plan of the Kaibokan *Shimushu*

ment agrees with Fukui's '*Japanese naval vessels at the end of the War*', p69-71, *Sekai no kansen* No 4/1959 p8-10, and 12/1966 p6-7, *History of shipbuilding in the Showa period — before and during the War (Shava Zosenshi-Senzen, Senji)*, Vol 1 p565 and Seiji Higashi's 'History of changes to the *Kaibokan* in drawings' in *Maru Special* No 28 p 20-31.

3 The Model 94 depth-charge thrower had been introduced in September 1934 as standard weapon in the Japanese Navy under the designation 'Type Y launching device, depth-charge twin launching device'. It would be used either as a single-side thrower, or for both sides simultaneously. Two firing tubes in the form of a Y at 50° inclination ran from the central part. The width, measured from the outside edge to the outside edge of the tubes, was 1.484m, the height from the base plate to the top of the centre part 1.083m. The floor area of the base late was 90cm × 50cm (35in × 20in). The thrower weighed 680kg (1500lb). When using the Model 95 (1935) depth charge, the depth charges could be hurled a distance of 75m (246ft) with simultaneous firing. The duration of flight was then 4.5 seconds. With a single firing, the range became 105m (344ft 6in) with 5.0 seconds flight duration. The Model 95 (1935) depth charge had a cylindrical shape. It was 77.5cm (2ft 6in) long, 45cm (16in) in diameter, and its all-up weight of 160kg (325lb) included 100kg (220lb) of Type 88 explosive. The sinking speed was around 1.9m or 6ft a second. Detonation depths of 30m (98ft), 60m (196ft) and 90m (295ft) could be set.

4 In contrast to the figure of 12 depth charges stated on p69 of 'Japanese Naval Vessels at the end of the War', Fukui states 18 depth charges on p20 of his book '*The Japanese Warships*', (published later), and the same number in table 9 of the appen-

dix to this book. This also agrees with the information on coastal defence ships in *Sekai no kansen* 7/1959, p51, and with the two sources named in note 2.

5 The classification *Gunkan* was a sub-division of the large section *Kantei*. In 1945 the following ships were classed as primary warships:
Battleships (*Senkan*)
Aircraft carriers (*Kokubokan*)
Cruisers, first and second class (*Itto* and *Nito Junyokan*)
Seaplane carriers (*Suijokibokan*)
Submarine tenders (*Sensuibokan*)
Minelayers (*Fusetsukan*)
Training battleships (*Renshusenkan*)
Training cruisers (*Renshujunyokan*)
The ships belonging to the *Gunkan* did not carry their normal class designation, but were designated *Gunkan*.

6 The Model 93 (1933) Sonar was installed in ships of the Third Programme and later. This was an active device. The soundwaves were transmited by a piezo-electric transmitter and then picked up again. The shortest locating distance with a submarine at a depth of 30m (98ft) was 200m (656ft). This figure rose to 250m (820ft) at a depth of 60m (196ft), and to 400m (1312ft) at a depth of 100m (328ft). On CD 22 (CD = symbol for *Kaibokan*) the following figures were given as longest locating ranges for a submarine travelling at 7.5 knots:
Own speed 0 knots = 4200m (4592yds)
Own speed 12 knots = 3000m (3280yds)
Own speed 14 knots = 1800m (1968yds)
These figures illustrate that the capability of the device deteriorated very rapidly when its own speed was raised.

British Naval Guns 1880-1945 No.13

by N J M Campbell

6in BL Mk XXII This rather heavy 50 calibre gun was internally similar to the much more widely used Mk XXIII. It was developed for the G3 battlecruisers and was mounted from 1927 in the battleships *Nelson* and *Rodney*. The gun was of normal taper wound wire construction with a hand operated Welin screw breech block and when new had no inner A tube and was known as Mk XXII*. On lining with a tapered inner A tube it became Mk XXII. Some years later Mk XXII** was introduced and this had inner A and A tubes but no wire. In all 40 guns were made including 2 experimental prototypes, and of the total 6 were Mk XXII**.

Originally 100lb shells were fired but from about 1942 112lb were used as in Mk XXIII. The Mk XVIII twin mounting allowed + 60° to − 5° elevation with loading at + 5°. It was hydraulically powered from a self-contained unit and had powered rammers but the rate of fire was slow at 5rpm. Flash precautions were very thorough. Revolving weight was *c*85 tons with a 14ft mean roller path dia.

6in BL Mk XXIII Introduced from 1933 in *Leander* this gun was mounted in all subsequent 6in cruisers up to and including *Superb* in 1945. It was also intended for the *Tiger* class as originally designed, and but for the war would have been adopted as a heavy field gun after years of Army indecision. The Mk XXIII was built with A tube, jacket to 115in from the muzzle, breech ring and breech bush screwed into the jacket. The Welin screw breech block had a hand-operated Asbury mechanism. On lining with a tapered inner A tube the gun was known as Mk XXIII*, the reverse nomenclature to that of Mk XXII. A modified gun with power worked breech mechanism was intended for the quadruple turrets originally proposed for the *Belfast* class and was to be Mk XXIV, but this mark was later adopted as a coast defence gun. In all 469 Mk XXIII were made.

The *Leander*, *Perth* and *Arethusa* classes had twin Mk XXI mountings, the *Southampton* and *Gloucester* classes triple Mk XXII and later cruisers from the *Belfast* class to the *Superb* triple Mk XXIII, with the triple RP10 Mk XXIV in the *Tiger* class as originally designed. This last was to have 60° elevation but otherwise generally resembled Mk XXIII apart from RPC. Mk XXI and XXII were short trunk turrets and XXIII long trunk. All 3 had hand ramming and were otherwise powered by a self-contained hydraulic system. The rate of fire was 6-8rpm and preferred loading angle + 7° to + 5°.

Mounting	Elevation	Loading	Rev Weight	Mean Roller Path dia
XXI	+60°−5°	+12½°−5°	95 tons	13ft 9in
XXII	+45°−5°	+12½°−5°	150/155 tons	19ft
XXIII	+45°−5°	+12½°−5°	175 tons	19ft

6in BL Mk XXIV An Army coast defence gun with the same performance as Mk VII* (100lb shell, MV 2890fs) but built with a loose barrel. It is believed that about 140 were made in World War II.

6in N5 This gun originally known as 6in QF Mark V, was developed from 1944 after some abortive work in 1942-43. It was clear that a 6in BL gun had become an anachronism and that any new design should be QF with separate ammunition loaded at one rammer stroke. It was originally intended for triple 80° elevation Mk XXV turrets in the projected *Neptune* class and then for the twin Mk XXVI in the *Minotaur* class designs of 1947. These were in turn abandoned and the first two experimental guns were not completed until 1949.

After extensive trials ashore and in the trials cruiser *Cumberland* the N5 in a modified Mk XXVI twin turret was eventually introduced in *Tiger* completed in March 1959, 15 years after the start of the gun's development. It was also in her sister ships *Blake* and *Lion*.

In its final form it was a loose barrel gun with hydraulically operated horizontal sliding breech block, and steel cartridge cases replaced brass. The staff requirement of continuous fire at 20rpm could be met but the muzzles in particular got excessively hot and water cooling had to be used. The 2 guns in a turret were not fixed together.

The mountings allowed 78½° (?80°) elevation with power loading at any angle, and 3 of those afloat had RP15 hydraulic control and 3 RP53 electric. It is believed that initially at least the turrets in *Tiger* and one in *Lion* had hydraulic control and the other in *Lion* and those in *Blake* electric.

5.5in BL Mk I Designed by Coventry Ordnance Works for Greece, this gun was introduced with the former Greek light cruisers *Birkenhead* and *Chester* and was adopted for further manufacture in 1914-18; 246 guns were ordered including those taken over, but only 81 were actually completed. It was of normal wire wound contruction with a tapered inner A tube and Welin screw block with Holmstrom mechanism, and was mounted in *Hood*, *Furious*, *Hermes*, *Birkenhead*, *Chester* and *K17* though not in other 'K' class submarines for which it was

Southampton's Mk XXII triple 6in 'Y' turret is hoisted on board by John Brown's 150-ton hammerhead crane at their Clydebank shipyard on 3 July 1936. The turrets were usually delivered by coaster from Vickers-Armstrong's works, Barrow supplying west coast yards and Elswick east coast.
Upper Clyde Shipbuilders/courtesy of Ian Buxton

PARTICULARS OF 6in GUNS

	6in BL Mk XXII	6in BL Mk XXIII
Weight inc BM (tons)	9.0125 (XXII** 9.023)	6.906
Length oa (in)	309.728	309.8
Length bore (cals)	50	50
Chamber (cu in)	1750	1750
Chamber length (in)	40.809	41.0
Projectile (lb)	100	112
Charge (lb/type)	31 SC150	30 SC150
Muzzle Velocity (fs)	2960	2758
Range (yds)	25,800/45°	25,480/45°

	6in N5	5.5in BL Mk I
Weight inc BM (tons)	c6.85	6.230
Length oa (in)	c315	284.728
Length bore (cals)	50	50
Chamber (cu in)	c1720	1500
Chamber length (in)	47	36.46
Projectile (lb)	129.75	82
Charge (lb/type)	34.5 MNF2P/S 224-058	22.54 SC115, 22.25 MD19
Muzzle Velocity (fs)	2513	2790
Range (yds)	25,330/42.7°	17,770/30°

originally intended. During World War II it was also in the AMCs *Laurentic* and *Montclare* and in emergency coast defence batteries.

There were a number of different transferable mountings:

Mounting	Elevation	Ships
PI	+15° −7°	*Birkenhead, Chester*
PI*	+25° −7°	*Furious, Hermes,*
		Laurentic, Montclare
PI**	+25° −7°	*K17*
CPII	+30° −5°	*Hood*

Elevation in *K17* may have been limited to 20° by height above deck.

5.5in BL Mk II A 42 calibre gun intended for World War I DAMS, which did not get beyond the design stage, though it had been intended to build 1100. New guns would have been Mk II* with an A tube, taper wire and full length jacket, becoming Mk II on lining with an inner A tube. Weight without BM would have been 5.625 tons. Later 5.5in BL Marks were Army gun-howitzers of World War II.

Bermuda receives her Mk XXIII triple 6in 'A' turret at
Clydebank on 11 May 1942. Note the roller path supporting
the final 157-ton revolving weight. The roof plates will only be
fitted after the guns have been shipped.

Upper Clyde Shipbuilders/courtesy of Ian Buxton

BOOK REVIEWS

THE SHIP OF THE LINE, VOLUME 1
The development of the battlefleet 1650-1850 by Brian Lavery
Published by Conway Maritime Press October 1983
224pp (30cm × 25cm) 110 illustrations, 18 line drawings and 8 graphs, index
ISBN 085177 252 8 (£20)

There has not been a full coverage of the British sailing ship of the line since John Fincham's History of Naval Architecture in 1851. That book was inadequate in its treatment of the earlier years relying too much on the prejudiced views of John Charnock. Brian Lavery has spent many years in his research and has published several important articles on sailing warships as well as editing the Conway edition of *Deane's Doctrine of Naval Architecture*.

The Ship of the Line Volume 1 traces the development of the ship of the line against the background of political and economic pressures. Operational history is only covered in sufficient depth to show how experience in war was used to influence future designs.

The graphs are particularly valuable in showing how the various categories of ship grew in size, altered in characteristics and often supplanted the next rate above. Despite the subtitle, there is fairly full coverage from 1588 onwards. In these earlier years the debate was between 'high charged' and 'low charged' ships. By the mid-seventeenth century there was argument concerning the relative numbers of two and three deckers.

The early years of the eighteenth century were an unfortunate period for British ship design, confined by the straightjacket of the establishment rules and by the concept of rebuilding. It is interesting to read that ships dismantled for rebuilding were still listed even when they had been no more than piles of used timbers for years. The appointment of Sir Thomas Slade as Surveyor in 1755 followed soon after by Admiral Lord Anson's return to the Board of Admiralty led to a more successful era.

The ships of the French Revolutionary Wars were fully up to their job. The British three deckers were very good as were most of the 74s. The Royal Navy fell behind the French in the introduction of the big two decker of 80 guns. This was probably due to lack of resources in timber and in shipbuilding labour though the topic is not fully explored.

There are some inadequate treatments of technical matters. For example, on page 94, it is said that the 74-gun *Invincible*, a 1747 prize from the French, had a speed of 13 knots compared with 11 for British ships. The condition of wind and bottom state are not given and, if all else was equal, an extra two knots speed implies some 65% more power (or reduction of resistance). This could only be explained by the effects of fouling.

Sir Robert Sepping's pioneer work on the development of timber structures is not given the credit it deserves and this reviewer finds the comment on page 149 that Seppings was 'an engineer rather than a naval architect' impossible to understand. One hopes that Volume II will cover the structural characteristics of wooden hulls more fully.

It should be brought out that much of Seppings' work was inspired by the acute shortage of big timbers for shipbuilding. His structural style enabled effective use to be made of short pieces. Seppings used iron diagonals in frigates and this was extended to the battlefleet by Edye, Sir William Symonds' professional assistant.

The main text of the book finishes at page 156 and is followed by an invaluable set of annexes. First, there are 35 pages of ship lists giving build particulars of all line of battle ships from 1618, divided into classes.

Then follow detailed appendices on numbers, specifications, armament and dimensions as well as two or three big documents reproduced in full. The references are fully documented and anyone wishing to challenge the author's views will have a great deal of reading to do.

At last, we have a real reference book for the ships that won British supremacy at sea and led to the creation of the British Empire.

D K Brown

OTHER BOOKS RECEIVED

Victoria's Navy: The heyday of steam by Colin White (Kenneth Mason, October 1983) 176pp, 220 prints and photographs, index, £11.95, ISBN 0-84937-284-7, 10in/24.5cm × 7in/18cm. The companion and follow up volume to the same author's *The end of the sailing navy* (Kenneth Mason, 1980) for which see the full review in *Warship* 20 by D K Brown. The index is for both volumes, format and chapter topics being identical. The evocative Victorian and Edwardian illustrations, almost all from the RN Museum, Portsmouth (of which the author is now deputy director), are the essence of this book, the text being no more than an outline link for the period 1870-1910. For a pictorial book, full of nostalgic *Illustrated London News* engravings in particular, the captions really should have been more detailed and this editor for one cannot see why Victorian lacks its initial capital letter. Pedantry apart this is an appealing synthesis of the period with a welcome emphasis on sailors as well as ships, not least the original Player's Navy Cut seaman from the 1885 turret ship HMS *Hero*.

Destroyer! German Destroyers in World War II by M J Whitley (Arms and Armour Press, October 1983) 310pp, 44 photographs, 14 maps, 15 line drawings, 7 appendices, bibliography, index, £12.95, ISBN 0-85368-258-5, 9in/22.8cm × 6in/15cm. This subject receives the exhaustive and infinitely painstaking treatment from an author well known to readers of *Warship*. See the publisher's advertisement in issue 29 for a full listing of battle plans and drawings included (limited by the format and not therefore fully detailed) though the book is 310pp long not 336pp. Even the dustjacket is used to illustrate camouflage schemes. The first and surely the last English language history of Hitler's 40

powerful but flawed destroyers, the first third of the book covers design and construction before a chronological account of their many varied and often little known operations. The maps and action tracks, enhanced by silhouettes of the participating ships, are pleasing to the eye though they lack scales. The technical appendices list the statistics (metric only) and summarise the careers of all the ships. One can think of only two omissions from this excellent work, there is no personal quotation from destroyer men or any discussion of the signal failure of 4th Flotilla (5 destroyers) to stay with *Scharnhorst* on Boxing Day 1943.

Le Porte-Avions Arromanches 1942-1978 by René Bail and Jean Moulin (Charle-Lavauzelle, Paris-Limoges, 1983) 92pp, 162 photographs and plans, no index, bibliography, 12in/30cm × 9in/22.5cm, 119 francs (approx £10). First of a pictorial 'Vie des Navires' series devoted to the light fleet carrier HMS *Colossus* which became France's *Arromanches* in 1946 serving until 1974 and broken up in 1978. Captions in English and French of carrier operations, especially Indochina 1948-54 and Suez 1956, and a look at her 8 sister ships.

A's & A's

GERMAN NAVAL RADAR (*Warship* 21, 22 and 27)
From Erwin Sieche, Vienna, Austria
Warship-reader Michael Bullen has found in his personal collection some pictures and plans of German naval radar equipment, thus adding new facts to the above mentioned theme:

Tirpitz: the Drüppel photographs RM 794 and RM 3752 clearly show that she also carried the huge FuMO 26 on the forward rangefinder tower since spring/summer 1944. Furthermore RM 794 shows a further variant of the radar equipment of the foretop rangefinder tower: both FuMO 27 and RuMBAnt 7 *Timor* removed and the latter replaced by the large FuMO 24/25 bedspring. Inscription on an official plan (Bundesarchiv RM 25/4-6) indicates that *Tirpitz* carried this configuration between July 1943 and her next refit in spring/summer 1944.

Mr Bullen also has successfully located the passive FuMBAnt 4 *Sumatra* aerials on *Scharnhorst*, *Lützow* and *Admiral Hipper*.

Scharnhorst: Bundesarchiv plans RM 25/5-1 and RM 25/5-11 show them where they should be – on the forward spotting top screen.

Lützow: the *Sumatra* loops can be seen on the front side

and the flank of the second level of the armoured spotting top in the picture on page 9, *Warship* 21. See drawing.

Admiral Hipper: the *Sumatra* loops can be detected on the corners of the spotting top screen (IWM pictures CL 2770 and CL 2771; both showing the blasted *Hipper* at Kiel). With this knowledge one can also trace them on the Drüppel photograph RM 542 showing the cruiser about 1942 in Norway. This indicates that *Admiral Hipper* received her passive equipment during her early 1942 refit.

The picture of *Z 39* in *Warship* 22, page 155 shows a lot of interesting electronic equipment. From top to bottom: At the masthead a FuMO 81 *Berlin-S*, on the tiny spur below a FuMBAnt 3 *Bali* and on the next spur below the aerial *Fliege* the set FuMB 26 *Tunis*. The real nature of the vertical cone on the crossyard, a device that can be found on many pictures, is unclear, it might perhaps be an infra-red detector. The vertical tube between the crossyards, also familiar on most German minor warships, is for protecting and hiding away signal flags. The forward searchlight sponson carries four FuMBAnt 4 *Sumatras*. The active antenna is rather a FuMO 24/25 than a FuMO 21 as stated. The number of passive antennas clearly mirrors the needs of the last year of the war.

The antenna configuration shows that the lefthand destroyer in the picture on page 3, *Warship* 21 is certainly not *Z 39*, as was first assumed.

MAJESTIC PREDREADNOUGHT PT 2 (*Warship* 28)
From Ian Sturton, Southampton, Hants
I have unearthed the accompanying photograph, which might be an 'A & A' to the alteration note at the foot of p281 (Issue 28). It illustrates a 6in Army howitzer specially fitted on the foreturret of *Majestic* or *Prince George* for the beginning of the Dardanelles Campaign, but removed by April 1915.

Submarine
DESIGN AND DEVELOPMENT

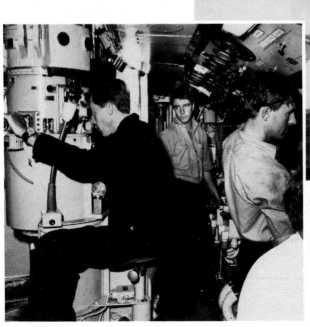

Zeppelin!

A Battle for Air Supremacy in World War I

Ray Rimell

Foreword by Air Marshal Sir Frederick Sowrey

The complete story of the Zeppelin raids over Britain, their devastating effect on the public, the counter-measures and their final defeat is told for the first time in *Zeppelin!* Ray Rimell has spent many years researching the archives, interviewing witnesses and talking to service personnel, both English and German, who actually participated in the battles. The careers of the airships are fully documented and the aircraft and weapons are described in detail, together with the damage they inflicted. Over 300 illustrations – the vast majority of which have never been published – maps and diagrams illustrate the text and there are extensive appendices.

300 x 230mm (12" x 9¼"), 256 pages, 300 illustrations, 15 maps and diagrams. ISBN 0 85177 239 0. £25.00 (+ £2.50 p & p when ordering direct) February.

Available from your local bookseller or by post from

Conway Maritime Press Ltd.
24 Bride Lane, Fleet Street,
London EC4Y 8DR

EDITORIAL

The 'Hunt' class minehunter HMS *Brocklesby*, 13 June 1983.   *L & L van Ginderen*

Mine warfare is seldom the foremost preoccupation of navies or indeed of those who write about them yet now and then it causes headlines and tensions that reverberate around the world. Such has been the case in Central America with the covert CIA-sponsored mining off Nicaragua's Pacific ports. These operations cause more than just physical damage, and in this instance, apparently 13 ships of several nations were damaged, they can sour relations between states far and wide and cause domestic dissension in the country at whose behest the mining is done. In a way mining evokes the same kind of outrage at sea that chemical warfare arouses on land. Its immediate tactical value may be outweighed by the lingering diplomatic complications and the continuing presence of unswept fields.

The mere threat of mining can influence naval deployments as witness the longstanding belief that Iran can mine the Straits of Hormuz. British minesweepers were sent to the Mediterranean partly because of the US Navy is still woefully deficient in both numbers of minesweepers and their quality. American reliance on helicopters and aircraft both for minelaying and minesweeping has meant that there is no naval organisation specifically devoted to the task; a paradoxical state of affairs when the 1972 mining of Haiphong was the most successful (at least in the short term) operation of its kind since 1945.

Minelaying is militarily cheap and relatively simple compared with missile or torpedo engagements. Almost any craft, airborne, surface or underwater can be quickly adapted to lay mines, and of course they can be laid from the shore. Operation Starvation, the US mining offensive against Japan in 1945, sank or damaged one ship for every 23 mines laid quite apart from its disruptive effects and Japanese resources tied up in mine-counter measures. In the European theatre RAF Bomber Command virtually closed the Baltic in a minelaying campaign also completely overshadowed by the simultaneous strategic bombing campaign.

An excellent illustration of the potency of minelaying comes in Frank Abelsen's account of the Norwegian second class gunboat *Tyr*. An historic leftover even by 1940, she nevertheless laid mines that did damage to the German invasion fleet out of all proportion to her own military value. Substantially more Axis warships and more Royal Navy ships were sunk by mines in 1939-45 than by any other single cause, even air attack.

The mine is the submarine's second weapon and as far as the modern US submarine is concerned, two can be carried for every one torpedo. NATO's future barrier strategy against the Warsaw Pact underwater fleet relies heavily on the US Mark 60 Captor encapsulated torpedo, really a tethered deepwater ASW mine that releases a torpedo on command. This ambitiously advanced piece of technology, product of research going as far back as 1961, has still to be operational but remains a relatively inexpensive item. The Pentagon's 1984 Fiscal Year defence budget proposals aimed to buy 500 for $151.4 million or $302,800 per unit, not a large amount compared with its submarine target.

Stocks of mines remain closely guarded secrets. Estimates of Soviet holdings run up to the half million mark (almost more than were laid by all the combatants in World War II), but a more reliable statistic is that the Warsaw Pact possesses 408 mine-countermeasures vessels to NATO's 235. Another bleak shortfall for a defensive alliance, in an area where numbers can never be too high.

The complexity and cost of minehunting forced France, Belgium and Holland into the 1974 Tripartite minehunter project for 45 vessels, but the number in service is not yet in double figures. At least, however, the current orders by the US Navy (for 14 mine-countermeasures vessels) and the Royal Navy for both glass reinforced plastic minehunters and trawler-minesweepers (the Extra-Deep Armed Team Sweeping concept) are beginning to provide modern ships capable of detecting and neutralising an unpleasant range of sea mines.   **Randal Gray**

We apologise for the non-appearance of the advertised article on 'Hunt' class MCMV and hope to publish it at a later date.

Marconi Class Submarines at War

By Pierre Hervieux

Da Vinci in 1940. She was the top scoring Italian submarine of
World War II.
Author's collection/courtesy of A Fraccaroli

The six boats of this class were built under the 1938
programme, they were a Bernadis design, derived from
the *Marcello* class. Compared with the earlier class the
beam was reduced and length increased as well as
range. More powerful motors provided for a slight
improvement in speed. The diving limit was 330ft and
one less gun was carried to compensate for the lower
stability of the new hull dimensions. These boats are
considered to have been the best Italian ocean-going
submarines built before World War II. During 1941–42
the conning tower was modified in all the boats, size
was reduced and the periscope sleeves were lowered.

Only half the class *(Marconi, Bianchi* and *Da Vinci)*
served in the Mediterranean before being transferred
to the Atlantic. Admiral Sir James Somerville's Force
H attacked the French warships at Mers-el-Kebir on 3
July 1940 and on the day before at 2330 (all times
given are German) *Marconi* (Capt Chialamberto)
launched torpedoes and missed the destroyer HMS

Baracca in Italian waters before being moved to the Atlantic 1940.

Author's collection/courtesy of A Fraccaroli

Voritgern (1917, 1090 tons) off Gibraltar. Force H was again attacked by *Marconi* on 11 July east of Gibraltar and this time the destroyer HMS *Escort* (1934, 1405 tons) was torpedoed and sunk 36° 20′N/03° 46′W during Operation MA 5. On 25 July 1940 the Italian proposal for establishing a base for Italian submarines in occupied France to operate in the Atlantic was accepted by the Germans. As a result on 1 September 1940 the new Italian base, named BETASOM, opened at Bordeaux under the command of Rear Admiral A Parona. *Malaspina* (Capt Leoni) forced the Gibraltar Strait on 3 August 1940 operated in the area of the Azores and then proceeded to Bordeaux. On her way she torpedoed and sank the British tanker *British Fame* (1936, 8046 tons, 0550, 37° 44′N/22° 56′W) on 12 August. This tanker belonged to the dispersed convoy OB 193. On 19 August an 8000-ton unidentified cargo ship was missed with one torpedo (0120, 39° 20′N/21° 25′W). From 17 August *Bianchi* (Capt Giovannini)

operated off Gibraltar claiming to have torpedoed and sunk an anti-submarine trawler on 25 August (0603); in fact she missed her.

From 27 August a second wave of Italian submarines was moved in two groups from the Mediterranean to Bordeaux, among them were *Baracca* (Capt Bertarelli) and *Torelli* who operated in the area between Portugal, the Azores and Madeira. The *Marconi* operating off NW Spain. On 4 September *Maslaspina* reached Bordeaux, being the first of 32 Italian submarines to be based in the French harbour for the next three years. On 19 September 1940 *Marconi* torpedoed and sank the Spanish trawler *Almirante Jose de Carranza* (1918, 330 tons, 0315, 43′N/09′W).

On 23 September *Da Vinci* (Capt Calda) was transferred to the Atlantic and like her sister boats passed safely through the Gibraltar Strait and operated in the area of the Azores and Madeira. On 28 September 1940 *Marconi* arrived at Bordeaux. On 1 October *Baracca* sank with gunfire the Greek cargo ship *Aghios Nicolaos* (1915, 3687 tons , 0415, 40′N/16° 55′W) and arrived at Bordeaux on 6 October, the *Torelli* having arrived on the 5th. On 9 October the *Malaspina* was the first to proceed to the North Atlantic from Bordeaux. In the course of October *Baracca* and *Marconi* followed. On 20 October *Malaspina* claimed to have torpedoed and sunk (?) an 8000-ton unidentified cargo ship from the dispersed convoy OB 229, 59°N/29°W. *Da Vinci* reached Bordeaux on 31 October. On her way to Bordeaux, *Bianchi*, last boat of the class, got into difficulties. On 4 November she had to put in to Tangier after being bombed by a London flying boat of No 202 Squadron RAF and depth charged by the destroyer HMS *Greyhound* and damaged. On 8 November *Marconi* in attempting to maintain contact with the convoy HX 84 was depth charged by the destroyer HMS *Havelock* but was able next day to put a finishing torpedo into the Swedish cargo ship *Vingaland* (1935, 2734 tons, 55° 41′N/18° 24′) which had been set on fire by a German FW 200 Condor plane. *Baracca* torpedoed and sank the British cargo ship *Lilian Moller*

TABLE 1: MARCONI CLASS OUTLINE

	Builders	Laid down	Launched	Completed
Guglielmo Marconi	CRDA, M	19.9.38	30.7.39	20.2.40
Leonardo Da Vinci	CRDA, M	19.9.38	16.9.39	7.4.40
Michele Bianchi	OTO, M	15.2.39	3.12.39	15.4.40
Luigi Torelli	OTO, M	15.2.39	6.1.40	15.5.40
Alessandro Malaspina	OTO, M	1.3.39	18.2.40	20.6.40
Maggiore Baracca	OTO, M	1.3.39	21.4.40	10.7.40

CRDA,M = Cantieri Riuniti Dell'Adriatico, Monfalcone.
OTO,M = Odero, Terni, Orlando, Muggiano (La Spezia).

Displacement	1191 tons surfaced/1498 tons submerged.
Displacement	251ft (76.50m) OA × 22ft 4in (6.81m) × 15ft 6in (4.72m)
Machinery	2 sets CRDA diesels, 3600hp/2 sets Marelli electric motors 1500hp.
Oil	118 tons
Maximum speed	17.8 knots surfaced/8.2 knots submerged
Range	2900 miles at 17 knots surfaced, 10,500 miles at 8 knots surfaced, 110 miles at 3 knots submerged, 80 miles at 4 knots submerged, 8 miles at 8 knots submerged.
Armament	3.9in (100mm) 47-cal gun, four 13.2mm AA machine guns (2×2). Eight 21in (533mm) torpedo tubes (4 forward, 4 aft) with 12 torpedoes.
Complement	7 officers plus 50 petty officers and seamen

Malaspina arriving in Bordeaux on 4 September 1940.
Author's collection/E C P Armées

(1913, 4866 tons) belonging to the dispersed convoy SLS 53 on 18 November (1740, 57°N/17°W). On 13 December *Bianchi* left Tangier for Bordeaux where she arrived on the 18th.

OPERATIONS IN 1941

Da Vinci operated in the North Atlantic for the first 18 days of January west of North Channel, without success. *Malaspina* and *Torelli* were deployed against convoys. The former had no success, but *Torelli* torpedoed and sank the Greek cargo ship *Nemea* on 15 January (1919, 5101 tons, 2120 52° 33′N/24° 13′); 28 minutes later she torpedoed and sank the Norwegian cargo ship *Brask* (1911, 4079 tons 52° 45′N/23° 59′W). The following day at 0100 *Torelli* sank with torpedo and gunfire the Greek cargo ship *Nicolaos Flinis* (1904, 3111 tons) 53°N/24°W. On 28 January 2100 she torpedoed and sank a fourth ship, the British SS *Urla* (1924, 5198 tons, 2100, 54° 54′N/19′W). Between 16 January and 22 February *Marconi* operated unsuccessfully off Portugal. By the end of January *Baracca* operated west of the North Channel and Ireland without scoring. In mid-February she was relieved by *Bianchi* which on the 14th torpedoed and sank the British SS *Belrest* (1925,

4517 tons, 21° 54′/21′W), a straggler from convoy SC 21. On the 19th *Bianchi* was ordered to operate against convoy OB 287 but failed to reach it that day because of an inaccurate FW 200 Condor sighting report. She encountered a stubborn adversary on the 23rd (2242) the British Ocean Boarding vessel HMS *Manistee* (1920, 5368 tons) which had already been damaged by a torpedo from *U 107*, but the crew succeeded in getting the ship under way again at 8 knots within 30 minutes of the hit. At 1056, *Bianchi* also fired but missed as did *U 107* with three duds! It was not until the morning of the 24th after further attempted attacks by both Axis boats that *U 107* (Capt Hessler) finally sank *Manistee* with a double fan salvo at 59° 30′N/21′. On the same say *Bianchi* was more skilful and luckier when at 0345 she torpedoed and sank the British SS *Linaria* (1924, 3385 tons, 61°N/25°W) from the dispersed convoy OB 288 which had been found by another Condor on the 22nd.

Following *U 47*'s contact report *Bianchi* was ordered to attack convoy OB 290 but did not come up. On the 27th (0145) she attacked and slightly damaged with gunfire the British SS *Empire Ability* (ex-German *Uhenfels*, 1931, 7603 tons) from convoy OB 290. Shortly later, at 0447, *Bianchi* torpedoed and sank the British SS *Baltistan* (1937, 6803 tons at 51° 52′/19° 55′), a straggler from the same convoy. On 18 April *Da*

Marconi arriving in Bordeaux on 28 September 1940.

Author's collection/E C P Armées

Vinci, *Torelli* and *Malaspina* began patrolling west of Ireland. On the 22nd *Torelli* sighted a homewardbound convoy but was unable to call in U-boats. The same happened with an outwardbound convoy next day. Between 9 and 30 April *Baracca* operated unsuccessfully west of Gibraltar. On 3 May (2120) at 55°N/21°W

Marconi in Bordeaux with a modified conning tower, July 1941.

Author's collection/E C P Armées

Malaspina (Capt Prini) launched torpedoes and missed the British passenger liner *Lycaon* (1913, 7350 tons). Six days later *Torelli* was deployed without success against a Condor-sighted convoy west of Iceland. *Bianchi* and *Malaspina* were likewise against another convoy.

An Italian submarine group of 7 boats operated against convoys W of Gibraltar between 25 May and 16 June. Among them was *Marconi* (Capt Pollina) which on 30 May torpedoed and sank the Royal Navy tanker *Cairndale* (1938, 8129 tons) 35°N/09°W). Then on 1 June (1452) *Marconi* sank with her 3.9in gun the unmarked Portuguese trawler *Exportador* (1917, 318 tons, 36°N/09°W). Then on the 6th she attacked convoy OG 63 between 0422 and 0427 launching torpedoes at a tanker and three cargo ships. Two of the latter were hit and sunk, they were the British *Baron Lovat* (1926, 3395 tons, 0425, 33° 30′N/11° 30′W) and the Swedish *Taberg* (1920, 1392 tons, 0427, 35° 36′/11° 12′W).

Between 24 June and 17 July an Italian submarine group operated against convoys West of Gibraltar. On 28 June (1254) *Da Vinci* (Capt Calda) torpedoed and sank the British tanker *Auris* (1935, 8030 tons, 34° 27′/11° 57′W) sailing independently. *Bianchi* left Bordeaux on 4 July to join this group but was torpedoed and sunk by the British submarine *Tigris* (Capt Bone) the next day at 45° 03′N/04° 01′W. Repeated radio calls between 12 and 18 July drew no reply. Also on the 5th

Torelli (Capt De Giacomo) sighted one small convoy proceeding westward to which *Da Vinci*, *Baracca* and *Malaspina*. Only *Torelli* was able to make an unsuccessful attack on a destroyer. On 7 July *Torelli* sighted another outwardbound convoy to which *Da Vinci* and *Baracca* were directed, but they did not find what was probably HG 66. But a week later at 2215 *Malaspina* torpedoed and sank the Greek Cargo ship *Nikoklis* (1921, 3576 tons, 36°N/21°W) from the dispersed convoy OG 67. On 17 July she torpedoed and sank the British cargo ship *Guelma* (1928, 44402 tons, 1695, 30° 44′/17° 33′W). Next day it was reported that agents had seen convoy HG 67 from Gibraltar. *Malaspina* and

Torelli arriving in St Nazaire on 23 December 1941 with part of the crew of the German auxiliary cruiser *Atlantis*. Note the modified conning tower.

Author's collection/E C P Armées

Torelli in Bordeaux on 5 October 1940.

Author's collection/E C P Armées

TABLE 2: SHIPS SUNK BY THE 6 MARCONI CLASS SUBMARINES

Da Vinci	17 merchant ships = 120,243 tons (the Italian top score of World War II)	
Torelli	7 merchant ships = 42,871 tons	
Marconi	1 destroyer, 1 RN Fleet Oiler = 9534 tons	20,292 tons
	6 merchant ships = 10,758 tons	
Malaspina	3 merchant ships = 16,384 tons	
Bianchi	3 merchant ships = 14,705 tons	
Baracca	3 merchant ships = 8987 tons	
TOTAL	39 merchant ships	
	1 destroyer = 223,482 tons	
	1 RN Fleet Oiler	

Torelli, together with 3 other Italian boats, were concentrated against them but the convoy evaded them.

On the 21st *Torelli* succeeded in torpedoing and sinking the Norwegian tanker *Ida Knudsen* (1925, 8913 tons, 2134, 34° 34′N/13° 14′W). On 9 August convoy HG 69's departure from Gibraltar was also reported, *Marconi* and two other boats were directed against it along with several U-boats. On 11 August (0335, 37°N/10°W) *Marconi* fired at but missed the British sloop *Deptford* (1935, 990 tons) and the corvette *Convolvulus* (1940, 925 tons), part of HG 69's escort. *Marconi* continued to send shadowing reports despite interruptions until she was driven off on 14 August. That same day at 0001 *Marconi* destroyed with gunfire the independent cargo ship *Sud* (1901, 2589 tons, 41°N/18°W) with 25 rounds of 3.9in. *U 126* (Capt Bauer) finished off the wreck with a torpedo. The operation was broken off the next day (15 August). *Marconi* was redirected during 20–24 August to hunt vainly for convoy HG 70 (reported to have left Gibraltar on the 18th). *Baracca*, *Da Vinci* and the other Italian boats had a similar fruitless search for convoy HG 71 (4–6 September). On 8 September *Baracca* (Capt Viani), in taking up a new patrol line, was compelled to surface west of Gibraltar by depth charges from the British escort destroyer *Groome* and, after a short gun engagement, she was sunk by ramming at 0930 in position 40° 15′/20° 55′W. *Baracca* was probably responsible for sinking with her gunfire the small Panamanian cargo ship *Trinidad* (1939, 434 tons, 46° 06′N/17° 04′W) on 5 September. Convoy HG 72 set out from Gibraltar on the 10th being attacked by *Da Vinci* and *Torelli*, but they were driven off by the escort. On the 18th they were redirected towards convoy HG 73, *Torelli* established a brief contact the next day and again during the evening of the 20th only to receive depth charge damage from the destroyer HMS *Vimy* during the night of the 21st-22nd. On the 23rd *Da Vinci* kept contact for a while. Nothing was heard from *Malaspina* after her departure from Bordeaux on 7 September. It is now known that the submarine attacked by *Vimy* was not *Malaspina*; this attack took place at 2115 on 21 September (37° 46′N/19° 18′W) and in addition according to the *Commando Sommergibili*'s orders, *Malaspina*'s position that day would have been about 180 miles farther to the east. *Marconi* left Bordeaux in 5 October and later received orders to attack convoy HG 74 (sighted after midnight on 23 October by *U 71*. *Marconi* was last heard from at 1130 on the 29th when she gave her position as 42° 55′/21° 55′W. She probably sank, by unknown cause, about 300 miles west of Gibraltar. It has been stated that *Marconi* was sunk on 28 November by *U 67*. This is certainly wrong for according to German sources *U 67* was not at sea between the end of September and mid-December. *Marconi* failed to answer radio calls made until 5 November.

On 14 December *Torelli* was in the South Atlantic resucing part of the crew from the German auxiliary cruiser *Atlantis* (sunk by the cruiser HMS *Devonshire* on 22 November) and brought them into St Nazaire.

OPERATIONS IN 1942

Between 20 February and 24 March 1942 the *Da Vinci* group (5 boats) operated east of the Antilles (Caribbean). At 0027 on 20 February the British cargo ship *Scottish Star* (1917, 7224 tons, 13° 24′N/49° 36′W), was torpedoed and sunk by the *Torelli*. On 25 February *Da Vinci* (Capt Longanesi-Cattani) torpedoed and sank the Brazilian cargo ship *Cabedelo* (1932, 3557 tons, 16°N/49°W). Next day *Torelli* sank with torpedo and gunfire the Panamanian tanker *Esso Copenhagen* (1939, 9245 tons, 10° 32′N/53° 20′W). On 28 February *Da Vinci* sank with torpedo and gunfire the Latvian cargo ship *Everasma* (1920, 3644 tons 17°N/48°W). On 11 March at 0056am *Torelli* launched and missed the

The 100m (3.9in) deck gun forward of a *Marconi* class submarine's conning tower in Bordeaux. These boats made heavy use of their gun armament, in conjunction with torpedoes.
Author's collection/E C P Armées

British SS *Orari* (1931, 10,350 tons, 13°N/57°W); this *Plymouth merchant ship was damaged on two other occasions and also survived.*

After returning to Bordeaux *Torelli* sailed again on 2 June to attack shipping off the Bahamas. Two days out into the Bay of Biscay (0227, 4 June) while running on the surface she was attacked by a plane using a searchlight and flying very low. Surprise was complete when it machine-gunned the boat and dropped bombs that exploded underneath. The heavily damaged boat made for the Spanish coast. The Spanish authorities obligingly towed her to Aviles for five days of repairs. She returned to Bordeaux on 14 July. This was the first time an Italian submarine had been attacked by night by a radar-fitted aircraft in the Bay of Biscay. In June *Da Vinci* sank four ships off West Africa. On the 2nd she sank with torpedo and gunfire the Panamanian sailing vessel *Reine Marie Stewart* (1919, 1087 tons, 07° 16'N/13° 20'W, 2250). On the 7th she torpedoed and sank the British SS *Chile* (1915, 6956 tons, 04° 17'N/13° 48'W). On the 10th it was the turn of the Dutch cargo vessel *Alioth* (1937, 5483 tons, 00° 08'/18° 52'W). On the 13th torpedo and gunfire dispatched the British SS *Clan Macquarrie* (1913, 6471 tons, 05° 30'/23° 30'W). On her return to Bordeaux *Da Vinci* was temporarily modified to carry a CA type midget submarine. This entailed removal of the deck gun and the installation forward of the conning tower of a cell fitted with clamps (shackels) to carry the CA. These could be freed while submerged and could be retrieved by the carrier submarine (known as Kangaroo) while awash. Tests showed that the midgets needed improving before they could be considered operational. The midget was destined to attack ships in New York and Freetown, the attack on New York being scheduled for December 1943 but never took place because Italy's surrender came first. *Da Vinci* left Bordeaux on 7 October and operated without success for the last five days west of the Cape Verde Islands under the command of Captain Gazzana. She switched to the NE coast of Brazil until 14 November with far greater success. On the 2nd *Da Vinci* sank with torpedo and gunfire the British SS *Empire Zeal* (1914, 7000 tons, 00° 30'S/30° 54'W). Next day at 0105 the Italian submarine was forced to crash dive by gunfire from the Dutch ship *Frans Hals* (1941, 6626 tons, 01°S/32°W) after a torpedo had missed. On 4 November *Da Vinci* sent the Greek ship *Andreas* (1919, 6566 tons, 2208, 02° 00'S/30° 30'W) to the bottom with torpedo and gunfire. The same combination accounted for the brand new Liberty ship *Marcus Whitman* (1942, 7176 tons, 0012, 05° 40'S/32° 41'W) at 0012 on the 10th and for the Dutchman *Veerhaven* (1930, 5291 tons, 03° 51'S/32° 41'W) at 0012 on the 10th and for the Dutchman *Veerhaven* (1930, 5291 tons, 03° 51'S/29° 22'W) at 0611 on the 11th.

OPERATIONS IN 1943

Torelli left Bordeaux in February 1943 and operated off the Brazilian coast without luck. She was attacked by aircraft off Fernando de Noronha on 16 March,

shooting one down with her 13.2mm AA guns, but she was left damaged, unable to submerge and leaking fuel. She returned to base. *Da Vinci* sailed, for the last time from Bordeaux on 20 February to operate in the Indian Ocean. Outwardbound in the South Atlantic she torpedoed and sank, on 14 March the British liner *Empress of Canada* (1922, 21,517 tons, 01° 13'S/09° 57'W). Then on the 19th at precisely midnight she torpedoed and sank the British SS *Lulworth Hill* (1940, 762 tons, 10° 10'S/01° 00'E). Reaching the Indian Ocean on 17 April she torpedoed and sank the Dutch cargo ship *Sembilan* (1922, 6566 tons, 31° 30'S/33° 30'E). Next day torpedo and gunfire sank the British SS *Manaar* (1942, 8007 tons, 30° 59'S/33° 00'E.) On the 21st the same means sank the US Liberty ship *John Drayton* (1942, 7177 tons, 32° 10'S/34° 50'E) and lastly the British tanker *Doryssa* (1938, 8078 tons 37° 03'S/24° 03'E). On her return voyage *Da Vinci* signalled Bordeaux on 22 May that she would arrive in a week's time. But next day at 1145 (GMT) the frigate HMS *Ness*, escorting a convoy, obtained a submarine contact th her asdic. She and the destroyer HMS *Active* dropped depth charges until the contact was lost. The submarine was *Da Vinci* and she was destroyed about 300 ыiles west of Vigo in Spain.

This left *Torelli* as the sole survivor of the class and she was extensively modified to carry cargo to the Far East by the end of May 1943. On 18 June she sailed from Bordeaux on the long voyage to the Indian Ocean with 130 tons of mercury, special steel in bars, 20mm gun mountings, a new pattern of 500kg aircraft bomb. Near St Helena *Torelli* escaped undamaged from an aircraft attack but was obliged to lengthen her course with the unpleasant result that she ran out of fuel in the Indian Ocean. After an unsuccessful rendezvous with a refuelling U-boat, BETASOM was able to organise a second successful one. A replenished *Torelli* kept on, was met by the Italian colonial sloop *Eritrea* and reached Sabang (Sumatra) on 26 August 1943. When Italy surrendered, *Torelli* was about to leave Singapore for Bordeaux with a valuable cargo. She was seized by the Japanese on 10 September. She was then handed over to the Germans who renamed her *UIT 25* and kept the boat until 10 May 1945 when she was handed back to Japan and enrolled into the Imperial Navy on 15 July unarmed as *I-504*. Found at Kobe on 2 September, she was scuttled off this harbour by the US Navy on 1 April 1946. *Torelli* had been a lucky vessel like the cargo ship *Orari* she missed! Compared to her sisters *Malaspina* and *Marconi* who disappeared without known cause, she survived serious damage three times, once from the destroyer HMS *Vimy* (21 September 1941) and twice from aircraft attacks (4 June and 16 March).

GRAF ZEPPELIN Part I

By M J Whitley

Despite the relatively advanced state of aircraft development in Germany during the First World War, little progress was made in the field of shipboard aviation, mainly due to the existence of the Zeppelin fleet, of which great things were expected. However, the only naval use made of the Zeppelins was for reconnaisance on a limited scale and they were more frequently employed on air raids over the British Isles. The wide-scale use of aircraft from flying-off platforms mounted on the turrets of Grand Fleet battleships was never initiated by the High Seas Fleet and even the seaplane carrier, of which the Royal Naval put nine into service, appeared to have held little interest for the German naval staff. Only one ship, the light cruiser *Stuttgart*, was actually converted for this purpose late in the war, being equipped with two hangars aft and able to operate three floatplanes. As the conversion was not completed until May 1918, her operational service was almost non-existent and after the surrender she was allocated to Britain and scrapped.

A further project to convert the obsolete cruiser *Roon* into an aircraft mother ship never left the drawing board. Apart from *Stuttgart*, only the raider *Wolf* made operational use of a scout floatplane but another brief use of shipboard aircraft does deserve mention even though it was only of a temporary nature. In the summer of 1916, an air attack on the port installations of Reval in the Gulf of Finland could only be carried out by using torpedo boats to ferry the low endurance floatplanes to a starting point offshore within their flying range. Four aircraft were so transported, one per torpedo boat, shipped on the after torpedo tubes. This was just one special operation and cannot truly be categorised as 'naval aviation'.

Only one attempt at producing a true aircraft carrier was seriously made. This was to have been the conversion of the Italian liner *Ausonia* which had been lying incomplete at the Blohm & Voss yard since her launching in April 1915. Her reconstruction would have followed the lines of that carried out to produce the British *Argus* except that the German ship would have had a proper bridge, funnel and superstructure on the starboard side. This was an advance on the *Argus* design whose retractable wheelhouse and horizontal smoke ducts in lieu of funnels led to problems in operational use. In another respect, however, the German design was behind the times for separate landing and flying off decks were envisaged, despite the availability of a flush deck from stem to stern. A mixture of floatplanes and wheeled fighters, totalling about 30 aircraft were to be accommodated. The ship was coal fired, with twin-shaft 18,000hp geared turbine machinery giving a speed of 21 knots. Curiously, both British and German conversions were from Italian liners. The German project came too late, however, for by late 1918, the war had been lost and it is doubtful if any work was actually carried out on the ship.

The collapse and surrender of Germany in November 1918 put an end to any further experiments and the Versailles Treaty of 1919 effectively killed any hope of future German naval aviation by prohibiting aircraft, their development and aircraft cariers. This situation pertained until the late 1920s and 1930s, when in a changed political climate, clandestine experiments with aircraft began again.

These undercover activities were mainly directed at the future information of a land-based air force but the *Reichsmarine* did, in October 1928, lay the foundations of a naval air arm, when it obtained government approval for a few seaplanes for 'experimental' purposes. The excuse for this was the fact that the Versailles Treaty allowed the *Reichsmarine* to retain anti-aircraft guns. This was interpreted as also permitting aircraft to tow the necessary targets for training purposes! In this way, an organisation known as 'Air Service Incorporated' was formed as a cloak for its illegitimate activities with the Fleet. Although eventually killed off with the advent of Hermann Goering and his 'Everything which flies belongs to me' attitude, this service did constitute the basis of a naval air arm.

In January 1935 the *Reichsminister der Luftfahrt*, Erhard Milch had laid down the agreed strength, composition and dispositions of the Naval Air Arm. Included amongst these was the provision for three carrier-borne *Grüppen*, one for Reconnaissance (*Träger Aufklarungsgrüppe (M) 216*), one General Purpose (*Trägermehrzweckgruppe 286*) and one Dive bomber (*Trägersturzkampfgrüppe 266*). Each *grüppe* comprised a staff fight and three *staffeln*, identified in the usual manner, (ie *1/216,2/216,3/216* etc). Two *gruppen* were to be based at Barge and the dive bombers at Jever when disembarked. All were expected to form on 1 October 1938. Note that at this period, naval aircraft duties were primarily considered to be spotter/reconnaissance and torpedo bomber, no pure fighter role being included. However, from 1935 onwards the small band of trained naval airmen were continually commandeered by the expanding *Luftwaffe*, with the result that the *Reichsmarine* ended up with a truncated force capable of only a few duties. Moreoever, despite this agreement with the *Luftwaffe* that the naval air arm would comprise nine

Tugs manoeuvring *Graf Zeppelin* after her launch at Kiel in Hitler's presence on 10 December 1938.

squadrons of long-range flying boats, 18 multi-purpose squadrons, 12 carrier-borne and two shipboard catapult squadrons, such was the inter-service bickering that only a fraction of this force was available at the outbreak of war.

Thus international politics, treaty restrictions and inter-service rivalry combined with the Navy's seemingly low enthusiasm to delay the building of Germany's first aircraft carrier even though, by the 1930s the type was assuming greater importance in naval tactics, despite formidable opposition from the 'Big Gun' protagonists. Nevertheless the Naval Staff were alive to the possibilities of the type and were considering the construction of carriers at least as early as 1934. On 12 March 1934, the staff requirements for a proposed aircraft carrier were tabled. These were as follows:

MAIN REQUIREMENTS

(a) Theatre of operations, Atlantic & North Seas.
(b) Minimum flight deck length 180m (590ft 7in).
(c) Catapult for single aircraft on forecastle.
(d) Facilities for handling seaplanes.
The ship was to be patterned on *Akagi/Furious/Ranger*.

Displacement	About 15,000 tonnes
Speed	33kts (continuous)
Armament	9 × 150mm or 6 × 203mm guns
Range	12,000 miles
Armour	Cruiser scale
Aircraft	60 (⅓ with folding wings)
Catapults	2

Admiral Raeder's main criticism of this concerned the gun armament. He attached special importance to the astern firepower, being particularly worried about a running chase, for which he considered two triple 230mm (8in) mountings the minimum desirable. This would have caused severe constructional problems as no doubt he realised, for he was prepared to accept one triple 203mm with three more single guns each side in casemates. However, design calculations soon showed the 203mm armament to be impracticable and in any case, only the USA had this calibre in aircraft carriers. Whether it was realised at this time that carriers should rely on their own aircraft and other ships' guns for surface defence is not clear but the calibre had to be reduced to 150mm.

By April 1934, during a conference on future construction it was proposed that an aircraft carrier be included in the 1935 programme. The Treaty of Versailles remained a problem and in view of this, together with the fact that this was a completely new type of vessel (for Germany), the head of the *Marinekommandoamt* proposed that preparations be started, to allow an order to be placed by October 1935.

The formidable task of designing the new ship was entrusted to *Marineoberbaurat* Wilhelm Hadeler, formerly assistant to the Professor of Warship Construction at Berlin University. Hadeler gathered together a design team and made a start on the project, having obtained technical details of the USS *Lexington* and using the Royal Navy's *Courageous* design as a useful starting point. By June 1934 a sketch design had been prepared, which immediately attracted comments and demands for modifications from many sections of the Navy, who appeared to be unsure of their precise requirements of an aircraft carrier. This bickering and indecisiveness was to be a feature of the design process of many a German naval vessel, with consequent long delays before construction commenced. The 'M' type cruisers were a notable example of this and in the case of the carrier, this tortuous process was further complicated by the need to involve a second service, the *Luftwaffe*, whose C-in-C had no love at all for the *Kriegsmarine*.

In June 1935 the Anglo-German Naval Treaty was signed in an effort on the part of Great Britain to impose some form of control on Germany's rearmament, bearing in mind the Versailles restrictions' ineffectiveness. This agreement restricted the German Fleet to 35 per cent of the British but, strangely, did not mention the forbidden category of aircraft carrier by which the Germans inferred a right to legally build 38,500 tons of this category! The *Kriegsmarine* then decided to build two vessels to utilise this tonnage thus forcing Hadeler to re-cast his design, having by this time, arrived at a legend displacement of some 24,000 tonnes following changes in the staff requirements. The major operators of aircraft carriers were the USA, England and Japan and Hadeler was fortunate that relations between his country and Japan were improving steadily (the Anti-Comintern Pact was signed in November 1936) and in consequence he was able to send a team to Japan to inspect the Imperial Navy's *Akagi*. As a result of this visit, numerous alterations were made to the German design, including the provision of a third life and an extension of the flight deck. Later still, following the successful development of a catapult system by Deutschewerk, it was agreed during a conference on 10 April 1937, to install two such equipments at the forward end of the flight deck.

The design work continued and led to the unveiling of a 12,250 ton (standard) displacement vessel which was actually of 33,550 tonne full load displacement with a speed of 33.8 knots on 200,000hp obtained from a four shaft geared turbine installation utilising the new high pressure steam concept. An aircraft complement of about 40 machines was envisaged with a gun armament consisting of 16 150mm guns (capable of low angle use only) and 10, later 12, 150mm guns was originally to number only eight, in single mountings but a proposal to save weight by utilising twin mountings was misinterpreted and led to eight twin casemates in lieu of the intended four twins. This complicated ammunition supply arrangements and required larger gun crews.

DESIGN FEATURES
The basic design featured a hangar structure and flight deck built on the hull after contemporary US and Japanese practice, in contrast with the more recent British 'all one' concept. Her 250m (820ft 3in) long hull was divided into 21 watertight compartments and incorpo-

rated two hangars, one above the above. Three electrically powered 5.5 tonne lifts, each on the centre line, served both hangars. The upper hangar was 185m (606ft 11in) long and the lower one 172m (564ft 4in). Both were 16m (52ft 6in) in width but the lower one had slightly less head room. The flight deck itself, 242m (793ft 11in) in length, was constructed of steel with an anti-splinter protection function and overlaid with a wooden surface. This deck was the upper deck strength deck of the ship. At the forward end of the flight deck, two compressed air catapults capable of launching 5 tonne aircraft at 133km/hr (82.6mph) were installed but the catapult originally envisaged on the forecastle on the British *Courageous* pattern was finally deleted from the design. Each catapult could launch nine aircraft on its own reservoir of air, at a rate of one every half minute. Following this, 50 minutes were required to recharge the reservoirs.

Four arrester wires were provided aft and two emergency wires fore and aft of the centre life. Drawings of the ship in its original form also show four further arrester wires disposed fore and aft of the forward lift, possibly intended to allow recovery of aircraft when the ship was going astern as, it is believed, certain US carriers were originally equipped to do so. On the starboard side was positioned the island superstructure following common practice (except for a few Japanese ships). This was a long, low structure fitting the command and navigating bridges, charthouse etc.

Fore and aft of the island, the secondary armament of 105mm SKC/33 guns in twin mountings was disposed two forward (later three) and three aft. The four 4m flak directors in their distinctive spherical stabilised towers flanked the massive flat topped funnel that dominated the superstructure. A single 7m rangefinder on the bridge was fitted for main (low angle) armament that consisted of 16 150mm SKC/28 guns paired in casements. This provided one of the most distinctive features of the design and had probably been adopted following the pattern of the Japanese *Kaga* and *Akagi* but which, apart from the antiquated French *Béarn*, had not been used by any other nation building aircraft carriers. In fact it had by then also been abandoned by the Japanese themselves.

Internally, there were four main deck levels which were full beam, denoted from keel upwards, hold, lower platform, upper platform and tween deck, of which the latter was the main armoured deck. Above the tween deck, the lower and upper hangars effectively split all other decks up to flight deck level into gallery decks, except at the extremities, where mess decks or work shops closed off the ends of the hangars. These gallery decks were known as decks 'D', 'C', 'B' and 'A' moving upwards to the flight deck, with 'B' deck running the full length of the ship to form forecastle and quarterdeck for working the ship. Much of the ship's company and all *Luftwaffe* personnel were quartered on these decks around the hangar spaces. Officers' accommodation in the form of single and double cabins was on 'A' deck with the officers' mess right forward under the leading edge of the flight deck. The mess could be divided into

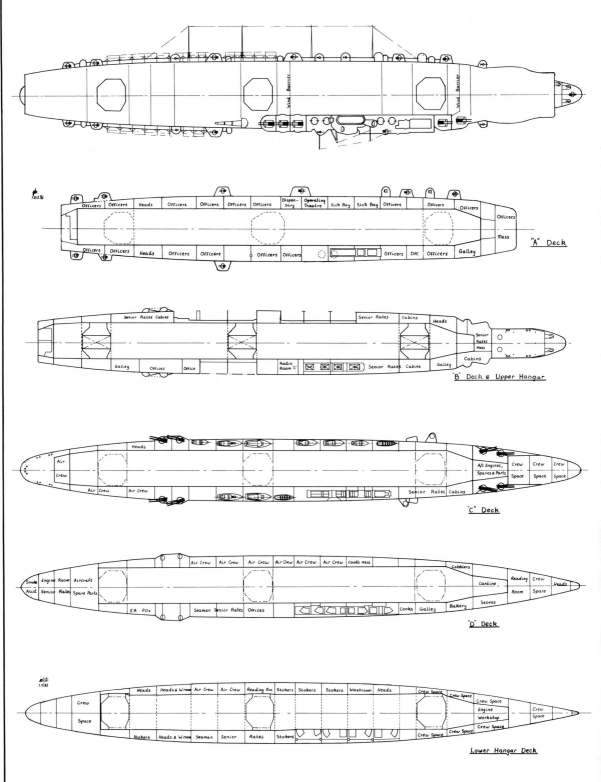

Deck plans for the *Graf Zeppelin*.

Author's drawing

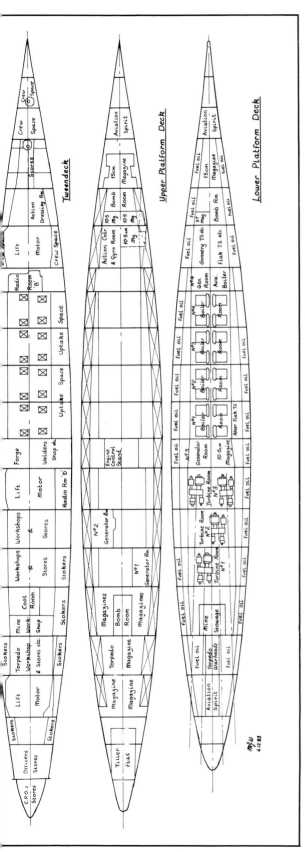

two parts – one Navy, one *Luftwaffe!* Also on 'A' deck to port was the sick bay, comprehensively equipped with an X-ray room, operating theatre, isolation room, two wards, dispensary and ancilliary facilities. The ship's complement numbered 108 officers (51 air force), and 1612 other ranks (266 air force).

Below the tween deck or armoured deck, the largest spaces were occupied by the main propulsion machinery and magazines. Four boiler rooms and three turbine rooms, together with four generator rooms and an auxiliary boiler room comprised the machinery unit, which extended from frame stations 66½ to 176 ie 44 per cent of the ship's length. On the platform decks forward and aft, the combined magazine and shell rooms for the 150mm guns served their respective guns via electrical bucket hoist systems whose supply route was of necessity complicated by the need to serve guns on the beam and thus be deflected around the hangar spaces. Also at the fore-ends was a separate magazine for bombs from which a lift conveyed the ordnance to the lower hangar deck. Aft was a large magazine for torpedoes with its associated warhead room below it, a magazine for mines and another for bombs. Lifts again conveyed the mines and torpedoes up to the lower hangar deck, via the torpedo workshop on the tween deck. The after magazine spaces for aircraft ordnance could stow 80–90 torpedoes or 220 mines with a normal stowage of 66 torpedoes and 48 mines. No provision appears to have been made for bombing-up on the flight deck except by cross transfer via the aircraft lifts.

ARMOUR PROTECTION
The ship's main vertical protection consisted of a 100mm waterline belt 4m (13ft 1in) deep extending from frame 57 to frame 177 (ie about 48 per cent of the waterline length) covering the machinery spaces and after magazines. Forward, this belt was reduced to 60mm (2⅜in) in the way of the forward 150mm magazines and then continued to the bows as 40mm (1⅝in), finally 30mm (1⅛in). Aft, the belt reduced only to 80mm (3⅛in) to the stern as protection for the steering gear. Inboard of the main vertical belt was a secondary 20mm longitudinal bulkhead which served as a torpedo bulkhead. The main horizontal armour on the tween deck was 40mm (1⅝in) thick, with the periphery increased in thickness to 60mm (2⅜in) and inclined at 45 degrees to join the lower side of the waterline belt. Closing off the armoured carapace so formed were transverse armoured bulkheads, 80mm (3⅛in) thick. Above the steering gear, 60mm (2⅜in) horizontal plate was employed. No protection was given to the hangar sides, other than splinter protection but the flight deck itself was given a degree of protection. This was predominantly 20mm but thickened adjacent to the lift shafts, especially the centre one where it was 38mm (1½in). This was undoubtedly for structural strength as well as for protective reasons. Around the funnel uptakes, the flight deck was 40mm whilst the vertical uptake protection was 80mm (3⅛in). Other armouring was spread rather thinly, the casemates having 30mm (1⅛in), flak directors 14mm and bridge control positions 17mm (³/₈in) protection. Total weight of armouring was approximately 5000 tonnes.

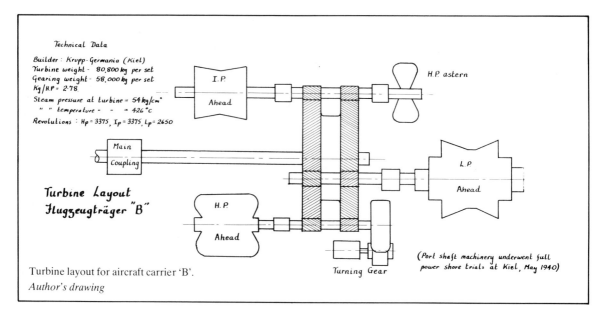

Technical Data

Builder : Krupp-Germania (Kiel)
Turbine weight - 80,800 kg per set
Gearing weight - 58,000 kg per set
Kg/H.P = 2.78
Steam pressure at turbine = 54 kg/cm²
"   "   temperature - - = 426°C
Revolutions : Hp = 3375, Ip = 3375, Lp = 2650

I.P. Ahead

H.P. astern

Main Coupling

L.P. Ahead

Turbine Layout
Flugzeugträger "B"

H.P. Ahead

Turning Gear

(Port shaft machinery underwent full
power shore trials at Kiel, May 1940)

Turbine layout for aircraft carrier 'B'.

Author's drawing

MACHINERY

The steam plant comprised 16 La Mont high pressure boilers, four in each of four boiler rooms. Each boiler, operating steam pressure 70kg/cm² at 450°C, had a rated capacity of 70 tonnes per hour and was equipped with two Saake ring oil burners, both at one end of the furnace under automatic Askania control. Economisers and air-preheaters were fitted, with forced circulation for which an efficiency of 85 per cent was claimed. Although these boilers were never to steam at sea aboard the carrier, they were basically similar to those aboard *Admiral Hipper* class heavy cruisers and would have undoubtedly suffered the same problems in service. Troubles experienced with the circulating pump and overheating of the air pre-heaters were eventually overcome but excessive corrosion of the superheaters caused by a carry over of 1 to 3 per cent continued despite alterations to the baffling in the steam drum. Corrosion also occurred in the economisers but the generator tubes themselves were relatively trouble free. The boilers for Aircraft Carrier 'A' were built by Deutschewerk, Kiel, those for 'B' by Germaniawerft.

The geared turbine installation had a designed power of 50,000hp per shaft on a four shaft arrangement, in three separate turbine rooms. The forward turbine room housed two turbine sets driving the wing shafts whilst the centre and aft turbine rooms contained the inner starboard and port turbines respectively. The turbines differed slightly between the two ships scheduled to be built, although initially both were to be identical. Those for '*Flugzeugträger A*' consisted of Brown Boverie & Co impulse/reaction type cruising and high pressure stages with straight reaction type intermediate turbines. Astern power was provided by a stern element in the forward end of the IP turbine, separated from the ahead blading by a diaphragm, whilst the astern element of the LP (low power) turbine was a double flow reaction stage at the centre of the casing. Like all German turbine designs,

separate casings were employed for each turbine stage due to the retention of single reduction (double helical) gearing, leading to layouts which were extremely wasteful in terms of weight and space. Efficiencies too were generally low.

The turbines for 'B' were built by Germania and were somewhat modified, being similar to those of *Prinz Eugen* except that the astern element in the IP turbine was removed and installed as a separate Curtis wheel on the forward end of the IP pinion. Comb type disengaging couplings were fitted to each shaft and could be operated at speeds up to 18 knots by synchronising turbine speed with trailing shaft speed.

Four boilers for '*Flugzeugträger B*' had been completed by Germaniawerft at Kiel and underwent trials before 'B' was cancelled. The electrical generating capacity of the design incorporated four generator rooms using both turbo- and diesel generation. These were distributed as follows:

Generator Room	Location	Diesel	Turbo
No 1	No 1 Turbine Rm Upper Platform dk Stb		2 × 460kw
No 2	No 2 Turbine Rm Upper Platform dk Pt	2 × 350kw	2 × 460kw
No 3	Lower Platform dk Pt amidships		1 × 460kw 1 × 230kw
No 4	Fwd of No 4 BR Lower platform dk Pt	2 × 350kw	

AC power for control circuits, particularly gunnery fire control, was provided by one 400kw converter and four 100kw sets, the 400kw vertical type motor alternator being in No 2 generator room.

Harbour steam supplies were provided by a separate auxiliary boiler room to starboard of No 4 generator space.

The main engine control stand and damage control centre was on the upper platform deck between No 3 turbine room and No 1 boiler room. Damage control arrangements were comprehensive, with the hull being divided into 21 watertight compartments. For fire fighting purposes, besides the sea water lines supplied by the main hull and fire pumps, and steam drenching, there were 20 gaseous extinguisher units that could flood compartments with 'Ardixine' gas to smother fire. This was not without its own hazards however, for it would also asphyxiate the crew and moreover could seep unnoticed through defective glands and seals into adjacent mess decks. This in fact occurred aboard *Admiral Hipper* when a number of men were found dead in their hammocks the following morning after firefighting activities the previous evening in nearby spaces.

An interesting feature of the propulsion plant was the provision of two Voigt-Schneider propeller rudders to assist berthing of the ship in harbour. These two units, powered by 450kw DC electric motors were installed in the fore-ends on the centre line and could be withdrawn through watertight doors in the ship's bottom when not in use. They could exert a lateral impulse of 7.7 tonnes and whilst not intended for use at sea, could, in emergency, be used for steering purposes at speeds not exceeding 12 knots, Furthermore, in the event of the main engines being destroyed, a speed of 3 to 4 knots could be obtained by using them to propel the ship.

The bunker capacity as designed was 5000 tonnes oil fuel, which calculations showed to be sufficient for an endurance of about 9600 miles at 19.1 knots steaming on two shafts (4 boilers) with 10,500hp each. At normal full power of 42,000hp per shaft and 16 boilers on line, a speed of 35.25 knots and an endurance of approximately 3020 miles was anticipated. However, practical results on ships in service with similar power plants later showed that the designed endurance figures for all classes of *Kriegsmarine* warships were wildly optimistic. This was due to several reasons. First, the calculations included only the minimum number of boilers flashed up to make the desired speed and ignored the need to keep part of the powerplant at short notice for steam under war conditions. Second, for stability reasons, many ships could not consume all fuel stowed. Third, in service, many of the high speed steam-driven auxiliary turbines were extremely avaricious consumers of steam and grossly inefficient. (This was particularly true of the Type 39 torpedo boats for example.) Thus it is unlikely that the endurance figures obtained on shore trials and design calculations given below would have been achieved in service:

Speed (kts)	36.5	24.2	19.15	15.3	15.3
Shafts (hp)	4×50,000	4×10,500	4×5000	4×2500	2×5500
Endurance	2645nm	6750nm	8340nm	8800nm	11,480nm

ARMAMENT

The disposition and type of the main gun armament was, as has been noted earlier, outdated. Not only were the 150mm guns suitable only for low angle use but the casemate installation would also probably have led to their being washed out in a seaway, particularly the forward mountings. British, Japanese and US carriers had by this time dispensed with low angle guns, relying on their escort to provide anti-ship defence. This continued use of separate L/A and H/A guns was common German practice at the time however and was also to be seen in the *Bismarck* class. Indeed it was even included in the designs of their successors. As far as German ships were concerned, it absorbed much extra weight and space, which could have been better employed elsewhere. By the time that the British, US and Japanese trends had become known, it would have been impossible to rework the design but the 150mm guns could and might well, have been omitted on entry into service and the weight saved used to augment the heavy flak.

Main fire control was exercised by means of the 7m rangefinder atop the bridge in conjunction with two director sights in the gunnery control stand below it. An auxiliary director sight for astern fire control was fitted immediately abaft the after flak director tower. The transmitting station for the 150mm guns was situated on the lower platform deck, port side, compartment 17. Also in this compartment were the associated amplifier, switch and power rooms.

The heavy flak armament, which consisted of the standard 105mm SK C/33 gun, was carried in twin mountings disposed on the starboard side, fore and aft of the island. Originally, the design incorporated five twin mountings with two forward and three aft but an extra mount was worked in on the flight deck above S2 150mm casemate. Allied with the provision of four tri-axially stabilised 4m base fire control towers, this made for a very respectable A/A outfit, but like the low angle guns, its disposition was open to question. Being all mounted on the starboard side, the engagement of, for example, low flying torpedo bombers approaching from the port beam would have been impossible if the carrier's own squadrons were taking off at the same time. Also, with the guns themselves so closely grouped, one hit could conceivably put 60 per cent of the heavy flak out of action.

Two flak control positions were provided at the fore and after ends of the lower funnel platform, which, in conjunction with the four range-finder towers and two separate flak transmitting stations, one in compartment XII and one forward in the same compartment as the low angle fire control station, provided comprehensive control facilities for air defence. There were however, a number of deficiencies in this system, caused mainly by its over-complicated layout, and poor weather proofing arrangements on the guns and electrical systems. The efficiency of gun installations was reduced by the long heating times for thyratron amplifiers – some three minutes and the use of large gyros for flak director stabilisation also led to long running up periods. Reliability and accessibility too were less than desirable, so that the flak control systems aboard *Scharnhorst* and *Admiral Hipper* with all these problems proved less effective than they might have been. The new carriers were designed with basically the same systems but in view of their scheduled later completion, it is likely that at least some of these deficiencies would have been rectified as was done, for example, with *Admiral Hipper*'s later near sister *Prinz Eugen*, whose flak directors were fitted with small gyro stabilisation and motor follow up giving a consequent decrease in reaction time.

The remainder of the flak outfit consisted of the standard 37mm and 20mm guns in twin and single mountings. A total of 22 37mm SK C/30 guns in twin mountings LC/30 were carried on sponsons around the flight deck, six to port, four to starboard and one on the forecastle. This gun was a hand-worked weapon in a stabilised tri-axial mounting, utilising large gyros, whose potential was limited by some of the defects referred to earlier in the context of gyro-stabilisation. Prototype mountings had not been tested under searching operational conditions with the result that some 300-400 had been built by the time defects became apparent. These were principally associated with poor weather proofing and the failure of the gyro-stabilisation system, 30 1.25m base portable rangefinders were provided for each mounting.

Seven single 20mm MG C/30 guns completed the short-range armament. This gun too was a hand-worked weapon, handicapped by its low rate of fire. Thus the designed armament could be summed up as useful in terms of weight of fire and accuracy but inadequately developed and distributed so that its full potential could not be realised. Nevertheless, in comparison with the British 'barrage fire' pompom and ineffective rifle calibre multiple .5 machine guns, it was a great advance and other combatant powers soon followed the lead to larger calibres.

AIRCRAFT

The designed aircraft complement was 43 machines whose types and mix varied through the ship's chequered development. Early drawings show what appear to be wheeled Heinkel He 60 biplanes embarked! Eventually, proposals crystallised into three types for three different missions: Fighter, Bomber, General Purpose (Recce/torpedo/Minelayer).

During the early stages of the carrier's development, *Luftwaffe* (and naval) aircraft were still in the biplane stage as typified by the He 51 and Arado Ar 68 single seat, fixed undercarriage fighters. These were armed with two machine guns and capable of about 306-330km/hr (190-205mph). In the floatplane reconnaissance role was the He 60 two-seat biplane equipped for catapult duty aboard the *Panzerschiffe* and light cruisers of the Fleet. With the probability of a true aircraft carrier entering service, companies such as Arado and Fieseler began to develop designs specifically intended for carrier operation. By 1937, the Arado concern, in competition with Fiesler had produced a naval version of the Ar 95, a coastal patrol/reconnaissance// light attack type that had not been accepted for use by the *Luftwaffe*. The navalised model, known as the Ar 95 was a fixed undercarriage two-seat biplane powered by an 880hp BMW radial engine and capable of a speed of 280km/hr. Modifications included a cockpit canopy, arrestor hook and catapult spools. Three prototypes were built but unfortunately the *Luftwaffe* preferred the Fieseler contender, which was faster and possessed a better range.

The Fieseler type, which owed something to the earlier Fi 156 'Storch', was a lean looking biplane of predatory appearance, powered by an in-line 1100hp Daimler-Benz 601B engine. The two-man crew were seated in tandem and, like its rival, given the comfort of a covered cockpit, open at the rear to allow the operation of a rear defensive gun. In the clean condition, ie without bombs or torpedo, the machine could achieve a top speed of 325km/hr (202mph) and it possessed, if anything, even better STOL characteristics than the Fi 156 due to the ailerons and full span automatic leading edge slats on both upper and lower wings. Large trailing edge flaps were incorporated on the lower wings in addition. Its defensive armament was limited to two 7.9mm machine guns but it could also carry a 1000kg bomb or one torpedo. This machine more than met *Luftwaffe* requirements for a carrier-borne torpedo bomber-/reconnaissance aircraft and Fieseler were awarded a control for 12 pre-production models (Fi 167A-0) to follow the two prototypes, (Fi 167 V1 & V2). These pre-production aircraft featured a few refinements and the addition of a dinghy for the crew. A production order did not follow for the carrier herself was suspended in 1940 and the completed machines used for a variety of trials before being formed into *Erprobungsstaffel 167* and posted to the occupied Netherlands for advanced coastal service trials until 1942. When work was resumed on the ship however, it was decided to use a modified Ju 87 (Ju 87E) for the tasks originally intended for the Fi 167 and as a result the surviving nine aircraft were surplus to requirements, being finally sold to Rumania for operations over the Black Sea.

TABLE 1: BOILER DATA	
Boiler design	La Mont
Builder	Krupp-Germania
Boilers per ship	16
Economisers	La Mont
Air pre-heater	Horizontal Streamlined
Normal evaporation	60 tonnes/hr
Maximum evaporation	70 tonnes/hr
Pressure at drum	70kg/cm (Max permissible 75kg/cm)
Temperature at S/H outlet	450°C
Feed water temperature	95°C
Efficiency	82.6%
Boiler heating surface	122 sq m
Superheater surface	146.8 sq m
Economiser surface	366.1 sq m
Air pre-heater surface	486 sq m
Radiant surface	29 sq m
Furnace volume	20.4 cubic m
Boiler width	3830mm
Boiler height	5305mm (to top of steam take-off drum)
Boiler depth	4098mm

Port broadside view of *Graf Zeppelin*, taken at Gotenhafen (Gdynia) in 1941. Note camouflage netting and reasonably good condition of the paintwork.

Drüppel

Arado persevered in the the naval fighter requirement and produced the Ar 197, a single seat fighter which could also carry 200kg (440lb) of light bombs. This design, still a biplane type, had maximum speed of 400km/hr (248mph) and was armed with two machine guns in the fuselage and two 20mm cannon in the upper wings. It was in fact very similar to the Fleet Air Arm's latest fighter, the Sea Gladiator, which entered squadron service in 1937. Unlike the British force however, which had to make do with what it could get hold of, and operated biplanes throughout the war, the *Luftwaffe* intended to go to sea with the best fighter available and it was once again unfortunate for Arado that Professor Messerschmitt had completed the first prototype of the Bf 109 fighter monoplane late in 1935, production versions of which began to enter service in 1937. The age of the biplane was at an end and the new monoplane far eclipsed the Ar 197 performance with the result that only three biplane prototypes were flown and tested before the project was abandoned.

Not surprisingly, the aircraft eventually chosen for the fighter role was the *Luftwaffe*'s premier machine, the Bf 109, modified for naval employment. (Quite whether the *Luftwaffe* would have been so generous if the Navy

TABLE 2: MAIN GUN ARMAMENT

15cm SKC/28k gun in 15cm Dop. LC/36

Calibre	149.1mm
Muzzle velocity	875m/s
Barrel length	55cal/8200mm
Liner length	52.4cal/7816mm
Constructional gas pressure	3050kg/mm²
Barrel life	1100rnds
Recoil force at 0° elevation	52000kg
Weight of breech & barrel	9026kg
Max range	22,000m
Ammunition	
Weight of shell	45.3kg
Weight of charge	14kg
Length of shell	655mm
Weight of cartridge	23.5kg
Length of cartridge	865mm
Mounting	
Elevation/depression	+35°/−10°
Training limits	±360°=720°
Elevation change per **handwheel revolution**	1.5°
Training change per **handwheel revolution**	6.0°
Weight of cast gun cradle	5109kg
Weight of base	2800kg
Weight of pedestal	13,620kg
Weight of training gear	892kg
Electric power	1300kg
Weight of shield	8627kg
Total weight of mounting	47,600
Armour	30mm fwd/30 side/ 30 rear
Armour type	Whn/A

TABLE 3: FLAK ARMAMENT

3.7 SK C/30 in twin mounting C/30

Calibre	3.7cm	Training charge per	
Muzzel velocity	1000m/s	handwheel revolution	4°
Muzzle energy	38mt	Weight of cradle, brake etc	
Barrel length	83 cal (3074mm)	(swinging mass)	243kg
Bore length	80cal (2960mm)	Weight of cast gun cradle	152.5kg
Constructional gas pressure	3450kg/cm	Weight of base	71kg
Barrel life	7500rnds	Weight of pedestal	2162kg
Recoil force (0° elevation)	1000kg	Weight of training gear	87kg
Length of rifling	2554mm	Weight of electric power	630kg
Type of rifling	Cubic parabola 50/35	Complete mounting	3670kg
Number of grooves	16	*2cm C/30 in 2cm Pedestal L30*	
Weight of barrel and breech	243kg	Calibre	2cm
Max horizontal range	8500m	Muzzle velocity	835m/s
Max vertical range	6800m (tracer 4800m)	Barrel length	65cal (1300mm)
Construction	Monobloc barrel with	Bore length	65cal (1300mm)
	drawn on breech ring.	Constructional sea pressure	2800kg/cm²
	Vertical sliding block	Barrel life	22,000rnds
	breech. Hydraulic brake	Recoil force (0° elevation)	250kg
	and spring recuperator.	Length of rifling	720mm
		Weight of barrel and breech	64kg
Ammunition		Max horizontal range	4900m
Weight of shell	742kg	Max vertical range	3700m
Weight of charge	365kg	*Ammunition*	
HE charge	Fp 02	Weight of shell	134g
Length of shell	162mm	Length of shell	78.5mm
Weight of cartridge	970kg	Weight of charge	39.5g
Length of cartridge	381mm	Weight of complete round	320g
Propellant	RPC/32	Length of complete round	203mm
Weight of complete round	2.1kg	Rate of fire	280rpm cyclic,
Length of complete round	516.5mm		120rpm practical
Fuses	E Nose fuse C/30	Magazine	20rnds
	Nose fuse C/34	*Mounting*	
	Ers St C/34 (Tracer)	Elevation/depression	+85°/−11°
Duration of tracer	12secs	Training limits	none
Rate of fire	160rpm cyclic.	Weight cradle, brake etc	
	80rpm practical	(swinging mass)	43kg
Mounting		Weight of mounting	
Elevation/depression	+85°/−10°	without sights	282kg
Training limits	±360°=720°	Weight of complete gun	420kg
Elevation charge per			
handwheel revolution	3°		

had had an independent air arm is very much open to doubt). Nor were the machines to be obsolete marks – Messerschmitt had been ordered to produce a carrier-borne version of the current Bf 109E (*Emil*), arguably the best version to be produced in the long production period of this famous fighter. Messerschmitt began work on the project and built one pre-production aircraft, designated Bf 109T-0 (the 'T' referring to *Träger* or Carrier) before concentrating on the *Luftwaffe*'s own land-based fighters and turning the project over to the Fieseler aircraft company for final detail design work.

Fieseler were also to produce the production versions. The carrier version was powered by a Daimler-Benz DB601N 12 cylinder engine of 1200hp giving the fighter a maximum speed (at 20,000ft) of 568km/hr (353mph). The 'T' version differed from the *Emil* mainly by the increased wing span achieved by adding about .6m (2ft) to each outer wing panel the provision of folding wings

which hinged just outboard of the gun bays. Catapult points and an arrestor hook completed the carrier conversion. Armament comprised two 7.9mm MG 17 machine guns in the fuselage and two more (or 20mm cannon) in the wings. Ten new airframes were transferred from the parent factory production line to Fieseler and completed as T-0s. Later an order was received for a production batch of 60T-Is, the definitive service version. After the suspension of *Graf Zeppelin* the fighter order too was suspended but some time later, production restarted with a modified design, T-2, with catapult points and arrestor hook deleted for land service. These

Detail close-up of her port bow at Gotenhafen. Note the empty casemates and sponsons. At the forward end of the flight deck can be seen the end of the port catapult track.

Archiv Gröner

TABLE 4: NAVAL AIRCRAFT

Arado Ar 197

Type	Single seat naval fighter
Powerplant	One 880hp BMW 132 De radial engine
Performance	Max speed 400km/hr at 2500m
	Cruising speed 355km/hr
	Service ceiling 8000m
	Range 695km
Weights	Empty 1840kg
	Maximum 2475kg
Dimensions	Span 11m, length 9.2m, height 3.6m
Armament	2 fixed 7.9mm MG in fuselage
	2 fixed 2cm cannon in upper wing
	200kg light bombs

Fieseler Fi 167

Type	Carrier-borne torpedo reconnaissance bomber
Powerplant	One 1100hp Daimler-Benz 601B
Performance	Max speed 325km/hr
	Cruising speed 270km/hr
	Service ceiling 8200m
	Range 1500km
Weights	Empty 2800kg
	Maximum 4850kg
Dimensions	Span 13.5m, length 11.40m, height 4.8m
Armament	One fixed forward firing 7.92mm MG17
	One flexible rear firing 7.92mm MG15
	One 1000kg bomb or one 765kg torpedo

Junkers Ju 87B

Type	Carrier-borne dive bomber
Powerplant	One 1200hp Jumo 211B Jumo 211Da
Performance	Max speed 340km/hr (at sea level)
	Cruising speed 282km/hr
	Service ceiling 8000m
	Range 790km
Weights	Empty 2710kg
	Maximum 4340kg.
Dimensions	Span 13.8m, length 11.1m, height 4.01m
Armament	2 fixed 7.9mm MG17 in wings
	One flexible 7.9mm MG15 in after cockpit
	500kg of bombs

Ju 87C, the naval version was a modified Ju 87B with slightly higher weights and presumably a little lower performance.

Messerschmitt Bf 109T

Type	Single seat naval fighter
Powerplant	One Daimler Benz DB 601N 1200hp
Performance	Max speed 568km/hr at 6150m
	Cruising speed 483km/hr
	Service ceiling 10,500m
	Range 660km
Weights	Empty 2000kg
	Maximum 2954kg
Dimensions	Span 11.18m, length 10.38m, height 2.6m
Armament	2 × 7.9mm MG17 in fuselage
	2 × 7.9mm MG17 or 2cm cannon in wings

Arado Ar 195

Type	Carrier-borne attack/reconnaissance
Powerplant	One 880hp BMW 132 De radial engine
Performance	Max speed 280km/hr
	Cruising speed 250km/hr
	Service ceiling 6000m
	Range 650km
Weights	Empty 2380kg
	Maximum 3745kg
Dimensions	Span 12.50m, length 10.5m, height 3.6m
Armament	One fixed forward firing 7.9mm MG17
	One flexible rear-firing 7.9mm MG15
	One 800kg torpedo or 500kg bomb

machines were issued for service in Norway, principally with *I Gruppe/Jagdgeschwader 77* where their performance was well suited to the short exposed airstrips typical of that country.

There was only one choice for the bomber role – the Junkers Ju 87 'Stuka', which was to become the standard *Luftwaffe* dive bomber. Entering service with the land-based air force in 1937, the Ju 87 had been sent to Spain for operational testing during the Civil War and had since been honed into a highly effective weapon that was later to symbolise the *Blitzkrieg* of 1939–41. The basis for the naval version was the Ju 87B, modified as the Ju 87C which was fitted with catapult points and manually folding wings. Jettisonable undercarriage facilitated emergency ditching. The pre-production model was designated Ju 87C-0 and the production model JuC-1. In the event the carrier's suspension led to the cancellation of the production order and the majority of the airframes converted to the Ju 7B-2. In 1942, following resumption of work on the ship, a new mark Ju 87E was proposed to combine the tasks of the Ju 87C and Fi 167 but the ship was cancelled again before this version left the drawing board.

Despite the hopes of the *Kriegsmarine* and the grandiose plans of Milch nearly five years earlier, on the outbreak of war in September 1939, only one carrier-borne *grüppe* had formed-*Trägergrüppe 186* at Kiel-Holtenau comprising three *staffeln, 4/186* equipped with Ju 87s, and *5&6/186* with Bf 109s. Nevertheless they *were* available and even if their aircraft were not all fit for sea service, sufficient machines could probably have been scrapped together to send a makeshift *grüppe* to sea. Unfortunately it was the carrier which was missing and in consequence the aircraft were utilised for the land offensive against Poland when the Ju 87s of *4/186* sank the destroyer *Wicher* at Hela on 3 September.

To be continued

The Type II U-boat

By David Westwood

Type IIB U-boats of the 1st U-boat or *Weddigen* Training Flotilla in late 1935. From left to right *U8, U10, U9, U11, U7*. All except *U7* (sunk in collision W of Pillau 18 February 1944) survived World War II only to be scuttled or scrapped afterwards.

When World War II broke out in September 1939, the German Navy possessed 57 U-boats, not all which were operational. Many historians and naval commentators have made much of this total without examining the type and role of the various submarines that made up that figure. In fact 30 of that total were of the Type II class, boats of restricted range (a maximum operational radius of 1500 miles), and limited offensive capability (they carried only five torpedoes or 12 tube-launched mines). However, memories of U-boat warfare in World War I had made other nations in Europe wary of the still new naval weapon, and the effect of prop-aganda and counter-propaganda at the time are still felt today.

John P Holland had designed his original boats at the turn of the century; during World War I developments of his original craft had wrought havoc against Allied and neutral merchant shipping. Germany saw the value of this new weapon, and had used it to great effect, supplementing surface operations, and later surpassing the more traditional methods.

Submarines, before the advent of nuclear power, were no more than submersibles; they were slow, vul-nerable to gunfire, and limited even more when they submerged. But they had one advantage over all their contemporaries – the ability to submerge and so con-ceal themselves. This was the edge they possessed, and in the words of Wilhelm Bauer, Germany's first sub-marine designer, this reduced the battleships to '*Eisen-kolosse*' or simply iron lumps with no future. But the U-boat's strategic role lay not in attacking and sinking warships but in cutting the economic lifeline which stretches some 3000 miles across the Atlantic between Europe and the Americas. It was in this field that the German submarine effort was eventually concentrated in the course of both World Wars, and which nearly cost the Allies the decision – twice.

THE UB II PREDECESSOR

Due to the limitations then inherent in submarine design, the original operational role of these craft had

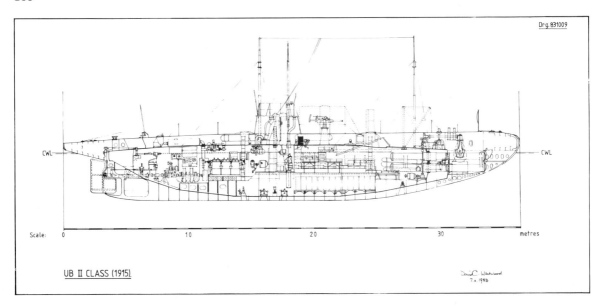

Drg. 831009

CWL   CWL

Scale: 0   10   20   30   metres

UB II CLASS (1915).

been seen as local, coastal patrols, with the occasional foray into enemy patrolled waters to lay ambush to traffic at nodal points, especially the entrances to harbours. The range restrictions of the early boats combined with their limited arament to produce boats of very reduced tactical value. The predecessor of the Type II U-boat was the World War I Type UB II design, ordered and built after the war had started. Its characteristics were typical of a coastal U-boat. In 1915, when the boats began to commission, German Navy submarine operations were being carried out off Flanders and elsewhere in the North Sea, and so the limitations of the boats had no serious effect. Longer range operations in the Atlantic were not then in full swing, and were to be carried out by larger boats, specifically designed for that purpose.

The UB II design was built by two constructors: Blohm & Voss, Hamburg, and A G 'Weser', Bremen. Thirty of the class were built, the first of them (UB 18) commissioning on 11 December 1915. The last of the class was accepted by the German Navy on 4 July 1916. (A comparison between the main characteristics of this class and the later Type II boats will be found at Appendix A). All UB II boats had twin 6-cylinder diesels, two electric motors and 122 battery cells. They were an improvement on the earliest German designs, and had twin hydroplanes fore and aft but they had only single propeller and rudder arrangements.

They were fitted with two 500mm (19.7in) torpedo tubes forward, arranged vertically, to improve the bow line of the boat. Some were also fitted with two lattice torpedo release tubes between tower and deck gun, above the waterline. In this latter case the internal tubes were modified to fire P-mines, of which 14 were carried; this was to allow the U-boat to carry out its secondary task of minelaying. There was also either a 50mm or 88mm gun, forward of the tower. The general

opinion of the boat was that it was adequate for its limited task, but was not a good sea-going vessel.

During the First World War, of the 30 boats of the class 17 were lost to enemy action or other cause off Flanders, 2 were lost elsewhere in the North Sea; 6 were lost in the Mediterranean, and 5 were used solely for training, and scrapped after the war. They did not contribute anything of great importance to the German submarine effort between 1915 and 1918, but served as an example of how quickly a small coastal U-boat could be designed and built. The boats built by Blohm &

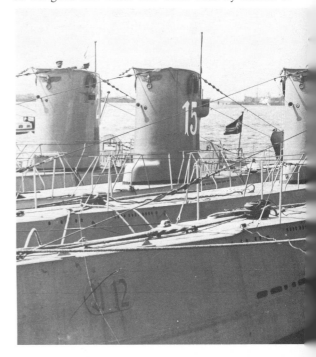

Voss, for example, were laid down and completed as follows:

Boat numbers	Date ordered	Date launched
UB 18 - 23	30.4.15	21.8.15 - 9.10.15
UB 30 - 41	22.7.15	16.11.15 - 6.5.16

(A maximum of ten months from order to launch.) This exercise was to be repeated in the case of the Type II boats 20 years later.

BETWEEN THE WARS

The war lost for Germany, the victorious Allies decided that the losers had to pay for the cost. The Treaty of Versailles was imposed upon Germany. Articles 188, 189 and 191 ruled that Germany was to have no submarines at all, and that any remaining boats were to be delivered to the victors; further, boats already in construction were to be destroyed as they lay. The sword was being turned into the ploughshare with a vengeance. This was further reinforced by the direction that all equipment and machinery formerly used for warship construction was to be converted at once to making trade goods.

The prohibition by the Treaty was total with regard to submarines, and the general effects of it were swinging. There can be little doubt that the Treaty conditions and French insistence that Germany maintain reparation payments, especially as the 1920s drew to a close were factors in the rise and power of Hitler and the Nazi party. Hitler came into power in January 1933; what had the designers and builders of U-boats been doing from 1922 to that date?

What they had not been doing was observing the strict letter of the Versailles Treaty. Although they had not flouted the Treaty openly, for that would have led to confiscations and sanctions, they had conspired to establish a commercial design firm, based in the Hague. Other design work was also done – abroad – particularly by Hans Techel in Kobe (Japan), designs which served as the basis for the later *I 1-3* and *21-24* boats. Interestingly enough, in Germany, it was a request from Argentina that led to the Hague firm being established. The Argentine Government asked the German Navy to design and build ten submarines for them.

The boats were to be built in Argentina, but the designs were to be wholly German, reflecting their importance and experience in the field. Krupp, one of Europe's largest armament manufacturers, was naturally involved, because the colossal conglomerate owned the yards of Germaniawerft at Kiel and A G 'Weser' in Bremen. In concert with the German Navy, Krupp decided that the way to circumvent the Treaty was to set up a commercial submarine design firm. This was *N V Ingenieurskaantor vor Scheepsbouw (IvS)*, established in the Hague under the command of Dr Techel, newly returned from Kobe.

Up to January 1933, *IvS* designed submarines for no fewer than 19 foreign countries, producing plans for 86 boats. Further, they had the satisfaction of seeing nine of these designs launched and commissioned. These were two designs for Turkey; one each for Spain, Sweden, Russia and Rumania, and three designs for Finland (5 boats in all were built).

It is with the last country, Finland, that the most effective work was done, leading to the Type II design.

CV 707 DESIGN FOR FINLAND

Finland first expressed interest in submarines to *IvS* in 1924, needing a design for a 100-ton minelayer. The Finns soon realised that the designed boat was rather small, even for limited operations in Lake Ladoga, so they asked for a larger boat to be brought out. (The small boat was completed and saw service in the Finnish Navy, having the distinction of being the then smallest submarine in service in the world.) But the larger design, CV 707 as it was known to *IvS*, of 250 tons planned displacement, was acceptable both to the Finns and eventually to the newly established *Kriegsmarine*.

The CV 707 was a more practical boat than the smaller *Saukko* (Pr 110 to *Ivs*). She displaced 248/297 tons, and had a range of 1500 miles. (No saddle-tanks were fitted initially, but see below for the incorporation of extra fuel capacity by this means.) Interestingly, her three bow torpedo tubes, now of 533m calibre (21in), were arranged in an 'eyes and mouth' layout, increasing her firepower by 50 per cent over UB II boats, yet retaining a practical bow form. She had clean, attractive lines, and an altogether seaworthy appearance. The three boats Finland commissioned were constructed in

Ten Type II boats in 1935, including *U2, U15, U16, U12, U14, U20* and others of the 'Weddigen' Flotilla with astern of *U14*, their new depot ship *Saar*.
Drüppel/courtesy of M J Whitley

Finnish yards, but under German supervision; needless to say the German Navy kept a close eye on progress, with a view to making the decision whether to use the design if Germany were once more to have a submarine arm.

During the later 1920s and early 1930s the German Navy spent much time evaluating the next submarine family, as well as looking at modern designs for surface ships. Admiral Erich Raeder had been appointed Commander-in-Chief of the Navy in 1928, and his firm view was that Germany, having to build from scratch, would have to have a balanced navy of sufficient strength to enable her to fulfil her continental defensive role at least. Part of that balanced navy would be the submarine arm, and to the officers and technologists of that arm could get experience abroad which would later serve the new arm well. So it was that many of the personnel concerned with submarines, before Germany actually had any, spent a lot of time in Finland (and elsewhere), testing the *Vesikko* (as CV 707) was later named by the Finnish Navy. At this time the Navy became so involved in the commercial enterprise that another camouflaged organisation was established, within the Navy itself, called *Igewit*, which coordinated the efforts of the commercial and military interests.

While CV 707 was building numerous Germans,

apparently retired naval officers, arrived in Finland to observe and take part in the process. Needless to say, they all had official backgrounds, and were there simply to glean all the information they could. The Finnish Government did not seem to mind; indeed, so courteous were they to the German submarine builders that CV 707, launched on 10 May 1933, underwent sea trials under German supervision, and was not handed over to the Finns until 13 January 1936. She saw service from then to the end of Finnish participation in World War II, and is now laid up at Suomenlinna/Sveaborg in Finland.

The tacit approval of this Treaty avoiding activity was not limited to Finland. A similar situation existed in Turkish and Spanish dealings with *IvS*, and therefore indirectly with the German Navy. New political alliances were being formed, and the European treaty map was once more being redrawn. In recognition of this, but paying lip-service to the Versailles Treaty, the German Navy under Raeder planned ahead for the future fleet. The new government under Hitler, and the voting of special powers to it by the Reichstag on 24 March 1933, meant the hope that plans would become reality had a firm chance of realisation.

Raeder wrote after the war that Chancellor von Papen and the new German Government felt that

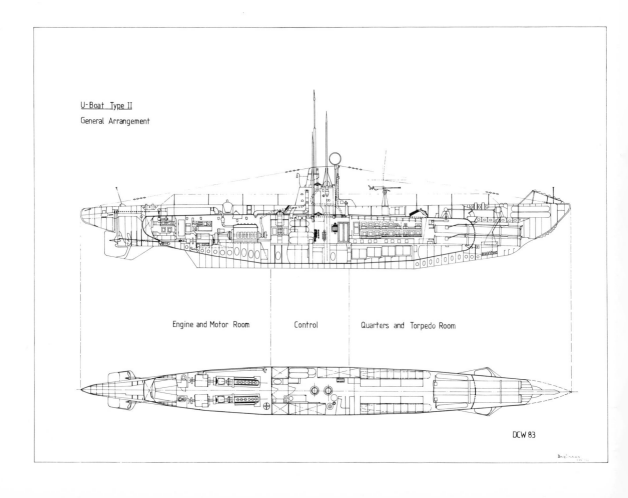

U-Boat Type II
General Arrangement

Engine and Motor Room   Control   Quarters and Torpedo Room

DCW 83

The Type IIB boat *U18* in smart pre-war paintwork at Kiel, rigged for surface running.

Drüppel/courtesy of M J Whitley

'small circumventions of the Versailles Treaty disarmament conditions were entirely permissible in the light of the international situation'. But the main problem lay with the attitudes of the supervising powers (Great Britain, France, Italy and Russia) rearmament on a scale far beyond the needs of defence, and especially the possession by Germany of a modern navy and the specifically prohibited U-boats. To free Germany from the restrictions of that Treaty in one unilateral move was not then politically possible, but the Germans felt that if they could convince Great Britain that they did not want parity with the Royal Navy, but would in fact impose limitations upon themselves as to the size and composition of the *Kriegsmarine,* then they might escape the shackles of Versailles by steps.

The Anglo-German Naval Treaty was, from start to finish, merely a discussion on how to present the German proposals to the world. Von Ribbentrop and his envoys opened the conference with the Foreign Office and Admiralty representatives by saying that if the British did not agree to Germany having 35 per cent of the tonnage of the Royal Navy except submarines, where they were to have 45 per cent, they were under instructions to return to Germany. The conference eventually endorsed the German proposal, as well as the further proviso that should Germany ask, the British were bound to agree to an increase in submarine tonnage to parity with the Royal Navy. This London Naval Agreement was signed in 1935, and the London Submarine Agreement (governing the conduct of submarine warfare) just over a year later. But it was the 1935 Treaty that gave Germany the *de jure* right to disregard the terms of the Versailles Treaty, and to build and commission submarines once more.

Raeder was against war with England. He said in his autobiography that in the First World War 'it was British and American seapower that brought us to our knees despite the great victories on land and the Russian breakdown' and his pre-war aim was that 'Such a situation should never be allowed to recur'. He intended, above all, to avoid conflict with Great Britain, and to build a new, ultra-modern navy that would be able to hold out against the navies of Germany's neighbours to the west and east – France and Poland.

TYPE II EMERGES

This permission to re-enter the submarine field did not, of course, surprise the German Navy, especially the so-called Anti-Submarine School (cover name for the embryo submarine arm). Once the 1935 Treaty had been signed, Germany immediately went ahead with the final construction of the U-boats that had been ordered months before the meetings in London took place. The first boats ordered and built for the new navy were of the Type II Class, designed on the basis of the UB II, and modified and improved by the experience gained in Finland through *IvS*. At the same time Type IA and early versions of the Type VII boats were also under construction.

Raeder now planned to get as many Type II boats into service as he could (within the agreed tonnage), and in the shortest possible time. The simplicity of the boats, and past experience helped, and he had a training flotilla and a service flotilla established before the end of 1935. The man he chose to command the 1st (*Weddigen*) U-boat Flotilla (and then the whole submarine service) was Captain Karl Dönitz.

The Type II was really no more than a refined version of the CV 707 design, and the first of the class *UI* was launched on 15 June 1935, and commissioned only 14 days later. Together with *U2-6* she went to the 1st Training Flotilla to form the basis of this new German U-boat Arm. By 28 September of that year the 1st U-boat Flotilla became reality, for *U7-9* arrived at their base, soon to be followed by another nine boats, *U10-18*.

As Dönitz wrote, after the war, the boat was 'A very simple and successful vessel, but very small'. As can be seen from the plans, the boat was little larger than the UB II design. But the reduced displacement of these boats meant that more of them could be built within the tonnage permitted by the London Naval Agreement than could be built of the larger 500- and 750-ton vessels. It also meant that the U-boat Arm would achieve a high strength in units, even if not in actual fighting power.

In all there were four versions of the Type II. The first, Type IIA, was the basis for development, and was like the initial *Vesikko* in having no saddle-tanks. This was modified in the other three versions of the Class (Types IIB, C and D), and the range of the boats was ultimately increased to 5650 miles. The operational area foreseen for these boats was the Baltic, the North Sea and the French waters of the English Channel. It had no future in the Atlantic, and indeed at the time there seemed no prospect for U-boat employment there anyway. The boats therefore, with their limits in range and firepower seemed insignificant to the British, providing no threat to the Royal Navy, especially as developments in Asdic seemed to reduce the submarine to impotence.

The most important function these boats were to perform was in fact not in the operational, but in the training sphere. Each Type II could be used to train crew after crew of new submariners for the German Navy, who would then progress to conversion courses on the larger Type IA, VII and IX U-boats. As early as 1936 Dönitz had realised that the Type II was 'too weak as regards armament, radius of action and speed'; equally disturbing was the fact that the Type IA was not coming up to expectations either, having an alarming tendency to go for the bottom, no matter what steering orders were passed. However, the Type II building programme continued, for the training function was essential in any event. Slowly U-boat tonnage approached the allowed tonnage under the Anglo-German Naval Agreement.

The class was built in fact until the last two boats were launched in January 1941 (*U151* and *152*), but by then it was obvious that the strategic naval battle was being fought far beyond the range of these little boats. In all three builders (Deutsche Werke and Germaniawerft at Kiel, and Flender-Werft of Lübeck) launched 50 Type II boats. Some were operational in the early part of the war, others renewed their opeational careers after a spell training in the Baltic, but the majority remained there, forming the training flotillas of the U-boat Training Units throughout the war. There were still Type II boats to be scuttled after the German capitulation in 1945, so the little boats made a contribution above the average.

CHARACTERISTICS

In the 90ft of the pressure hull there had to be squeezed three officers and 25 men, stores and consumables for up to three weeks on patrol. The hull already had two 6-cylinder MWM diesels and two SSW electric motors. To fuel the diesels there were nearly 12 tons of diesel oil inboard, as well as 62 battery cells beneath the forward compartment to provide underwater power for the electric motors. Two reserve torpedoes (or a number of mines) also had to be fitted in. There was little, if any, spare room in the boat.

There were three main compartments, with watertight doors and bulkheads between them. The forward compartment combined torpedo room, crew's quarters and battery space. Aft lay the control room and the attack centre (located in the tower above the control room). There the officers had their quarters, along with the boat's main controls and the radio room. Finally in the stern was the diesel electric room, housing engines and motors, gearing, shafts and electrical controls, and a minute machine-shop.

Externally the boats had a very low silhouette making the vessels almost invisible at night. The saddle-tanks broadened the hull overall cross-sections, but did not affect performance greatly. The design was undoubtedly suited to short-range patrol work in inshore waters and inland waters; nevertheless in the last days of peace some of the boats were stationed as sea well outside their intended operational areas. The shortages in numbers of the German Navy were critically obvious in the last quarter of 1939. The Type II boats were, then, up to the eve of war, 'political' boats in the sense that they increased numbers, but their fighting capacity was not that great. But they did serve as the backbone of the training side of the U-boat Arm for many years, and made a very important contribution to the eventual effectiveness of Dönitz's force when the Battle of the Atlantic began in earnest.

Two Type II boats stripped and pontooned for transit (their port and centre line torpedo tubes show to advantage) to the Black Sea in 1942. The lefthand boat is believed to be *U9* whilst the other is probably *U24*. Alongside is a third boat with camouflage screening above the hull, whose identity is uncertain. She does not appear to by a Type II and is possibly a captured enemy boat (the shape of her stern is distinctive).
Drüppel/courtesy of M J Whitley

Japanese 'Kaibokan' Escorts Part 2

By Hans Lengerer and Tomoko Rehm-Takahara

TYPE A, ETOROFU CLASS

More than four years passed before coast defence ships were again included in a building programme. At the liaison conference between the government and the Imperial Headquarters on 2 July 1941 the 'fundamentals of a national policy for the Japanese Empire in consideration of the altered situation' was agreed; this document emphasised strongly the need to push towards the South, and the inevitability of a war with the USA and Britain. In pursuance of this policy, and in recognition of Japan's great inferiority compared with the potential of the USA, the Navy decided to accelerate war production. As early as 15 August 1941 the complete execution of the 'emergency preparation programme' *(Shusshi junbi keikaku)* was decided. Even before that, on 28 July 1941, the 'rapid warship building programme for 1941' *(Showa 16 nendo senji kyuzo kansen senzo keikaku)* had been pushed through as part of this programme. This programme, known as the 'most urgent programme' *(Maru kyu keikaku)*, was aimed at strengthening the numbers of ships designed for defensive duties. It provided for the construction of 288 ships (actually 326, as the supplementary programme also officially belonged to the *Maru kyu keikaku*; among that number were 30 *Kaibokan*, with

Etorofu in May 1943.

CPL

building numbers 310–339. Fourteen units were to be Type A of 860 tons, and 16 ships to be Type B of 940 tons standard displacement, although in the budget all 30 ships were again stated to be of 1200 tons standard displacement; they were to cost 5,112,000 Yen (£513,756) per ship, or 153,360,000 Yen (£1,610,280) in total, 4260 Yen (£451) per ton.

When we consider that at this time Japan only possessed four ships of the *Shimushu* class for escort duties (the destroyers were intended for screening heavy ships) a figure of 30 *Kaibokan* appears to be more than a slight miscalculation: this figure exposes the total ignorance about the need to protect merchant shipping during a war. The Admiralty staff simply failed to recognise the significance of the escort ship, although the battle in the Atlantic made its importance quite obvious.

Although the Type A ships (*Etorofu* class) were allotted the primary role of convoy escort, and the secondary task of minesweeping, the Admiralty staff again demanded only 19.7 knots as top speed, three 120mm (4.7in) guns and one depth-charge thrower. Defence against aircraft and effective anti-submarine work could not be achieved with this armament.

In order not to delay the start of work on the 14 ships, the plans of the *Shimushu* class were adopted and

The Type A *Etorofu* class Kaibokan *Oki* leaving Uraga for final trials on 25 March 1943.

Author's collection

altered only slightly in spite of their complicated structure, which was not suitable for wartime mass-production. For this reason *Etorofu* class ships exhibited scarcely any differences from their predecessors. The alteration of the plans (basic planning number E 19) principally concerned simplification of the bow area, the stern, and the superstructure. The main dimensions were virtually identical, except that the overall length was shortened by 0.30m, due to the new bow shape, and the stardard displacement was increased by 10 tons to 870 tons at the same trials displacement.

The differences from the *Shimushu* class were as follows:

1 The bow was altered to a straight stem with a small overhang. The steel cables of the paravane gear were no longer led through holes in the fore foot, as on the *Shimushu* class, but were routed in roughly the same way as in German warships. The Japanese Navy decided to do this for the first time, because this design, in which the cables were held in outriggers at a predetermined depth, fixed at the bow and projecting out in the line of travel, was simpler.

2 The bridge no longer projected forward over the lower structure. The cladding consisted of thin steel plates, which protected the crew from machine gun and light machine cannon fire. The open rear extension of the bridge was extended to the forward tripod mast, which was connected to the lower structure by means of supports.

3 The ships completed by about June 1943 had the same forward tripod mast as on the *Shimushu* class, but on later ships it ended just above the 3m (9ft 10in) rangefinder in a platform, on which the aerial of a Type 22 radar was mounted. The topmast now only carried two yards.

4 The radio direction finder was fitted on the searchlight platform behind the searchlight.

5 The upper part of the funnel was no longer tapered, but had the same cross-section over its whole height.

6 The tripod mainmast was longer.

7 The stern was no longer raked aft but straight.

8 Instead of a semi-balanced rudder, a fully balanced rudder was used, and the shape of the stern underwater was simplified. This measure, in conjunction with the altered stern shape, reduced the turning circle and increased the speed.[7]

9 Instead of 18 depth charges, 36 of the Model 95 charges were carried.

10 The anti-submarine electronics consisted of a Model 93 sonar and a Model 93 hydrophone.[8]

Although minesweeping remained part of the ships' duties as before, some of the ships were only equipped with two paravanes, because of the increase in depth charge load to 60 units, which was decided on during the building period. The AA weapons were strengthened and radar fitted as on the *Shimushu* class. On a few ships, however, the number and position of the AA weapons differed somewhat from the standard equipment after the Battle of the Philippine Sea (five triple 25mm); for example, *Kanju* had only two 120mm AA guns in single mounts, but 21 25mm machine guns (5 triples, 2 twins, 2 single mounts) to compensate.

As a result of the simplified design, the building time for the hull was reduced to 70,000 man-days. Even after these alterations the ships were by no means suitable for mass-production and the building time was too long for the hopes of the naval design office to be realised. Moreoever, actual war experience made it clear that a specialist escort ship had to be more closely matched to her tasks in terms of armament and equipment. These considerations led to the suspension of building work.

The *Etorofu* class comprised 14 ships, begun between February 1942 and August 1943, and completed between March 1943 and February 1944. During the war eight of them were sunk.

TYPE B, MIKURA CLASS

Together with the 14 ships of the *Etorofu* class, 16 ships of a new class of *Kaibokan* were included in the 'urgent war programme'. The Admiralty staff demanded for the first time an adequate AA and ASW armament:
1 120mm AA as main armament.
2 Two sonar units and 2 hydrophones.
3 Four depth charge throwers and 120 depth charges.
4 One pair of large minesweeping devices (*Tankan shiki sokaigu*).
5 Speed of 19.7 knots.
6 Range of 5000 miles at 16 knots.

Planning of this type was begun at the beginning of 1942. At first it was intended to be a completely new design, but after further studies it was decided to adopt the *Etorofu* class hull, although in somewhat simplified form, to save time. The principle was to alter neither the displacement[9] nor the shape, but to undertake any possible simplifications in hull construction, because the ships were now to be used exclusively as escort vessels, and no longer as guardships for the North Pacific. In addition, the armament was to be matched more closely to the ships' intended role. The design drawings were therefore completed in a relatively short time (basic planning number E 20), and the ships of the *Etorofu* and *Mikura* classes were built alongside each other.

The differences compares with the *Etorofu* class consisted basically of structural simplifications and alterations of the armaments and equipment.
1 The reinforcement of the hull along the waterline was dropped.
2 Instead of the double floor, the plate thickness was increased, the joints between plates mostly welded, and

an electric welding process was used for the bulkheads and frames.
3 The oil-fired auxiliary boilers were not installed, as the ships were no longer intended for use in the North Pacific.
4 Accommodation, especially the officers' quarters, was considerably simplified; this could be done because by this time the coast defence ships were no longer rated as major warships. The number of scuttles in the area of the lower deck was also reduced as a result of battle experience.
5 While the *Etorofu* and *Shimushu* classes could be said to have a box-type bridge (with some limitations), the form of the *Mikura* class was closer to the form of a stepped bridge, with the front part projecting as far as the forecastle deck, and a high bulwark around the 3m range finder.
6 The superstructure deck was no longer full-length, but divided into two deckhouses.
7 The tripod foremast was the same shape as *Etorofu* class ships completed after about June 1943. The legs had a less severe rake, while the platform carrying the Type 22 radar unit aerial was slightly different, and the method of fixing of the topmast and its rake were slightly different.
8 The radio direction finder was set up in front of the searchlight on the deckhouse.
9 The 75cm searchlight was located on a small, round structure on the deckhouse.
10 The engine rooms and the funnel were moved further aft. The funnel was narrower and thinner, and the galley funnel was led upwards along the forward side.
11 The tripod mainmast was moved further aft, was longer, and upright. The relative distance between the masts was slightly increased by this alteration.
12 The fuel supply was reduced from 200 to 120 tons, with a corresponding drop in range from 8000 miles to 5000 miles at the same speed of 16 knots.
13 Instead of the three 120mm low angle guns in type G mounts, three 120mm/45 AA of the Year 10 model

The Type B *Mikura* at Tsurumi, Yokohoma as completed at the end of October 1943. She had Type 22 radar on her mainmast and high angle 120mm guns.

(10 nendo shiki) were installed. A single mount with shield was located on the forecastle abaft the breakwater as on previous types, while a twin mount without shield was fitted on the quarterdeck.

14 The depth charge load was increased to 120, and the storage rooms in the aftership were arranged below the lower deck. Two Model 94 depth charge throwers with Model 3 loading frames were fitted, along with two depth charge launchers at the stern. The three depth charge launchers situated on either side of the earlier types were omitted. The stern was lengthened by 1.07m (3ft 5in) to fit the larger depth charge rooms.

15 Large minesweeping gear was fitted on a bulge in front of the depth charge launchers on each side. The number of small minesweeping devices (paravanes) was reduced to two. They were again fixed in supports on either side of the superstructure abreast the funnel.

16 The anti-submarine and radar equipment was given due consideration from the outset, and all ships had at least one Model 93 sonar unit when completed, along with one Model 93 hydrophone and one Type 22 radar unit. The newly developed sonar Model 3 type 2 was fitted to the *Chiburi* first in early 1944[10] (the first Japanese ship to be so equipped).

17 The 6m (20ft) motor boat to starboard, previously fitted behind the 6m cutter, was omitted.

Overall, the *Mikura* class differed markedly from its predecessors, and was in many respects a completely different design. While the *Shimushu* and *Etorofu* classes retained much of the character of a gunboat, this type, with reservation, can be said to be the first real escort vessel fully equipped in terms of armament and equipment for ASW and AA work. The fact that they still retained the substantial minesweeping gear at the stern, as on the minesweepers, is proof, however, that the Admiralty staff had still not abandoned the idea of using these ships for minesweeping, and they had once more allotted to the ships a task which was extraneous to their design. The fitting of 2 depth-charge throwers was not exactly adequate for sinking submarines, and even the AA armament, and especially the light AA (four 25mm machine guns in two twin mounts), was inadequate, and the lack of air warning was a further weak point.

As a result of the simplifications listed above, the building time of the hull was reduced from 70,000 to 57,000 man-days. In spite of the saving of virtually 20 per cent, the building time was still considered to be too long and the design too complex, as the war situation was demanding more and more escort vessels. This fact, together with the weaknesses in equipment and armament, led to the Modified Type B. By this time eight ships[11] had been built; they had been started between October 1942 and September 1943, and completed between October 1943 and May 1944. The new type was the *Ukuru* class, whose thorough-going simplification was planned by all the yards working in cooperation.

Soon after the ships were commissioned a general increase in the AA weapons was carried out; the ships were fitted with ten 25mm machine guns (three triple,

one single mount), and thus possessed a total of 14 machine guns. Some ships, which were selected for special duties (submarine hunting groups), were fitted with four additional 25mm machine guns in single mounts. The tripod mainmast, on which the antenna of the (Type 13) air search radar was fitted as of autumn 1944, had to give way to the third triple: it was relocated about 3m farther forward. The arrangement of the machine guns differed only slightly from that of the earlier ships: two twin mounts fitted on platforms on both sides of the bridge: two triples on platforms abreast the funnel; the third triple on the centreline at the rear end of the deck superstructure; the single mount in front of the bridge. On a platform forward of and slightly below this was an 80mm trench mortar. At the stern a Model 94 depth charge thrower and one Model 3 loading frame were added. The new Model 2 (1942) type of depth charge was used from this time onward. Several ships were fitted additionally with the new sonar model 3 type 2. Towards the end of the war the large minesweeping equipment on the quarterdeck was removed.

The *Mikura* class comprised eight ships, five of which were sunk during the war.

MODIFIED TYPE B, UKURU CLASS

During the battles for Guadalcanal, which lasted roughly six months, (August 1942 – February 1943) the Japanese Navy lost many small warships, and the losses among merchant ships also increased greatly. The only means of reversing the trend was to mass-produce escort vessels, in order to patrol the main shipping routes, and to protect the convoys. Early in 1943 the Japanese Navy decided to mass-produce the coast defence ships. With the *Mikura* class as the starting point, a new ship was designed under the basic planning number E 20 B; she differed extensively from the Type B, principally in her hull lines, her equipment and the design and production methods – this was the *Ukuru* class. Basically the ships were a modified and simplified form of the *Mikura* class in which the ASW and AA armament had been strengthened, and the structure of the hull simplified as far as possible.

To this end, studies were made of the absolute simplifications that had been carried out since the end of 1942 in merchant shipbuilding and which were to be introduced for the first time in warship building. Although the alterations to the design plans were completed in less than 2 months (April to end of May 1943), and all possible simplifications were included, the first ship, the *Hiburi*, completed on 27 June 1944, nevertheless gave very satisfactory results, and even the speed hardly suffered compared with the *Mikura* class. Indeed, a greater loss of speed had not been expected, in spite of the considerable doubts which had been expressed initially, as the Technical Research Office *(Gijutsu kenkyusho)* had found by experiments involving model ships that there would be hardly any increase in drag even with simplified shapes and at maximum speed (if the same block coefficient as on the earlier ships were retained). At cruising speed the drag was increased by 5 per cent. This shape of hull was also used on the Type D destroyers (*Matsu* class and especially *Tachibana* class) and the first class transports *(Itto Yusokan)* as well as the coast defence ships of Types C and D.

The differences between Type B, the *Mikura* class, and the modified Type B, the *Ukuru* class, were essentially as follows:

1 In order to permit construction of the ships in sections, the shape of the hull was simplified as far as the limits of practicality allowed. The aim was to minimise the use of shaped steel, of which there was already a shortage, and curved plates, and to use those shapes and material thicknesses which were already used in the construction of the standard merchant ships being built. Instead of the rivetted joints used until then, welding was to be extended even to those joints which provided the basic strength of the hull. The increase in the straight and flat, the reduction of the curved, and the virtually complete omission of double-curvature plates (horizontal and vertical), resulted in ribs which were (almost exclusively) either straight or had a single change of direction. The hull consisted now of just flat plates, and single-curved plates joined to them. The time-consuming work of making cast components and forming sheets was considerably reduced.

The adoption of the simplified ship's form dispensed with the overhanging stem of the bow, which became instead a straight definite bow. The forward frames were no longer curved, but entirely straight. The slight change of sheer at the forecastle also began with a

A Type B Mikura class Kaibokan in May 1945(?).

Author's collection

sharp angle, which was the typical solution to the direct joining of sheets at different angles. The area where the forecastle deck sheer strake had previously curved gently to meet the deck plates was made perfectly straight, in spite of the potential tension problem, thus producing a further sharp angle between deck and outer plating. The camber of the forecastle deck disappeared; it was made quite flat. The disadvantage of this design was that the water could no longer run off adequately. The odd-looking angle at the step-down of the deck was omitted, the hull sides being flat. The bow lines were fuller, while the transition from the stem to the keel was a simple angle. The earlier elliptical shape of the stern was replaced by a transom stern. The reduction in performance, which in fact was hardly apparent, and the reduced durability, were expected to some extent. Also, bearing in mind the size and fitting out of various compartments, disadvantages and inconveniences had to be accepted, in order to allow more rapid construction.

The officers' and crew's quarters was again simplified, and the single cabins for the officers were replaced by communal areas. These measures did indeed achieve shorter building times and savings in materials, but their effect on operational capability and morale were a major drawback. By contrast with British and American escort ships, habitability was considered a side issue, and from this class onward was terribly neglected. In addition the protective measures against an outbreak of fire or the spreading of fire into other areas of the ship were greatly increased, and as these measures resulted in very spartan crew compartments the ships' endurance was limited compared with Allied escorts.

2 The form of the bridge was also altered to allow rapid building. The cross-section was hexagonal, and there were no more rounded shapes.

3 The lookout post, or crow's nest, on the topmast of the forward tripod mast, was omitted.

4 The tripod mainmast was arranged in such as way that a 25mm triple could be installed on the deck superstructure behind it.

5 The superstructure was lengthened.

6 The funnel was no longer round or oval, but hexagonal.

7 The three 120mm AA guns (1 twin, 1 single mount) were arranged as on the *Mikura* class in 'A' and 'Y' positions. The difference was just that the ships of the earlier phase, which were laid down up to about June 1944, had the same protective shield as the *Mikura* class on the forward mounting, while the others had a modified version of new shape.

8 The ships were fitted with five 25mm triple gun mounts, which were installed as on the *Mikura* class after the alteration in armament. The AA bandstands at the bridge position and abreast the funnel were no longer supported by three narrow stanchions, but by a single, broad, pierced support. The single AA gun in front of the bridge, and the 80mm trench mortar were also built in at the same time. Some of the ships were later fitted with a further four 25mm machine guns in single mounts, which were set up on the forecastle.

9 The nine ships built by the Hitachi shipbuilding company, based in Sakurajima, and which have already been mentioned in connection with the *Mikura* class[11], were fitted with three Model 94 depth-charge throwers, three Model 3 loading frames, two depth-charge rails,

one pair of large minesweeping devices, and one pair of paravanes.

On the remaining ships this equipment was omitted entirely, and they were fitted instead with 16 Model 3 depth charge throwers (1943)[12].

After completion most ships had the minesweeping equipment removed.

10 From the outset the foremast platform was designed to take the aerial for the Type 22 radar unit, while the aerial for the Type 13 was installed either to the front, to the side, or to the rear of the mainmast after completion.

11 The underwater locating equipment consisted of a sound navigation and ranging unit (Sonar) Type 93 – on later ships this was changed for two Type 3 Model 2 Sonar units – and an underwater listening unit (hydrophone) Type 93.

12 The number of generators was reduced from 3 to 2.

This simplified design was applied to the Type A vessels approved in the Urgent War Programme of 1941, but only to those ships which had not yet been started. This double alteration in the design plans explains the confusion in the building numbers in the Programme mentioned above concerning the ships of the *Etorofu*, *Mikura* and *Ukuru* classes. In total 29 ships of the improved Type B ships were built together with those approved in later programmes. Four were uncompleted at the end of the war, and 20 were cancelled.

On average four months were required to build each ship. The hull form, greatly simplified compared with conventional shapes, and the use of sectional building methods, reduced the required man-days to 42,000.

TABLE 6: CLASS TECHNICAL DETAILS

	Etorofu	*Mikura*	*Ukuru*
Basic Planning number	E 19	E 20	E 20 B
Building number	310	320	332
Standard displacement	870 tons		940 tons
Trial displacement		1020 tons	
Length between perpendiculars		75.2m/237ft 11in	
Waterline length	76.2m/250ft	77.5m/254ft 4in	76.5m/251ft
Overall length	77.7m/255ft		78.7m/258ft 5in
Waterline beam		9.1m/29ft 10in	
Side height		5.3m/17ft 5in	5.34m/17ft 5in
Average draught	3.05m/10ft		
Machinery	2 No 22 type 10 diesels ((4200bhp))	as *Etorofu*	
Speed	19.7kts		19.5kts
No of propellers and rpm	2 × 510rpm		2 × 510rpm
Fuel	207 tons		120 tons
Range	8000nm/16kts		5000nm/16kts
Armament	3 × 12cm	3 × 12cm (1×2, 1×1)	as *Mikura* except
	4 × 25mm (2×2)	4 × 25mm (2×2)	6 × 25mm (2×2)
	36 Mod 95 depth charges	120 Mod 95 depth charges	
	Mod 94 thrower	2 Mod 94 throwers	
	Mod 3 loading frame	2 Mod 3 loading frame	16 Mod 3 loading frame
Additional armament	as *Shimushu* class	10 × 25mm	
		8cm army mortar	
Sensors	radar as *Shimushu* class plus Mod E 27 radar intercept receiver (all classes) on tripod mast		
	behind bridge		
	Mod 93 sonar	Mod 93 sonar (2 Type	
	Mod 93 hydrophone	2 after April 1944	
		all classes)	
		Mod 93 hydrophone	
Crew (according to budget)	147	150	

TABLE 7: CLASS OUTLINES

5	310	*Etorofu*	Hitachi, Sakurajima	23.2.42	29.1.43	15.5.43
6	311	*Matsuwa*	Mitsui, Tamano	20.4.42	13.11.42	23.3.43
7	312	*Sado*	Tsurumi	21.2.42	28.11.42	27.3.43
8	313	*Oki*	Uraga Dock	27.2.42	20.10.42	28.3.43
9	314	*Mutsura*	Hitachi, Sakurajima	25.7.42	10.4.43	31.7.43
10	315	*Iki*	Mitsui, Tamano	2.5.42	5.2.43	31.5.43
11	316	*Tsushima*	Tsurumi	20.6.42	20.3.43	28.7.43
12	317	*Wakamiya*	Mitsui, Tamano	16.7.42	19.4.43	10.8.43
13	318	*Hirado*	Hitachi, Sakurajima	2.11.42	30.6.43	28.9.43
14	319	*Fukue*	Uraga Dock	30.10.43	2.4.43	28.6.43
15	321	*Amakusa*	Hitachi, Sakurajima	5.4.43	31.9.43	20.11.43
16	323	*Monju*	Mitsui, Tamano	15.2.43	31.7.43	30.11.43
17	325	*Kanju*	Uraga Dock	8.4.43	7.8.43	30.10.43
18	330	*Kasado*	Uraga Dock	10.8.43	9.12.43	27.2.44
19	320	*Mikura*	Tsurumi	1.10.42	16.7.43	31.10.43
20	322	*Miyake*	Tsurumi	22.2.43	30.8.43	30.11.43
21	329	*Awaji*	Hitachi, Sakurajima	1.6.43	30.10.43	25.1.44
22	326	*Nami*	Hitachi, Sakurajima	10.8.43	3.12.43	28.2.44
23	327	*Kurahashi*	Tsurumi	1.6.43	15.10.43	19.2.44
24	328	*Yashiro*	Hitachi, Sakurajima	18.11.43	16.2.44	10.5.44
25	329	*Chiburi*	Tsurumi	20.7.43	30.11.43	3.4.44
26	334	*Kusagaki*	Tsurumi	7.9.43	22.1.44	31.5.44
27	331	*Hiburi*	Hitachi, Sakurajima	3.1.44	10.4.44	27.6.44
28	332	*Ukuru*	Tsurumi	9.10.43	15.5.44	31.7.44
29	333	*Daito*	Hitachi, Sakurajima	17.4.44	24.6.44	7.8.44
30	335	*Okinawa*	Tsurumi	10.12.43	19.6.44	16.8.44
31	336	*Amami*	Tsurumi	14.2.44	13.11.44	8.4.45
32	337	*Aguni*	Tsurumi	5.2.44	21.9.44	2.12.44
33	338	*Shinnan*	Uraga Dock	24.5.44	5.9.44	21.10.44
37	339	*Shonan*	Hitachi, Sakurajima	23.2.44	19.5.44	13.7.44
35	5251	*Yaku*	Uraga Dock	24.5.44	5.9.44	23.10.44
36	5252	*Kume*	Hitachi, Sakurajima	26.5.44	15.8.44	25.9.44
37	5253	*Chikubu*	Uraga Dock	8.9.44	24.11.44	31.12.44
38	5254	*Ikuna*	Hitachi, Sakurajima	30.6.44	4.9.44	15.10.44
39	5255	*Kozu*	Uraga Dock	20.10.44	31.12.44	7.2.45
40	5256	*Hotaka*	Uraga Dock	27.11.44	28.1.45	30.3.45
41	5257	*Shisaka*	Hitachi, Sakurajima	21.8.44	31.10.44	15.12.44
42	5258	*Ikara*	Uraga Dock	26.12.44	22.2.45	30.4.45
43	5259	*Sakito*	Hitachi, Sakurajima	7.9.44	29.11.44	10.1.45
44	5260	*Ikino*	Uraga Dock	3.1.45	11.3.45	17.7.45
45	5262	*Mokuto*	Hitachi, Sakurajima	5.11.44	7.1.45	19.2.45
46	5264	*Habuto*	Hitachi, Sakurajima	3.12.44	28.2.45	7.4.45
47	4701	*Inagi*	Mitsui, Tamano	15.5.44	25.5.44	16.12.44
48	4702	*Habushi*	Mitsui, Tamano	20.8.44	20.11.44	10.1.45
49	4703	*Ojika* ex *Oga*	Mitsui, Tamano	7.9.44	30.12.44	21.2.45
50	4704	*Kanawa*	Mitsui, Tamano	15.11.44	20.1.45	15.3.45
51	4705	*Uku*	Marinearsenal, Sasebo	1.8.44	19.11.44	25.1.45
52	4707	*Takane*	Mitsui, Tamano	15.12.44	13.2.45	26.4.45
53	4709	*Kuga*	Marinearsenal, Sasebo	1.8.44	19.11.44	25.1.45
54	4711	*Shiga*	Marinearsenal, Sasebo	25.11.44	9.2.45	20.3.45
55	4712	*Io*	Marinearsenal, Sasebo	25.11.44	12.2.45	24.3.45

Note: Fates follow on p180.

However, efforts continued to reduce this time to 30,000 once the yards had gained some experience.

The desired number of ships was not achieved. The reasons were as follows: First, the emphasis was switched to Types C and D; and second, there were problems with the main engines, since diesels simply could not be built fast enough.

Towards the end of the war this type was used as a command ship for Type C and D vessels.

During the war seven ships were sunk. The remainder were used almost exclusively for minesweeping and repatriation duties, and thereafter were distributed among the Allies as spoils of war. Five ships were passed to the hydrographic office as weather stations and survey ships; later they were also used for patrol duties and remained on the effective list until 1966. One ship, the *Kojima* (ex-CD *Shiga*), was given to the town of Chiba, where she still serves the population of the Inage area.

NOTES
7 The power of the diesel engines on the *Shimushu* class was raised to 4500bhp (3310kW) by raising the revolutions. On the *Etorofu* class the same diesels (Model 10 Nr 22) produced 4200bhp (3089kW) at 510rpm. The top speed remained the same, nevertheless.
8 Hydrophones are passive locating devices, ie listening systems, which register sounds which are detected in the water (shaft, propeller, engine noises, etc). They can be used to indicate the direction only, and not the range. The Model 93 (1933)

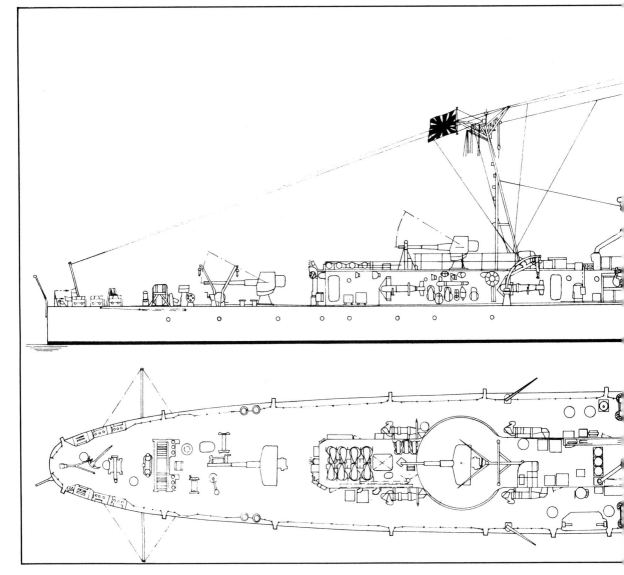

Sketch 3 Type A, *Etorofu* class: *Iki* after completion (June 1943). Very similar to the *Shimushu* class when completed, but with command bridge extended farther forward, different bow shape, some ships with tapered funnel etc.

hydrophone had 15 microphones, which were attached close to the bow in the form of an ellipse. If the speed of the submerged submarine was 3kts, the system's performance was as shown in the table:

Own speed (kts)	Kagero	Hatsutsuki	Shimakaze	Arashi
0				5500 (5)
6		5000 (3)		
8	3200 (1)			
12	1400 (3)	2600 (3)	6000 (3)	4000 (5)
14	1000 (1)	2000 (3)		
18				3000 (5)
20				2000 (5)
22			4000	

Note: All distance figures in m. Figures in brackets indicate the variation in direction in degrees.

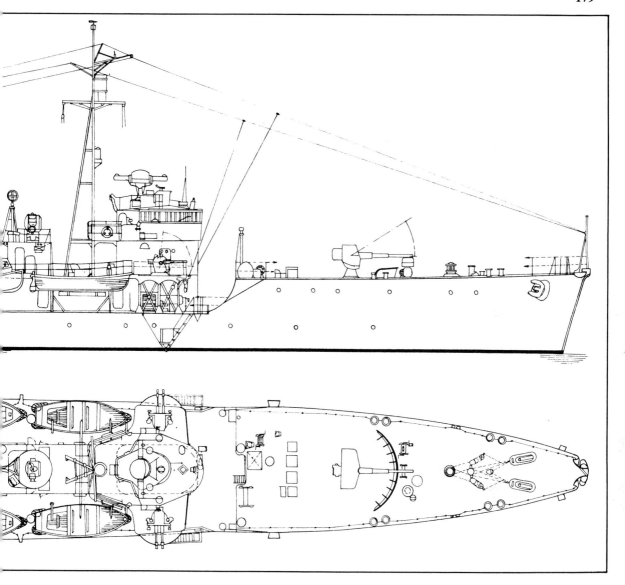

9 Although the standard displacement rose by 70 tons to 940 tons, the increase was almost entirely the result of increased equipment and alterations to the armament.

10 The performance of the Model 3 Type 2 Sonar *(3 Shiki 2 gata suichi tanshingi)* was, in the example of *Hiburi*, (a ship of the *Ukuru* class), as follows (pertaining to a submarine travelling submerged at 3 knots):

Own speed (kts)	Range (m)	Submarine's depth
10	3500	30
	3000	60
14	2500	30
	1200	60
16	1000	

11 In this text only *Mikura, Miyake, Awaji, Nomi, Kurahashi, Yashiro, Chiburi Kusagaki* are included as *Mikura* class. Officially, however, the ships *Hiburi, Daito, Shonan* (urgent war programme), *Kume, Ikuna, Shisaka, Sakito, Mokuto, Habuto* (modified fifth programme), built by the Hitachi shipbuilding AG at the Sakurajima yard, and also the ships *Otsu* and *Tomoshiri*, which were not finished at the end of the war, were also classed as *Mikura* class. The reason for this lies exclusively in their minesweeping devices, and the use of depth-charge throwers and loading frames of the *Mikura* class. As far as the hull was concerned, they were identical to the *Ukuru* class, and hence it seems more appropriate to class them as such.

12 The Model 3 depth-charge launcher was a device intended especially for coast defence ships. The special feature was that half of the firing tube lay below the upper deck, which considerably simplified the loading process. The installation was admittedly rather complex. The total weight was 370kg, the firing tube was inclined outwards at an angle of 50°. The performance was the same as that of the Model 94. The depth-charges were brought from the storage compartments onto the loading ramp with a dredging lift; the slow rate of hoisting using the manually-operated davits was thereby eliminated. In front of the loading ramp they could either be thrown over the rollers

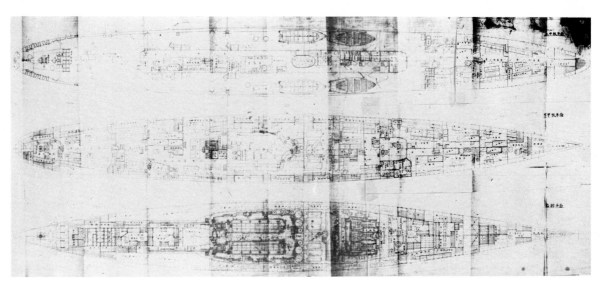

The upper, middle and hold decks of the *Etorofu* class.
Author's collection

Sketch 4 Type A, *Mikura* class: *Yashiro* after alteration of the light AA weapons and fitting of Type 13 and Type 22 radars.

onto the depth-charge thrower, or over the run-off frames over the stern.

This was a well thought-out and effective system; the efficiency of the British Hedgehog thrower was not yet achieved, however. The method of working, the installation and the arrangement of the throwers is shown in sketch 6.

FATES

5 Repatriation. To USA, 5.8.47 BU at Harima, Kure.
6 Sunk 22.8.44 US submarine *Harder* 14° 15′N/120° 05″0 23 miles W of Manila.
7 Sunk 22.8.44 US submarine *Haddo* as *Matsuwa*.
8 Repatriation. Tsingtao 29.8.47 to China as *Chang Pei*.

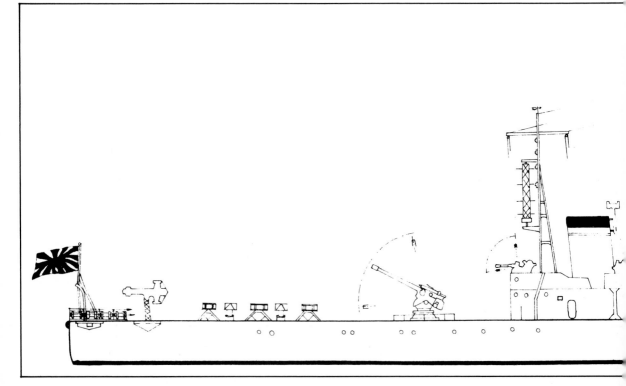

9 Sunk 2.9.43 US submarine *Snapper* (08° 40′N/151° 31′0, 85 miles NNW Truk Island).

10 Sunk 24.5.44 US submarine *Raton* (01° 26′N/149° 20′0, South China Sea – Dutch-East Indies area).

11 Repatriation. Shanghai 31.7.47 to China as *Lin An*.

12 Sunk 23.11.43 US submarine *Gudgeon* (28° 49′N/122° 11′0 Eastward of China Sea, 70 miles S of Shushan island).

13 Sunk 12.9.44 US submarine *Growler* (17° 54′N/114° 49′0, South China Sea – 250 miles E of Hainan Island).

14 Moderate damage 1.3.45 from US aircraft. Repatriation, 16.7.47 Singapore to England.

15 Sunk 9.8.45 US and British carrier aircraft (38° 26′N/141° 30′0, Bay of Onogawa, near Miyazaki, N of Honshu).

16 Severely damaged 3.4.45 by US aircraft in Hongkong. BU Japan.

17 Sunk 15.9.45 Russian aircraft off Ubrisan (North Korea).

18 Bow separated 22.6.45 by torpedo from US submarine *Crevalle*; emergency repair in Ominato, 20.8.45 to Sasebo, BU there.

19 Sunk 28.3.45 US submarine *Threadfin* (31° 49′N/131° 44′0 near Kyushu).

20 Planned for repatriation, struck mine 21.8.45 at Moji, out of action, not repaired, BU in Sasebo.

21 Sunk 2.6.44 US submarine *Guitarro* (220° 34′N/121° 51′0 between Formosa and Yosho Island).

22 Sunk 14.4.45 US submarine *Tirante* (35° 25′N/126° 15′0 West of Quelpart island – East China Sea).

23 Minesweeping, to England 14.9.47, bought back and BU in Nagoya.

24 Minesweeping. Tsingtao 29.8.47 to China as *Cheng An*.

25 Sunk 12.1.45 US carrier aircraft (10° 20′N/107° 50′0 South China Sea)

26 Sunk 7.8.44 US submarine *Guitarro* (14° 51′N/119° 59′0, 60 miles W of Manila).

27 Sunk 22.8.44 US submarine *Harder* (14° 15′N/120° 05′0, 35 miles WSW of Manila).

28 Minesweeping until 1947. *Ukuru Maru*, 1947 observation ship MSF. *Satsuma* 1954 (PL 109) JMSDF.

29 Minesweeping, sunk 16.11.45 after striking mine in the straits of Tsushima

30 Sunk 30.7.45 US carrier aircraft (35° 30′N/135° 21′0 NNW Maizuru).

31 Repatriation, to England 10.9.47, bought back and BU at Hiroshima.

32 Severely damaged 27.5.45 (bow removed) not repaired, BU.

33 Minesweeping until 1947. Became *Shinnan Maru* MFS. Became *Tsugaru* (PL 105) JMSDF 1954.

34 Sunk 26.2.45 US submarine *Hoe* (17° 08′N/110° 01′0, S of Hainan Island).

35 Sunk 23.2.45 US submarine *Hammerhead* (12° 30′N/109° 29′0, off Indochina).

36 Sunk 28.1.45 US submarine *Spadefish* (33° 56′N/123° 06′0, Yellow Sea).

37 Minesweeping until 1947. Became *Chikubu Maru* 1947. Became *Atsumi* (PL 103) JMSDF 1954.

38 Minesweeping until 1947. Became *Ikuna Maru*. (Observation ship weather station, transport ministry). Became *Ojika* (PL 102) JMSDF 1954.

39 Minesweeping. To USSR 28.7.45 at Nakhodka.

40 Repatriation, to USA 19.7.47, bought back and BU Uraga.

41 Repatriation. Shanghai 6.7.47 to China as *Hui An*.

42 Minesweeping, damaged in Kaguchi Passage 1.8.45. Sunk after end of the war, raised and BU.

43 Minesweeping, moderate damage 27.6.45 in Chokyo Passage off Nagoshia (S Korea). BU Sasebo.

44 Repatriation. To USSR 29.7.47 at Nakhodka.

45 Sunk 4.4.45 by mine in Shimonoseki straits, 4 miles off Buzaki Lighthouse.

46 Repatriation. Singapore 16.7.47 to England.

47 Sunk 9.8.45 US carrier aircraft (38° 26′N/141° 30′, off bay of Onagona N of Honshu).

48 Repatriation. To USA at Kure 6.9.47 bought back BU Kure.

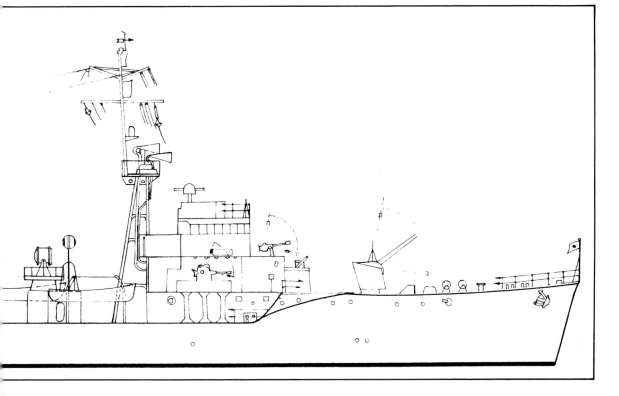

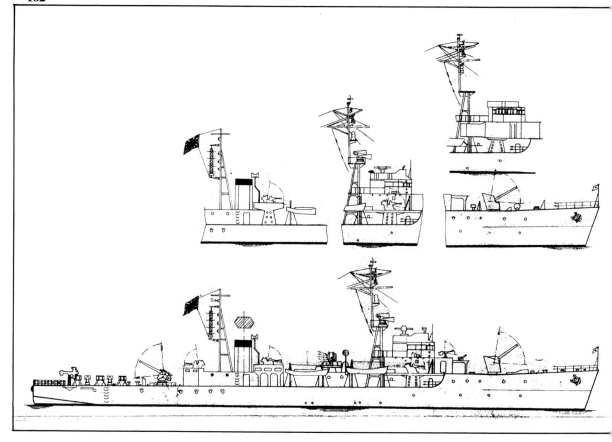

Sketch 5 Type A, *Ukuru* class: *Shonan* with depth-charge throwers and *Mikura* class minesweeping devices after reinforcement of the light AA weapons.

Small sketch, right bottom and centre: *Shisaka;* compare shape of the bridge and the protective shield.

Small sketch, left: Shape of the 25mm machine gun platform on the *Amami* and other ships.

Small sketch, top right: Appearance of *Kanawa* before delivery to the Royal Navy.

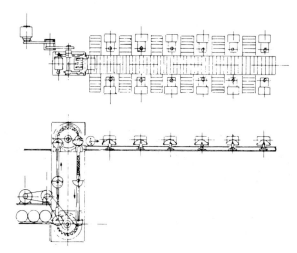

Sketch 6 Details of the depth charge system (in this case 12 throwers), and especially the supply line from the storage compartments aft.

49 Sunk 2.5.45 US submarine *Springer* (33° 58′N/122° 58′0, Yellow Sea)
50 Repatriation. Singapore 14.8.47 to England.
51 Slightly damaged by US carrier aircraft 28.4.45. Slightly damaged 9.5.45 by mine W of Straits of Shimanoski. Repatriation, to USA at Tsingtao 4.7.47.

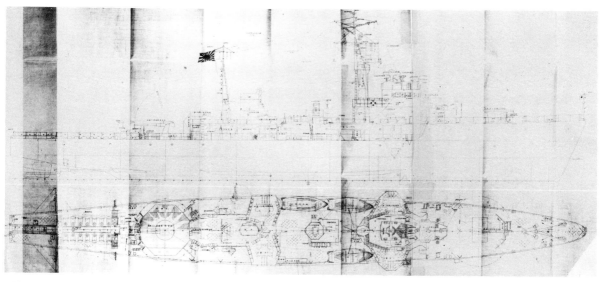

Elevation and upper deck 1:50 plans of the *Ukuru* class *Uku*.
Author's collection

The Type B *Ukuru* class *Amami* on her trials off Yokohama in
April 1945. She has Type 22 radar on the mainmast.
Author's collection

52 Damaged by bomb hit close to Maizuru from carrier aircraft
30.7.45. BU Kure.
53 Struck by mine in Fukugowa gulf 25.6.45. Not repaired, BU
Maizuru.
54 Minesweeping. Became *Shiga Maru* 1947, MSF 1948.
Koyima (PL 106) in JMSDF in 1955.
55 Repatriation, hotel ship in Senzaki from 4.46. BU Sasebo.

184

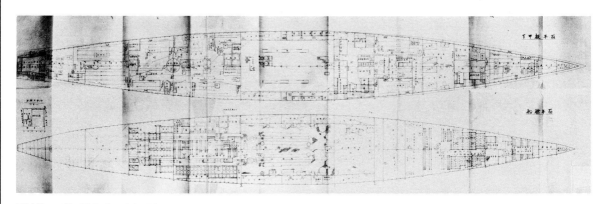

Middle and hold decks of the *Ukuru* class *Uku*.
Author's collection

The Type B *Mikura* class *Awaji* off Awajishima (Osaka Bay)
after her completion in January 1944.
Author's collection

The Gunboat Tyr

By Frank Abelsen

When England, France and USA began to build ironclads between 1850 and 1860 wooden warships rapidly became obsolete. The Royal Norwegian Navy therefore went into its gunboat period. The Navy Commission fleet plan of 1855 envisaged building 12 steamgunboats. It was later intended to build the gunboats in three classes.

In the Navy's new fleet plan of 1877 we find 12 first class gunboats, 24 second class gunboats and 46 third class gunboats.

But the Navy's budget for the new construction was reduced during the following years, and the value of the existing warships was reduced by technological developments.

The decay of the Navy was a fact. Some of it could be attributed to the Navy Department and the Army Department being united into the Defence Department

in 1884. The Army was much bigger than the Navy and considered to be the main force. Consequently, an Army officer headed the Defence Department.

At this time it was also said that the Navy's main task was to enfilade the land approach to Kristiania, the capital of Norway, from the fjord within Oscarsborg, the coastal defence fortification in Oslo-fjord. The Navy was forced by financial economies into sheltered waters as a defensive coastal defence force.

The first class gunboats had to be constructed with very good sea-going qualities for duty along Norway's northern coast. Only four were built and they were all of different design. The third class gunboats were, for economy's sake, converted from 18 old row gun-barges.

In the years from 1874 to 1887 seven second class gunboats were built at the Carljohansvern Shipyard in Horten, the main naval base in Norway. They were *Vale, Uller, Nor, Brage, Vidar, Gor* and *Tyr*.

This class was modelled after the British gunboat

General arrangement (1:50) of the gunboat *Tyr* 1946.

The Naval Museum, Norway

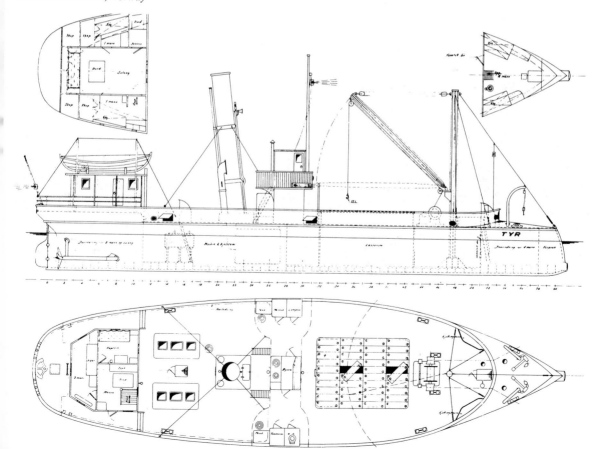

Pl XXXIX

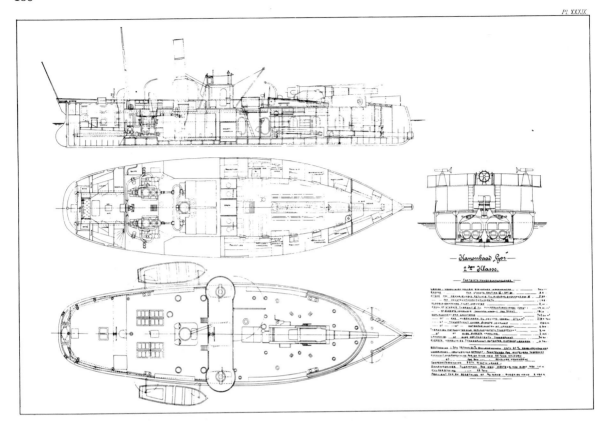

General arrangement of the second class gunboat *Gor*.

The Naval Museum, Norway

HMS *Staunch*. Advocates of the 'skerries-tactic' saw this type of gunboat to be 'nearly' ideal. They should lie behind islets and skerries (reefs), waiting in ambush with their heavy guns. *Gor* and *Tyr* were the first warships built of steel in Norway. The remaining ships were built of iron.

All their names came from the Scandinavian mythology. *Tyr* was the son of Odin, and he was the proper god of war. He ruled over victory in battle. The day of the week, Tuesday, in Norwegian 'Tirsdag', comes from *Tyr*, and there are many place names in Norway derived from him.

CHARACTERISTICS

The gunboat *Tyr* was launched on 16 March 1887 at the Carljohansvern Shipyard in Horten. Her total cost was 356,557,00 Norwegian crowns. *Tyr* had a displacement of 294 tons, and her dimensions were, length (oa) 31.8m (104ft 4in), beam 8.5m (27ft 11in) and draught 2.2m (7ft 3in). Her machinery consisted of two vertical compound steam engines and two cylinder tube boilers with a pressure of 6.5kg/cm². This gave 450ihp and a maximum speed of 10.5 knots. The bunkers held 22 tons of coal and she had an action radius of 750 miles at 8 knots. The complement was 44 men. This class was originally armed with one 27cm (10.6in) L/13 muzzle loading gun from Armstrong, as the main armament.

Gor and *Tyr* were on the other hand armed with one 26cm (10.5in) L/30 breech loading gun from Krupp as the main armament. This gun weighed 25.2 tons and the mountings about 14 tons. The heavy armament claimed nearly 14 per cent of the largest displacement which was disproportionately large. Their whole firepower lay in this sole gun. The gunboat could not catch any enemy, but had to wait until a vessel came within range. Then the gunboat could be very dangerous.

The big gun could fire a steel- or cast iron shell of 275kg (606lb) with a charge of 87kg (191lb) prismatic brown powder, and the muzzle velocity was 520m/sec. With the explosive composition of 10.5kg (23lb) the steel shell could at quite close range, penetrate wrought iron plating of 52cm (20.4in). The range was 4000m at 5° elevation, and the gun crew numbered 13 men. They needed 6 minutes to fire a round. The gun was mounted on a slide-mounting which was fixed to the deck. So traversing meant moving the ship. Between the mounting and the gun-carriage there was a hydraulic break, filled with a mixture of glycerine and water. The advance of the gun-carriage had to be done with a tackle.

Tyr had as secondary armament, one Hotchkiss 57mm quick-firing gun, which is now exhibited at the Norwegian Naval Museum in Horten, and two Hotchkiss 37mm revolver-guns. In addition *Gor* and *Tyr* had one 356mm (14in) underwater torpedo tube for Whitehead torpedoes, mounted in the bow.

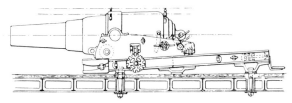

Armstrong 270mm (10.6in) L/13 muzzle loading gun, original main armament of Norwegian second class gunboats.

Drawing from The Norwegian Sea Defences 1814–1914

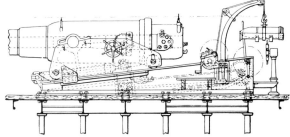

Krupp 260mm (10.2in) L/30 breech loading gun, *Tyr*'s main armament.

Drawing from The Norwegian Sea Defences 1814–1914

SERVICE CAREER

Tyr took part in the yearly division cruise and torpedo exercises. She also joined the mobilisation exercise in September 1895. But in 1900 the gunboat was laid up until the mobilisation in 1905. *Tyr* was then stationed with the Hvaler division.

By this time the gunboat-age of the Navy was ending. This type of ship was out of date. From 14 April 1910 *Tyr* served as a tender to the first Norwegian submarine *Kobben*. This duty went on until 31 December 1913.

Tyr, as well as gunboats of the third class, were afterwards converted into minelayers intended for laying

Armstrong 267mm (10.5in) L/19 no 3 gun aboard the gunboat *Brage* 1905.

The Naval Museum, Norway

temporary mine-barriers in closed waters. *Tyr* was equipped with mine-tracks to take 55 contact mines. Their heavy guns were taken on shore and replaced with a Belgian 120mm quick-firing Cockerfill gun. The secondary armament was replaced with one 76mm quick-firing gun, probably a Bofors L/50, and two 37mm quick-firing guns, probably Hotchkiss.

At the outbreak of World War I *Tyr* was again stationed in the Hvaler-division, as a minelayer in defence of Norwegian neutrality. The division had its base at the Hvaler islands, farthest out in the Oslofjord. The unit's role was to disarm and demolish drifing mines, and to pick up dead bodies. During the war 222

dead bodies were picked up around the Norwegian coast. The defence of neutrality was rounded off from 13 November 1918 to 1 April 1919 with guard duty and the seeking of drifting mines. After this was *Tyr* was laid up as too old for naval duty.

In the autumn of 1939 at the outbreak of World War II, *Tyr* and her sister ships were again fitted out for the defence of neutrality. The Royal Norwegian Navy consisted of essentially the same ships as in 1914, except for 19 ships built since 1918 of which only five were of modern design. On 8 April 1940 the Navy consisted of 111 ships. Of these there were 62 real warships, but 43 of them had been built between 1874 and 1918. The remainder were 49 hired whalers, trawlers and coastal passenger steamers, used for guard duties.

WORLD WAR II

Tyr was assigned to the Bergen Squadron with the Second Minelayer Division. Her captain, F Ulstrup, also commanded the division. The gunboat/minelayer was stationed at the small seaport of Klokkarvik in the Lerøy guard section.

In the night of 8/9 April, at about 0030, Captain Ulstrup was informed that the Rauøy and Bolærne forts in the outer Oslofjord were engaging unknown warships. Captain Ulstrup immediately gave orders to clear the ship for action and to get the mines ready for laying. When the first German warships from Group 3, the Bergen Group entered the Korsfjord, *Tyr* went out to lay the mines in the strait between Sotra island and Lerøy. Without being observed by the German force, *Tyr* managed to lay seven mines before the warships were too close for comfort. After that *Tyr* went northward and laid 16 mines at the southern end of Vatlestraumen, a very narrow strait at the southern approach to Bergen. This minelaying also went unobserved by the Germans.

But the German warships (the cruisers *Köln* and *Königsberg*, the gunnery training ships *Bremse*, and depot ship *Carl Peters*, the torpedo boats *Leopard* and *Wolf* and five S-boats) passed the minefields without detonating any of the mines. The return voyage was a different story.

When the cruiser *Köln*, in the evening of 9 April, went out from Bergen to go back to Germany, she put out an Oropessa sweep. Several moored contact mines were cut and the minefield was discovered. But that did not prevent the German transport *Sao Paulo* of 5000grt hitting one of *Tyr*'s mines later that evening. *Sao Paulo* sank immediately with heavy loss of human life and war material.

The Germans had no minesweeper in the area. So the German vessels *Schiff 9*, *Cremon* and launches from *Carl Peters* were ordered to sweep the waters around Vatlestraumen. They sailed from Bergen on the evening of 10 April. *Schiff 9* hit a mine at 19.25 and went down within one or two minutes. *Cremon* hurried to pick up survivors but five minutes later also hit a mine as did one of the launches. The mines from *Tyr* also sank the German 8500grt cargo ship *Liège* on 27 April and in middle of May another cargo ship hit a mine and sank.

Hotchkiss HK 57mm L/44 gun.
The Naval Museum, Norway

The gunboat *Gor*.
The Naval Museum, Norway

After the minelaying *Tyr* carried on with the guard duty in the southern approach to Bergen. She spotted a German S-boat near the island of Skorpo. *Tyr* opened fire and the S-boat replied with her 20mm machine gun. The S-boat manoeuvred clear of the gunfire from *Tyr* which took cover near a small island. *Tyr* carried on southward, but was attacked by three S-boats, one of them being hit by a 37mm shell from *Tyr*. The second S-boat stopped to help the damaged boat while the third S-boat carried on with the shooting. After a while the German S-boats withdrew from the fight and disappeared to the northward.

During the evening of 16 April *Tyr* withdrew into Uskedal, a small seaport on the outer Hardangerfjord. Captain Ulstrup was now commander of the newly established Hardangerfjord Sea Defence Section. The command of *Tyr* was taken over by the second officer, Sub-lieutenant K Sandnæs.

During the battle at Uskedal in the night of the 19-20 April *Tyr* managed with her 120mm gun to damage the German *Schiff 18* so seriously that the ship was run aground. From her were landed German troops, north of Uskedal, and *Tyr* was then in the middle of Storsund just out of Uskedal and fired upon the German positions ashore. The German soldiers fired back with their heavy machine guns and at the same time the gunnery training ship *Bremse* opened fire from the western entrance of Uskedal. The situation was now so dangerous that *Tyr* withdrew from the engagement and went back to the port. *Tyr* received orders to go out again to assist the Norwegian torpedo boat *Stegg* which was engaging *Bremse*.

As soon as *Tyr* showed up in the strait *Bremse* started firing at her again. *Tyr* therefore steamed across the strait and into a bay where she took cover. Sub-lieutenant Sandnæs saw that further fighting was hopeless and received orders to prepare to destroy the ship. The crew went ashore to get some rest. When they tried to move weapons and ammunition ashore, two German S-boats came into the Storsund at high speed and came alongside *Tyr*. The Norwegian crew hid on the island while the Germans took over *Tyr*. A German trawler came and took *Tyr* under tow back to Uskedal.

IN GERMAN HANDS

The German force left the area at Uskedal in the morning of 20 April after the Norwegian force had retreated. *Tyr* was sailed to Bergen under German flag and with a German crew. The German Admiral Schrader decided on 30 April to lay a minebarrier in the entrance of Sognefjord to catch the Norwegian warships, which still operated in the fjord. The minelayers *Try* and *Uller*, also captured by the Germans, were to be used for the tak. The ships had about 80 mines on board and were commanded by *Korvetten-Kapitän* Borchardt.

Norwegian intelligence in this area was very effective and the two minelayers were observed throughout their advance. Two Norwegian aircraft, F-312 and F-334, took off and attacked *Tyr* and *Uller*. They dropped nine bombs without hitting either ship, but three Germans aboard *Uller* were wounded by a splinter. After the attack *Tyr* and *Uller* continued towards the Sognefjord where they began to lay the mines. In the night another Norwegian aircraft, F-58, made two dive bomber attacks. One 250kg bomb and four 50g bombs were dropped, but there was no direct hit. One bomb exploded close to *Uller* which was so damaged that she took in water. *Uller* was therefore grounded at the southern end of Losneøy. *Tyr* only received minor damage. The aircraft was exposed to heavy gunfire from the minelayers without being hit and it returned to the base.

The minelaying stopped and the crew of *Uller* were taken onboard *Tyr*. Thereafter *Uller* was fired on until she began to burn. Early in the morning *Tyr* sailed southward towards Bergen. But once again she was followed by coast watchers. When *Tyr* steered down the Fålefotsund, a very narrow strait between Hissøy island and the mainland, the crew from a Norwegian guardboat were waiting for her and opened fire with machine guns from both sides of the strait. How many of the estimated 36 German soldiers were killed or wounded is not known. The Germans replied with the 120mm gun and small arms without hitting any of the Norwegians. The shooting stopped when *Tyr* was out of range and the ship continued towards Bergen.

Details of *Tyr*'s subsequent war service under German command are not extant. She was perhaps laid up, because the Germans were of the opinion that the minelayers were hopelessly old. But some of *Tyr*'s sister ships were used by the Germans. *Gor* and *Vale* were used as 'kondensatorschiff' for delivering distillated water. *Vale* was also for a while used as a tug-boat under the 'Hafenkapitän-Bergen'. *Vidar* was captured by the

The car ferry M/S *Bjøorn West*, ex-gunboat *Tyr*.
Photographed by Lars-Helge Isdahl

Germans at Melsomvik on 14 April 1940, entered the *'Hafenschutzflotille Kristiansand-süd'* as *NK-31* and was used as a minelayer. *Nor* was also laid up during the war.

POST-1945 CAREER

After the German capitulation in 1945 the old minelayers were returned to the Royal Norwegian Navy. They were immediately discarded, but *Gor* was used as a water barge until she was condemned and was later broken up. *Nor* was sold in 1949 and was renamed *Flatholm*. She exists today as a lighter.

Tyr was sold in 1946 to the P/R Tyr in Bergen and was rebuilt into a heavy lifting crane ship at the Gravdal Shipyard in Sunde. In 1949 she was sold again, and this time to Brødrene Wilhelmsen A/S in Åsane and completely rebuilt into a car ferry. Renamed as M/F *Bjørn-West* she started her new duty as a car ferry between Knarvik and Steinestø) north of Bergen. The old steam engine was replaced with a 375bhp Deutz diesel motor. This motor was again changed with a 400bhp Wickmann diesel in 1970.

Bjøorn-West was named after the famous Norwegian Milorg Company that operated in the Matre mountains in the winter of 1945. The ferry was taken over by *'A/S Bergen — Nordhordland Trafikklag'* in 1971. This company changed its name to 'Bergen-Nordhordland Rutelag' in 1974. In August 1980 *Bjørn-West* was bought by the A/S Saki (Fredrik Odfjell) Company at a cost of 275,000 Norwegian crowns.

The ship is now used as a supplementary ferry, when other ferry owners need extra help during the summer season. The ferry has also been used to carry heavy rolling-stock to the head of a fjord in Western Norway. It is to be hoped that this ship, which has served her country for nearly a century, will continue to sail for many years to come.

REFERENCES

Den Norske Marine 1865-1950 Særtrykk av Norge på havet.
Det Norske Veritas, skipsliste 1947-1980.
Mineleggerne Gor og Tyre, Rolf Scheen Norges forsvar nr. 10-1960 (artikkel).
Norges Sjøforsvar 1814-1914, Kristiania 1918
Norges Sjøkrig 1939-1940, Rolf Scheen (bind 1-2).
Norges Sjøkrig 1940-1945, bind I, bind III E A Steen, Oslo 1956.
Norges Skipsliste 1947-1980, Sjøfartsdirektoratet.
Sjømilitæret Samfunds Marinekalender 1814-1934 Oslo 1934.
Skipet, organ for Norsk Skipsfartshistorisk selskap Nr. 4 1980.
Skipsbygging på Horten gjennom 150 år Marinens Hovedverft 1968.
Gors og Tyrs artillerimateriell (prlt. G Mørch).
Norsk Tidsskrift for Søvæsen, 5. årgang 1886-1887 Horten 1887.
Haandbog i Søartilleri Horten 1894.
Egne notater.

The Reborn Battleships

by Norman Friedman

The battleship *New Jersey* off the Lebanon on 25 September
1983. She fired 312 16in shells in all.

UPI/Popperfoto

For a quarter century the United States Navy was unique
in the world in having retained four battleships in
reserve. One of them, *New Jersey*, has now been back in
service for over 18 months. *Iowa* should be recommissioned before this article is in print, and the Navy is
seeking funds to recommission the other two ships.
From the Navy's point of view, these ships are an expression of uniquely American naval priorities. They are also

a considerable bargain, since the cost of modernisation
appears to have been less than the price of a new frigate.
The Navy has, however, had to contend with repeated
charges that the battleships are being brought back into
service, not for some vital military role, but out of a
misguided nostalgia. After all, they are unique in the
world, and they are 40 years old.

The recommissioned battleships should fill two complementary primary roles. First, they restore a level of
fire support that the Marines have sorely missed. The
United States now possesses only six ships carrying guns
with calibres greater than 5in: four battleships and two

New Jersey off the Lebanon on 25 September 1983.

UPI/Popperfoto

heavy cruisers (with a third, the much-used *Newport News*, probably good only for cannibalisation). For many years the Marines have noted nervously that the 5in gun of a destroyer actually has a smaller calibre than a standard Soviet weapon, the 130mm (5.1in). This disparity was actually used to justify the development of the ill-fated US 8in lightweight gun. For some years in the 1960s US shipbuilding plans included a specialised Amphibious Fire Support ship (LFS) armed with the new gun and assault rockets, but it never materialised, and Marine Corps amphibious forces actually declined in carrying capacity after Vietnam.

Some even imagined that the United States would never again have to land troops on hostile shores. However, post-Vietnam experience suggested otherwise. Moreover, in the decade since Vietnam, it has become increasingly clear that neither the United States *nor* the Soviet Union may be able to control events in the Third World short of local warfare. That is, the rate of crisis may be increasing, although without any threat of escalation into general war. That is exactly the political climate that demands increased shore bombardment capability – as in Lebanon. In this sense the reappearance of the 16in gun at sea is extremely timely.

BATTLESHIPS AND CARRIERS
Second, as a unit in the Surface Action Groups (SAGs), the battleship can help project US seapower into an increasingly turbulent Third World. Although a SAG clearly cannot match a carrier battle group's capability, only one carrier in three can be on station at any one time, allowing for one under refit and one working up or coming home. This figure can be improved temporarily in an emergency, but the US Navy must plan for sustained deployments. The limitations of the carrier force were particularly highlighted by the decision to maintain major naval forces in the Indian Ocean, following the Soviet invasion of Afghanistan in December 1979. At the time, with 12 active carriers, the United States was maintaining two in the Mediterranean and two in the Western Pacific. The Indian Ocean carrier or carriers had to come from those fleets. However, the two deployed fleets (Sixth and Seventh) were already at a

Two gunners mates stand beside a 16in imitation shell aboard *New Jersey* 29 September 1983. The US Navy still has over 21,000 16in shells.

UPI/Popperfoto

bare minimum of strength. Ideally, carriers should always operate in pairs, so that even the current goal of 16 is short of what it would take to form three deployed fleets. SAGs can go part of the way to make up the difference.

Indeed, under some circumstances long-range gunfire

New Jersey fires for the first time since Vietnam 1969 on 14 December 1983. She fired 11 rounds (out of 71 from 3 ships) against Syrian AA positions inland after US reconnaissance jets were fired at. The photograph is an extreme enlargement from a colour slide taken by USMC 1st Lieutenant Bob Dillon from the Marine position at the airport.

UPI/US Marine Corps

may be preferable to carrier air attacks. For example, they do not risk the loss of valuable pilots, as in Lebanon. Some would suggest that it is peculiarly disheartening to the victims of shelling that they cannot hope to do anything about the attack. They can at least shoot back at aircraft. This is hardly to suggest that the gun can somehow be revived in such a way as to supplant aircraft, but only that, within its niche, the gun remains valuable.

It can be argued, too, that the battleships are potentially extremely valuable as fleet flagships, replacing the missile cruisers of the 1960s and 1970s, the last of which,

New Jersey off the Lebanon on 13 January 1984. Two days later she fired on Druze positions with her 16in and 5in guns.

UPI/Popperfoto

Oklahoma City, was retired in 1979. Such a configuration was studied in 1981, but rejected for the time being as too expensive. However, a flagship conversion would be a viable possibility for a future large battleship refit. See the earlier article (Issue 19) on the command cruisers for the continuing significance of flagship capacity at sea. Certainly fast battleships such as the *Iowa*s were valuable as flagships within wartime and postwar fast carrier task forces.

Battleship survivability is an important element of all of these proposals. Anti-ship missiles, such as Exocet, are now the common coin of Third World navies. Although a fleet at sea should be able to deal relatively easily with such weapons, the prospect of surprise attack remains sobering. Carriers have always been vulnerable, in that by they have on board large masses of explosives and highly inflammable jet fuels. A battleship is different. She has only very limited volumes of explosives, primarily well below the waterline. The new missile installations are all above deck, unconnected to magazines or other explosive concentrations below. A small missile would be unlikely, then, to do very much damage. Massive side armour (7in–12in for the *Iowa*s)

would help a battleship resist most current forms of attack. Note that there are so few armoured warships in the world that there are very few armour-piercing weapons. In this sense, the gross obsolescence of the battleship is a major asset. This is not to say that a ship like *New Jersey* cannot be sunk, only that sinking her is no trivial matter.

GUNFIRE SUPPORT

From the Marine's point of view, the 1960s and 1970s were extremely depressing times. They had long believed that naval gunfire was essential to the success of any opposed landing. Although they hoped to achieve a measure of surprise through techniques such as helicopter assault, they were uncomfortably aware of the decline of the heavy (8in and 16in) gun in the active and then in the reserve fleets. There were two attempts to solve this problem: an abortive Landing Fire Support Weapon, which would have been compatible with Terrier missile launchers; and the 8in lightweight gun. The gun was actually built, and mounted aboard the destroyer *Hull*, but it was cancelled due to lack of funds. It was suggested, too, that a single 8in gun, incapable of firing smothering salvoes, would be relatively ineffective. The Navy did continue to develop a guided version of the 5in destroyer shell, which (by default) would be the only available future fire support weapon, but it, too, was afflicted by high costs. Such fiscal issues will presumably become more pressing as the Reagan Administration is forced to reduce defence spending over the next few years.

The continued existence of the four battleships was the only bright spot in this gloomy picture. As the war in Vietnam escalated, naval gunfire support became more and more valuable, and by 1966 the Department of Defense was considering recommissioning either one battleship or two heavy cruisers. Senator Richard B Russell was a strong advocate of the battleship. However, the then Chief of Naval Operations, Admiral David L MacDonald, strongly opposed it, and the decision to recommission *New Jersey* was not announced until the day after he left office, the following year. Modernisation was purposely made extremely austere, to avoid criticism that the ship was intended more as an admiral's flagship than for shore bombardment. Thus, although the ship had served as a flagship in the past, her admiral's quarters were deliberately not overhauled. It was claimed at the time that 80 per cent of all naval targets in Vietnam were within 16in gun range of the coast, and during her brief deployment *New Jersey* fired 5688 16in shells, compared to 771 during the whole of World War II.

Even so, critics of battleship reactivation remained active. In particular, as a Congressman, Melvin Laird had criticised the battleship decision. He became Secretary of Defense after Richard Nixon became President in January 1969. Some argued at the time that Secretary Laird personally ordered *New Jersey* decommissioned in 1969, as she was preparing for a second Vietnam deployment. The Navy Department went so far as to consider disposing of all four surviving battleships in 1973; the *New Jersey* and *Missouri* were to have been preserved as memorials. However, they were retained in view of their unique shore bombardment capability. They were, moreover, relatively youthful in terms of time spent in active service. *Missouri*, for example, was commissioned in 1944 and decommissioned in 1955, after only 11 years. Her sister ships were all laid up in the late 1940s, as part of a series of economy moves, and were recommissioned for Korea, then withdrawn in 1957-58. As of 1977, the Board of Inspection and Survey estimated that each had at least 15 remaining years.

MODERNISATION DECISION

It is difficult to trace the precise origins of the decision to modernise and recommission the battleships. As early as 1975, an analyst at the Center for Naval Analyses suggested that battleships might replace carriers in forward areas in time of crisis. They would be better able to survive an initial Soviet surprise attack, even though they would have nothing like the firepower of a carrier. They might, moreover, be able to engage Soviet ships at considerable distances, using guided shells. In 1969, in connection with the recommissioning of *New Jersey*, the Naval Ordnance Laboratory experimented with sub-calibre shells that could be fired from a 16in/50 gun. It appeared that a 280mm round could reach about 100,000 yards (50nm). At this time many thousands of such shells remained, non-nuclear relics of the Army 'atomic cannon' programme. In combat the ship fired only 16in rounds, but the potential to reach beyond twice conventional gun range remained and, indeed, remains now.

By about 1977 there was some Navy interest in recommissioning. The Board of Inspection and Survey examined all four ships and found them fundamentally sound. Early in 1980 one battleship, *New Jersey*, was tentatively included in the FY81 (Carter) budget, along with the proposal to refurbish the aircraft carrier *Oriskany*. Some regarded the battleship as a rival to the carrier project; others suggested that the battleship had been included as a kind of sacrificial lamb, in the expectation that one or the other, but not both, would be killed in committee. In fact both died, but the battleship came quite close to realisation. At this time it was estimated that an austere refit, incorporating NATO Sea Sparrow missiles for self-defence, would cost $225 million in FY80 dollars, or $270 million in FY81 funds; modernisation would take 12–15 months.

A retired USAF fighter pilot and Washington defence consultant, Charles E Myers, is credited with publicising the merits of a battleship under the designation 'interdiction assault ship'. He was particularly interested in the all-weather capability inherent in 16in guns. It is not clear at this remove whether Myers originated the idea or whether he was an early proponent, eg of an idea originated by the Marines, who certainly wanted the ship. Certainly the battleship was part of the official Navy budget request by February 1980. It did not survive the process of budget-cutting, but funds for *New Jersey* were included in the Reagan Administration's FY81 Supplemental budget.

New Jersey with a helicopter overhead just after she first fired into Lebanon. She can operate 3 helicopters.

UPI

NEW JERSEY CONVERSION

Out of a total cost of about $326 million, $170 million went for rehabilitation. The rest bought a variety of new systems: four octuple armoured box launchers for Tomahawk land-attack and long range anti-ship missiles; four quadruple launchers for Harpoon anti-ship missiles; four Phalanx close-in defensive guns; improved communications (to cruiser standard); SLQ-32 defensive ECM gear; and a new SPS-49 air search radar. The stern was cleared to provide one operating helicopter spot and three parking spots. Four twin 5in/38 guns were landed to make space for the Tomahawk launchers. The ship was converted to use Navy distillate fuel, rather than black oil, and her firefighting facilities were improved.

Once the project had been approved, it moved very rapidly. The design team was assembled aboard the ship at Long Beach, and given a very short time to complete work. Deadlines were also used to force the hands of the many offices within the Office of the Chief of Naval Operations. In other cases, each branch might have many chances ('chops') to review a given project, each 'chop' adding delay. In this case, everyone was allowed only a single 'chop'. As a result, *New Jersey* was converted on time and to cost, a salutary example for other shipbuilding projects.

The austerity of the conversion was justified, at the time, by the urgent need to reinforce US amphibious forces, and by the expectation that more might be accomplished in a future second and third phase. After all, a battleship is an enormous platform, and her sheer size invites proposals for installations such as the Aegis air defence system and a flight deck, aft. More recently the phase two plan has been abandoned, although the ships will receive better command and control systems. Thus it is most unlikely that the radical proposals for VSTOL flight decks and heavy batteries of vertically-launched missiles (either cruise or defensive) will ever materialise. The deterrent is the sheer cost of such radical alterations as the removal of No 3 turret.

New Jersey was funded under the FY81 and FY82 budgets, the latter providing long-lead funds for *Iowa*, which was fully funded under FY83 and should be recommissioned in April 1984, well ahead of the originally planned date of January 1985. Preliminary work began in October 1982. In theory, two battleships provide a minimum force sufficient to support simultaneous Marine operations in both oceans. However, at least one ship will always have to be refitting or working up, so three is a more realistic figure. The Navy failed to obtain funds for *Missouri* in FY84, but will try again in the current (FY85) budget. As this is written, it is not clear whether *Wisconsin* will be refitted.

New Jersey has now been in service for a little over a year, proving her versatility in each of the numbered fleets, and firing her 16in and 5in guns in anger for the first time in 14 years off Lebanon (14 December 1983 – 26 February 1984). There, the loss of US carrier attack aircraft proved Myers' point: no one can shoot down or capture a 16in shell. On the other hand the effectiveness of *New Jersey*'s shelling, and the spotting arrangements for it, is something of a mystery.

As a footnote, it may be worth noting that Congressional critics of the battleship programme suggested the two surviving *Des Moines* class cruisers as alternatives. Studies showed that they were deficient in the deck area required to fit cruise missile launchers: only a very large ship has sufficient area sufficiently isolated from the blast of heavy guns. The project manager of the design felt that the best alternative was, alas, long gone: he wished the two *Alaska*s had not been broken up in 1961, after so little active service. After all, in a world of unarmoured ships, even they would have been well-protected. As it is, then, the battleships seems to have been the best alternative. If the Navy has its way, they will remain in service through the rest of this century, and will see their 60th birthdays.

The Building of HMS Duke of York

by Ian Buxton

Duke of York was the third ship of the *King George V* class of battleship; 35,000 tons standard, ten 14in and 16 5.25in guns. Her hull and machinery were ordered from John Brown's Clydebank yard on 28 April 1937 as Contract No 554. She was laid down on 5 May 1937, launched 28 February 1940 and completed 4 November 1941. All photographs are from the author's collection courtesy of Upper Clyde Shipbuilders Ltd (Clydebank Division).

Duke of York's forward structure takes shape in July 1938. The protective bulkhead runs beneath the line of shadow cast on the deck plating, outboard of which is the cellular air/liquid/air anti-torpedo sandwich. Inboard are electrical breaker spaces and the ring main. The two nearest ladders lead down to what will become the damage control centre and low power rooms on the lower deck. Forward of the transverse bulkhead on frame 119 is 'B' turret space.

A view from aft also taken in July 1938. Plating being laid amidships is covering the after machinery spaces at middle deck level, ie two below the upper deck. 'Y' turret will be installed between the two transverse bulkheads. The liner *Queen Elizabeth* can be seen approaching the launching stage on the next berth.

1 The starboard outer shaft bracket being lifted into place, ready for the palms to be rivitted to the supporting structure. Since the light cranes seen in the earlier photographs, could not lift such loads, sheers had to be rigged; the legs are clearly seen.

2 So that's how it was done. Tongued and grooved cemented side armour plates 15in thick and weighing some 40 tons were fitted after launch, and fixed with armour bolts through the shell plating tapped into the back of the plate. Photograph taken on 29 March 1940.

3 Curved armour 11-13in thick for 'B' twin 14in barbette surrounds in ring bulkhead. The planing mechanism for machining the roller path is being dismantled. The time is May 1940 so that the ships behind the destroyer *Noble* (launched 7 May) and the destroyer depot ship, *Hecla* (launched 14 March).

3

Superstructure erection in the region of the wardroom and planking of the upper deck are well under way (about August 1940). Casemates for the after twin 5.25in gun mounts are nearly complete. The compressed air main to operate the rivetting and caulking tools is visible. The destroyers behind are probably *Nerissa* and *Nizam*.

1

2

3

1 Machinery long since shipped and uptakes installed, the foward funnel is fitted in May 1941.

2 What it's all about. The 92-ton lefthand 14in gun for 'B' turret is lifted by Clydebank's 150-ton cantilever crane in July 1941. The trunnions and pins are clearly visible near the rear of the gun to permit elevation to 40°, but necessitating a 12-ton balance weight around the breech. Holes in the 7in rear of the turret are for ventilation.

3 Looking more like a battleship in June 1941, but directors, some 5.25in mounts and close range armament have yet to be fitted.

4 Forward superstructure with 8-barrelled pompoms and their controllers, 44in searchlights, 20in signal projectors, main director with Type 284 radar and two Mark V high-angle directors with Type 285. The 20mm Oerlikon gun pits are still empty.

5 Just what the modelmaker ordered. A midships view taken on 6 September 1941, two months before completion but with RN ratings already aboard.

4

5

Almost ready to leave (6 September 1941)) boats shipped,
aircraft/boat cranes stowed, Carley floats and flotanets fitted.
The destroyer *Onslow* lies on the port side.

Duke of York leaves Clydebank on 7 September 1941,
assisted by the tug/tender *Paladin*, drawing 31ft amidships.

Arethusa Class Cruisers Part 1

By Alan Pearsall

Arethusa at sea August 1915. She never had a mast aft. Her only boats in this picture are the two sea boats forward. Commodore Tyrwhitt's broad pendant can just be seen at the truck, while at the port yardarm is the Red Ensign flown by British ships to avoid confusion with the Imperial German Ensign. She has the AA gun aft.

NMM

Trywhitt's *Arethusa* was perhaps the most famous cruiser of the 1914-18 War. Her seven sisters took a prominent part in the sea war. Yet the eight ships are relatively unfamiliar, even to students of warship design. They were all completed after the outbreak of war had imposed censorship, and, unlike their immediate successors, they all disappeared relatively quickly after the war. Technically as well as historically, however, they were an important and formative design, and richly deserve the fuller description now attempted, while the illustrations will, in addition, support their claims to be regarded as among the more handsome warships of the steam era.

To understand the background of their design is almost to review the development and purpose of the cruiser in the Royal Navy. From its inception in the 1880s the type had evolved into larger and smaller classes. Their purpose was, in fleet work, to scout ahead and around seeking information about the enemy and foiling the similar efforts of their opposite numbers. Cruisers were also employed in the protection of trade and possessions overseas. Usually operating independently. In both cases the larger cruisers acted as powerful supports to their smaller consorts. The qualities required were speed, radius of action and reasonable armament, but always with regard to size, because it will be clear that numbers of ships were often as useful as individual size and power. Thus we find attempts – not always successful – to design small and powerful cruisers which could be built in quantity.

In the late nineteenth and early twentieth centuries, the advent of torpedo craft introduced a new element. The early destroyers needed a larger warship in support, to provide quarters for the flotilla commander and his staff and to watch over the affairs of the sometimes frail torpedo craft. The high speed of the latter, however, complicated the naval architect's problem even more, and, in the Royal Navy, a third group of cruisers appeared to meet this need – the so-called 'scouts'. Between 1904 and 1912 large armoured cruisers, medium cruisers and these light fast 'scouts' were all built, often contemporaneously.

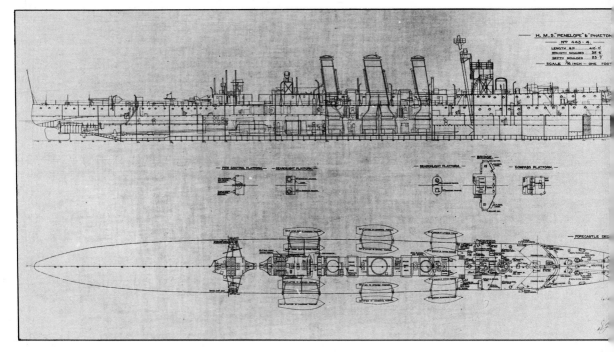

¹⁄₁₆in = 1ft elevation and deck plans of the *Arethusa* class cruisers *Penelope* and *Phaethon* as completed 1914–15.

NMM

By contrast, the German Navy built only a few armoured cruisers and otherwise followed a steady line of development of light cruisers, each group being slightly larger and faster than its predecessor. Both navies agreed, however, that, for light cruisers, the 4in gun was most suitable, and this was the armament of the British 'P' class of 1898, the 'Gems' of 1903-4, and the various scouts from 1904 onwards.

By 1912, the development of the destroyer had produced a situation where the existing flotilla cruisers of the 'scout' and *Boadicea* types were becoming barely adequate, and service opinion of them was unfavourable. Their speed of about 25 knots was now becoming too slow for accompanying destroyers that could maintain nearly 30 knots at sea, while their armament of 4in guns now gave support only by numbers rather than calibre. German destroyers certainly retained the 3.4in gun rather longer than did British, but, on the other hand, they tended to be rather faster than British equivalents. A case therefore existed for further development of the 'destroyer cruiser'.

Meanwhile another line of development had run its course. The 'Town' class had been built first under the 1908 Programme as a more powerful fast cruiser and successive versions had followed, until it was felt that the type had become rather large although in other respects excellent ships. In some of them, an armoured belt instead of a protective deck, was introduced for the first time in small cruisers.

The advent to the Admiralty of Winson Churchill brought not only that inquiring and forceful mind to bear on these problems, but also that of the equally forceful Lord Fisher, upon whom Churchill relied for much technical advice. The combination, in fact, added another reason for an improved cruiser design, when they decided that the battleship of the 1912 Programme should be a fast division capable of 25 knots, thus emphasising the Fleet's weakness, which the appearance of the battlecruisers had already indicated, in having no cruisers of any greater speed. This contradiction, however, produced a disagreement on the cruisers of 1912 between Churchill and Fisher.

DESIGN HISTORY

Churchill had the Director of Naval Construction produce a design based on the *Active*, the latest 'scout'. The original proposals were for a 'Super-*Active*' of 3500 tons, oil-fired for 30 knots, armed either with ten 4in guns, or two 6in and four 12pdrs, the latter subsequently being modified to two 6in and four 4in. However, another proposal was made, for a 'Super-*Swift*' with six 4in and 40 knots, and this was strongly supported by Fisher, if it did not actually emanate from him. Fisher disliked small cruisers anyway, holding the view that they lost their speed quickly in a seaway, and, worse still, that they would be 'all gobbled up by an armoured cruiser, like the armadillo gobbles up the ants – puts out its tongue and licks them up one after another – and the bigger the ant, the more placid the digestive smile'. The 'Super-*Swift*' could escape, however, and draw the enemy on to another of Fisher's great visions, the Big Submarine.

Churchill, supported by Jellicoe, held out for the 'Super-*Actives*', pointing out that they were fast and

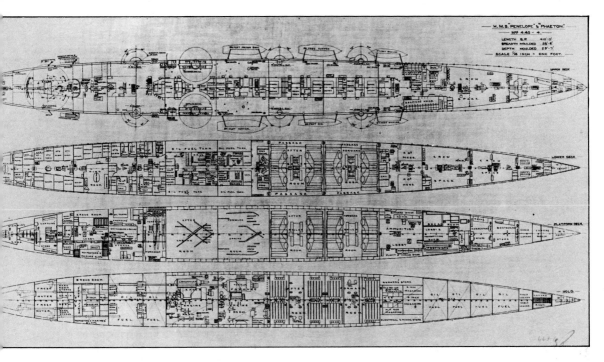

powerful enough to be 'destroyers of destroyers', and that it was intended to continue in these ships the fitting of armoured belts as in the later 'Town' class. From these views, they could not be shaken.

The question of numbers also arose acutely. For some years past, the estimates had provided only for four or five light cruisers each year, a number which was barely sufficient to keep pace with German construction without allowing either for the much wider British responsibilities or for the inferior position of the defender against an attacker with the choice of place and time of attack. Even in 1912, Churchill proposed 'chucking two *Dartmouths* and a *Blonde* and scraping round to get four "Super-*Actives*" instead'. But a paper by Troubridge pointed out the inferiority of the British position and the programme was increased to eight ships both in 1912 and 1913. These 16 additional light cruisers were, as it turned out, just in time.

The design was, of course, prepared in the office of the Director of Naval Construction, then Sir Philip Watts, by the cruiser section under W H Whiting, S V Goodall, later to be DNC himself, doing the detailed work, which took place in the first half of 1912. The result was conventional in outline, based very much on the *Active*, but rather larger, faster, oil-fired and armoured. The new features were thus to be incorporated in a tried framework, in the best form of technical development. The hull form was tested at Haslar, after which the beam was reduced by a foot, though the full results were not available until the contracts had been let, and the *Caroline*s embodied the test results to the full. The hull was very fine, with a square section and bilge keels. The original stipulation that the side must be straight where it was armoured was waived, as the design developed, again to the improvement of the hull

form. This condition was intended to avoid complicated arrangements where the belt ended and a protective deck began fore and aft, but it was decided instead to continue the belt right up to the stem and further aft at 2in thickness. The main belt was 3in High Tensile (HT) steel, and the plates, some very large, were all worked so that they formed part of the strength of the ship, thus saving a good deal of weight. A 1in deck was fitted aft over the steering engine compartment. The upper deck amidships was also in 1in HT steel, although this was as much for strength as protection, as the impossibility of carrying the lower deck through the boiler rooms required deep web frames, extra cross beams and other measures to ensure the strength of the hull, a problem accentuated by the intention to carry fuel in the ends and thus creating a high hogging bending movement. In an attempt to ensure dryness forward, increased flare was given to the forcastle.

MACHINERY

The machinery of the new cruisers also broke new ground. The enterprise of the Italians in their light cruiser *Quarto* was, it was thought, being followed by the Germans in using fast-running destroyer-type turbines in larger ships, and the *Arethusa*s consequently became the first British major warships to be so equipped. The power required to reach the desired speed of 30 knots was high even by battleship standards. Although geared turbines were considered, they were not felt to have proved themselves and four screws were to be fitted, each driven by a 7500shp direct drive turbine running at 590rpm which could give 1000shp at 650rpm for some hours when required. The outer shafts were driven from the forward engine room, the inner from the after. Forward of the engine room were

Undaunted in the Clyde 1914, second ship of the class. She alone had no searchlight platform on the mast and her 4in guns still have no shields.

NMM

two boiler rooms, each with four Yarrow water-tube boilers working at 235lb per sq in. When tenders for the machiner were called for, a curious episode occurred, as all the tenderers quoted to the Admiralty specification, but also submitted alternatives, professedly more economical. As a result, all the six vessels with Parsons turbines also had cruising turbines fitted geared to the outer shafts, to run at a more economical speed. The other two ships had Brown-Curtis turbines, but no cruising turbines.

ARMAMENT

There was much discussion over the armament. The first draft suggested two 6in and four 12pdrs, but this seems quickly to have been replaced by a wholly 4in armament, either ten, as in the *Active* or 12, but in either case to be a new mark of quickfiring gun instead of the ordinary breechloading (BL) guns hitherto used. These guns were to be mounted, again as before, along both sides. Twelve guns, it was found, meant too many men to be carried, and ten became the armament finally approved, with men to fight seven, ie both forecastle and quarter-deck guns (two each) and one side of three. Two single torpedo-tubes were also to be carried. However, there were those who remained unhappy about 4in guns only and it would be interesting to speculate on the success of the *Arethusa*s if they had been completed with their original armament.

Despite the great shortage of light cruisers in 1914-15, the immediately preceding *Active*s and *Blonde*s, upon which the design was based, took a very

minor part in the war, hardly comparable, say, to the early 'Town' class. Late in 1912, however, following the appointment of Rear-Admiral Sir Archibald Moore and Controller, it was again proposed to fit a 6in gun fore and aft, each replacing two 4in. Only minor alterations were necessary, principally raising the conning tower, bridge and funnels $3\frac{1}{2}$ft. The bigger guns meant a slight increase in weight, but the advantage of making the ships rather more than large destroyers was well worth this handicap. Although this proposal was approved by by Bridgeman, then First Sea Lord, and by Churchill, the argument was reopened when the armament of the 1913 cruisers came to be discussed, as there was the question of using the redundant 4in on these ships.

Even at this stage, the all 4in armament was still in the field, although, already, advanced thinkers had gone to an all 6in armament too. In favour of the 4in it was asserted that they could cope with any German destroyer (and indeed light cruisers), that the cruiser would not be tempted to engage superior enemies, that a mixed armament was unsatisfactory in a small ship, and that 6in shell was too heavy to be handled in such small and lively vessels. The advocates of the 6in, however, believed in fitting the largest gun reasonably possible and thus producing more powerful ships, with a marked superiority over destroyers, while a single-calibre armament needed fewer men yet gave greater fighting power. In the end, a curious compromise was reached, after a conference of cruiser admirals. The 1913 cruisers, the *Caroline*s, were to have two 6in aft to allow the ship to protect herself from a chasing cruiser, while eight 4in forward and on the sides would deal with destroyers from wherever they might come. It was suggested that the *Arethusa*s should also be fitted with this extremely odd, for a British ship at least, arrangement of guns. The DNC, however, strongly opposed this suggestion, as the extra weight involved in extending the superstructure was serious in itself, and would also adversely affect the trim. The original modification was therefore allowed to remain. The weight problem was one which became increasingly serious both for the *Arethusa*s and their successors.

The torpedo armament also caused some trouble. It was feared that the 21in torpedo proposed would not stand being fired from the upper deck. The original intention was therefore to fit submerged tubes, but no room could be found for them. A lower deck mounting was suggested, but, again, space could not be found for a training tube, while the deck height was insufficient for loading. An upper deck mounting had therefore to be accepted, at first only with single tubes, but twin tubes were soon fitted to make up the salvo of two which seems to have been considered all that was needed at this time – as in contemporary destroyers and the 'E' class submarines. The final armament was two 6in Mark XII on PIX mountings, six 4in Mark V, one 3in AA and four 21in torpedo tubes. Fire control arrangements were of the rudimentary pre-director

Phaeton goes on her 1914 trials in the Clyde looking throughly disarranged. The two ensigns may be noted. She has sponsons under each 4in gun, and poles up on the radio aerials, as well is the full complement of boats.
P A Vicary

type, there being a control position on the bridge and another at the after end of the superstructure, with voice pipe and 'navyphones' to guns and tubes. Each control position had a rangefinder and two searchlights. An armoured conning tower was, as was then customary, provided on the forecastle, with an armoured tube to the transmitting station below. There were magazines and shell rooms fore and aft, with a long supply route to the broadside guns.

The design as a whole was a very finely balanced one. It will be clear from the foregoing that there was no space to spare, and the weights were equally closely drawn. Although there was a Board margin of 20 tons when the design was approved by the Board in July 1912, it quickly disappeared under the usual small additions and alterations, and, indeed, the *Caroline*s once again started the tendency to enlarge, by being 10ft longer.

Invitations to tender were sent out in July 1912 and orders were placed in September. One ship was allotted to Chatham Yard and another to Devonport, while the remainder were to be built by contract by Fairfields (one), Vickers (two) and Beardmores (three). Each of these firms was to engine its ships, but for dockyard-built ships, an attempt was made to help the Thames Ironworks Co, then in the hands of a receiver, in the hope that they could, with such a contract, surmount their difficulties. But the hope was vain, and eventually the Chatham ship was engined by Fairfields and the Devonport one by the Parsons Company.

Three views of the *Arethusa* when new shows the handsome appearance of the class to good advantage. She has not been fitted with the centre pair of davits and the whaler lies at the boom. She has canvas screens along the waist. The rigging of the radio aerials shows well in the quarter view.

NMM

TURBINES AND BOILERS

Six of the ships had Parsons impulse-reaction turbines, with cruising turbines fitted on the outside shafts. *Arethusa* and *Undaunted* engined by Fairfields were fitted with Brown-Curtis short type turbines without cruising turbines. Designed shp was 30,000shp at 590rpm for 28 knots, with an eight hour overload to 650rpm for 40,000shp and 30 knots. Although these turbines ran at a much higher speed than previous designs, and the builders all expressed misgivings about the low weights specified by the Admiralty, no serious trouble was experienced in the upshot, and similar machinery was fitted in subsequent light cruisers. The cruising turbines, however, do not appear to have been much used, as they took 20-25 minutes to connect up.

Eight Yarrow water-tube boilers were provided working at 235lb per sq in and with a heating surface of 42,400 sq ft, and with forced draught. Succeeding light cruisers again had similar installations.

OIL FUEL

The use of oil fuel was one of the *Arethusa*s great advantages over their predecessors, both in giving higher speed and in avoiding the delay and exhaustion of coaling. But several difficulties were found. The original scheme was to use all the double bottom for fuel, as well as four tanks forward of the fore magazine, two between after engine room and after magazine and two (known as 'peace tanks') over the engine rooms above water. It was first of all felt that the fuel under the boilers might heat dangerously when the boilers were fully extended. Then it was found that some of the oil was so viscous that heating had to be fitted in the tanks. Finally the peace tanks were seen to be a possible danger, as even if the fuel was used first, the vapour left could be dangerous in action. They could also have an adverse effect on stability. In practice, they were filled with 50 tons or so instead of their full capacity of 150 tons, the fuel was used first, and then the tanks were filled with water. Such tanks were not repeated, and their omission contributed to the improved accommodation of subsequent classes. The total oil stowage was 810 tons.

FUEL CONSUMPTION

The fuel consumption of all the *Arethusa*s and their direct-drive successors seems to have been similar, using about 550 tons a day at 29 knots and 260 tons at 24, with 96 at 16 on main engines, and only 60 on the cruising turbines at that speed. The subsequent geared-turbine cruisers saved about 100 tons a day at the higher speeds.

Expressed in the customary manner, the radius of action of the class was:
100 miles at 29 knots (1½ days)
1700 miles at 24 knots (3 days)
3200 miles at 16 knots (8 days)
5000 miles at 16 knots (13 days) cruising turbines.

Names were given to the ships from traditional frigate sources and none, indeed, had been out of the Navy List very long. The Chatham ship, laid down in No 7 Dry Dock on 28 October 1912, became *Arethusa* and gave her name to the class. The *Aurora* at Devonport was actually begun four days earlier, while the contract ships, *Undaunted* at Fairfields, *Phaeton* and *Penelope* at Barrow and *Galatea, Inconstant* and *Royalist* were all laid down by June 1913. The first launch was in September 1913, and when war broke out on 4 August 1914, three of the ships were very near completion – the *Arethusa* was actually commissioned at Chatham on 11 August by Captain B S Thesiger, *Aurora* and *Undaunted* followed within the next month.

The trials of the *Arethusa* were highly unsatisfactory, not only because she did not apparently make her speed, but also because they were run in shallow water in the Thames Estuary, with unreliable bearings as marks; some defects also developed. The DNC therefore demanded that the next ships should be properly tried as much depended on them, with the *Caroline*s coming on fast, and further developments of the type in prospect. Furthermore, it was never expected that the

*Arethusa*s would make their full speed without some trials of propellers to achieve the best design. And, of course, there was the extra weight, such as 37 tons more in the machinery, 29 tons in the 6in guns and five for twin tubes. Both *Aurora* and *Undaunted* were therefore tried on the Polperro (Cornwall) and Skelmorlie measured miles respectively, where they reached 28½ to 29 knots with the full 40,000shp.

No extensive trials of propellers were undertaken, so that this was the most usual performance of the class. When they went into service, they were found to be very wet forward, but were good sea boats, and never seem to have abandoned an operation on account of bad weather. One complaint was indeed recorded in 1915, but the DNC held this to be only what might be

1 *Galatea* at anchor with short topgallant mast. She could be distinguished by the wings to the upper bridge. The motor boat in the after davits shows well.

IWM

2 *Inconstant* in her early days, also with short topgallant mast.

IWM

expected from a small ship in the North Sea. The *Arethusa*s trimmed by the bow, which may partly explain their wetness, and the 10ft longer *Caroline*s were apparently much drier. All the later 'Cs', however, were liable to take water badly over the forecastle, and trawler bows were eventually fitted to the last ones. *To be continued*

BOOK REVIEWS

DÖNITZ – THE LAST FÜHRER
Portrait of a Nazi War Leader by Peter Padfield.
Published by Victor Gollancz February 1984.
525pp (23.5cm × 17.5cm) 32 photographs, 2 maps,
index ISBN 0 575 03186 7 (£12.95).

Mr Padfield has written a long account of the life and career of the late Grand Admiral Karl Dönitz (1892-1980). In it he argues that Dönitz became a fanatical Nazi whose U-Boat Arm was a tool for German world domination. Further he alleges that Dönitz gave tacit, if not active approval to the genocide programme. He also states that the U-boat threat was a mere chimera, never posing a serious threat to Great Britain and her will to continue to fight.

The military argument appears sporadically throughout the work, with a concentration (strangely) in the last pages on Dönitz's appreciation of the naval situation and U-boat strength and capabilities on the eve of the Second World War. Could the U-Boat Arm have brought Great Britain to her knees if all available submarines had been concentrated in the Atlantic at the start of hostilities – assuming that Dönitz had had the 300 U-boats he stated were necessary for the task? Mr Padfield says no.

In the initial period of the U-boat war, up to the middle of 1940, the sinking figures were low, but they began to rise dramatically, especially when the French west coast bases had been secured. By the end of 1941 they had once more begun to fall. On 11 December 1941, in the euphoria of the immediate aftermath of Pearl Harbor, Hitler declared war on the United States and Dönitz ordered the start of Operation *Paukenschlag* ('Drumbeat') and sinkings rose to unprecedented heights.

This was in fact one of Dönitz's most serious mistakes, and was compounded by the decision to undertake 'tonnage war' rather than the far more worrying form – economic warfare directly mounted against shipping around the one American springboard into Europe – the British Isles. The author does refer to the two forms of warfare, but fails to explore them; there is little doubt that fear of the effects of concerted U-boat warfare was very much in Churchill's mind at the time. From the evidence in the Public Record Office and elsewhere the disruption of the eastbound Atlantic convoys could have caused the withdrawal of British participation in the Second World War.

The results off the East Coast of the United States were undoubtedly encouraging, but when forced by the institution of convoy there to return to the North Atlantic convoy routes, the Allies were still unsure of their ability to deal with the menace until the resounding successes of spring 1943. Mr Padfield seems to be unaware of the main axiom of the Principles of War, which states that once the aim is selected it must be maintained.

The author also puts too much significance on the figure of 300 U-boats that Dönitz considered necessary to close the Atlantic to shipping bound for England. His appreciation (see above) was an example of frustration if not consternation at war being declared by Great Britain long before Hitler had said the massive Z-Plan Fleet need be ready (between 1946 and 1948). Both Grand Admiral Raeder and Dönitz were in agreement that the only resort lay in U-boats because they took less time to build. Therein lies Dönitz's reasoning – at least eventually there would be something for the Navy to do in the war; as it was they could merely demonstrate that men of the *Kriegsmarine* would show others how to die well.

The further argument that had there been 300 boats, then all resources of the Royal Navy would be concentrated on one single route, is an over-simplification, as well as a recipe for disaster. Incidentally, the comment that aircraft carriers would be included in escorts is countered by two factors: First, there was no efficient anti-submarine bomb in service at the time, and second, the *Courageous* sinking. Only three years later did the escort carrier begin to take a toll of U-boats, and by then the enemy had been forced away from the main northern convoy routes, submarine detection and attack techniques having undergone a revolution.

Mr Padfield argues in addition that had the Royal and Allied Navies been in any danger of losing the convoy war, the United States would have entered the war to combat the German threat. Here his knowledge of American history and politics is sadly lacking.

The real heart of the book lies however not in a detailed examination of the naval aspects of the Grand Admiral's life, but in the relationships between him and the Nazis. The early descriptions of his life are recounted to show a strict Prussian upbringing, yet demonstating that Dönitz as a young man was fascinated by the more esoteric things in life. There is also significant reference to the question of whether Dönitz was actually mentally unstable. This last point is both extraneous (surely a succession of Commanding Officers would have noticed), and as hurtful to his remaining family as are the allegations of rabid Nazism that follow.

The more serious allegation against Dönitz was, and is, that the September 1942 *Laconia* Order was a *carte-blanche* for U-boat commanders to shoot merchant ship survivors in the water. It seems strange that there was only one such incident during the war, and the very order caused problems of wording before it was transmitted. There is no doubt that at least some of the evidence adduced at the International Military Tribunal at Nüremberg was of dubious origin, especially as it came from deserters from the German Armed Forces. The claim that the Nazism allegation is further supported by the rhetorical nature of some of Dönitz's exhortatory speeches and his *assumed* presence at a genocide briefing by Himmler requires a lot of faith in any historian of the period – especially in view of the *débâcle* over the Hitler Diaries.

There is no doubt that Dönitz was not an entirely simple character, but Mr Padfield fails to publish the evidence so vehemently promised when talking to Mr Ludovic Kennedy ('Timewatch', February, BBC 2). It is not enough to throw mud; an historian must make it stick. Equally, no responsible historian should shrink from the unpalatable truth, even if it does cause a change in opinion; regrettably Mr Padfield has failed to alter this reviewer's opinion, but he had caused a number of further questions to be asked.

The books reads racily, with a journalistic flow, and can thus be assimilated readily, but the melange of fact, surmise and suspicion makes it a book for the specialist professional historian rather than the general reader.

David Westwood

OTHER BOOKS RECEIVED

The Great War at Sea 1914-1918 by Richard Hough (OUP, October 1983) 353pp, 41 photographs, 11 maps, index, £14.50, ISBN 0 19 215871 6, 9½in × 6in. A strange offering from OUP since it is no more than a popular, compressed version of Arthur Marder's famous five volumes on the *Dreadnought to Scapa Flow*. The post-Jutland period, more than half of hostilities, receives a handful of pages. The Grand Fleet and High Seas Fleet dominate to the exclusion of all else, especially the activities of the other major navies.

US Naval Developments by Jan S Breemer (Frederick Warne, February 1984) 194pp, photographs, 59 figures, tables and organisation charts, index, £14.95, ISBN 0 7232 3234 2, 9¾in × 6¾in. A compact fact-filled guide to the US Navy of the 1980s with a foreward by Norman Polmar. Four appendices detail its ships, aircraft, weapons and sensors. Chapter 5 refreshingly covers recruitment and manning problems.

The US Merchant Marine: in search of an enduring maritime policy by Clinton H Whitehurst, Jr (Naval Institute Press/Arms and Armour Press, March 1984) 330pp, 25 photographs, 39 tables and bibliography, glossary, index, £20.95, ISBN 0 87021 737 2, 9in × 5¾in. The first general survey of American shipping to be published since 1954. Clinton H Whitehurst and other specialist contributors from the industry provide 20 essays that cover history, government involvement, technology, the American seaman, ports, US-owned foreign flag shipping, inland movement of goods and rival fleets (especially the Soviet Union). Since 1954 the US merchant fleet has shrunk from 1123 ships to 500 (late 1982) and its world ranking from first place to eleventh. This is a comprehensive and strategic study taking in the Rapid Deployment Force and the naval role of merchant ships.

Sea Power in the Falklands by Captain Charles W Koburger, Jr, US Coast Guard Reserve (Retd) (Praeger, March 1984) 188pp, 19 photographs, 12 maps, index, £14.95, ISBN 0 03 069534 1, 9½in × 5¾in. A vigorously written analysis of the Falklands War from an American observer that has two particularly interesting chapters on Operation Rosario (the original Argentine invasion) and the *Armada Republica Argentina*. This short account has no revelations or axes to grind and is all the better for that.

A's & A's

CHINESE BATTLESHIPS *(Warship 29)* From Peter H Kuntz, Durmersheim, Germany

In the above cited article, the author states, that these two ships were the biggest warships completed for a foreign navy in Germany before World War I.

This is not quite true: In June 1900 AG Vulkan of Stettin completed the armoured cruiser *Yakumo* for the Japanese Navy. She was far bigger than the Chinese ships, having 10,288 tons in loaded condition. This ship served in the Japanese Navy for 46 years!

HMS QUEEN ELIZABETH *(Warship* 29, photograph p 31) From N J M Campbell, Ryde, Isle of Wight and J Dixon of Altrincham, Cheshire.

Aircraft were supplied to battleships of the Grand Fleet during the second half of 1918. Late October figures give the 5 *Queen Elizabeth*s as carrying a total of 3-1½ Strutters and 7 single-seaters, probably Camels as the Pup was being phased out, with platforms on B and X turrets. These platforms were not all identical, and some did not have the rails over the gun barrels which were needed for the 1½ Strutter.

Decapping armour was not fitted and the light line of

B turret is believed to be due to sunlight falling on the edge of the 13in face plate where it joined the 11in armour of the rest of the turret.

The 3 patches visible on the photographs (on the shelter-deck screen above No 3 6in gun near the scuttles just above the open skylight and on the screen above as J Dixon has helpfully pointed out) were from hits by Turkish field guns on 5 March 1915. The damage report gives 18 hits by 2.8in percussion fuzed shrapnel from mobile guns. Next day there were 3 hits by 11in from the old battleship *Hairredin Barbarossa*, all on the side armour below water and causing very little damage. On 18 March there were 5 hits from 5.9in howitzers firing HE shell.

After Jutland *Warspite* had similar patches on her port quarter near the blanked off casemates. These scars remained with both ships until their reconstruction in the late 1930s.

COASTAL FORCES MISCELLANY From G M Hudson, Halifax, W Yorks.

In *Conway's All the World's Fighting Ships 1922-46*, reference will be found on page 67 to the first MTBs built for the Royal Navy since the First World War; the

60ft British Power Boat *MTB 1-12, 14-19*. Among the details of these 18 boats appears a note that, *MTB 1* was ex-*MTB 7*, *MTB 7* was ex-*MTB 13* and *MTB 19* was ex-*MTB 1*. A comment on these renumberings may be of interest.

The original *MTB 1*, was involved in extensive 'first of class' trials, from early 1936 until 1939. During this period she was under the charge of British Power Boats (BPB). She was commissioned temporarily on 23 June 1936, under Lieutenant-Commander G B Sayer RN and on 30 June, with *MTB 2*, also temporarily commissioned for the occasion, took part in a special demonstration for King Edward VIII. With the King, accompanied by the First Sea Lord and Commander Lord Louis Mountbatten, on board, *MTB 1* carried out a high speed attack, during which a practice torpedo was fired at the destroyer HMS *Amazon*. *MTB 1* was the first of His Majesty's Ships, in which King Edward VIII embarked after his accession and, after this exercise, she paid off and returned to BPB control.

By the end of 1936, the remaining boats of the 1935 Programme, *MTB 2-6*, had been accepted into service and it was decided to send a flotilla of this type to the Mediterranean, based on Malta. In order to bring the 1st MTB Flotilla up to full strength – six boats – and also present a logical numerical sequence, *MTB 7*, the first boat of the 1936 Programme, was renumbered *MTB 1 (ii)* in April 1937, becoming the Senior Officer's boat (Lt-Cdr G B Sayer RN). *MTB 1 (i)* then became *MTB 7 (ii)*.

A similar situation occurred in 1938. As *MTB 7 (ii)* ex-*MTB 1 (i)* was still running trials under BPB control, *MTB 13*, a 1937 Programme boat, which was still under construction at Hythe, was redesignated *MTB 7 (iii)* whereupon *MTB 7 (ii)* ex-*MTB 1 (i)* became *MTB 13 (ii)*. This enabled the 2nd MTB Flotilla, shipped in freighters to Hong Kong in September 1938, to comprise *MTB 7-12*.

The final MTB renumbering of the original boat took place in June 1938 when *MTB 13 (ii)*, ex-*MTB 7 (ii)*, ex-*MTB 1 (i)* became *MTB 19*, presumably as a result of the number '13' being considered unlucky. (This is borne out by an explanation of pendant numbers prior to 1948, where no pendant number '13' appears to have been in use, with one exception. For some reason *S 13* did get used; surprisingly there was a *MA/SB* (later *MGB 13*!).

It was however the following year before *MTB 19* was finally accepted by the Royal Navy, joining *MTB 14-18*, to form the 3rd MTB Flotilla. Originally intended for Singapore, these six boats actually joined the 1st Flotilla at Malta for the outbreak of World War II, before returning, via French rivers and canals, to Portsmouth on 8 December 1939.

The renumbering of the original *MTB 1* was by no means over when she finally entered service as *MTB 19*. Whilst the five most modern boats of the 1st MTB Flotilla, *MTB 14-18*, were ready to operate from their new base at Felixstowe by early 1940, the six older boats, *MTB 1-5* and *19*, were no longer considered fit for front line operations. (*MTB 6* had been lost through heavy weather off Sardinia on the return journey from

Malta to Portsmouth.) Consequently, in the late summer of 1940, these six boats were reclassified as Motor Attendant Craft and were renumbered *MAC 1-6* respectively.

It is understood that MAC were used as dispatch boats by Captains (Minesweepers), at Sheerness, Dover, Portsmouth, Harwich, and Grimsby, for visiting their flotilla at sea. These were requisitioned trawlers, presumably at that time in the war, not fitted with short-range radios.

The final reclassification and renumbering of these craft occurred in 1942. After service as MAC, several of these boats served on air/sea rescue duties during 1941/42, before being converted for target service duties in 1942. In her ultimate role, the original boat was again renumbered, becoming *C/T 06* and, as such, she appeared on the 'sale lists' issued postwar by the Director of Small Craft Disposals.

Naval Books

Conway Maritime offer an unrivalled range of authoritative and well-illustrated titles on naval subjects. A free catalogue is available, but some of the leading titles are listed below:

MERCHANT SHIPS AT WAR
The Falklands Experience
Captain Roger Villar RN DSC
The Falklands War is now distant enough to allow an objective appraisal of its achievements and lessons; this book is the first to study what is probably the most outstanding facet of the whole campaign – the rapid requisition, conversion and deployment of a highly varied fleet of nearly 50 merchant ships.
9½" x 7¼", 192 pages, 135 illustrations. ISBN 0 85177 298 6. £9.50 (plus £1.25 p + p)

US NAVAL WEAPONS*
by Norman Friedman
This exhaustive study by an acknowledged expert on the subject discusses the development and function of every weapon system employed by the US Navy from the birth of the 'New Navy' in 1883 to the present day.
12¼" x 8½", 288 pages, 200 photos, 150 line drawings. ISBN 0 85177 240 4. £18.00 (plus £1.80 p + p)

NAVAL RADAR*
by Norman Friedman
A layman's guide to the theory, functions and performance of seaborne radar systems, from their introduction just before the Second World War to the present day, including a catalogue of every major piece of radar equipment to have seen service with the world's navies.
11" x 8½", 240 pages, 200 photos, 100 line drawings. ISBN 0 85177 238 2. £18.00 (plus £1.80 p + p)

CARRIER AIR POWER
by Norman Friedman
A penetrating analysis of how carrier warfare operates, with extensive data on the ships and their aircraft.
12" x 9", 192 pages, 187 photos, 32 line drawings. ISBN 0 85177 216 1. £12.50 net (plus £1.50 p + p)

ANATOMY OF THE SHIP:
THE BATTLECRUISER HOOD*
by John Roberts
The first volume of this new series. Every aspect of the *Hood* is covered in a degree of detail never previously attempted for a recent capital ship, and the standard of line drawings has been highly praised.

9½" x 10" landscape, 128 pages, 24 photos, 320 line drawings. ISBN 0 85177 250 1. £8.50 (plus £1.25 p + p)

ANATOMY OF THE SHIP: THE AIRCRAFT CARRIER INTREPID*
by John Roberts
The second in this new series, this volume covers the *Essex* class aircraft carrier which is now being refurbished in New York as a floating Air-Sea-Space museum.
9½" x 10" landscape, 96 pages, 20 photos, 300 line drawings. ISBN 0 85177 251 X. £8.50 (plus £1.25 p + p)

SUBMARINE BOATS
The Beginnings of Underwater Warfare
by Richard Compton-Hall
"Cdr. Compton-Hall has produced a book whose research and many rare photographs and drawings will delight both the technically-minded and the general reader." *Daily Telegraph*
9½" x 7¼", 192 pages, 173 photos and drawings. ISBN 0 85177 288 9. £10.50 (plus £1.50 p + p)

CONWAY'S ALL THE WORLD'S FIGHTING SHIPS 1860-1905*
The first complete listing of all warships between the first ironclad and the *Dreadnought*. "... must rank with the all-time great naval reference works ..." *The Navy*. "... all the thoroughness and attention to detail we have come to expect from Conway Maritime ... excellent value". *Ships Monthly*
12¼" x 8½", 448 pages, 471 photos, 506 line drawings. ISBN 0 85177 133 5. £24.00 (plus £2.00 p + p)

CONWAY'S ALL THE WORLD'S FIGHTING SHIPS 1922-1946*
The second in this highly acclaimed series, the 1922-1946 volume covers all significant warships built between the Washington Treaty and the end of the wartime construction programmes. With over 1000 illustrations, it is the ultimate reference book on the navies of World War II.
12¼" x 8½", 464 pages, 506 photos, 530 line drawings. ISBN 0 85177 146 7. £30.00 (plus £2.00 p + p)

CONWAY'S ALL THE WORLD'S FIGHTING SHIPS 1947-1982*
Part I: The Western Powers
Part II: The Warsaw Pact and Non-Aligned Nations
"For those readers who already have the first two volumes, we do not need to make any further recommendation. To those new to these works we strongly advise you to make an inspection." *Model Boats*
Part I: *12¼" x 8¼", 304 pages, 280 photos, 250 line drawings. ISBN 0 85177 225 0. £25.00 (plus £2.00 p+ p)*
Part II: *12¼" x 8¼", 256 pages, 250 photos, 240 line drawings. ISBN 0 85177 278 1. £25.00 (plus £2.00 p + p)*

A CENTURY OF NAVAL CONSTRUCTION: The History of the Royal Corps of Naval Constructors
by D K Brown R C N C
This behind-the-scenes history of the Royal Navy's designers offers a new insight into the factors governing British warship design from the nineteenth century to the Falklands conflict.
9½" x 6", 384 pages, 92 photos, 20 line drawings. ISBN 0 85177 282 X. £20.00 (plus £2.00 p + p)

DESTROYER WEAPONS OF WORLD WAR 2*
by Peter Hodges and Norman Friedman
A detailed comparison between British and US destroyer weapons, including mountings, directors and electronics. "... one of the greatest possible additions to the ... range of naval books ..." *The Navy*
9½" x 7¼", 192 pages, 150 photos, 73 line drawings. ISBN 0 85177 137 8. £7.50 (plus £1.25 p + p)

BATTLESHIP DESIGN AND DEVELOPMENT 1905-1945
by Norman Friedman
The first layman's guide to the design process and the factors governing the development of capital ships. "... an eye-opening study of an extremely complex business ..." *Nautical Magazine*.
10" x 8", 176 pages, 200 photos, plans and line drawings. ISBN 0 85177 135 1. £8.50 (plus £1.25 p + p)

MODERN WARSHIP DESIGN AND DEVELOPMENT
by Norman Friedman
"... never before have the problems and parameters of modern warship design been set out so comprehensively, informatively and clearly ... the book should be read by everyone with a concern for the modern naval scene, professional or amateur, uniformed or civilian." *Journal of the Royal United Services Institute*
10" x 8", 192 pages, 167 photos, 65 line drawings. ISBN 0 85177 147 5. £9.50 (plus £1.25 p + p)

*These titles are available in North America from the Naval Institute Press, Annapolis, Md 21402.

from your Local Bookseller or by post from
Conway Maritime Press Limited
24 Bride Lane, Fleet Street, London EC4Y 8DR

(when ordering direct please add the posting and packing charge noted after the price)

EDITORIAL

The Aegean Campaign of late 1943 is not one of the best remembered naval episodes of the Second World War yet over forty years later it holds more than historical significance.

The Aegean or Dodecanese Campaign lasted from the Italian surrender in September to the Allied (mainly Greek) evacuation of Samos by caique into neutral Turkey in late November. At a time when the Allies were winning the war on all other fronts, Hitler's determination to hold on to Crete and Rhodes (thus deterring Turkey from entering the war) resulted in a crushing local defeat for the largely British forces involved. The takeover of Rhodes and its strategic airfields by 7000 Germans from 25,000 Italians, who understandably expected but did not receive massive Allied help, proved to be decisive while the British ad hoc seizure of smaller neighbouring islands (especially Kos and Leros to the north) ultimately proved futile.

Kos fell in two days (3-4 October) and Leros in five (12-16 November) to brilliantly improvised German amphibious and airborne attacks launched from Athens and Crete. The cost to the Allies amounted to 4800 British Army casualties (3200 prisoners of war); 5350 Italian prisoners (many officers were shot out of hand by their former allies); 136 guns; 115 RAF aircraft; a crippled cruiser; 6 destroyers and 2 submarines sunk as well as 10 lesser warships. Three more cruisers, 4 destroyers and 4 submarines were heavily damaged. The Germans' decisive victory cost 12 steamers, 20 minor warships and 1 destroyer wrecked with perhaps 3000 troops killed or wounded. The *Luftwaffe* lost 156 planes winning a duel with the Royal Navy scarcely less severe than that off Crete 28 months earlier.

From a naval point of view the fascination and frustration of this campaign can be summed up in a single question. Why was the Royal Navy once more committed to transporting, supplying, defending and finally trying to evacuate isolated garrisons with too few ships in the teeth of hostile airpower given the enormous Allied superiority in the Mediterranean?

Even with all the evidence available, including the recently published volume 3 of *British Intelligence in the Second World War*, this is not an easy question to answer. At one level the Dodecanese campaign was bedevilled by American suspicions of Churchill's vision of an Allied push into the Balkans alongside the just opened invasion of Italy. This came to a head when first Eisenhower and then Roosevelt refused to divert any air support from the Italian Front after the fall of Kos. Roosevelt put it starkly 'strategically, if we get the Aegean Islands I ask myself where do we go from there'. The US P38 long-range Lightning fighter squadrons briefly giving cover to the cruisers and destroyers were withdrawn on 11 October and never returned despite Ultra intelligence of daily German postponements of Operation Leopard, the assault on Leros.

The loss of the US fighters forced the Royal Navy to abandon daylight sweeps into the Aegean. The destroyers lay up in neutral Turkish waters during the day, where the *Luftwaffe* was categorically ordered by Hitler not to bomb them (as the Enigma decrypts showed from 12 October) before returning at night to Haifa, Beirut or Alexandria. How desperate the British Chiefs of Staff became can be seen when at their suggestion the Foreign Secretary requested Turkey on 7 November to allow Allied aircraft to operate from Anatolia. Turkey refused and five days later, despite the fullest intelligence of German moves, the 25-ship landings on Leros began unintercepted and achieved tactical surpise. Not only did the destroyer force miss the invasion force due to the prohibition on daylight operation, but sweeps the following night by 6 destroyers also failed to find anything and a follow-up night landing on 15-16 November was reacted to only at dawn from Turkish waters. After land fighting as bitter as for Crete in 1941, the Allied garrison surrendered on the evening of the 16th.

These failures had been preceded by one before the invasion of Kos. The battleships *King George V* and *Howe* were at Alexandria after escorting the surrendered Italian Fleet there. They sailed for Home Waters on 1 October taking *Faulknor* (seen on this issue's cover) *Fury, Echo* and *Eclipse* as their destroyer screen. As a result two submarines were the only warships available to attack the invasion convoy which, right up to when in sight of Kos, was assumed to be Rhodes-bound. It is hard to avoid the conclusion that even the available naval forces were not best used. The first MTBs reached the Aegean theatre only on 6 October. Simultaneous events across the Mediterranean happened very quickly and the crisis of Salerno absorbed the aircraft of 4 British escort carriers, *Illustrious, Formidable* and *Unicorn* by mid-September. Command changes cannot have been helpful; Cunningham became First Sea Lord on 4 October and Vice-Admiral Sir Algernon Willis succeeded him as C-in-C Levant (15th).

A year later the British Aegean Force (including 7 escort carriers, 7 cruisers and 19 destroyers) would cover landings on the Aegean islands and mainland Greece when the Germans finally began evacuating everywhere except Crete and Rhodes. By that time, however, hostilities between Greek Royalist and Communist guerilas were a year old and the legacy of their civil war continues to haunt Greece today. The lessons of 1943 are also not without relevance to her problems with her NATO ally Turkey and their potential adversary – the Soviet Union. The Aegean Crisis of 1975-76, coming after the Turkish invasion of Cyprus, demonstrated again that large garrisons on islands are simply hostages to superior air and naval power. It is sincerely to be hoped that the Aegean never again becomes a sea of conflict. **Randal Gray**

Nordenfelt Submarines

By John M Maber

The Rev George William Garrett (1852–1902) stands in the hatchway of his 1879 submersible *Resurgam* in the Britannia Engine Works and Foundry, Birkenhead.

Author's collection

In March 1880 the magazine *Scientific American* reported under a heading 'The Garrett Submarine Torpedo Boat':

> 'This is a new torpedo boat, invented by the Rev G W Garrett, England and besides being capable of being used as a most formidable weapon afloat has the power of sinking and remaining under water for very many hours, and thus can enter any blockade port unperceived. No compressed air is carried, but the air in the boat is maintained at its normal composition by a chemical apparatus invented by Mr Garrett. When under water, also, no smoke or gas is given off, although an engine of considerable power is kept in motion. Various experiments with the vessel have been made in the Great Float, Birkenhead before setting off on a voyage to Portsmouth . . . The boat, the inventor tells us, is in every way a success, and will easily perform what has been expected of her, and thus become one of the most deadly weapons of naval warfare.'

This report, based on one which appeared originally in the *London Graphic*, referred to Garrett's steam-driven submarine *Resurgam* which had been put afloat by crane at Birkenhead in 1879. In this craft, engined with a single-cylinder horizontal return connecting rod engine driving a single screw, steam was taken, when running on the surface, at the then high pressure of 150lb per square inch (psi) from a large coal-fired boiler occupying the greater part of the cylindrical centre section of the boat. Preparations for diving involved sealing the furnace and ashpit doors, followed by shutting down the forced draught blower and the conning tower. Thereafter, in diving trim, steam was taken off the boiler utilising the latent heat in the same manner as Lamm's smoke free tram, patented in 1872 and subsequently adapted for service as a fireless locomotive in explosive works and depots.

Garrett planned his craft so that a minimum reserve buoyancy of about 100lb was maintained as a safety margin but in practice of course the residual positive buoyancy depended upon how much coal and feed water was embarked. There were apparently no ballasting arrangements and *Resurgam*, which floated more or less awash with only the light casing and conning tower clear of the water, was to be taken down when under way by the action of diving planes, positioned either side amidships and controlled manually from the conning tower. With but one pair of planes, and these amidships, there would have been a complete lack of longitudinal stability although the boat might have been able to 'porpoise' along alternately diving and coming awash, a mode of progress made necessary for navigation in any case by the absence of a periscope.

Built by Cochran & Co, the boiler makers then of Birkenhead, *Resurgam* was 'launched' into the Great

Float with the aid of a 50-ton crane all but ready for sea on 10 December 1879 and later the same day moved out into the Mersey unde her own power. In the meantime, it had been decided, probably to attract Admiralty interest in the project, that the craft should be steamed round to Portsmouth where a demonstration could be arranged. Thus with Garrett in command *Resurgam* departed that evening, it being intended that preliminary diving trials should be undertaken in Liverpool Bay en route for the South Coast. Planning appears to have been somewhat ad hoc, as also was the navigation, but eventually *Resurgam* reached Rhyl in North Wales where a base was established to carry out certain modifications before embarking on further trials. The craft remained in the area for some weeks during which time Garrett used most of this remaining funds to purchase the small steam yacht *Elfin*, both to provide accommodation and to

Nordenfelt I on the slipway at Ekensberg near Stockholm before her launch in 1885.

Author's collection

serve as an escort when required. Eventually, late in the evening of 24 February 1880 *Elfin* left Rhyl with *Resurgam* in tow bound for Portsmouth. Thirty-six hours later, however, in boisterous weather the tow parted and *Resurgam*, without crew or power, drifted off in a sinking condition eventually being lost to view.

In the absence of the submarine the Admiralty quickly lost any interest that might have been aroused and Garrett found himself for the time being without employment and lacking further reources. Thus he approached the Swedish millionaire engineer Thorsten Nordenfelt with a proposal that the latter should take over the development of his (Garrett's) submarine patents. Nordenfelt apparently proved enthusiastic in considering Garrett's ideas and saw in the submarine the ideal vehicle for Whitehead's 'locomotive' torpedo. In the event their working relationship was put on a formal basis in 1881 when Garrett became Nordenfelt's assistant for submarine design and construction.

The problem with the primitive locomotive torpedo was to bring it within effective range of the intended target, a task rendered risky albeit even suicidal by the invention of the quick-firing gun and the later development of a more accurate weapon of this type by Nordenfelt himself. Thus he now found himself in a position to take advantage of Garrett's practical experience which he put to good use in the design of his first submarine torpedo boat, laid down at Ekensberg, near Stockholm, in 1882.

NORDENFELT I

Known as *Nordenfelt I*, this 64ft long craft displaced 60 tons in surface trim and was of cigar-shaped hull form with concentric circular frames made up from wrought iron angle bar of 3in by 3in by 3/8in section spaced 2ft apart. On this frame the hull itself was built up of iron plates ⅜in thick apart from the bottom plating over the length of the mid-section of the craft which was of ⅝in thickness, the overall strength of the structure being considered adequate to withstand diving to about 50ft over the keel without distortion. The maximum diameter of the hull was 9ft but sponsons amidships increased the beam to 11ft.

Internally, of course, the thickness of the plating together with the depth of the frame webs restricted the useful space to that available within a maximum diameter of about 8ft. Forward, the cylindrical return tube marine boiler occupied much of this available space thus making difficult any communication with the fore end of the craft. Working at a pressure of 100psi, although designed to withstand 150psi, this large boiler supplied steam not only to the propulsion and auxiliary machinery, but connected also with heat exchangers in

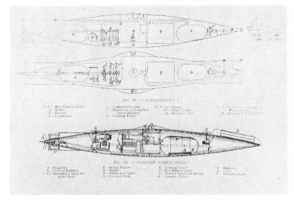

Above: Elevation and section of *Nordenfelt I*. Below: Elevation of a Turkish Nordenfelt.

Author's collection

the bottoms of a pair of accumulators holding in all some 8 tons of hot water at a nominal 150lb pressure. Utilising the latent heat on Lamm's 'fireless' engine principle (as in Garrett's boat) this was claimed to be sufficient for about 14 miles at 4 knots.

The 100hp twin cylinder compound engine driving a single screw took steam at 100psi when running on the surface and exhausted via a surface condenser back to the boiler feed system. When preparing to dive the funnel was housed and shut off together with all other openings, while the furnace and ash pit doors were sealed to prevent the noxious combustion gases escaping within the craft. With the forward and after accumulators now opened up and connected through to the boiler, steam would be flashed off as the pressure dropped from the nominal 150psi thus to enable the engine to continue working. The exhaust condensate returned via the hot well to the feed system in the normal way. In order to extract the maximum stored energy, the system was fitted with a large capacity air pump thus producing the high degree of vaccum required to work the steam down to below atmospheric pressure. This made necessary in turn an engine with large diameter cylinders to utilise the steam at this low pressure. There remained the problem of heating the eight tons of water in the accumulators which involved, in fact, circulating steam through the heat exchangers for 48 hours or more in order to raise the required pressure of 150psi! Fore and aft trim could be regulated by adjusting the water levels in the two accumulator cisterns.

In surface trim Nordenfelt's craft lay with some 3ft of freeboard amidships but preparations for diving involved first admitting some four tons of water to a centrally placed ballast tank to bring the boat awash with some 600lb to 800lb of residual buoyancy. The boat was then to be taken down by the use of small vertical propellers positioned each side amidships in the sponsons mentioned above and driven by a 6hp twin cylinder engine controlled either by a hand regulator or by an automatic throttle valve. Water pressure via an open-ended pipe acted against a weight causing the throttle valve to close as depth increased, hopefully to bring about a measure of stable depth control. With the craft dived and under way it was intended that trim should be assisted by a pair of hydroplanes acting forward, pendulum controlled via a steam-powered servo system. However, it was found in practice that surging in the ballast tank, boiler and accumulator cisterns, coupled with an inherent lack of longitudinal stability due to the siting of the vertical propellers amidships, rendered the task well nigh impossible for more than a few minutes at a time. When dived, of course, the vessel would have been blind.

A centrifugal blower provided forced draught for the boiler so that when preparing for an attack the tall funnel could be unrigged and stowed before trimmed down awash for the initial approach against the intended target. Smoke and furnace gases were then discharged below the surface, sufficient positive pressure being maintained by the blower, thus reducing the chance of detection.

Following her launch and completion of fitting out, *Nordenfelt I* was towed to Landskrona in southern Sweden for preliminary trials that were run during 21–25 September 1885 in the presence of a large number of observers including 39 representing European and other naval powers. Only limited success only was achieved, however, although the craft ran well in a semi-submerged condition with little more than the tiny conning tower awash. Once fully dived, stable depth keeping proved elusive and in general the opinion of the observers was that the craft had, at best, potential as a semi-submersible torpedo boat. The armament comprised a single 14in torpedo tube[1] for launching a Whitehead or a Schwartzkopf torpedo, placed well forward within a fairing external to the pressure hull, and a Nordenfelt 25mm QF gun.

Closed down trials showed the air within the boat to be sufficient to meet the needs of the three-man crew for some six hours although on the other hand subsequent experience demonstrated that the sealing of the furnace and ash pit doors was far from satisfactory. In fact the effects of carbon monoxide and carbon dioxide were to make themselves only too frequently apparent. Drowsiness was noticed amongst the more sensitive crew members and on occasion men became unconscious. Indeed George Garrett himself fell victim to the escaping fumes which left him unfit for duty for some three weeks!

The Landskrona trials were followed by further lengthy trials run in England, in Southampton Water, where a mass of data was gathered to be utilised in new designs of submersibles planned by Nordenfelt. Despite the problems encountered during these prolonged exercises, Lieutenant-General Sir Andrew Clarke, the Inspector General of Fortifications, who had been present at Landskrona, realised the potential of the submarine in a coastal defence role and recommended the purchase of a Nordenfelt boat at a cost of £9000 to permit a thorough investigation of the question. The British government of the day evinced no further interest in the matter, however, and the proposal was quickly forgotten. Nordenfelt was fortunate in 1886, therefore, in being able through the agency of the famous arms dealer Basil Zaharoff to dispose of his No1 to the Greek government for the same sum (£9000), the craft being demonstrated to the apparent satisfaction of her new owners during trials in the Bay of Salamis later in that year. By this time the sealing arrangements for the furnace and ash pit doors had been substantially improved although in all probability the boat saw little service under the Greek flag, other than in a semi-submersible role, and she was broken up soon after the turn of the century.

NORDENFELT II

In the meantime, in 1884, with only limited construction resources available in Sweden, it seems probable that Thorsten Nordenfelt had approached the Barrow Shipbuilding Co with proposals, possibly involving some form of partnership, for the building of submarines incorporating his patents. At a time beset by economic problems and declining trade the Barrow company had achieved some success in building warships so Nordenfelt's proposals offered a further welcome diversification. Presumably terms were agreed for building a Nordenfelt type submarine as a speculative venture since records exist of Yard No 143 which was put afloat at Barrow on 14 April 1886. In the absence of any prospective purchaser the craft was registered initially as a merchant vessel, presumably while preliminary trials were run.

Larger than her predecessor, the new steel-hull submarine displaced 160 tons but retained the same cigar-shaped hull form, albeit with a 12ft diameter circular section amidships and an overall length of 100ft. In fact, the general design was essentially similar to that of the earlier craft although in an attempt to improve longitudinal stability, the vertical diving propellers were arranged one forward and one aft, each driven independently by a 6hp engine. The boiler was sited aft of amidships while the two hot water accumulators were replaced by a single cistern forward. Aft of the boiler the twin cylinder compound engine of 250hp, taking steam at 100psi, was mounted in line with the run of the bottom plating at an angle of about 4 degrees to the horizontal, the drive to the single screw being via an inclined propeller shaft and a pair of universal joints. Bunkers abreast the boiler held briquettes (blocks of compressed coal dust) for ready use in addition to which 8 tons of fuel were stowed in a bunker beside the hot water cistern, sufficient in all for 900 miles at economical speed without refuelling. Designed speeds were 11 knots in surface trim and 5 knots dived.

Preparations for diving included closing all openings and sealing the furnace and ash pit doors while water ballast tanks forward and aft, each of 15 tons capacity,

The Turkish Nordenfelt *Abdul Hamid* (nicknamed the 'Whale Ship') off Constantinople in 1888. Her external torpedo tube and the 25mm Nordenfelt guns are highly prominent as well as the vertical diving screws. Behind her is an *Osmanieh* class broadside ironclad (one of four British-built and launched 1864–65).

Author's collection

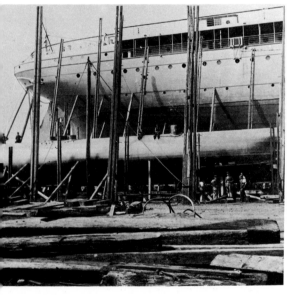

Nordenfelt IV, destined for Russia, building at the Barrow Shipbuilding Company (later Vickers).

Vickers Shipbuilding & Engineering Ltd

were fitted to trim the boat down. An additional 7-ton ballast tank amidships under the central compartment served to regulate buoyancy thus allowing compensation for fuel burned off. Once awash the vertical propellers could be brought into use to take the boat down while maintaining a horizontal attitude, obviously a delicate operation. As in *Nordenfelt I*, bow hydroplanes, worked manually or automatically under the influence of a pendulum, were fitted to help overcome the problem of trim control while running awash or dived. Apart from the commander, the crew numbered six who, with the boat on passage or running closed down for diving, worked in two watches. Unlike Garrett's *Resurgam*, no means were provided in the two Nordenfelt submarines for air purification.

The weapon fit comprised two mechanically-launched 14in Whitehead torpedoes carried in a pair of external

tubes on the bow and two 25mm Nordenfelt machine guns, one forward and the other aft of the conning tower.

In the meantime the Turkish government, fearful of Russian intentions while at the same time not wishing to be outdone by the nation's neighbour and arch rival Greece which had purchased *Nordenfelt I*, had shown more than a passing interest in acquiring a pair of submarines to strengthen its defences. Subsequent events remain something of a mystery but it would seem that on 23 January 1886 the Turkish government placed an order for two submarines with the Des Vignes Co of Chertsey on the Thames. Whether this company had the facilities for building a submarine is a matter for conjecture, but it would appear likely that the order resulted first in the acquisition from the Barrow Shipbuilding Co of *Nordenfelt II* which became the Turkish Submarine Boat No 1, later renamed *Abdul Hamid* after the reigning Sultan.

Dismantled, *Nordenfelt II* was shipped out in sections to Constantinople (Istanbul) and once assembled was re-launched on 6 September 1886. In the event the recruitment of a Turkish crew proved a problem and trials in the Golden Horn on 5 February 1887 had to be run as best as Nordenfelt's assistants, Captain George Garrett[2], Mr P W D'Alton and a Mr Lawrie, could manage on their own. However, the craft behaved well on the surface and indeed proved successful running awash as a semi-submersible; on the other hand, once dived she proved difficult to handle suffering the same lack of longitudinal stability as her predecessor. The re-arrangement of the vertical diving screws forward and aft instead of athwartships appears to have done little to improve matters while free surface resulting from the lack of baffles within the boiler and hot water accumulator or adequate sub-division in the ballast tanks served only to compound the issue.

Torpedo trials too proved abortive since release of the weapon disturbed the trim of the boat, bringing the bow up violently as the torpedo left its tube. In the event, the trials crew managed to retrieve the situation and bring the craft to the surface but the exercise was not repeated.

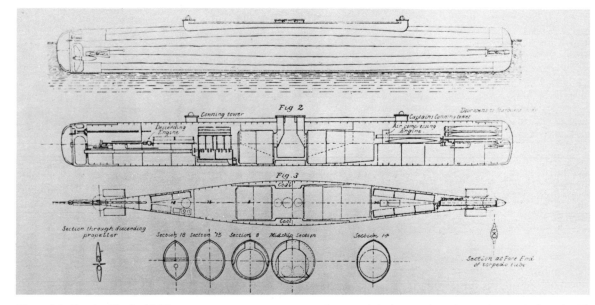

Plans of the Russian *Nordenfelt IV*.
Author's collection

Although accepted, and indeed eventually paid for, by the Turkish government, Submarine Boat No 1 *(Abdul Hamid)* never commissioned for service and remained laid up under cover on shore in the Constantinople Naval Arsenal until eventually broken up, probably during the First World War.

THE SECOND TURKISH NORDENFELT
Named *Abdul Medjid*, the second submarine too was shipped out in sections to Constantinople and, once re-assembled[3], entered the water on 4 August 1887. Following a trial run to Ismid some 60 miles distant, however, the lack of a Turkish crew resulted in the boat being laid up with *Abdul Hamid* in the Naval Arsenal, eventually to be broken up.

NORDENFELT IV – FOR RUSSIA
Meanwhile, back at Barrow, plans had been drawn up for building an improved Nordenfelt submarine, in all probability once again to be built as a speculative venture although it seems likely that the Turkish government made known its interest early as a potential buyer. Whatever the actual circumstances surrounding the origin of the project, the Turkish government did secure an option on the vessel the keel of which was laid as Yard No 149 in 1886. The 1887 edition of *Brassey's Naval Annual* includes under 'Turkish Ships' a drawing of the Submarine Boat *Nordenfelt*, unmistakeably this craft. The design radically departed from Nordenfelt's earlier boats, the cigar-shaped configuration being abandoned for a hull form of circular cross section amidships tapering in plan to a narrow vertical elipse forward and aft. Thus the draught was the same throughout the length of the craft bringing increased buoyancy at the extremities in an attempt to ease the problem of longitudinal stability. At the same time, in order to minimise surging, the craft was designed with nine separate ballast tanks holding in all 35 tons of water this being the quantity required, with fuel and all stores embarked, to reduce the residual buoyancy to about 500lb in preparation for diving.

Somewhat larger than her predecessors *Nordenfelt IV*, in fact actually named *Nordenfelt*, was 125ft long overall with a beam (maximum diameter) amidships of 12ft. The surface displacement worked out at 160 tons in light condition and that submerged 243 tons. She entered the water at Barrow on 26 March 1887 and immediately demonstrated some miscalculation in her design since she trimmed down heavily by the stern and had to be ballasted forward to correct the error.

With the frames spaced some 20in apart and plating $5/16$in thickness the structural strength seems to have been considered adequate to withstand the pressure at a depth of 100ft. Over the turtle backed casing, exposed when running on the surface, plating one inch thick provided protection against small arms and light gunfire. Aft of amidships a tandem pair of two cylinder compound engines, built by Plenty & Sons of Newbury and designed for 1000hp at a pressure of 150psi, drove on to a four throw crankshaft directly coupled to the four bladed screw positioned in an aperture forward of the rudder. The estimated speed in surface trim was given as 12 knots. There were two cylindrical locomotive boilers holding in all 27 tons of water, the after one being 10ft 6in long and the forward unit a massive 18ft in length. Each had two furnaces and the fuel (coal briquettes) was stowed in side bunkers abreast the stokehold between the boilers. As in the earlier boats, of course, once shut down for diving steam was flashed off at a steadily reducing pressure although in this case there were no separate hot water cisterns. Preparations for sea involved firing both boilers and then discharging steam, as soon as sufficient pressure became available, direct from the after unit into the lower part of the forward boiler, thus to accelerate heating the mass of water therein. On reaching full working pressure (150psi) this forward boiler, with its furnace fires banked, was isolated from the steam system ready for reconnecting when preparing to dive. Thus, for running on the surface, the after boiler only provided steam for the main and auxiliary machinery.

The coal bunkers provided stowage for 8 tons of fuel, sufficient for about 1000 miles at 8 knots, although for extended passage three of the nine ballast tanks could be pressed into service as temporary bunkers enabling 20 tons to be embarked, presumably adequate for some 2500 miles at an economical speed. There was no electricity the crew having to rely upon candles and oil lamps for internal lighting, although this primitive means would also have provided an indication of any dangerous rise in the carbon dioxide content of the air within the boat. No means were provided for purifying the air.

Glass-domed conning towers in 1in thick steel, 2ft high and 2ft 6in in diameter, served for working the boat when shut down, the forward one as the command position[4] equipped for control of the 'descending' propellers and the after lookout as the engineer watchkeeper's station with an all round view of the horizon. Preparations for diving involved stowing the two funnels and, as in the earlier craft, sealing all openings including the uptakes and the furnace and ash pit doors which were bolted into position against an asbestos seal. With residual buoyancy reduced to about 500lb the boat could be forced to submerge by the downward thrust of the vertical propellers. Submerged the maximum speed was about 5 knots.

The weapon fit comprised a pair of 14in internal torpedo tubes mounted one above the other in the bow and protected at their forward, outboard, ends by a hinged door worked from inside the boat and opening to starbord. In all four Whitehead torpedoes were carried. It had been intended in addition that a pair of Nordenfelt 2-pounder quick-firing guns should be added[5] for self-defence, but in all probability they were never fitted.

On completion *Nordenfelt IV* was registered with the Board of Trade as a merchant ship and following preliminary handling trials steamed south to Southampton, arriving after a stormy passage which appears to have been weathered to the satisfaction of those concerned. However, certain modifications were called for, presumably seen to be necessary in the light of sea experience, and this work which included the provision of a light casing to form a weather deck between the two conning towers was undertaken locally in June 1887 by Oswald Mordaunt & Co of Woolston.[6]

Basin trials took place within the confines of Southampton's Outer Dock (now the Princess Alexandra Dock) and were followed by open water trials run in the relative shallows over the Mother Bank Shoal off Ryde, Isle of Wight. The first demonstration for service representatives took place on 26 May 1887 with the craft running awash in the closed down state for an hour and a half, following which it was claimed that stored steam sufficient for 24 miles remained in the boilers. Steaming awash in the course of the demonstration the *Nordenfelt* evoked considerable interest by circling around the ironclad battleship *Invincible* then lying at anchor in Cowes Roads. After surfacing the funnels were erected and the boilers fired with the vessel soon enabled to increase speed to 14 knots. Being painted a neutral grey she showed herself to be a difficult target, in particular while running slowly awash when the raised casing and two small conning towers proved almost impossible to detect at more than a few hundred yards distant.

In surface trim too her performance appears to have been completely satisfactory, a speed of 14 knots being maintained over the measured mile in Stokes Bay without difficulty at 1300 indicated horse power (ihp). On 23 July 1887 she put in an appearance at the Naval Review held at Spithead to honour Queen Victoria's Golden Jubilee and there created considerable excitement in the midst of the ironclads and the few remaining wooden men-of-war, albeit all but the small training brigs fitted with full powered steam machinery. Among other guests on this occasion Tsar Alexander III of Russia was evidently impressed by what he saw!

Once fully submerged, however, the performance of *Nordenfelt (IV)* was much less favourable, all the faults in her predecessors being repeated including the violent changes of trim due to the effects of free surface in the boilers, and to a lesser extent in the tanks, such that while undergoing trials near the Mother Bank she frequently touched bottom. As demonstrated by Nordenfelt's first submarine, the hydroplanes, in this boat fitted both forward and aft, did little to control trim or to assist effective depth keeping.

Trials continued intermittently throughout the summer of 1887 and culminated in semi-official demonstration of the submarine's capabilities on 19 December. Despite the problems encountered when dived, the *Engineer* in its issue of 23 December 1887 followed up these trials with an enthusiastic leading article lyrical in its praise of the Nordenfelt submarine concept. The writer looked to the future with a suggestion that 'We may – we hope we shall – have quite a little fleet of Nordenfelts when Christmas comes round again. When once Columbus had shown the way to America, the water was freely traversed'. Two months later[7] the same journal reported that the United States government had '... decided in favour of Nordenfelt boats as a permanent arm.'

The *Army and Navy Gazette* too had no hesitation in telling its readers that the Nordenfelt submarine had '... a great and assured future before it, that with a gun or two on her turtle back and working as an above water torpedo boat, she certainly possessed many advantages over the ordinary first class torpedo boat, and that her powers of submerging should make her the more valuable craft . . . .'

In the meantime, in a move aimed at improving future prospects by diversifying their armament interests, the directors of the Barrow Shipbuilding Co had invited Thorsten Nordenfelt to join the company which in the ensuing reorganisation in 1888 became the Naval Construction & Armaments Co Ltd. The new organisation acquired by purchase Nordenfelt's patents although in fact no further submarines to his designs were to be built at Barrow or indeed anywhere in the United Kingdom.

By this time the Turkish government appears to have lost interest in submarines and Nordenfelt was fortunate in being able to persuade the Russian Imperial government to consider buying his latest submersible. Despite continuing problems with depth and trim control the Russians appear to have been satisfied with her performance during trials although they did stipulate that completion of the sale should be subject to a demonstration of craft's capabilities in the deeper waters off Kronstadt, commenting that 'Any boat might undertake trials in shallow water which could not be repeated in deep water!'[8]

Escorted by Nordenfelt's yacht *Lodestar* the submarine left Southampton en route for the Baltic and Kronstadt in November 1888. For much of the time in fact *Nordenfelt IV* towed *Lodestar* and it was steaming thus that the former stranded on the Horns Reef off Jutland on an ebbing tide apparently through mistaking lights on the Danish coast. Attempts were made to refloat the submarine at high water but these and subsequent efforts proved of no avail and with *Lodestar* herself grinding her bottom on the reef there seemed little chance of success. Leaving the wreck for the time being Captain Garrett and the crew made their way as best they could to Esbjerg.

Refloated some two weeks later the battered *Nordenfelt IV* was brought into Esbjerg where her owners (Naval Construction & Armaments Co Ltd) hoped to have the boat declared a constructive total loss on the grounds that the prospective buyer would be most unlikely to complete the purchase. Eventually the submarine was abandoned to the insurers although this had to await settlement of a dispute over the payment of salvage dues. Attempts made to find a buyer proved unavailing and a few years later, the insurers having settled with the Naval Construction and Armaments Co, the now derelict hulk was broken up for scrap. In the meantime, being once again without work, George Garrett abandoned his submarine interests and migrated to the United States where he died in 1902.

AFTERMATH AND CONCLUSIONS

Nordenfelt continued his association with the Barrow company but, like Garrett, took little further interest in submarine development although two boats, reputedly of Nordenfelt type but designed by a Frenchman named d'Equevilley, were built in 1890 for the German Imperial Navy which seems to have negotiated a licence in 1885 to make use of Nordenfelt's submarine patents. Presumably this arrangement followed the Landskrona trials at which *Nordenfelt I* had been demonstrated in September of that year. Built at Kiel (Howaldswerke) and Danzig (Kaiserlichen Werften) respectively these two submarines were attached to the local torpedo flotillas at Kiel and Wilhelmshaven but little is known of their performance apart from a statement that 'In a semi-submerged condition these boats were moderately

good, but their speed did not come up to expectations[9] . . .'. The Howaldt boat was 114ft long with a maximum diameter of a little under 11ft, the hull form like the early *Nordenfelt*s being cigar shaped. In surface trim she displaced 212 tons. A photograph believed to show this craft has appeared in a number of works since it was first published by Lieutenant-Colonel Alan H Burgoyne in 1903[10].

Very little information concerning Nordenfelt boats' trials, other than that made public by Nordenfelt himself, reached the press or contemporary technical journals at the time and it was not until 1901 that P W d'Alton, Nordenfelt's former assistant but subsequently Chief Engineer to the Central London Railway, was able at last to comment on the performance of the Turkish *Abdul Hamid (Nordenfelt II)*:

'She had the fault of all submarine boats, viz, a total lack of longitudinal stability. All submarines are practically devoid of weight when under water. The *Nordenfelt*, for example, weighed for a couple of hundredweights less than nothing when submerged, and had to be kept down by screw propellers provided for the purpose. The Turkish boat was submerged by admitting water to tanks aided by horizontal propellers, and raised by blowing the ballast out again and reversing the propellers. Nothing could be imagined more unstable than this Turkish boat. The moment she left the horizontal position the water in her boiler and the tanks surged forwards and backwards and increased the angle of inclination. She was perpetually working up and down like a scale beam, and no human vigilance could keep her on an even keel for half a minute at a time. Once, and we believe only once, she fired a torpedo, with the result that she as nearly as possible stood up vertically on her tail and proceeded to plunge to the bottom stern first. On another occasion all hands were nearly lost. Mr Garrett was in the little conning-tower. The boat was being slowly submerged – an operation of the utmost delicacy – before a committee of Ottoman officers, when a boat came alongside without warning. Her wash sent a considerable quantity of water down the conning tower, the lid of which was not closed, and the submarine boat instantly began to sink like a stone. Fortunately Mr Garrett got the lid closed just in time, and Mr Lawrie, the engineer, without waiting for orders blew some water ballast out. It was an exceedingly narrow escape.'[11]

The *Engineer*, likewise, having abandoned its former enthusiastic stance, was now scathing in its criticism of *Nordenfelt IV*:

'To all intents and purposes the Nordenfelt was a total failure as a submarine boat. She began badly. As soon as she was launched from the stocks at Barrow it was seen that a mistake had been made in calculating weight, as she was down by the stern, drawing 9ft aft and about 4ft 6in forward. This would have been partially rectified by her torpedoes, but she never had one on board. Extra

Nordenfelt IV on basin trials at Southampton in 1887.
Author's collection

ballast had to be put in forward, and it was always held, rightly or wrongly, that this made it all the more difficult to keep her on an even keel when submerged. The extra weight carried militated greatly against her speed as a surface boat. Another mistake was that the water-ballast tanks were too large, or perhaps it would be more correct to say that they were not sufficiently sub-divided. When she was in just the proper condition to be manoeuvred by her horizontal propellers the ballast tanks were only about three quarters full, and the water being left free surges backwards and forwards in them. It must not be forgotten, however, that ample tank capacity was necessary because the quantity of ballast needed depended on the number of tons of coal and stones on board. Sub-division would, however, have prevented the surging of the ballast water. If, for example, the boat was moving forward on an even keel at, say, two knots, if a greaser walked forward a couple of feet in his engine room, her head would go down a little. Then the water surged forward in the tank and she would proceed to plunge, unless checked, and in shallow water would touch the bottom, as she did on the Mother Bank in the Solent . . . The Nordenfelt was always rising or falling, and required the greatest care in handling.'

Probably Nordenfelt himself had been over-optimistic while being at the same time obstinate in failing to learn by experience, so that the same faults were repeated in each boat in turn until eventually he lost interest in the submarine. During the period of his involvement in submarine design he lectured at length to the Royal United Service Institution and took part also in discussions at the Institution of Naval Architects where in 1888 he soundly condemned proposals by Lieutenant G W Hovgaard of the Royal Danish Navy that battery/electric motor propulsion should be employed under water than stored steam.

Despite the fact that Nordenfelt's association with 'diving boats' was a brief digression in his long career as an engineer and entrepreneur, his involvement remains significant because *Nordenfelt II*, launched nearly one hundred years ago, was the first submarine to be built at Barrow. In 1897 the Naval Construction & Armament Co Ltd, became Vickers, Sons & Maxim Ltd whose successors, Vickers Shipbuilding & Engineering Ltd, continue in business today, building submarines, as part of British Shipbuilders. Nordenfelt himself died in 1920 but he is probably remembered more for his machine gun rather than for the submarines which featured so prominently in the technical press of the 1880s.

NOTES

1 Installed during the period that *Nordenfelt I* was in United Kingdom waters for further trials.
2 Garrett had been granted a temporary commission as a Commander in the Imperial Ottoman Navy although he appears to have worn the uniform of a Captain, complete with fez. See Chapter 6 of *Submarine Boats* by Cdr Richard Compton-Hall (Conway Maritime Press, 1983) for further treatment of the *Nordenfelt*s.
3 Although some accounts claim that the second Turkish boat was not reassembled, the *Engineer* for 24 February 1888 refers to the '. . . two submarines . . .' leaving Constantinople.
4 Accounts differ concerning the respective roles of the two conning towers.
5 and 6 *The Scientific American*, 21 January 1888.
7 The *Engineer*, 24 February 1888.
8 *Submarine Warfare* Herbert C Fyfe (London, 2nd edition 1907).
9 *The Evolution of the Submarine Boat, Mine and Torpedo* by Commander Murray Sueter, RN (Portsmouth, 1907).
10 *Submarine Navigation, Past and Present* by Lt-Col Alan H Burgoyne, MP (London, 1903) (cf Murray Sueter who claims this photograph to show a later Howaldt boat of 1897).
11 *Submarine Warfare op cit*

WARSHIP PICTORIAL

Saving the last 'Flower' class Corvette HMCS Sackville

By Thomas G Lynch

HMCS *Sackville*, 29 December 1941, during anchor trials off St John, NB. The Builder's house flag and Red Ensign still fly.
MARCOM Museum

Much has been written about the 'Flower' class corvettes of World War II fame over the intervening 40 years, but the story of the concept, evolution and glories of these ships is not the subject of this article. Rather, this story is of the closing chapter in the corvette saga, not inappropriately occurring in the Dominion of Canada. The early portion of the story is not unique in itself, but is unique in entirety since the subject ship has served with her original owners for forty years. That ship is HMCS *Sackville*, the former K 181.

Sackville was the product of the enormous decision made in the first year of the war to build warships in Canada. This decision had been extremely risky, since Canadian yards after nearly a decade of neglect during the Depression, were scarcely capable of ship repair, let alone ship construction. Furthermore, very few had ever built a steel hulled vessel over 100ft long. But build them they did.

Sackville was one of only two corvettes built in Atlantic Canada, both being built by St John Shipbuilding and Drydock Ltd, St John, New Brunswick. HMCS *Amherst* was the first vessel, being hull number 10 and *Sackville* carried hull number 11. Both were of the first batch of 'Flowers', with the short forecastle, foremast before the bridge and among the

first 55 Canadian corvettes to be fitted with Mk II minesweeping gear.

Both vessels followed the Canadian decision to name corvettes after small towns in Canada, something that was at odds with the Admiralty decision on flowers for theirs. Hence Canadian sailors were spared the embarrassment of serving in a *Pansy* or *Hollyhock* that their RN counterparts suffered!

CONVOY ESCORT 1942–44

Sackville was launched at St John on 15 May 1941 with Mrs J E W Oland as sponsor. She underwent trials off St John during the month of December and was commissioned into the Royal Canadian Navy on 30 December 1941. In January she sailed to Halifax, arriving on the 12th. Work-ups occupied the remainder of January and she did her first duties as a fisheries patrol vessel at the end of the month. Escort duties began in February and her first action occurred with the rescue of 29 survivors from the torpedoed Greek ship *Lily* of 5719 tons on 9 March, due south of Newfoundland. She landed these in Halifax, where the disgrace of her career ended also. Her first captain was relieved, the crew exchanged with her sister corvette HMCS *Baddeck* and Lt Alan Easton RCNR appointed as her new captain. *Sackville* never looked back.

In April 1942 *Sackville* joined the newly-formed Escort Group C-3, based in St John's, Newfoundland.

During this spell of time, some of the most savage battles in the Atlantic war were fought, *Sackville*'s most hectic being on 2–3 August 1942. During the convoying of ON-115, *Sackville* encountered three different U-boats on the surface in near-blinding fog, only effectively engaging them through the blessing of her new Type 271 radar. The first was depth-charged to the surface by a shallow pattern at an angle of 40° until nearly a third of the forward hull was exposed. Another pattern of two then detonated, seeming to lift the entire U-boat out of the water before it slid back under the surface. The second attack brought oil and debris to the surface before the target disappeared from both sight and the probing beam of asdic. Two hours later at about 0900,

Sackville's last sail-past, 16 December 1982. As can be seen, the dramatic changes to the ship between 1964 and 1976 altered the ship to the point where she was barely recognisable as a corvette.

CAF Photo

radar discovered another contact at about Red 080°. Four minutes later the U-boat was engaged by depth charges, but asdic contact was lost in troubled water.

Next day (3 August) dawned, with fog cutting visibility to virtually zero. After a seemingly endless day without attacks, at 1502, the asdic reported high-speed hydrophone effect. *Sackville* at the time was standing guard while her sister corvette HMCS *Agassiz* attempted to tow the torpedoed *Belgian Soldier*. A sweep by the Type 271 radar detected several contacts that could not be identified because of the fog, but one contact to starboard was particularly interesting. Course was altered and three minutes later a shadowy grey form resolved into a U-boat, crossing the ship's bows from starboard to port at about 8 knots. The wheel was put hard to port and full speed rung for, but the submarine began to submerge inside the ship's turning circle at the same time. However, the 4in gun on the forecastle was

Sackville in June 1944 during her Bermuda work-ups. She had just completed her forecastle extension refit at Galveston, Texas.

CNCT Photo

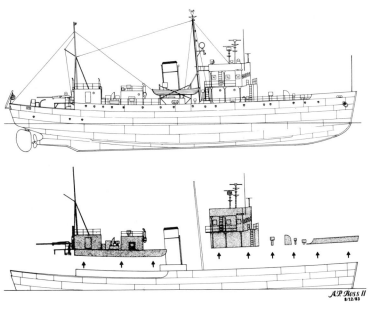

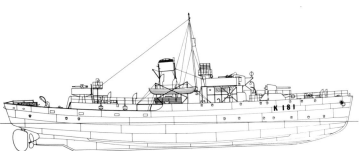

11 October 1983: *Sackville* sits high
and not so dry in Scotia Dock,
Halifax Industries Limited for a
well-earned below the waterline
refit.

J D Sargeant

able to engage the U-boat at full depression. A hit at the
base of the conning tower was obtained, but the second
shot went screaming over the U-boat as it submerged
deeper. Engagement with .303in Lewis and 0.5in
Browning guns was spectacular, but ineffective and the
submarine was lost in the depths below a thermal
gradient.

After the war *Sackville*'s probable kill was discredited
after comparison with captured German documents.
U 43 had been badly damaged and barely made France,
only to be repaired and lost on 31 March 1943.
However, the record of one badly damaged, one
damaged and another driven off was remarkable for the
limited effectiveness of a corvette.

Sackville's closest brush with death happened in
September 1943 while part of Escort Group Nine in
support of the beleaguered combined convoy ONS
18/ON 202. The U-boats had renewed mid-ocean
wolfpack tactics and launched their new secret
anti-escort GNAT or acoustic torpedo with remarkable
success. HMCS *St Croix*, a Canadian destroyer, the
destroyer HMS *Itchen* and the corvette HMS *Polyanthus*
were sunk and the frigate HMS *Lagan* had her stern

blown off. Five merchantmen were sunk as well. Against this, one U-boat was sunk by ramming and seven others sunk or damaged by depth charges and shellfire. However, even when faced with renewed wolfpack tactics and a demoralising new weapon aimed at escort vessels, Allied warships were able to keep losses very low and crushed Axis hopes that the supplies for the forthcoming invasion could be strangled. Allied technology largely neutralised the GNAT threat within weeks with the 'Foxer' and later, the CAT noisemakers. The U-boats never regained the initiative lost in May 1943.

Sackville transferred to Escort Group C-2 for the balance of World War II in October 1943. She underwent two refits: one split between Liverpool, Nova Scotia, and Halifax between 14 January to 2 May 1943. However the most important occurred between 14 January and 7 May 1944 in the Todd Galveston Dry Docks Inc facilities, at Galveston, Texas. Here the curse of the short forecastle was finally done away with, when the forecastle was extended aft to just abaft the funnel, near frame station 60. The foremast was shifted to behind the bridge and the familiar open-bridge of the later corvettes made its appearance. She worked up in late May through June 1944 off the Bermuda station and made the crossing to Londonderry, Northern Ireland, at the end of June. Soon after leaving on the westward leg, the No 1 boiler ruptured and she was forced to return to Londonderry for temporary repairs. She sailed for Halifax, limping on one boiler with convoy ONS 248 on 11 August.

The boiler was judged to be irrepairable while in the ship and so it was decided she would finish the war as a training ship for the Halifax officer training unit, HMCS *Kings* in September. *Sackville*'s life seemed nearly over.

MINEFIELD SUPPORT VESSEL 1944–46
In Ottawa the Naval Board decided on 7 August 1944 that the coastal craft, *Rayon D'or* should be purchased outright and converted for maintenance of the signature-recording controlled-loop minefields off Halifax, Sydney and St John, New Brunswick. However, in October an investigation by the Construction Superintendent, Halifax of *Sackville* as a possible alternative postponed the decision on *Rayon D'or*, the latter found to be in less than ideal shape after six years of war. His report of the same month stated that *Sackville* was far superior and since there would be a requirement for controlled-loop craft after the war, the conversion of the corvette at $50,000 was a bargain. *Rayon D'or* was returned to her owners and the conversion of *Sackville* began in Halifax in late October 1944. *Sackville*'s old pennant number, K 181 disappeared since she was now a local defence craft and she re-appeared with Z 62 in May 1945.

The conversion entailed the removal of No 1 boiler and associated auxiliary equipment, re-arrangement of boiler lines and the building of a cable tank in the former boiler space. On the forecastle, the 4in BL and platform, hedgehog and other small structures were removed. In place, a second larger steam winch was installed, two samson posts and derricks were erected ahead of the modified bridge and a large cable sheave fitted at the very bows.

All this work took time and the German surrender saw *Sackville* still slumbering in the dockyard. The completed ship entered service in late May and in September she began lifting the acoustic controlled-loop minefields in St John, New Brunswick, dumping the unwanted portions in a deep hole in the Bay of Fundy. She returned to Halifax with 7100ft of good cable which was discharged at the former French Cable Wharf in Dartmouth, NS. The ship then lifted the field at Sydney and paid off on 6 April 1946 into inactive reserve.

RESEARCH VESSEL 1953–82
The ship recommissioned on 4 August 1950 as a reserve depot ship. An extensive refit was undertaken to correct defects in the hull caused by inactivity over four years and remained in reserve until 1953 until she was re-activated into the Canadian Naval Auxiliary Fleet as a research vessel. She, with her civilian crew, transported oceanographers and geologists from the Ministry of Energy, Mines and Resources to the Gulf of St Lawrence where several summers were spent surveying the ocean bottom and currents of the area. Several cruises off the Greenland-Baffin Island coast, the last with a research crew on the 600-ton *Vena*, owned by Columbia University were undertaken to investigate alternative fishing grounds to the Grand Banks. All of these were under the supervision of the Fisheries Research Board, the last finished in September 1960.

The ship then entered extensive research studies with the Bedford Institute of Oceanography, Dartmouth, NS in 1961, still manned and administered by the Superintendent, Auxiliary Services. The ship was refitted in 1964 and a large lab facility added at the stern while an oceanographers' hut was put in at the forecastle break on the starboard side.

The ship undertook various tasks for oceanographic survey of the bottom, coastal shelves, magnetic abnormalities and fields, thermal currents and thermoclines, plus fisheries-related studies. In 1964 a passive flume stabiliser system was installed by George T Davie and Sons, Lauzon, PQ and then a 150hp Voith-Schneider Vertical Axis propeller was installed by the same firm in December 1964 between frames 30-36 at the bows. The latter proved too weak to hold the ship in any current and increased fuel consumption to a horrible level through increased drag. This was removed during refit at Dartmouth Marine Slip in April 1967.

By 1975 Bedford Institute was receiving newer research ships of a specific design better suited to their needs. *Sackville* was in turn required by the Defence Research Establishment, Atlantic, Dartmouth, NS. This change in roles saw *Sackville* come full circle. Designed and used as an anti-submarine escort warship, she now was working for a research group whose largest task was keeping the Canadian Navy at the forefront of anti-submarine warfare.

Sackville undertook her last major refit in 1968, when the old naval bridge was removed and a modern,

23 October 1983: the port-lower view of the hull in Scotia Dock. The propeller shaft awaits its cap. The very fine condition of this 42-year-old hull can be seen. The doubler plates can be seen forward of the shaft plates, below the bisecting rivet line.

Lyncan

The 2pdr and 20in searchlight platforms nearing completion, 2 April 1984.

Lyncan

enclosed two-deck structure erected. The forecastle break was extended from station 60, just abaft the funnel to the end of the old deckhouse (station 89) and the new, enclosed space given over to additional accommodation. This additional top hamper made the corvette's normally-vicious behaviour in rough weather worse, with prolonged swings in roll in a quartering sea.

By 1981 *Sackville*'s age was a concern as well as the limited room for expansion to more refined ASW research. Vessels like the ultra-quiet *Quest* and *Endevour* were the ships of the future. Oddly, the hull was in excellent shape, since *Sackville* had been the recipient of one of the first mass-produced cathodic protection systems devised by the-then Naval Research Establishment in the 1950s. Her final refit was deferred in January 1982 and the cards were on the table. *Sackville* would be disposed of within a year if not reprieved. So would end the career of the last 'Flower' class corvette in Canadian service.

A group of determined veterans, spearheaded by the Naval Officers Association of Canada was formed that same spring to save the last corvette. By mid-1982, a

tentative agreement was reached between the Department of National Defence and the newly-named Canadian Naval Corvette Trust (CNCT) to maintain *Sackville* in inactive reserve until the CNCT could raise the necessary monies to satisfy the government the ship would not become a burden upon the taxpayers of Canada.

A two-part organisation was established, the larger part established in the financial centre of the country, Toronto, and a smaller, dynamic group in Halifax to oversee the actual restoration of the ship. The former was tasked with the raising and administration of the Trust's monies and has succeeded very well.

On a foggy, drizzling 16 December 1982, the foghorns and whistles echoed and re-echoed in Halifax harbour as the former corvette made her final sail-past, reviewed by the-then Commander, Maritime Command, Vice-Admiral J A Fulton. Her long decommissioning pennant trailed in the harbour waters a full ship-length astern, *Sackville* was ending a long, useful career and about to enter an even more exciting second one.

RESTORATION BEGINS

Sackville sat at her berth at Jetty Nine at the extreme south end of HMC Dockyard until the late spring of 1983. Minor stripping out of some interior spaces in the waist areas began. A prime contractor was found in Eastern Marine Services, Porter's Lake, NS, and extensive stripping of the waist, lab and bridge began in the late summer. The largest project was moving the electrical distribution and AC/DC converter from the large lab space at the stern down into the generator room in the former petty officers' mess aft of the engine-room. This was largely completed by September. Meanwhile, the mechanics of obtaining the ship had been followed and the ship became the unofficial property of the CNCT in August. An official ceremony was planned for

October, but the green light to start major alterations was given.

The first items were the forecastle bulwarks. This was a straightforward torching operation. Then the large lab was stripped and gutted. However, the removal was interrupted on 11 October 1983 when the ship was towed up-harbour for an underwater refit. Entering the Scotia Dock at 0915, the ship sat high and dry by 1130. A year's idleness had seen marine growth rampant and kelp and seaweed hung down from the waterline like a South Seas hula skirt. A hydrojet blasting was necessary to remove this before it dried and this was followed by a sand-blasting to get the hull down to good, sound, bright steel. It should be noted that Halifax Industries Limited did this work at cost, also not charging docking fees as part of their corporate donation.

Because of possible galvanic interaction between dissimilar metals, the bronze-sulphur propeller was removed and a cap welded over the intact shaft. This item will be polished and displayed at jetty-side when the ship is completed. Doubler plates were added under the engine room where minor corrosion had occurred in the past, all outlets through the hull were plated over and the old active cathode protection system was removed. After final clean-up, the ship was treated to an anti-corrosion coating, followed by two coats of a coal-tar epoxy anti-fouling paint. Seventy new-style passive, non-sacrificial anode bars were installed along the line of the bilge-keels, roughly the number used on a modern *Iroquois* class destroyer! The ship will not need a further underwater servicing for at least seven years, other than a yearly scraping by underwater divers.

With the blanking off of through-the-hull openings, a radiator had to be fitted in the engine room, starboard side, to cool the *circa* 1963 Cummins diesel emergency generator. This unit has been very well maintained. So the ship now has an independent source of power that can be utilised in time of power failure or mooring the

The stripped forward seamen's messdeck. The navel pipes are centre in the photo.

Lyncan

ship at locations where shore-side power is unavailable.

On 28 October the completed ship was turned over officially to the CNCT by Senator Henry Hicks, representing the federal government. Accepting the ship was the National Chairman, Edmund C Bovey. Also present, the new Commander, Maritime Command, Vice-Admiral James C Wood presented a cheque for nearly $24,000 raised in less than two months by the officers and men of Maritime Command from coast to coast. This was accepted by the Halifax Working Group Chairman, Commodore Andrew McMillin. The Maritime Command contribution grew to over $41,000 by December 1983.

The ship returned to Jetty Nine on 31 October and the destruction of the laboratory began in earnest. By 21 November the lab was ready to remove. A floating crane, loaned by the Navy on 27 November, removed the roof and bulkhead sections which had been collapsed inward by the 23rd. The final sections were removed by 1400 and the crane was moved forward to remove the bulwark sections stacked on the forecastle. The following day, some 30 tons of surplus anchor chain was extracted from the chain lockers by hoisting it out, 40ft at a time by a shore-side Sagadore crane. The resultant funds generated by the sale of the scrap and chain were recycled into the restoration effort.

The gutting out of the waist areas and bridge began in earnest in November and December. The first reconstruction project was the building of the 2pdr and 20in searchlight platforms at the aft of the former deckhouse. This was completed in February 1984 and the temporary plastic film and wood framed structure removed from over the completed structure. During February-March, the intervening deck in the bridge structure was removed, leaving it a huge hollow shell. After careful measurement, it was found that the 'new' 1944 bridge could be constructed *within* the gutted shell, less the bridge wings. This also identified a need for a false deck, 17⅜ higher than the weather deck. Both were constructed from ⅜in steel plate and angle iron donated by DOFASCO Canada as part of their corporate gift.

By mid-March the wheelhouse bulkheads had been raised. The overhead deck was in place by mid-April and a quiet fortnight ensued in which the only work was the sectioning of steel to be removed in May. Structural strips were left to keep the old bridge from collapsing and 34ft of ship side and upper deck plating was earmarked for removal to open up the ship's waist area once more.

Final destruction of the two-deck bridge structure began on 7 May. With the new wheelhouse structure complete inside the old, extreme care was necessary in lifting off each section. One slip and a half ton of scrap steel could crush the new wheelhouse before it ever saw the light of day! The entire lift of the old structure was completed on 8 May.

The floating crane returned on the 14th to remove the waist area sections. The starboard side was first, then the port, both being accomplished within four hours. With the removal of all this steel (some 30 tons) draught forward decreased from 10ft to 8ft 6in and the stern decreased by 9in. This will again increase with the addition of the 4in gun and platform, hedgehog, depth-charge throwers, etc over the next eight months.

The next immediate work was the construction of the bridge wings, starting on 22 May. After this, the bridge overhang that housed the Type 127 asdic plot and depth recorder to port (within the overhang) and a minute chart space to starboard will be built. The fitting out of the wheelhouse and open bridge space, including two 20mm Oerlikons on the bridge wings will be done concurrently with the fabrication of the 4in gun platform. Indeed the latter, plus the Carley float launch platforms at the stern, will be the last major steel additions to the ship. The destructive phase of the restoration is over.

7 May 1984, the destruction of the old bridge began.
CAF Photo

The triple-expansion engine with one cover removed. Volunteer labour is largely responsible for the restoration of this area. In turn, training upon non-critical, but similar equipment provides good experience.
Lyncan

WEAPONS AND EQUIPMENT

Where have the necessary weapons and accessories come from? The list is endless and incomplete.

4in BL Mk IX gun on CP1 mount: Although a dime a dozen in 1945, there were only two left in Britain. One was at Whale Island (Portsmouth) and the other in the Imperial War Museum (London) and both were definitely not available! Here in Canada the picture was even more bleak . . . apparently not one example had been kept by any museum! However, in the late fall of 1983 a 4in BL on CP1 mount was 'discovered' to be gracing the front lawn of the Legion Branch in Amherstberg, Ontario. Protracted negotiations finally saw the Legion branch turn the gun over to the CNCT in a very tight vote in March of this year. It is in transit at the time of writing and will be refurbished with technical aid from the armourers of the Maritime Warfare School in their spare time. It should be ready to mount by late fall.

2pdr Vickers Mk VIII pom-pom on Mk VIII mount has created problems. Once plentiful, very few examples still exist and the only one in Canada is privately owned and held at LaHavre, N.S. Negotiations have been protracted and so far inconclusive.

20mm Oerlikons: The actual weapons are held by the Canadian War Museum, Ottawa. These will be transferred under permanent loan agreements to the ship this fall. However, the Mk IIa mounts are missing and unless spare units can be found, the truly expensive task of building these in a machine shop will be the only route left open.

Hedgehog A Mk II hedgehog with Mk 8 stabiliser is held by the Canadian War Museum also, complete with 24 inert mortar rounds. This is in the process of being transferred as well.

27ft whaler and Carley floats: None of these exist in the Navy's inventory, so Naval Engineering Unit, Pacific (NEU(P)) volunteered to build a 27ft whaler to traditional standards on a spare time basis. Carpenters in training volunteered and the whaler was completed in November 1983. To prove its worth, NEU(P) won the New Year's Whaler Race at Esquimalt, British Columbia, hands down! This, plus new 10 and 20-man Carley floats will be shipped to Halifax this fall. It should be noted that these tasks have been accomplished at no cost to the taxpayer of Canada.

Radar: The Type 271P radar is an expensive, complex item to build from scratch, so aid and technical expertise was sought from the Combat System Engineers of the Maritime Warfare School. In their own spare time, these people are preparing detailed building plans that Eastern Marine Services will be able to use in construction of the 'lantern' and RDF hut immediately below it. Additionally, they will help in the mock-up of

The 34ft section of the ship's side plate and upper deck removed, 14 May 1984.
CAF Photo

the instrument cases and dials on both the 271 and the SW2C radars.

Radio Room: This task is well in hand thanks to a group of 'ham' radio operators. They assure the CNCT that they will install a complete radio suite. Equipment includes a PV 500H W/T transmitter, a FR-12-T W/T set and MSL W/T receiver to name a few pieces. Plans tentatively call for an operating 'ham' station in the radio room after 1985.

Other ASW Gear: Fortunately the Canadian Navy found a use for Mk IV depth charge throwers after the war, when the Mk 43 ASW torpedo was adopted in 1952. The Mk IV thrower was modified with a 45° inclined tray and two additional guides to toss the Mk 43 over the side, warhead down for proper entry into the water. These were fitted in the *Restigouche* and *MacKenzie* destroyer classes and luckily were only replaced in the past few years by the Mk 32 mod 5 triple ASW torpedo tubes. Termed Mk (NC)2 throwers, these are being restored to Mk IV configuration and will be shipped to *Sackville* very shortly. Likewise, it has proved necessary to manufacture 50 dummy 300lb depth charges, commonly classified as Mk VIIs. These will be fitted in stern racks and traps fabricated by Eastern Marine this fall and ready racks between the throwers, port and starboard. Luckily, plans for these survived the intervening 40 years.

10in and 20in searchlights: These have been fairly easy to find, with several offered by various sources. The 20in

has been found within Maritime Command lay-by stores and several 10in lights have surfaced in Reserve divisions.

INTERIOR AND PAINTWORK

Restoration of interior spaces was not envisaged in Phase I planning. However, this has changed in two areas: the former seamen's mess and the engine room.

Because of the relative simplicity of gutting the former seamen's mess, this was done in March by Halifax Working Group volunteers. The Fleet School of Maritime Command had expressed an interest in undertaking the restoration of this area through the use of volunteers in their spare time, if the CNCT would provide the furnishings. Accordingly, a drive is on-going for kit items, hammocks, cap boxes, kit bags and respirators, to name a few. Tables, benches and hammock nets will be fabricated and hopefully the mess will be restored to a very close approximation of a 1944 mess deck.

Hundreds of important, but smaller items have been donated by individuals from coast to coast, too numerous to mention. Needless to say, *Sackville* upon completion in May 1985 will truly represent the early 'Flower' class corvette, modified and altered throughout the war years and at its best (or worst, depending upon who you talk to!) in late 1943–early 1944.

A bit about the painting of the ship. A modified Western Approaches scheme of off-white overall, with a Western Approaches Blue 'soft-wave' panel down both sides and camouflage panels on the upper works vertical surfaces was picked as representative of the little escort vessels of late 1943. White counter-shading will be done as per Admiralty Fleet Orders of the day. Finally, as a last touch, the once familiar white K 181 pennant number will adorn the ship's sides and duck-like stern.

The target date for completion is 1 May 1985 in time to participate in the Battle of the Atlantic Sunday ceremonies that year. It is planned to have the ship moored in mid-harbour during the 75th anniversary of the Canadian Navy ceremonies and possible participation in the fleet sail-past planned for July. However, when all the hurrahs are complete in mid-1985, the ship will be put on permanent display for the general public. The place has yet to be fixed as contractual problems have arisen with the proposed site, the Maritime Museum of the Atlantic. Governed by the Nova Scotia Museum, which is, in turn, governed by the provincial Department of Education, the Museum has suffered from severe cutbacks with the 'Zero Growth' budgets of the provincial government. Unless these problems can be resolved, it will be unlikely that the ship will be displayed at the government piers on Lower Water Street.

The second alternative is to house the ship within HMC Dockyard. This would mean that public access would be limited to controlled guided tours, since she would be on Department of National Defence property. However, several distinct advantages, especially in the field of security and control of vandalism are apparent. However, this is just in the primary investigation stages

and cannot be speculated upon. Let it rest that *Sackville* will find the very best home available!

Some $800,000 are required for the restoration and maintenance fund. Up to 1 May 1984, some $223,000 was either spent or committed to the restoration, a figure that was within $1000 of projections and estimates made by Eastern Marine's Bill Wallace. An estimated $410,000 overall will be required to complete Phase I restoration. Current fund-raising has yielded $402,000 to date, but this includes gifts in kind and pledges. A closer approximation of actual cash could be close to $325,000 raised as of 1 May 1984.

When completed and open to the public, *Sackville* will serve as an international reminder of that most savage of sea battles, the Battle of the Atlantic, the small, makeshift ships and green men who stemmed the tide of world domination by oppressive powers . . . but only just. Perhaps she also acts as a caution to those people and leaders of the future should war ever break out again in the cold, grey Atlantic, that tiny, primitive, stop-gap escorts of her type will not be capable of stemming the tide. Time and technology have precluded the cheap fix in naval warfare. Sail on, *Sackville*, so that none may be lost to time and attrition!

The cleared starboard waist. The bulwark cap rail remains to be fitted as well as finishing, grinding and priming. The depth-charge throwers will be installed this summer.
CAF Photo

The last pieces of the old structure are hoisted off on 8 May 1984.

CAF Photo

The ship-lap, hand-built 27ft whaler fabricated by the shipwright apprentices at CFB Esquimalt, BC for *Sackville*.

SACKVILLE SHIP PARTICULARS

	1944	1965	1982
Length (pp)	190ft	190ft	190ft
(OA)	205ft 1in	205ft 3in	205ft 3in
Beam	33ft 1in	33ft 1in	33ft 1in
Draft (bows)	8ft 3in	9ft 2in	10ft
(Deepest)	13ft 5in	13ft 9in	13ft 9in
Displacement:			
(standard)	950t	1085t	1130t
(full load)		1350t	1350t
Engine	1 triple-expansion steam engine at 2720ihp		
Boiler (after June 1944)	1 Scotch Marine return tube. Built by Dominion Bridge Co, Vancouver, BC, 1940. 3 furnace oil. Boiler maximum pressure (water test:) 335psi. ops pressure: 225psi		
Speed (at 133rpm)	16kts	11.5kts	13kts
Range	3450nm at 12kts	3225nm at 10kts	11.5 days at 11.5days to 40% reserve
Consumption (full speed)	2.81 barrels	3.64	2.81
Crew (officers)	6	10	10
(men)	79	20	22
Pennant no (approx dates)			

1941—44	1944–46	1950–53	1953–59	1959–64	1964–82
K 181	Z 62	532	AN 113	ALC 113	AGOR 113

British Naval Guns 1880-1945 No 14

By N J M Campbell

5.25in QF Mk I This 50 calibre gun was built with an autofretted loose barrel, jacket to 99in from the muzzle, removable breech ring and sealing collar. It was necessary to dismount the gun to change barrels which weighed 1.654 tons, and the horizontal sliding breech block was hand operated with SA opening. Separate QF ammunition was fired, the brass cartridge case with SC charge weighing 41lb. A total of 267 guns were made of which 6 were lent to the Army.

Ship trials were carried out in *Iron Duke* in 1939 and it was mounted in short trunk Mk I twin mountings in the *King George V* class battleships and in long trunk Mk II twin mountings in 9 of the first 11 of the *Dido* class cruisers, the exceptions being *Scylla* and *Charybdis*. RP 10 Mk II mountings which also had power operated loading trays, were in the last 5 *Dido*s and late in the war the 2 after mountings in the cruiser *Argonaut* were converted to RP 10 as were the Mk I mountings in the battleship *Anson*. All mountings were powered by individual hydraulic systems, had separate HA and LA shell hoists and +70° to −5° elevation. The gunhouses were cramped and the rate of fire was about 7 or 8rpm instead of the intended 10-12. There is no doubt that the less powerful US 5in Mk 12 was a better AA weapon.

Revolving weights were 77.5 tons for Mk I, 84-96 for Mk II and 95 for RP 10 Mk I_x in the battleship *Vanguard*. This last had a larger gunhouse, the hydraulic pump and electric driving motor were moved to the fixed structure and joy-stick local control was fitted.

5.25in QF Mks II, III, V The desirability of increasing the MV of Mk I from 2672fs was discussed on more than one occasion, but in the event this only applied to the above Army guns which were in single 70° mountings and intended for AA and coast defence, though only 3 guns in the Tyne area were ever mounted in the latter role. Mk II had a stronger breech ring and block, allowing 22 instead of 20.5 tons/in² (crusher guage) working pressure and MV of 2850fs at the price of much reduced life. Mk III had a Probertized chamber and forward banded shell but was not introduced to service, while Mk V and Mk II modified for improved AA mountings.

5.25in QF Mk IV A Mk I gun with an upward opening breech block on the lines of that of the 4.5in QF Mk V gun. Two experimental guns were ordered in January 1944. Apart from a higher rate of fire performance was

to be as in Mk I. Sketch drawings of the Mk III mounting belong to the postwar era and indicate fixed ammunition and 70rpg per minute.

5.2in QF Mk I Only 6 guns were made and 4 mounted in the 1923 submarine *X1* to enable her to engage a destroyer if surfaced. The twin mounting allowed 40° elevation and the 42 calibre gun was built with tapered inner A tube, A tube, jacket over the rear part of A and breech ring. Horizontal sliding SA breech mechanism was fitted and separate ammunition fired.

5.118in BL Vickers Mk A This 130mm 53.4 calibre gun was made by Vickers for Russia and was considered for DAMS in the First World War, but turned down as it would have made too many different calibres. With an 81.3lb projectile and tubular NC charge MV was 2700fs.

5.1in QF Experimental Two of these 50 calibre guns were built in 1931 for trails as a possible armament for destroyers, and one was mounted in *Kempenfelt* but was found to be too heavy. One gun had a monobloc autofretted barrel and the other a two tube one. Separate ammunition was fired and with a 70lb projectile MV was 2693fs or with a later 62lb one *c*2790fs. The mounting was a 4.7in CP XIV with a new cradle.

5in BL Mks I to V These were 25 calibre guns differing in construction. Mk I of which 77 were made, had an A tube taking the breech block, and 5 hoops including the trunnion hoop over the breech end. It was withdrawn after the failure of a 6in Mk II in the corvette *Cordelia* in 1891. The other guns all had an A tube and jacket which took the breech block and included the trunnions. The Marks differed in the number and arrangement of hoops and tubes over the A tube between jacket and muzzle and originally neither Mk II or III were chase hooped to the muzzle. Altogether 150 Mk II, 225 Mk III, 100 Mk IV and 82 Mk V were made. They were not often used as the main armament of ships other than sloops, though *Iris*, *Mercury*, *Caroline*, *Pylades* and *Garnet* were so armed. They were carried together with 6in by many of the masted cruisers and in a few ironclads still mainly armed with RML. They were originally intended as the secondary armament for the battleships *Nile* and *Trafalgar* and were in the cruisers *Scout* and *Fearless*, but were replaced in both classes by the far more effective 4.7in QF. A total of 112 guns

The erection shop at Elswick works near Newcastle on 31
March 1941. In the foreground are Mark I twin 5.25in turrets
destined for the cruiser *Cleopatra* building at Hawthorn
Leslie's yard downriver. In the background are Mark II twin
4.5in mountings for the carrier *Implacable*.

Vickers

were kept in store for armed merchant cruisers.
Mountings were usually VCPI (20° elev), VBI (15°), or
VBII (22°).

Some surplus naval guns were used as coast defence
drill guns but they were very rare as active coast
defence armament. About 50 guns, mostly Mk V,
included in the above totals, were used by the Army on
'over-bank' carriages for field defences largely in India.
They must not be confused with the later 5in medium
field guns known as 60pdrs. Another possible source of
confusion is the Australian coast defence armament
which included EOC Pattern D of 31 calibres and MV
1987fs.

5in BLC Mks I/IV, I/V Twelve guns converted as naval
drill guns with Welin breech blocks and single motion
BM. A breech ring was added and the trunnions
repositioned. MV was increased to 1905fs. One gun
still survives in the Ordnance Museum at Priddy's
Hard, Portsmouth.

5in BL Mk VI Three Bethlehem 51 calibre stock guns
mounted in a naval coast defence battery at Scapa Flow
in the First World War. With a 50lb shell and 18.2lb
MD16 charge MV was c3135fs.

5in BL Mk VII A Bethlehem 51 calibre gun similar to
Mk VI but of improved construction. A total of 150
were ordered for DAMS but cancelled at the end of the
First World War.

A Mark I twin 5.25in turret being erected at Vickers-Armstrong's Elswick works 14 January 1942 for the cruiser *Sirius* building at Portsmouth Dockyard.

Vickers

and vertical sliding breech block. The bore was chromium plated 0.005in deep for 162.25in from the muzzle. Barrel life was exceptional and could reach 4600 EFC while the rate of fire was up to 22rpm.

Mountings in *Delhi* were power worked base ring Mk 30 – the modification has not been found – with RPC, enclosed shields and 85° elevation. US lists give Mk 30/80 for escort carriers. This was an open mounting, also power worked, but without integral hoists and only 27° elevation. British lists usually indicate Mk 37/2 which was generally similar but allowed 85° elevation though the overhang of the flight deck would have limited this.

5in QF Mk NI A 70 calibre water-cooled fixed ammunition gun of the later 1940s intended as the Navy's medium calibre DP gun, and particularly for a new projected type of large destroyer. Accurate performance figures have not been found but judging from the 70 calibre USN F, MV would have been *c*3400fs with a 70lb shell. The fixed round was *c*65in long and one design of single 90° mounting had a total weight of 77 tons with a max continuous rate of fire of 66rpm though higher figures are sometimes quoted.

5in QF Mk N2 A 56 calibre version of the above intended for single and twin 90° mountings. Little reliable data has been found, but there appear to have been later total weight limits of 55 and 92 tons for single and twin mountings and some designs had the continuous rate of fire reduced to 40rpm. It was a more practicable conception than NI but like it remained experimental.

5in BL Mk VIII A 41 calibre field gun intended as a replacement for the 60pdr but eventually rejected as too heavy. With a 56lb shell MV was 2700fs.

US 5in Mk 8 Twenty-two of this 51 calibre BL gun were supplied in 1941 with 10 former Coast Guard cutters under Lend-Lease in 1941. The particular version appears to have been Mk 8/7 in most ships. This had a taper liner, A tube and full length jacket with a hoop and locking ring. There was a breech bush and also a liner locking bush, and the Welin block had Asbury BM. The P mountings were Mk 15 allowing 20° elevation.

US 5in Mk 12 This famous 38 calibre separate ammunition QF was probably the best dual purpose gun under the conditions of the Second World War, and it seems that if supplies had been available much greater use would have been made of it, as shown by a 1944 proposal to mount 6 twins in the battleship *Nelson*. In the event 53 guns were supplied, the rearmed cruiser *Delhi* having 5 single mountings while of Lend-Lease ships the 23 *Ameer* class escort carriers had two and repair ships *Assistance* and *Diligence* one each. The guns were Mk 12/1 with an autofretted monobloc barrel weighing 1.783 tons, secured to the housing by a bayonet joint,

PARTICULARS OF 5.25in AND 5in GUNS

	5.25in QF Mk I	5.2in QF Mk I	5in BL Mks IV, V
Weight inc BM (tons)	4.293	3.425	2.005
Length oa (in)	275.5	230.65	139.15
Length bore (cals)	50.0	42.0	25.0
Chamber (cu in)	894	630	504
Camber length (in)	30.6	26.014	19.05
Projectile (lb)	80	70	50
Charge (lb/Type)	18.05 SC 140 21 NF/S 198-054	10.78 MC 16 11.36 SC 109	15.5SP 4.45 Cord 7.5
Muzzle Velocity (fs)	2672	2300	1750
Range (yds)	24,070/45°	17,288/40°	8700/19°51
Ceiling (ft)	46500/70°	-	-

	US 5in Mk 8/7	US 5in Mk 12/1
Weight inc BM (tons)	5.045	3.200
Length oa (in)	261.25	223.75
Length bore (cals)	*c*50.6	38.0
Chamber (cu in)	1200	654
Chamber length (in)	*c*38.9	28.66
Projectile (lb)	50	55
Charge (lb/Type)	24.5 NC	15.2NC
Muzzle Velocity (fs)	3150	2600
Range (yds)	15,850/20°	18,200/45°
Ceiling (ft)	-	37,200/85°

For US guns MV at 90°F charge temperature, not 80°.

The stern galleries of *Duke of Wellington* early in her career as
a harbour service ship at Portsmouth *CPL*

Duke of Wellington Class
Steam Battleships

By Andrew Lambert

The *Duke of Wellington*'s figurehead.
CPL

The great mid-nineteenth century developments in naval design and technology led to many ships being converted from one generation to the next. Sailing ships were fitted with steam power, and wooden steamships were adapted into ironclads. One class of British capital ships above all others serves to illustrate the rapidity of the changes that took place in the period 1845–1865. One ship in particular was substantially modified no less than three times before entering service: first while still a sailing ship, then into a steamship and finally to the pioneer coast defence turret ship.

The four ships that eventually made up the *Duke of Wellington* class were originally ordered in 1841 as First Rate sailing ships of the line of the *Queen* class, mounting 116 guns on three decks. The *Queen* class had been designed by the Surveyor of the Navy between 1832 and 1847, Captain Sir William Symonds. Symonds' designs were based on very different principles from those that had guided British naval architecture for the preceding century. He favoured a wide beamed hull with steeply rising floors and no ballast. This form produced very fast ships, especially in light winds, however they tended to roll heavily in adverse conditions and were considered inferior gun

platforms. In essence Symonds' ships possessed a fragile balance of qualities that required fine tuning and skilled seamanship before they demonstrated their superior sailing.

Symonds had been appointed by the Whig administration of 1830–41. When the Tory Government of 1841–46 took office he was subjected to an uncommon level of official hostility. Admiral Sir George Cockburn, the Senior Naval Lord, eventually suspended all work on first and second rate ships designed by Symonds on 9 December 1844. At this stage the *Duke of Wellington* class had not been laid down, although the dockyards had collected much of the timber required to build them and begun to shape it to the original design. Wooden shipbuilding in the years after 1815 had become a lengthy process dominated by the need to ensure the complete seasoning of all the timber employed. This was the only policy that would produce durable ships, the larger the ship the more time needed to build it.

The returning Whig Government of 1846–52 did not end Symonds' discomfiture. They appointed a Committee of Reference on Shipbuilding to examine the state of naval design. The members of the Committee were, almost to a man, implacably opposed to Symonds' design principles. Consequently their deliberations and conclusions were dominated by sharply worded criticism. The Admiralty then ordered Symonds to modify some of his ships along the lines proposed by the Committee. He refused, and retired.

MODIFICATIONS

This did not prevent the *Duke of Wellington* class ships being modified. The Assistant Surveyor, John Edye, recast the design to include an additional 5ft in the bow and modified hull lines. At this stage the four ships became a separate class from the three *Queen* class ships, which were too far advanced for such modifications. Once the new design had been accepted the ships were rapidly built, two were advanced until ready for launching, the other pair placed in frame. At this stage they were again suspended, this time on the advice of the new Surveyor, Captain Sir Baldwin Walker (1848–61) in early 1851.

A new factor had brought about this second suspension. With the first trials of the pioneer seagoing screw propeller ship *Archimedes* in 1841 the ultimate possibility of fitting steam power into line of battleships had been established. Unlike the paddle-wheel the screw did not mask large parts of the broadside or greatly affect performance under sail. Following experiments with the large screw frigate *Arrogant* and the old 74-gun battleships *Ajax, Blenheim* and *Hogue* the steam battleship had become a practical proposition. When the remarkable performance of Stanislas Dupuy de Lôme's 90-gun steamer *Le Napoleon* (launched 1850) became known the end of the sailing battleship was assured. Therefore Walker suspended all work on sail of the line. His thoughts then turned to the construction of an entirely steam driven battlefleet, rather than one composed of sail with a leavening of steamers. The success of the first British purpose-built

The *Marlborough* under sail and steam during her 1858–64 commission as flagship of the Mediterranean Fleet.
CPL

steam battleship, *Agamemnon* of 91 guns (launched 1852), only served to confirm the wisdom of Walker's policy and the timely nature of its adoption by the incoming Tory Government.

DUKE OF WELLINGTON

Walker considered that the three-decked 120-gun ship was a far superior fighting machine to the 90-gun two-decker because of their concentrated broadside fire at close range. Therefore he wanted to prepare a steam-powered three-decker with the least delay. The *Duke of Wellington*, then still bearing her original name of *Windsor Castle,* was awaiting launch at Pembroke Dockyard. So in December 1851 Walker sent his assistants Isaac Watts and John Abthell to inspect the ship and ascertain her suitability for conversion into a steamship. Their report was favourable and the ship was recast as a 131-gun steamer, using the 780hp (nominal) engines by Robert Napier that had been removed from the iron frigate *Simoon* on her conversion into a troopship. The conversion entailed cutting the ship apart in two places and adding 23ft amidships and 7ft at the stern. At 240ft overall she was then the longest capital ship in existence.

Windsor Castle was launched on 14 September 1852. On the same day the Duke of Wellington died, and so the ship was renamed to honour his memory. Completed by mid-1853 *Duke of Wellington* proved to be an outstanding ship, the more so bearing in mind her already chequered design history. The outbreak of the Crimean War the next year saw a British fleet enter the

Marlborough at Portsmouth on returning from her 1858–64 commission in the Mediterranean.
CPL

Baltic to blockade the coast of Russia. Vice-Admiral Sir Charles Napier, the Commander-in-Chief, flew his flag in the *Duke*, the most powerful warship in the world. He reported to Walker that she also 'sailed like a witch'. For the following two years the *Duke* carried the flag of Rear-Admiral Sir Richard Saunders Dundas, who had replaced Napier in 1855. Thereafter she served as a receiving ship at Portsmouth until 1902, when she was sold to the shipbreakers Castle of Charlton. The early end to her active career would seem to indicate that her conversion had been unduly hurried, to the detriment of her timbers and the unsatisfactory performance of her second-hand engines.

Duke of Wellington in dock at Keyham (Devonport) in March 1854. She flies the pennant of Commodore Sir Michael Seymour shortly before proceeding to Portsmouth where she became Vice-Admiral Sir Charles Napier's flagship for the Baltic campaigns of the Crimean War.
CPL

MARLBOROUGH

When Walker decided to create an all steam battlefleet he selected the *Marlborough* for conversion into a steamship, starting work in mid-1853. As she was only complete in frame it was possible to add 5ft to her bow to improve the lines of entry over those of the *Duke*. Her launch, begun on 1 August 1855, took more than a week to complete as she became stuck on the ways. This indicated the rapid growth in launch weights brought on by the steam era.

Marlborough commissioned in 1858 as flagship of the Mediterranean Fleet and remained on that station for 6 years flying the flags of three admirals. With new engines of 800hp (nominal) by Maudslay, Son & Field the *Marlborough* proved a more powerful steamer than the

---

DUKE OF WELLINGTON CLASS PARTICULARS

Name	Builder	Laid down	Converted	Launched
Duke of Wellington	Pembroke	5.1849	19.1.1852	14.9.1852
(ex-*Windsor Castle*)				
Marlborough	Portsmouth	1.9.1850	9.6.1853	1.8.1855
Royal Sovereign	Portsmouth	17.12.1849	25.1.1855	25.4.1857
Prince of Wales	Portsmouth	10.6.1848	27.10.1856	25.1.1860

DIMENSIONS (ft and in)

	Queen	(Design)	(Built)	Marlborough	Royal Sovereign
Length, overall	204	210	240½	245½	240½
Length, of keel	166ft 5¼in	171ft 1in	201ft 1⅛in		
Breadth, extreme	60	60	60	60	62
Depth in hold	23¾	24⅔	24⅔	25ft 2in	25ft 2in
Displacement	4502t		5829t	6065t	5080t

ARMAMENT
Duke of Wellington (21.8.1852)

Gun Deck	10 × 8in/65cwt
	26 × 32pdr/56cwt
Middle Deck	6 × 8in/65cwt
	30 × 32pdr/56cwt
Main Deck	38 × 32pdr/42cwt
Upper Deck	20 × 32pdr/25cwt
	1 × 8pdr/95cwt
	131 guns = 382 tons

Marlborough would have carried all 8in guns on the gun deck and all 32pdrs on the middle deck.

MACHINERY

Duke of Wellington	780nhp by Napier (ex-*Simoon* iron frigate). 1979 indicated horse power on trials in Stokes Bay 11.4.1853 = 10.15kts.
Marlborough	800nhp by Maudslay, 2683ihp on trials in Stokes Bay 12.5.1856, not rigged = 11.886kts.
Royal Sovereign	800nhp by Maudslay, 2796ihp on trials in Stokes Bay 12.8.1858, not rigged = 12.253kts.
	As a turret ship 2460ihp = 11kts.
Prince of Wales	800nhp by Penn, 3352ihp on trials at sea 31.10.1860, not rigged = 12.569kts.

The average cost of these ships was £130,000. *Royal Sovereign* cost a further £180,000 to convert.

Prince of Wales as the training ship *Britannia* in the River Dart at the turn of the century.

Duke although being more heavily laden she was not her equal under sail. Both ships were considered successful. The major fault in *Marlborough* was her overcrowded upper deck battery. Walker always packed too many guns into his upper deck batteries as he considered that the plunging fire of these pieces at close range was a three-decker's greatest advantage. In *Marlborough* they were so badly arranged that the lower rigging was set alight during gunnery drill. Paid off in 1864, the *Marlborough* spent the next 60 years as a receiving ship at Portsmouth with the *Duke*. She was sold in 1924 but capsized off Brighton while on tow to the breakers.

ROYAL SOVEREIGN

The third ship of the class to be launched, *Royal Sovereign*, had been too advanced to follow the plan of the *Marlborough* and had to be completed to the same design as the *Duke*. She saw no service as a steam battleship. But on 4 April 1862 came the order to convert her into a turret ship to try out the ideas of Captain Cowper Coles. For this she was cut down to the lower deck, leaving a barge-like hull of extreme beam to length ratio. This was then completely placed in 4½in–5½in iron plate and fitted with four turrets, the foremost carrying two guns, the others one. Originally these were 10.5in smoothbores, but in 1867 9in muzzle loading rifles were installed.

Completed on 20 August 1864, *Royal Sovereign* was the first British turret ship. Intended only for coastal operations her longest voyage was to Cherbourg in 1865, where she made a terrific impression on the French. Thereafter she served as a gunnery tender to HMS *Excellent* until 1873. Her low freeboard, lack of masts and low coal capacity made her quite unsuited to fleet duty and so she was considered primarily experimental. She was scrapped in 1885.

One of the principle reasons behind the conversion of *Royal Sovereign* had been to ascertain the suitability of turrets for installation on the cut down hulls of wooden battleships. In this respect *Royal Sovereign* was a complete success, but the cost of her conversion nearly equalled the total price of the similar iron-hulled *Prince Albert*. As Edward Reed stated plans were prepared for further conversions along the lines of *Royal Sovereign*, but they were held back to await an emergency that never arose.

PRINCE OF WALES

The last ship of the class, *Prince of Wales*, was completed after the plan of *Marlborough*. She saw no sea service, and after her trials her machinery was removed into the ironclad *Repulse*, a broadside ship converted from a 90-gun ship of the *Bulwark* class. On 3 March 1869 she replaced the original *Britannia* as the officer cadets training ship in the River Dart, assuming that name for the remainder of her stationary life. Hulked in 1909 she was eventually sold out of the service on 13 September 1914.

The design history of the *Duke of Wellington* class demonstrates the fluid state of naval architecture in the period 1845–1865, a period marked by more significant developments than any other two decades in the history of the warship. *Royal Sovereign*, having begun her life as the last word in sailing battleship design became one of the most powerful steam battleships in the following decade. And she actually began her active career as the precursor of the early twentieth century armoured battleship. This might appear a remarkable career, but it should be remembered that the hull of such a ship represented an enormous investment, both in labour and scarce materials, which the politicians and admirals of the transitional era were unwilling to abandon lightly.

NOTE
For the first full length study of the evolution, development and active service of the wooden steam battleship and an assessment of its place in the history of the modern warship see the author's recently published book *Battleships in Transition: The Creation of the Steam Battlefleet 1815–1860*, available from Conway Maritime Press at £11.95.

Japanese 'Kaibokan' Escorts Part3

By Hans Lengerer and Tomoko Rehm-Takahara

The Type C escort *CD 1* leaves Kobe harbour on her maiden voyage at the end of February 1944.   *Author's collection*

The Type C coastal defence ships were demanded by the Naval General Staff somewhat before the *Ukuru* type, at the end of March 1943. The reasons for this are clear when it is realised that even with such a severe simplification as in the modified Type B there was a time limit, which it was not possible to undercut. The imminent shortage of steel[13], the lack of suitable diesel engines, and the situation of the dockyards, whose capacity was stretched to its limit (some of them were overloaded with repair work), contributed further to the requirement for a smaller, even further simplified class. The *Ukuru* class alone would not be enough.

The reduction in size was also necessitated because these ships were to be constructed by small yards using rapid-construction methods. Such yards had little or no experience of building warships. The design considerations for this new class were based strongly on studies of the growing losses in the Japanese merchant navy. It was belatedly recognised that any reduction in losses could only be achieved by organising the merchant ships into convoys and providing escorts. This situation was serious enough in itself to accelerate the commissioning of coastal defence ships; the failures in the Solomons, and in particular the battles around New Georgia (central Solomons) in mid-1943, which claimed the loss and the damage of many small warships, led to mass production of the *Kaibokan* in even greater numbers. Planning was completed in June 1943 and from February 1944 the ships were delivered at a rapid rate, which had been considered impossible earlier. The situation was so serious that the authorities wanted to

have the coastal defence ships constructed in unlimited numbers, restricted only by the number which the yards were capable of building. The choice of main engine and hull form were the problem areas in planning. At that time there was scarcely one diesel engine which was suited to mass production, and only one engine gave what could be considered satisfactory results: the 23 *Go Otsu* 8 *Gata* diesel (No 23 model B8) used in the Type 13 submarine chaser. However, this ship had a speed of 16 knots at a trials displacement of 460 tons, and even though its hull shape was not very efficient, it would have been very difficult to maintain that speed with twice the displacement. Initially, therefore, it was planned to raise the power to more than 1900bhp by means of a turbo-charger. In fact, however, no turbo-charging was used; instead the output power was increased by raising the propeller revolutions to 350rpm, which gave a speed of 16.5 knots.

TYPE C

The following points were demanded and influenced the size of the ship: good seaworthiness in all weather

The Type C escort *CD 8* on trials in February 1944.   *CPL*

conditions, and full operational capability in all conditions. The *Sokuten* class minelayer was used as a basis, as its 750 tons trials displacement was considered to be the smallest ship suitable for open sea use. This class was known to be fairly seaworthy and robust, so initially the trials displacement was set at 800 tons, and later raised to 810 tons. The side height and draught of the hull were generous, and the length reduced where possible. The midship coefficient became large, the prismatic coefficient became small. Hence the central area became broader, and a shape was evolved which was low in drag.

In terms of their hull the Type Cs can be termed smaller versions of the *Ukuru* class, in which structural simplifications were carried out to the greatest possible extent. The construction methods of the standard Type 2E freighter were largely adopted: sectional building methods and welding; as this vessel had achieved the greatest degree of simplification at that time. The production of the Type 2E freighter was studied closely, and it was decided after model experiments to adopt its hull shape. This was a very risky decision but it later turned out to be justified: the Type C's performance was generally satisfactory. Although the design was drawn up under pressure of time (for the reasons already mentioned), these vessels had adequate stability and seaworthiness. Only the longitudinal or trim stability gave cause for concern, as the ships pitched considerably, dipped too low at the bow, and took in much water; ie they were nose-heavy. This defect was alleviated towards the end of the war by adding extra ballast in the aftership.

The ships' fittings and equipment were also simplified and shaved down whenever possible. This process went so far that, for example, the coathooks were rivets set at an angle, and the blackboard was replaced by part of a wall being painted black. The latter measure was a kind of fire protection, an aspect given ever greater attention after June 1944. The crew and store rooms were very large like those in the *Ukuru* class. The weight proportion of the equipment, which had amounted to 6 per cent in the *Shimushu* class, therefore fell to 4.6 per cent in the Type C.

In the construction of the hull electric welding was again used, after a fairly long gap. After the disaster which struck the Fourth Fleet on 26 September 1935, when an unusually powerful typhoon tore the bow from the destroyer *Hatsuyuki*, and severely damaged other ships, electric welding was not used again for joining the strength members; the Japanese Navy returned to rivetted joints. Practical experiments in welding procedures, strength of the joints and various material types did not provide satisfactory results. Until 1942 electric welding was only used for relatively unimportant parts. However, in view of the undisputed time and space savings offered by welding, there was a tendency to use the method again after the start of the war. Without doubt mass production was only possible with the use of electric welding and sectional building. Sketches 10a–10c show how the welding was used. The number of portholes was reduced to a minimum. In comparision with the *Ukuru* class, the standard displacement dropped by 195 tons to 745 tons, and the overall length from 78.77m to 67.5m (221ft 6in). The use of a diesel engine producing only 1900bhp reduced the speed from 19.5 knots to 16.5 knots. The range was 6500 miles at 14 knots.

ARMAMENT

The main armament consisted of one 120mm AA gun[14] on the forecastle, and one on the quarterdeck. In contrast to Type A, the only forward gun was fitted with a guard shield, and even then not on all ships. The ships carried six 25mm machine guns in two triple mounts as light AA weapons, fitted on platforms on both sides of the funnel. After the first ships were completed (up to about *CD 21*) the general reinforcement of the AA weapons was decided on, and the ships were strengthened by two double and two single mounts. For the twins, platforms were added at the bridge position to starboard and port. The single mounts were set up on the centreline, one at the after end of the deck superstructure, the other on a platform in front of the bridge. On a pedestal in front of this stood the 80mm Army trench mortar. Some of these ships, which were allotted to the escort group command, were fitted with an additional four 25mm machine guns in single mounts. On later ships the bulwark was higher at the machine guns and AA command position, in order to provide better protection against fire from other ships. The shield on the gun was also altered in some cases.

Some ships possessed a projecting platform at the stern, on which rails were fitted. It might have been that they were to be used in the final phase of the war to lay mines, and thus harass the Allied landings on the Japanese home islands. The depth-charge throwers were reduced in number to 12 units, with the depth-charge capacity remaining the same. Before they were installed, the thrower arrangement was tested using a wooden mock-up, because the assembly, projecting far below the upper deck level, was not exactly simple. The transport of the 100 depth charges stowed in a storage compartment was similar to that of the *Ukuru* class, and used the special lift system so that rapid throwing was possible. Next to the throwers there was again a run-off frame. Minesweeping devices were no longer fitted.

The hydro-acoustic equipment comprised two (Sonar) Type 3 model 2 (one Type 93 model 2 unit on the ships completed before April/May 1944), and one underwater listening unit (hydrophone) Type 93 model 2. From autumn 1944 the aerial for the Type 13 radar unit was mounted on the aft mast, while the Type 22 began to be fitted shortly after the first vessels had been completed; it was already fitted on ships completed after April 1944.

The strength of the armament becomes clear when we realise that the weight proportion compared to the trials displacement on the *Shimushu* class was 11 per cent, but 16.8 per cent on the Type C.

Externally the Type C differed from the *Ukuru* class in the following ways:

1 The longer forecastle.

2 The larger sheer of the forecastle – as on *Ukuru* class the rise was no longer curved, but completed flat.

3 The lower funnel – the latter was diagonal, straight, and stood roughly in the centre of the deck superstructure

4 The form of the deckhouse. While the *Mikura* and *Ukuru* classes had what we could term a single deckhouse, on the Type C it was only a rectangular substructure, which served as support for the searchlight platform.

5 The support system for the forward AA stands – while they were supported by a broad support on the *Ukuru* class, this support now took the form of two narrow turrets.

6 The slight inclination of the forestem.

Of the 132 Type C ships included in the wartime programme, 53 ships were finished by the end of the war (of which 26 were sunk), even though the yards chosen to build them were those which had formerly constructed submarine chasers, or which had no experience of warship building (eg Nihonkai, Toyama; the newly fitted Kyowa yard, Osaka). The average building time was reduced to 3 months, and the man-days to 28,000.

TYPE D

Soon after work began on the plans of Type C it became clear that it would not be possible to fit out the required number of ships with diesel engines, as production of the engines was insufficient. The fact that the Type 23 model B 8 diesel planned for the class No 1 ship was to be altered for mass production did not change the situation. The use of other engines did not seem advisable, because they did not possess the reliability of this design. Hence, although the diesel was considered desirable from the point of view of low fuel consumption, the turbine, with its high fuel consumption, was the only solution.

Planning work on these ships began on 14 June 1943, and as the deadline for building to begin was October, approval was obtained in the notably short time of just over a month, on 20 July 1943. The ships, designed under the basic planning number E 22, were termed Type D and designated class No 2, because they were given even numbers. As in the case of Type C (and before that the *Ukuru* class), the use of improved simplified design features and equipment were the principal aims in design. As a result of this the hulls of these two Types (C and D) were fundamentally identical. Admittedly the dimensions were slightly increased over Type C, especially the draught, as the fuel capacity was larger. Also, of course, there were differences in terms of the propulsion system, the engine room, the use of only one propeller, and other small improvements and simplifications. The drive system was the impulse type geared turbine as used in the standard wartime freighter Type 2 A, with a performance of 2500bhp and two Kampon water tube boilers of Type No 0 mod B 15. The higher power (by 600bhp), compared with the Type C, produced an extra knot of speed. This turbine was selected because it was simple to construct. It had not been deemed to be suitable for warships, but the situation at that time provided no other way out. The use of only one propeller represented a considerable simplification, and proved to be a wise decision.

The trials displacement rose by 90 tons, on account of the enlarged fuel capacity (240 tons, against 106 tons). Nevertheless the range fell to 4500 miles at 14 knots because of the much heavier consumption; this was 2000 miles less than the Type C. This fact made the escorting of a convoy between Japan and Sumatra the largest duty the ship could perform, as with the Type No 1.

ARMAMENT

Armament consisted again of two 120mm AA guns in A and Y positions, both mounted on pivots, and only the forward one with a guard shield. Two 25mm triples were fitted as light AA weapons. After the June 1944 naval Battle of the Philippines, the machine gun armament was increased by two twin and two single mounts. They were fitted in the same way as in the Type C. Some of the ships were fitted with an additional four 25mm machine guns in single mounts, which were located on the quarterdeck. These ships were those allotted to the escort group command. In front of the bridge a platform was added for the 80mm Army trench mortar.

The hydro-acoustic equipment and depth charges, depth-charge launchers and run-off frames were the same as in the Type C. Some of the ships also had still the Type 93 sonar unit, while others did not have the Type 13 radar. On the later ships the aerial of the Type 13 radar unit was fixed to the rear mast. Below the tripod mast was situated the radar compartment, as on the Type C. The searchlight pedestal, which was free-standing on the first ships, was simplified and built onto the radar compartment. On the subject of the searchlight, it should be mentioned here that it was hardly ever used, and its inclusion was, as in the case of the minesweeping devices, not relevant to the ships' planned tactical uses.

The form of the shield on the 120mm AA guns was altered, and the rear AA gun also received a shield. The bulwark was raised, as on the Type C. Because the machine guns and radar equipment were strengthened, the crew also had to be increased. At the same time, radar and sonar rooms had to be set up, so the living

1 The Type C escort *CD 17* on the day of her completion (13 April 1944).
CPL

2 US submarines took the greatest toll of the Kaibokan. A periscope view of another (Type C) victim.
Author's collection

3 A Type C Kaibokan throws up flak in defence of a convoy surprised off Hong Kong by US Army bombers.
Author's collection

quarters shrank, and the accommodation for the crew sank to a new low. The planned crew numbers are given in table 8. In fact, there were 173 men on board *CD 45* (Type C) in February 1945, and 169 in *CD 84* (Type D).

The overall result was that the Type D was basically the same as the Type C, and here again stern ballast had to be fitted to compensate two bow-heaviness.

Externally the Type D differed from the Type C in the following points:
1 The shape and position of the funnel; it was of oval shape, greater height, and stood in the middle.
2 The arrangement of the galley funnel – it was taken from the deck superstructure, which was behind the funnel, forward to the funnel, ran up on the starboard side, and ended just above the funnel.

3 The position of the searchlight. The earlier searchlight platform at the centre frame position had made way for the funnel; the searchlight was moved aft onto the deck superstructure.

As a result of the shortage of oil (fuel) the ships laid down after January 1945, and also those not completed at that time, were fitted with boilers which were converted to coal firing. Consideration was also given as to how the boilers of those ships already commissioned could be converted to coal firing. During the building and repair periods some ships were indeed converted, and carried on after the war with coal.

Of the 143 planned ships, 63 were completed by the end of the war, 25 of which were sunk. To shorten the building time, a full-scale model had been made, and precise tests carried out. This procedure eliminated any problems with the simplified ship's form. As a result of the tests, the Kure naval arsenal calculated the building time at 20,000 man-days (70 days). But this target was not achieved because the material supply, especially in 1945, was very low. The number of man days rose to an average of about 28,000, the same as for Type C.

While Types A, B and B modified had been built in large shipbuilding yards and naval arsenals, it was medium-sized and small firms that produced Types C and D. In particular, Nihonkai, Niigata iron works, Naniwa Dock should be mentioned here, and the Kyowa yard, which was set up as a special yard for *Kaibokan* in 1943 but was very soon closed again, should not be forgotten. Some of the shipyards were fitted out for mass production of the *Kaibokan* and enlarged.

THE END OF KAIBOKAN CONSTRUCTION

If we consider Japanese warship building during World War II, then it becomes quite clear, that the year of 1943 and the first half of 1944 were the zenith of production. After operation 'Sho' (Battle of Leyte Gulf), in which the main forces of the Japanese were *de facto* destroyed, action by the remaining ships was rendered impossible, and as the supply routes to the South were cut off, only the smaller warships could be built on account of the shortage of shipbuilding materials and fuel. From summer/autumn 1943 on, the transporters, transport submarines, destroyers of class D, coastal defence ships and MTBs (*Gyoraitei*) were given priority. At the beginning of 1945 first priority was given to everything which was connected with the preparation for the decisive battle over the Japanese home islands. On 2 February 1945 the commission for (urgent) war armament acceleration (*Kinkyu sembi sokushin bukai*) determined the war armaments programme (*Sembi keikaku*). This programme included the production of the special attack weapons (submarines of the HA 201 type, *Koryu*, *Kairyu*, *Kaiten* and *Shinyo* explosive boats). The vice naval minister laid down the sequence of production for naval armament in a proposal dated 26 February 1945. Based on this proposal the design department of the Navy (*Kaigun kansei hombu*) defined the degree of urgency for the building, repair and production (radar, sonar, AA weapons, and Army weapons used by the Navy only) for the various classes of ships and types of weapons.

The coastal defence ships were allotted priority rating 3 (out of 8), in respect of building and 'major repair' (longer than a month), and priority rating 2 in respect of 'minor repairs' (less than a month). As early as March 1945, however, increased production of the *Koryu*s and *Kairyu*s was decided on; the building of warships was stopped to a large extent. Building of coastal defence ships was stopped; ships whose construction had been approved in earlier programmes were not ordered, and the contracts of ships already ordered were annulled. The last ship completed during the war was the *CD 204* laid down on 27 February 1945.

THE COASTAL DEFENCE BOATS

As the war situation deteriorated, the Japanese began to investigate the building of coastal defence boats *(Kaibotei)* in the summer/autumn of 1944 for the final

The Type C *CD 77* in August 1947 after minesweeping duty. Her guns have been removed but the Type 22 radar is visible at the mainmast.

Author's collection

decisive battle in defence of the Japanese home islands. The plans, which were completed at the beginning of 1945, included two types: Type A with steel hulls and Type B with wooden hulls. The latter were to be built in far greater numbers than type A because of the shortage of steel.

In respect of the boats' intended duties, the two classes were identical. Originally they had been conceived as *Kaiten* (human torpedo) carriers, but during their planning more depth-charge equipment was included, to make them suitable for submarine hunting at the same time. They were also to take over the patrolling of the coastal waters: the task of the auxiliary patrol boats, whose building had been stopped.

It was planned to use the boats to take the *Kaiten* Type 1 to the regional bases, or to the neighbourhood of the enemy landing groups. The *Kaiten* were to be transported on sliding hoists on the quarterdeck, and let down to the water over the stern. If there was no necessity to transport the *Kaiten*, the boats were to be used for anti-submarine warfare and escort duty. Four depth-charge throwers for one broadside and 60 depth charges were planned. With this equipment, patrol duties could be carried out at the same time. For detecting the submarines there were to be two Type A and one Type B hydrophones of Type 93 and one Type A and two Type B sonars of Type 3. For aerial surveillance the boats were to be fitted with Type 13 radar, and a 40mm machine cannon of the latest Type 5 for anti-aircraft work, plus six 25mm machine guns in single mounts.

The war programme for 1943/44, approved by means

TABLE 8: CLASS TECHNICAL DETAILS				
	Type C	**Type D**	**Kaibotei A**	**Kaibotei B**
Basic Planning number	E 21 B	E 22	E 24	E 25
	2401	2701	1851	1701
Standard displacement	745t	740t	270t I[1]	285t I[1]
			278t II[2]	280t II[2]
Trial displacement	810t	900t	282t II	290t II
Length between perpendiculars	63.0m/206ft 8in	65m/213ft 3in	46m/150ft 11in	35m/114ft 10in
Waterline length	66.0m/216ft 6in	68m/223ft 1in	48.5m/159ft 1in	37.5m/102ft 5in
Overall length	67.5m/221ft 6in	69.5m/228ft 1in	51m/167ft 4in	40.25m/132ft 1in
Waterline beam	8.4m/27ft 7in	8.6m/28ft 3in	5.4m/17ft 9in	6.09m/20ft
Side height	5.0m/16ft 5in	5.2m/17ft 1in	3.5m/11ft 6in	3.6m/11ft 10in
Average draught	2.9m/9ft 6in	3.05m/10ft	2.30m I[1] 7ft 7in	2.43 I[1] 8ft
			2.36m II[2] 7ft 9in	2.45m II[2] 8ft 1in
Machinery	2 Diesel No 23B	1 Turbine K0255F	2 diesels (8000bhp)	2 diesels (800bhp)
	Type 8 (1900bhp)	(2500shp)		
Speed	16.5kts	17.5kts	15kts	12.5kts
No of propellers and rpm	2 × 360	2 × 460	2 × 500	2 × 500
Fuel	106t	240t		
Range	6500nm/14kts	4500nm/14kts		1500nm/10kts
Armament		2 × 12cm/1		1 × 40mm/1
		6 × 25mm/3		6 × 25mm/1
Depth charges		120 Model 2	2 Kaiten II	1 Kaiten II[2]
		12 Model 3 throwers		
Additional armament		2 × 12cm/1		
		12 × 25mm (2×3, 2×2, 2×1)		
		1 × 8cm Army mortar		
		120 depth charges		
Sensors		Radar as *Shimushu* class	Type 13 radar	
		Sonar and hydrophones as *Ukuru* class	Mod 3 sonar	
			2 hydrophones	
Crew	125	141	?	?

of the special war budget of 1944/45, included 20 coastal defence boats of class 1 (Type A) with the building numbers 1851–1870, and 60 coastal defence boats of class 101 (Type B) with the building numbers 1701–1760. The Type B boats were allotted to the wooden shipbuilding yards, which also produced the auxiliary submarine-chasers *(Kusen tokumutei)* and the auxiliary patrol boats *(Shokai tokumutei)*. The building of auxiliary patrol boats was stopped in favour of the coastal defence boats. As in the case of the coastal

TABLE 9: CLASS OUTLINES

Running No	Building No	Name	Builder	Laid down	Launched	Completed
56	2401	CD 1	Mitsubishi, Kobe	15.9.43	29.12.43	19.2.44
57	2402	CD 3	Mitsubishi, Kobe	15.9.43	29.12.43	29.2.44
58	2403	CD 5	Tsurumi	23.10.43	15.1.44	19.3.44
59	2404	CD 7	Tsurumi	23.10.43	18.1.44	10.3.44
60	2405	CD 9	Mitsubishi, Kobe	15.10.43	15.1.44	10.3.44
61	2406	CD 11	Mitsubishi, Kobe	15.10.43	15.1.44	15.3.44
62	2407	CD 13	Tsurumi	18.11.43	9.2.44	3.4.44
63	2408	CD 15	Tsurumi	18.11.43	21.2.44	8.4.44
64	2409	CD 17	Tsurumi	15.12.43	26.2.44	13.4.44
65	2410	CD 19	Tsurumi	15.12.43	28.2.44	28.4.44
66	2411	CD 21	Nihonkai Dock	1.12.43	31.3.44	18.7.44
67	2712	CD 23	Nihonkai Dock	10.2.44	20.5.44	15.9.44
68	2413	CD 25	Tsurumi	1.2.44	14.5.44	2.7.44
69	2414	CD 27	Tsurumi	16.2.44	3.6.44	20.7.44
70	2415	CD 29	Tsurumi	2.3.44	26.6.44	8.8.44
71	2416	CD 31	Tsurumi	3.3.44	4.7.44	21.8.44
72	2417	CD 33	Tsurumi	26.5.44	22.7.44	31.8.44
73	2418	CD 35	Tsurumi	30.5.44	3.9.44	11.10.44
74	2419	CD 37	Nihonkai Dock	5.4.44	5.8.44	3.11.44
75	2420	CD 39	Tsurumi	10.6.44	13.8.44	27.9.44
76	2421	CD 41	Tsurumi	1.7.44	8.9.44	16.10.44
77	2422	CD 43	Mitsubishi, Kobe	10.4.44	22.6.44	31.7.44
78	2423	CD 45	Nihonkai Dock	25.5.44	5.10.44	23.12.44
79	2424	CD 47	Tsurumi	15.7.44	29.9.44	2.11.44
80	2425	CD 49	Tsurumi	31.7.44	15.10.44	16.11.44
81	2426	CD 51	Mitsubishi, Kobe	1.5.44	20.8.44	21.9.44
82	2427	CD 53	Tsurumi	15.8.44	29.10.44	28.11.44
83	2428	CD 55	Tsurumi	20.8.44	4.11.44	20.12.44
84	2429	CD 57	Tsurumi	10.9.44	15.11.44	13.1.45
85	2430	CD 59	Tsurumi	25.9.44	22.11.44	2.2.45
86	2431	CD 61	Marinearsenal Maizuru	1.4.44	25.7.44	15.9.44
87	2432	CD 63	Mitsubishi, Kobe	1.7.44	20.9.44	15.10.44
88	2433	CD 65	Nihankai Dock	10.8.44	30.11.44	13.2.45
89	2434	CD 67	Marinewerft Maizuru	15.6.44	15.9.44	12.11.44
90	2435	CD 69	Mitsubishi, Kobe	24.8.44	28.11.44	20.12.44
91	2436	CD 71	Tsurumi	5.10.44	3.12.44	12.3.45
92	2437	CD 73	Tsurumi	8.10.44	10.12.44	5.4.45
93	2438	CD 75	Nihonkai Dock	18.10.44	20.2.45	21.4.45
94	2439	CD 77	Tsurumi	2.11.44	18.12.44	31.3.45
95	2440	CD 79	Tsurumi	6.11.44	30.12.44	6.5.45
96	2441	CD 81	Marinearsenal Maizuru	7.8.44	15.10.44	15.12.44
97	2443	CD 85	Tsurumi	20.11.44	27.1.45	31.5.45
98	2444	CD 87	Tsurumi	27.11.44	15.2.45	20.5.45
99	2448	CD 95	Tsurumi	27.11.44	14.4.45	4.7.45
100	2503	CD 205	Niigata	10.5.44	15.8.44	30.10.44
101	2504	CD 207	Naniwa, Osaka	17.5.44	24.8.44	15.10.44
102	2507	CD 213	Mitsubishi, Kobe	24.9.44	15.1.45	12.2.45
103	2508	CD 215	Niigata	20.7.44	10.11.44	30.12.44
104	2509	CD 217	Mitsubishi, Kobe	1.12.44	26.2.45	17.7.45
105	2510	CD 219	Naniwa, Osaka	2.9.44	30.11.44	25.1.45
106	2511	CD 221	Niigata	11.9.44	26.12.44	2.4.45
107	2513	CD 225	Niigata	22.11.44	26.3.45	28.5.45
108	2514	CD 227	Naniwa, Osaka	5.12.44	10.2.45	15.6.45
109	2701	CD 2	Marinearsenal Yokosuka	5.10.43	30.12.43	28.2.44
110	2702	CD 4	Marinearsenal Yokosuka	5.10.43	30.12.43	7.3.44
111	2703	CD 6	Marinearsenal Yokosuka	5.10.43	15.1.44	15.3.44
112	2704	CD 8	Mitsubishi, Nagasaki	20.10.43	11.1.44	29.2.44
113	2705	CD 10	Mitsubishi, Nagasaki	20.10.43	11.1.44	29.2.44
114	2706	CD 12	Marinearsenal Yokosuka	5.10.43	15.1.44	22.3.44
115	2707	CD 14	Marinearsenal Yokasuka	5.10.43	25.1.44	27.3.44
116	2708	CD 16	Marinearsenal Yokasuka	5.10.43	25.1.44	31.3.44
117	2709	CD 18	Mitsubishi, Nagasaki	1.11.43	11.1.44	8.3.44
118	2710	CD 20	Mitsubishi, Nagasaki	1.11.43	11.1.44	11.3.44
119	2711	CD 22	Mitsubishi, Nagasaki	1.11.43	27.1.44	24.3.44
120	2712	CD 24	Mitsubishi, Nagasaki	1.11.43	27.1.44	28.3.44
121	2713	CD 26	Mitsubishi, Nagasaki	1.2.44	11.4.44	31.5.44

TABLE 9: CLASS OUTLINES (continued)

Running No	Building No	Name	Builder	Laid down	Launched	Completed
122	2714	CD 28	Mitsubishi, Nagasaki	1.2.44	11.4.44	31.5.44
123	2715	CD 30	Mitsubishi, Nagasaki	15.2.44	10.5.44	26.6.44
124	2716	CD 32	Mitsubishi, Nagasaki	15.2.44	10.5.44	30.6.44
125	2717	CD 34	Ishikawajima	25.3.44	6.7.44	25.8.44
126	2718	CD 36	Fujinagata	20.3.44	16.9.44	21.10.44
127	2719	CD 38	Kawasaki, Kobe	2.4.44	15.6.44	10.8.44
128	2720	CD 40	Fujinagata	20.3.44	15.11.44	22.12.44
129	2721	CD 42	Mitsubishi, Nagasaki	15.4.44	7.7.44	25.8.44
130	2722	CD 44	Mitsubishi, Nagasaki	15.4.44	7.7.44	31.8.44
131	2723	CD 46	Kawasaki, Kobe	1.5.44	30.6.44	29.8.44
132	2724	CD 48	Fujinagata	15.5.44	18.1.45	13.3.45
133	2725	CD 50	Ishikawajima	8.7.44	9.9.44	13.10.44
134	2726	CD 52	Mitsubishi, Nagasaki	15.5.44	7.8.44	25.9.44
135	2727	CD 54	Mitsubishi, Nagasaki	15.5.44	7.8.44	30.9.44
136	2728	CD 56	Kawasaki, Kobe	1.6.44	30.7.44	27.9.44
137	2730	CD 60	Kawasaki, Kobe	16.6.44	15.9.44	9.11.44
138	2732	CD 64	Mitsubishi, Nagasaki	8.7.44	5.9.44	15.10.44
139	2733	CD 66	Mitsubishi, Nagasaki	8.7.44	5.9.44	21.10.44
140	2734	CD 68	Kawasaki, Kobe	3.7.44	30.9.44	20.11.44
141	2736	CD 72	Ishikawajima	18.8.44	23.10.44	25.11.44
142	2737	CD 74	Mitsubishi, Nagasaki	1.8.44	2.11.44	10.12.44
143	2738	CD 76	Mitsubishi, Nagasaki	1.8.44	18.11.44	23.12.44
144	2741	CD 82	Mitsubishi, Nagasaki	6.9.44	18.11.44	31.12.44
145	2742	CD 84	Mitsubishi, Nagasaki	6.9.44	18.11.44	31.12.44
146	2751	CD 102	Mitsubishi, Nagasaki	1.9.44	4.12.44	20.1.45
147	2752	CD 104	Mitsubishi, Nagasaki	1.9.44	16.12.44	31.1.45
148	2753	CD 106	Ishikawajima	18.9.44	7.12.44	14.1.45
149	2756	CD 112	Kawasaki, Senshu	10.5.44	5.9.44	24.10.44
150	2759	CD 118	Ishikawajima	8.6.44	20.11.44	27.12.44
151	2762	CD 124	Kawasaki, Senshu	29.6.44	12.1.45	9.2.45
152	2763	CD 126	Kawasaki, Senshu	7.11.44	25.2.45	26.3.45
153	2725	CD 130	Harima	22.2.44	24.5.44	12.8.44
154	2766	CD 132	Harima	10.4.44	25.6.44	7.9.44
155	2767	CD 134	Harima	26.5.44	29.7.44	30.9.44
156	2769	CD 138	Harima	27.6.44	1.9.44	23.10.44
157	2772	CD 144	Harima	1.8.44	10.10.44	23.11.44
158	2775	CD 150	Harima	4.9.44	15.11.44	24.12.44
159	2777	CD 154	Harima	12.10.44	26.12.44	7.2.45
160	2778	CD 156	Harima	17.11.44	25.1.45	8.3.45
161	2779	CD 158	Harima	28.12.44	25.2.45	13.4.45
162	2780	CD 160	Harima	27.1.45	10.4.45	16.8.45
163	2793	CD 186	Mitsubishi, Nagasaki	4.11.44	30.12.44	15.2.45
164	2795	CD 190	Mitsubishi, Nagasaki	20.11.44	16.1.45	21.2.45
165	2796	CD 192	Mitsubishi, Nagasaki	5.12.44	30.1.45	28.2.45
166	2797	CD 194	Mitsubishi, Nagasaki	18.12.44	15.2.45	15.3.45
167	2798	CD 196	Mitsubishi, Nagasaki	31.12.44	26.2.45	31.3.45
168	2799	CD 198	Mitsubishi, Nagasaki	17.1.45	26.2.45	31.3.45
169	2800	CD 200	Mitsubishi, Nagasaki	31.1.45	19.3.45	20.4.45
170	2801	CD 202	Mitsubishi, Nagasaki	16.2.45	2.4.45	7.7.45
171	2802	CD 204	Mitsubishi, Nagasaki	27.2.45	14.4.45	11.7.45

FATES

56 Sunk 6.4.45 US Army aircraft (23°55′N/117′40′O, off Hsien tou)
57 Sunk 9.1.45 US carrier aircraft (27°10′N/121°45′O, off Wen chau, N of Keelung, China)
58 Sunk 21.9.44 US Carrier aircraft (15°25′N/119°50′O, N of Masintoc, Philippines)
59 Sunk 14.11.44 US submarine *Ray* (17°46′N/117°57′O, South China Sea, 250 miles W of Luzon)
60 Sunk 14.2.45 US submarine *Gato* (34°48′N/125°58′O, Yellow Sea)
61 Sunk 10.11.44 US Army aircraft at Ormoc Bay, Philippines
62 Sunk 14.8.45 US submarine *Tonsk* (35°42′N/134°35′0, Sea of Japan)
63 Sunk 6.6.44 US submarine *Rato* (08°58′N/109°30′, South China Sea SW of Cap St Jacques)
64 and **65** Sunk 12.1.45 US carrier aircraft (08°58′N/109°30′, Mekong Delta, South Vietnam near Cap St Jacques)
66 Sunk 6.10.44 US submarine *Seahorse* (19°27′/118°08′, South China Sea)
67 Sunk 12.1.45 US carrier aircraft (14°15′N/109°10′)
68 Sunk 3.5.45 US submarine *Springer* (34°38′N/124°15′)
69 Repatriation, 14.8.47 Singapore to England
70 Struck mine, 28.5.45. Main engine damaged, unfit for service. BU Sasebo
71 Sunk 14.4.45 US submarine *Tirante* (33°25′N/126°15′, East China Sea, W of Quelpart Island)
72 Sunk 28.3.45 US carrier aircraft (31°45′N/131°45′, off Kyushu, E of Kagashima)
73 Sunk 12.1.45 US carrier aircraft (11°10′N/108°55′, South China Sea, South Vietnam)
74 Repatriation, 4.9.47 Osaka to USA. Bought back and BU Kawasaki Senshu in Osaka
75 Sunk US Army aircraft (35°06′N/129°03′O, Sea of Japan)
76 Sunk 9.6.45 US submarine *Sea Owl* (34°8′N/127°18′0, off Makpo, South Korea, Straits of Tsushima)
77 Sunk 12.1.45 US carrier aircraft (11°10′N/108°55′0 South China Sea, South Vietnam off Cape Padarani)
78 Severely damaged 28.7.45 by US carrier aircraft, stranded off Owase

79 Sunk 14.8.45 US submarine *Torsk* (35°42′N/134°36′ off Amanite)
80 Minesweeping, 3.7.47 Shimizu to USA, BU Shimizu
81 Sunk 12.1.45, US carrier aircraft (14°15′N/109°10′, South China Sea, South Vietnam, North of Quinhan)
82 Sunk 7.2.45 US submarine *Bergall* (12°04′N/109°10′, South China Sea)
83 Repatriation, 16.7.47 Singapore to England
84 Repatriation, BU 1947
85 Repatriation, collision with sunken battleship *Hyuga*, raised, BU in Kure
86 Moderate damage 9.2.45 from striking mine 10nm from Cap St Jacques, taken to Saigon, BU there
87 Struck mine 10.8.45, Gulf of Nanao, bow above water
88 Sunk 14.7.45, US carrier aircraft, Mursran Bay, Hokkaido
89 Repatriation, 6.7.47 Shanghai to China, became *Ying Kom*
90 Severely damaged 8.3.45 US carrier aircraft (19°02′N/111°50′, lost in storm 16.3.45 off Wen'ch'ang, Kwantung Province)
91 Repatriation, to USSR 28.8.47 at Nakhotoka
92 Sunk 16.4.45 US submarine *Sunfish* (39°36′N/142°05′, off Todozoiki, Miyako Bay, Honshu)
93 Run aground off Odomari 10.8.45, lost
94 Minesweeping, to USSR 28.8.47 at Nakhodka.
95 Repatriation, to USSR 29.7.47 at Nakhodka
96 Repatriation, to China 29.8.47 at Tsingtao, became *Yu An*
97 Repatriation, to China 31.7.47 at Shanghai, became *Chin An*
98 Repatriation, to USA 29.7.47 at Nagasaki. BU at Kawanami 15.5.48
99 Minesweeping in harbour of Yokosuka near Buoy No 3, moderate damage 8.7.45, unfit for service, BU
100 Repatriation, to China 31.7.47 at Shanghai, became *Chang An*
101 Repatriation, to USA 4.7.47 at Tsingtao
102 Struck mine 18.8.45 in harbour of Fusan (Korea)
103 Repatriation, to China 6.7.47 at Shanghai, became *Liao Hei*
104 Minesweeping, to England 5.9.47 at Nagasaki, bought back, BU Nagasaki by Koyakishima
105 Sunk 15.7.45 US carrier aircraft (41°48′N/140°41′ off North Honshu)
106 Repatriation, to USSR 29.7.45 at Nakhodka
107 Engine damage in Kure, BU 30.4.48
108 Repatriation, to USSR 5.7.47 at Nakhodka
109 Near miss 30.7.45 from US carrier aircraft, harbour of Maizuru, raised, BU
110 Sunk 28.7.45, US carrier aircraft, near Toba
111 Sunk 13.8.45 US submarine *Atuk* (42°16′N/142°12′, off Shizunai, Hitaki province, Hokkaido)
112 Repatriation, to England via Singapore 16.7.47
113 Sunk 27.9.44 US submarine *Plaice* (29°26′N/128°50′, East China Sea, off Amami Oshima)
114 Minesweeping, to USA 5.9.47, bought back, BU in Sasebo
115 Repatriation, to China 6.7.47 at Shanghai, became *Tsi Nan*
116 Repatriation, to England 14.8.47 at Singapore
117 Sunk 29.3.45, US Army aircraft (14°44′N/107°16′, South China Sea)
118 Sunk 29.12.44, US aircraft (Lingayen Gulf, Luzon, Philippines)
119 Minesweeping, to USA 5.9.47 bought back from USA, BU by Sasebo
120 Sunk 28.6.44 US submarine *Archerfish* (24°44′N/140°20′, S of Ioshima)
121 Minesweeping, to USA 6.9.47 at Kure, bought back, BU by Harima in Kure
122 Sunk 14.12.44 US submarine *Blenny* (15°46′N/119°45′, 3 miles W of Hermana Major, Philippines)
123 Sunk 28.7.45, US carrier aircraft (Inland Sea, 100 miles W of Okinawa)
124 Repatriation, to England 16.7.47 at Singapore
125 Repatriation, to USSR 5.7.47 at Nakhodka
126 Repatriation, to USA 19.7.47 at Yokosuka, bought back, BU by Tsurumi
127 Sunk 25.11.44 US submarine *Hardhead* (14°22′N/119°57′, 60 miles W of Manila, Philippines)
128 Minesweeping, to China 29.8.47 at Tsingtao, became *Chan An*
129 Sunk 10.1.45 US submarine *Puffer* (27°01′N/126°34′, 100 miles W of Okinawa)
130 Repatriation, to USA 5.7.47 at Yokosuka
131 Sunk 17.8.45 US aircraft off Makpo, Korea (34°51′N/126°02′)
132 Minesweeping, to USSR 28.8.47 at Nakhodka
133 Severely damaged 11.5.45 by submarine torpedo off Wakayama (stern broken off) given up during repair in Osaka, BU
134 Repatriation, to USSR 29.7.47 at Nakhodka
135 Sunk 15.12.44 US carrier aircraft (19°25′N/121°25′, North point, Calayan Island, straits of Luzon, Philippines)
136 Sunk 17.2.45 US submarine *Bowfin* (33°53′N/139°43′, 5 miles off Mikorajima, off Honshu)
137 Repatriation, to England 14.8.47 at Singapore
138 Sunk 3.12.44 US submarine *Pipefish* (18°36′N/111°54′, South China Sea, E of Hainan Island)
139 Sunk 13.3.45 US Army aircraft, (23°30′N/117°10′, South China Sea, off Sient'ou, S of Namoa island)
140 Sunk 23.4.45 US carrier aircraft, (28°25′N/124°32′ South China Sea)
141 Sunk 1.7.45 US submarine *Hadda* (38°08′N/124°38′, Changsan, West Korea, Yellow Sea)
142 Sunk 14.7.45 US carrier aircraft,(42°21′N/140°59′ off Muroroa, North Honshu)
143 Minesweeping, to USSR 28.8.47 at Nakhodha
144 Sunk 10.8.45 Soviet aircraft, 7nm SSW Kumsusan, Korea
145 Sunk 29.3.45 US submarine *Hammerhead* (14°30′N/109°16′, South China Sea)
146 Minesweeping, to USSR 28.8.47 at Nakhodka
147 Minesweeping, to China 29.8.47 at Tsingtao, became *Tai An*
148 Repatriation, to USA 5.7.47 at Yokosuka
149 Sunk 18.7.45 US submarine *Barb* (46°03′N/142°16′, off Karafuto)
150 Repatriation, to China 31.7.47 at Shanghai, became *Choing Sha*
151 Minesweeping damage 10.4.45, off Futaoijima lighthouse, moderate damage, out of action, BU in Nagasaki
152 Repatriation, to England 14.8.47 at Singapore
153 Sunk 29.3.45 US Army aircraft, (14°44′N/109°16′, South China Sea)

(Fates continued on p256)

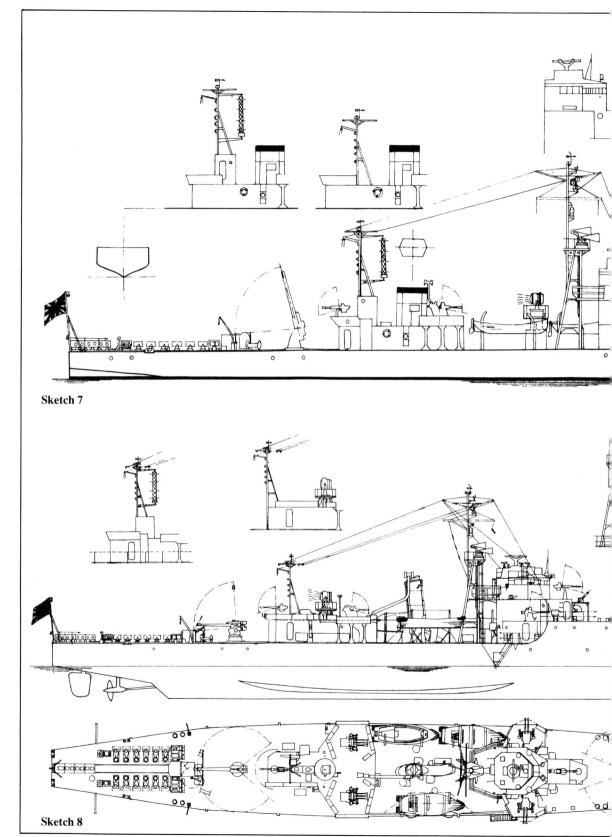

Sketch 7

Sketch 8

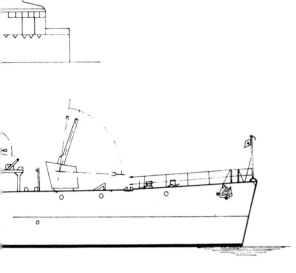

Sketch 7 Type C, class No 1: Appearance of the ships after about number 40.
1st and 2nd small sketch right: Bridge shapes of the first ships to be built.
3rd small sketch from right: Mast before installation of the Type 13 radar.
4th small sketch from right: Shape of the rear part of the deck superstructure differing from the main sketch.
Small sketch, left bottom: Stern shape (not to scale!).
Small sketch, right bottom: Cross-section of the funnel.

Sketch 8 Type D, class No 2: No 2 after strengthening of the light AA weapons.
Small sketch right: Small alterations to the bridge. Before fitting of the AA platforms and the mortar.
Small sketch, centre: Different arrangement of the mast on different ships.

Sketch 9 Type D body plan.

defence boats, the Type A auxiliary patrol boats had a steel hull, and those of Type B had a wooden hull. Type A was intended to have 200 tons displacement, a speed of 10 knots, and an action radius of 4000 miles at 8 knots, according to an order dating from 1943. On 22 April 1943 the building of Type A 90 boats and building of 300 Type B boats was demanded.

In the 84th session of parliament (December 1943) the funds for 62 boats were approved, and in the 86th

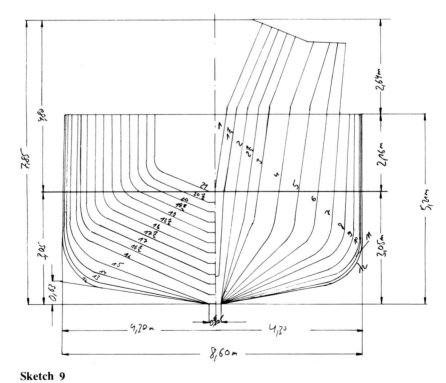

Sketch 9

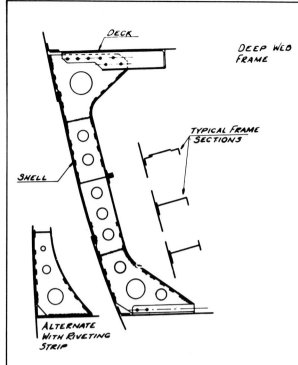

Sketch 10a

sessions (December 1944) the funds for 178 boats. However, work on them never started. Production of Type B was stopped by the Japanese on 29 May 1945. The approved funds were used to build the coastal defence boats.

The first boat, *CDa 113* (CDa symbol for coastal defence boat) was laid down on 11 February 1945 at Miho, Shimizu. Although the building of the auxiliary patrol boats was stopped, and work in the wooden ship yards was accelerated, only 22 boats had been started (by the end of the war), none of which had been

Sketch 10a A typical deep web frame of a *Kaibokan*. Rivetted at ends and intermittently welded to face plate and rivetting strip.

Sketch 10b Light frame from the after part of a *Kaibokan*. Intermittently welded to shell and rivetted to brackets. The side shell shown as welded in seams and rivetted to the gunwhale. The bottom shell seams are rivetted.

Sketch 10c. Longitudinal, transverse bulkhead of a *Kaibokan* floor.

Sketch 11 Coastal defence boat of Type A, class No 1 (approximate drawing, not to scale!).

1 The disarmed Type D Kaibokan *CD 52* before her handover to the USSR in July 1947.
Author's collection

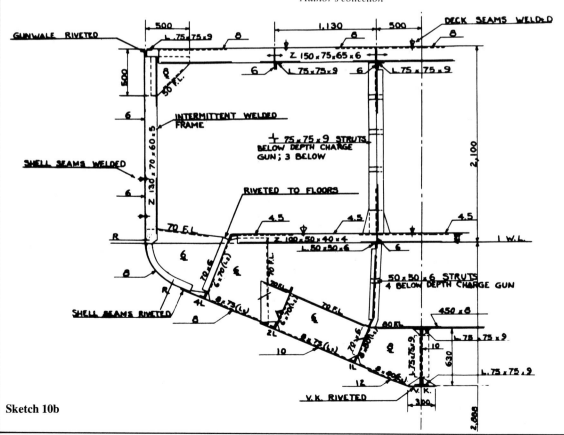

Sketch 10b

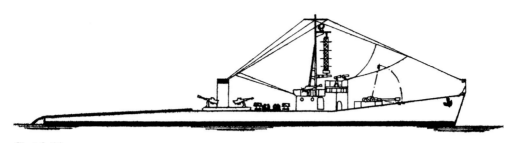

Sketch 11

1

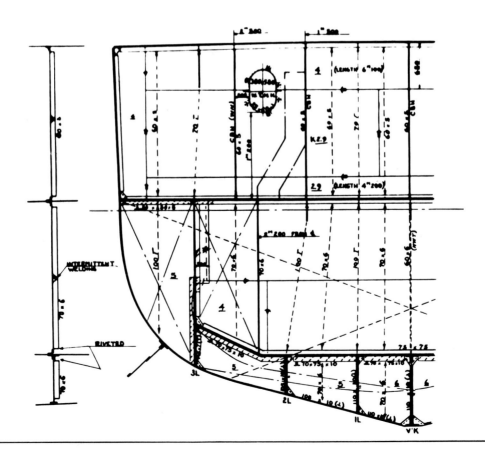

Sketch 10c

154 Repatriation, BU in Japan
155 Sunk 6.4.45 US Army aircraft (23°55′N/117°40′ off Hsient'ou, Kwangtung province, China)
156 Sunk 2.1.45 US Army aircraft (16°37′N/120°19′ off San Fernando, Philippines)
157 Sunk US submarine *Besugo* (04°32′N/104°30′, off Malaya)
158 Repatriation, to USA 4.7.47 at Tsingtao
159 Minesweeping, to England 10.9.47 at Innoshima, bought back, BU by Takuma
160 Minesweeping, to England 4.9.47 at Maizuru, bought back, BU by Iino
161 Repatriation, to USA 25.7.47 at Maizuru, bought back, BU by Iino
162 100% complete on 15.8.45, repatriation, to England 8.9.47 at Nanao. Bought back, BU by Mitsubishi
163 Sunk 2.4.45 US carrier aircraft, Seai Bay, Yellow Sea
164 Slightly damaged 24.7.45 US carrier aircraft in Tanube; handed over in Shimonoseki. BU 1.4.48 by Moji
165 Repatriation, to China 31.7.47 at Shanghai, became *Tung An*
166 Repatriation, to China 6.7.47 at Shanghai, became *Wei Hai*
167 Repatriation, to USSR 5.7.47 at Nakhodka
168 Repatriation, to China 31.7.47 at Shanghai, became *Hsi An*
169 Struck mine 17.5.45 in Gulf of Miyozu; moderate damage, out of action, handed over at Maizuru, BU by Iino 1.7.48
170 Struck mine outside Maizuru, moderate damage, out of action, handed over at Sasebo, BU 31.12.47
171 Slightly damaged 17.7.45 in accident in the Bay of Senzaki, E Coast of Honshu. BU 31.1.48 at Nagasaki

Summary: US submarines sunk 39 Kaibokan, US aircraft sank 35, storms sank 2, mines sank 3. Postwar 22 performed minesweeping and 59 sailed on repatriation duties. The Allies took over 67 ships (17 each to USA, China and USSR while Britain took 16) of which the American batch were bought back and scrapped in Japan.

TABLE 10: COASTAL DEFENCE BOATS (KAIBOTEI)

Running No	Building No	Name	Builder	Laid down	Launched	% Completion
1	1851	*CDa 1*	Kawanami, Uranosaki	15.4.45	15.6.45	65
2	1852	*2*	Kawanami, Uranosaki	24.4.45	29.6.45	
1	1701	*CDa 101*	Funaya, Hakodate	23.5.45	–	75
2	1703	*103*	Yamanishi, Ishinamaki	6.4.45	–	65
3	1704	*104*	Yamanishi, Ishinomaki	27.5.45	–	60
4	1709	*109*	Murakami, Ishinomaki	31.5.45	–	75
5	1713	*113*	Miho, Shimizu	11.2.45	–	85
6	1718	*118*	Koyanagi, Shizuaka	28.6.45	–	60
7	1719	*119*	Koyanagi, Shizuaka	10.8.45	–	40
8	1722	*122*	Ishikawa, Ujiyamada	17.5.45	–	35
9	1725	*125*	Goriki, Ujiyamada	2.7.45	–	70
10	1726	*126*	Goriki, Ujiyamada	2.7.45	–	50
11	1728	*128*	Nishi, Ujiyamada	29.5.45	–	70
12	1731	*131*	Shikoku Dock, Takamatsu	5.3.45	–	75
13	1732	*132*	Shikoku Dock, Takamatsu	25.3.45	–	60
14	1733	*133*	Shikoku Dock, Takamatsu	15.4.45	–	45
15	1737	*137*	Tokushima Tokushima	–	–	–
16	1738	*138*	Tokushima, Tokushima	–	–	
17	1739	*139*	–	–	–	
18	1741	*141*	Fukushima, Matsue	30.4.45	–	65
19	1744	*144*	Hayashikane, Shimonoseki	12.5.45	–	75
21	1748	*148*	Jinen, Moji	13.4.45	–	65
21	1751	*151*	Fukuoka, Fukuoka	9.6.45	–	60
22	1757	*157*	Saga, Takaoka	1.5.45	–	65

TABLE 11: WEIGHT DISTRIBUTION OF JAPANESE ESCORT VESSELS (tons)

	Shimushu class	Etorofu class	Mikura class	Ukuru class	No 1 class	No 2 class
Hull	388.10	383.00	386.00	378.00	295.00	315.00
Fitting	59.50	61.00	61.00	55.00	39.50	41.00
Ballast	–	–	25.00	40.00	–	15.00
Fixed Equipment	27.20	30.00	30.00	29.00	23.30	23.50
Gun	58.41	55.10	76.50	78.50	55.58	55.40
Torpedo (means ASW)	14.06	15.90	43.60	42.20	36.77	36.77
Navigation	1.90	2.70	2.70	1.20	1.20	1.20
Optical		1.20	1.30	1.40	1.31	1.36
Electric	35.00	37.90	38.70	34.10	29.00	25.40
Wireless	6.76	8.60	9.40	12.60	10.75	11.59
Machinery	177.70	197.70	169.00	167.60	130.40	123.00
Consumable equipment	65.53	65.60	77.70	80.80	72.72	60.50
Fuel oil	147.00	138.00	80.00	80.00	70.70	160.00
Light oil	0.33	0.60	0.60	0.30	0.30	0.30
Lubrication oil	13.30	13.30	8.00	7.10	8.00	1.00
Fresh water into hydrophone	–	5.00	6.40	5.60	5.70	5.70
Emergency equipment	–	0.30	0.30	0.50	0.30	0.30
Reserve	20.68	1.40	3.70	6.10	29.47	15.55
Total (trial displacement)	1020	1020	1020	1020	810	900

Notes: 1 Data given at the eve of the basic design (actual data may vary)
    2 Weight distribution for *Ukuru* class is based on armament with 16 x model 3 DC throwers, for the ships which had 2 x model 94 DC throwers 'Torpedo' was 41.00 and 'Reserve' 7.30.

launched (see Table 10). The boats were designated special boats *(Tokushutei)*, and were accepted into the warship register as small auxiliary service boats *(Tokumutei)* after the auxiliary minesweeping boats.

TRANSPORT CONVERSIONS

After the end of the war the repatriation of Japanese soldiers and civilian officials in war service, cut off on many islands in the Pacific and on the coasts of Asia, presented a major problem. The greatly depleted Japanese merchant fleet was not in a position to fulfill this task. The SCAJAP (Naval shipping control authority for Japanese merchant marine) did make 215 ships available (100 Liberty, 100 LST, 9 C-1 freighters and 6 hospital ships), but a further 150 former warships of the Imperial Japanese Navy were also used for transport duties. Of these the most numerous were 61 coastal defence ships. They were termed special transporters *(Tokubetsu yusokan)*, cancelled from the warship register and entered in the register for special transporters. As well as seven ships incomplete (*CD 97, 105, 107, 58, 78, 116* and *142*), *Urumi, Murotsu* and *CD 62* also received approval for completion. The first two were never completed, as they were no longer needed – an adequate amount of shipping space was available. *CD 62* sank in Kure harbour on 14 January 1946.

The warships, which were not equipped for carrying personnel or materials, were converted by a wide variety of methods. A typical example for the smaller warships is the conversion of *CD 105* and *CD 107* as special transporters. Incidentally *CD 107* was the last warship supplied to the Imperial Japanese Navy.

As Type C *Kaibokan* they had a crew of 9–14 officers and 196–245 petty officers and men. This number was reduced to slightly more than half. The ammunition storage rooms, the depth-charge storage compartments, and rooms for the hydro-acoustic equipment were converted to accommodate people. The superstructure was extended forwards. On the quarterdeck a large deckhouse was erected to house personnel, which also served to maintain the ship's centre of gravity.

The ships were intended mainly for transport duties from Taiwan and Central and Northern China. Hence the radius of operation could be reduced, and part of the fuel tanks taken out of service. The ship's interior space was thus increased, and could be used after conversion for additional supplies of food and drinking water.

The capacity of the ships was calculated at 100 crew and 443 'passengers'. The latter were to be accommodated as follows:

1 Crew* accommodation:
a) Upper deck in the forecastle
region 16 officers
b) Upper deck in the foreship
region 10 crew
c) Middle deck at the forward
mast position 34 crew
d) Middle deck at the rear mast
position 26 crew

e) Former rear ammunition
storage compartment 14 crew
Total: 16 officers and 84 crew = 100 persons.

2 'Passenger' accommodation:
a) In the deckhouse 93 persons
b) Middle deck below the officers' compartment 70 persons
c) Middle deck below the deck
house 78 + 48 persons
d) Former forward ammunition
storage compartment 58 persons
e) Former compartments for
hydro-acoustic equipment
(sonar, hydrophone) 40 persons
f) Former depth-charge storage
compartment 56 persons
Total 443 persons

*The captain's cabin was to form a reserve room.

Since the galley no longer sufficed for this number, a second galley was set up behind the first – this was located in the deck superstructure in front of the funnel. Temporary toilets were arranged on both sides on the upper deck aft.

The conversion work allowed 400–500 persons to be carried per journey; for a ship of only 800 tons standard displacement, this was a good performance.

In the months August–October 1946 Shizuo Fukui, a former commander (ship-building) set up studies into the full or partial conversion of coastal defence ships to passenger ships, in order to use them in civilian service. There are sketches in Fukui's book 'Japanese Naval Vessels surveyed', page 92, sketch 2 C (to 1) and sketch 2 D (to 2). Approval for neither project was granted.

NOTES

13 The Japanese Navy used DS (Ducol Steel) for the strength members of their ships, after experience with HTS (High Tensile Steel) and HHTS (Special High Tensile Steel). After the beginning of the war production of this steel was not sufficient to meet requirements, so that a return to HTS had to be made at the beginning of 1943. Even so, capacity was still insufficient, and mild steel was even considered for the hulls of destroyers. However, this did not come about, as in the autumn of 1943 the production of a steel with almost the same properties as the German St 52 (KM) started.

14 Specification of the 12cm LAG L/45 3-year type AA gun.

Barrel length	45 calibre = 5.4m
Max pressure	27kg/mm²
Barrel weight	2.86 tons
Total weight	6.69 tons
Shell weight	20.413kg
Powder weight	5.11kg
Initial velocity	825m/s

Ballistic data

Range		
Barrel elevation	5°	6028m
	10°	8604m
	20°	11,916m
	30°	14,278m
	30°	15,200m

Arethusa Class Cruisers Part 2

By Alan Pearsall

The original intention was to employ the first four as fleet cruisers, and captains were appointed to them on that basis. The outbreak of war, however, revealed only too clearly how short the Royal Navy was of powerful and fast light cruisers, and the *Arethusa*s were indeed just in time. It is said that Commodore Tyrwhitt visited the Admiralty and pointed out forcefully that the *Amethyst* of 1904, in which he then had his broad pendant, was obsolete and far too slow to keep up with the modern destroyers under his command. Whatever the truth of the story, he was certainly told to exchange ships with Captain Thesiger, who had been preparing to take the *Arethusa* after the German cruiser *Karlsruhe*. The indignation of the latter officer can be imagined, and he was no doubt supported by Captain A G Hotham of *Undaunted* and Captain H R Cooke of *Aurora* when they were ordered to turn over to Captain Cecil Fox and Captain Wilmot Nicholson respectively, as the former ship was to replace the lost *Amphion* with the 3rd

The wreck of the *Arethusa* near the South Cutler Buoy off Harwich in or after February 1916. The U-boat mine exploded under the boilers (killing 6 crew) so that, weakened in the most vulnerable spot, the ship broke in two. Hopes of salving her were not abandoned until August.
NMM

Royalist in an early (1915) camouflage painting, and lofty mast, unlike her two yard sisters.
P A Vicary

Flotilla and the latter was to take the new 10th Flotilla of 'M' class destroyers, all at Harwich. The indignant captains had, however, little destroyer experience and they were mollified by appointments to even newer light cruisers.

Jellicoe was also indignant at the removal of much needed light cruisers from his command, but he had to wait until the remainder of the *Arethusas* and the *Carolines* completed. Until then he had to make do with Commodore Goodenough's 1st Light Cruiser Squadron of six 'Town' class, the remaining nine of that class being actively engaged in chasing the German light cruisers on foreign stations. It was not until early 1915 therefore that the Grand Fleet received four *Arethusas* and the first *Carolines* to augment its cruiser force. The eighth *Arethusa*, the *Penelope*, joined the first three at Harwich. This 4-4 distribution lasted until early in 1918, when the three remaining at Harwich turned over their crews to new 'C' class ships and went to the Grand Fleet.

HELIGOLAND BIGHT AND 1914

Long before the last of the class commissioned, the first three had made their name, and they remained the best known of the eight. *Arethusa* joined Tyrwhitt's Harwich Force on 24 August and almost at once she was leading it in the sweep which resulted in the Battle of the Heligoland Bight on 28 August 1914, which was to be the only example of the type of action which everyone had expected to be almost a daily occurrence – a general light cruiser and destroyer scrum. *Arethusa* was in the middle of it, taking and giving hard blows, and eventually she limped back to Chatham Yard to repair. But her reputation was made. The world had been waiting for just such a battle, and the audacity of two small light cruisers (*Fearless* being the other) and some destroyers venturing so close to the vaunted fortress of Heligoland caught the public imagination. The phrase 'Saucy *Arethusa*' was inevitably revived and the Admiralty even ordered a plate to be fixed on her

Phaeton has had her topgallant mast cut down and the after searchlight platform placed over the after control. The two projecting flag lockers on the front of the bridges of her (and *Penelope* seen below right in mid-1918) show clearly.
IWM

quarterdeck with the words of the poem engraved thereon, much to the embarrassment of the 'bold mariners' of her crew.

But the Harwich Force continued to exploit the psychological advantage which she had gained. The constructors too were pleased with her trial by battle. The armour had not been pierced, and those shells which struck unarmoured parts had damaged nothing important. The drying room was said to be a shell trap, and here an extra section of 1in deck was urged, only to be ruled out on weight grounds. The 4in guns, however, had proved unsatisfactory, and the gun trials of other ships showed the same – the semi-automatic ejection of the cartridge case was uncertain. The difficulties were, however, only the initial troubles of a new mark.

Undaunted joined the Harwich Force in October, after some engine-room troubles. She too distinguished herself at once. With four 'L' boats of her destroyer flotilla on one of the patrols to Terschelling (maintained

Aurora in her March 1915 war paint.
G A Osbon

by the Harwich Force in the early part of the war) she encountered a division of four German torpedo boats and sank them all (17 October 1914).

Aurora joined later in October, but was obliged to wait until the Gorleston raid for any serious operation, but then she joined the others in a new venture – covering seaplane carriers from which raids on Germany were launched, with the hope also of tempting out German warships to drive off the intruders. Several

Undaunted still retains her mizzen mast forward of the searchlight platform in or after 1918 with a Sopwith Pup on a flying off platform above her forward 6in gun.
IWM

A Deperdossia monoplane on a temporary runway aboard *Aurora* in November 1915.
IWM

efforts of this type were made, several abortive, but on one, the three *Arethusa*s with some Grand Fleet armoured cruisers induced the guns of Heligoland to open fire on them, the only occasion on which those weapons ever came into action. Minelaying operations also were covered by the Harwich Force, and on one of these the *Undaunted* had the first of her two collisions, when she was run into by the destroyer *Landrail* while altering course in fog on 24 March 1915. They were also involved in the Yorkshire raid and the Dogger Bank action, besides countless sweeps and patrols in the southern North Sea. In 1915, during the first U-boat campaign, both *Aurora* and *Undaunted* took destroyers to the Irish Sea on anti-submarine duties.

OPERATIONS IN 1915

Of the other ships, only *Phaeton* had interesting experience in her early days. Like some of the others she did a trial voyage to Gibraltar where she calibrated her guns. From there, however, she was ordered to Marseilles, where she picked up General Sir Ian Hamilton and took him at high speed to the Dardanelles, where he was to command the troops intended to force the Straits. Reaching Mudros harbour (Lemnos) on 17 March, she took Sir Ian on his first examination of the Gallipoli peninsula. During the great bombardment of 18 March, the General watched the action from her, and she attended the mined battlecruiser *Inflexible* on her way to Mudros. The results of that action, however, convinced those on the spot that only a large-scale landing would suffice, and *Phaeton* was accordingly recalled, as her services were no longer needed.

Galatea had been for a short time leader of the 2nd Flotilla, but in February 1915 she hoisted the broad pendant of Commodore E S Alexander-Sinclair in command of a new 1st Light Cruiser Squadron (LCS) with *Inconstant* (to which Captain Thesiger was appointed), *Caroline* and *Cordelia*. *Phaeton* joined *Royalist* in June 1915 in another new light cruiser squadron, the 4th with *Comus* and *Calliope*, after a period of detached service. The 1st LCS was attached to the 1st BCS at Rosyth, while the 4th was at Scapa. They naturally participated in the fleet operations, though

never becoming so prominent as the Harwich group, to which *Penelope* was added in January 1915.

Various alterations had already been made. All the guns were quickly fitted with light spray shields to protect the gun's crews, and small sponsons were also provided to give more space. (The later five ships were built with these fittings). A blast screen was fitted before the after 6in to cover its supply hatch when the gun was firing before the beam. Other visible changes were small masts aft for the aerials and ensign, a wireless cabin under the bridge together with shelters for the gun crew, and Carley floats and splinter padding on the bridge. Alterations were also made in the after control, due in part to mechanical working of the searchlights, and in some ships it was moved forward.

In the spring of 1915, the Harwich Force ships were constantly sighting Zeppelins, and they were all fitted with ramps to carry a seaplane in the hope of catching one of the airships. Although it was possible to get the seaplane into the air in $2\frac{1}{2}$ minutes, the stratagem was unsuccessful, and was abandoned after a time. The main event of 1915 for the *Arethusa*s was the successful pursuit of the German minelayer *Meteor* on 9 August in which five of the class participated, the three Harwich ones actually finding the scuttling minelayer and rescuing the 43 survivors of the armed boarding steamer *Ramsey*, which she had sunk, while the two from the 1st LCS were approaching very near at hand.

EARLY 1916

The year 1916 was an eventful one for our eight ships. Operationally there was more of the sweeping, which involved now the northern part of the North Sea following the *Meteor* affair. In one of these, on her way home, *Arethusa* met her end. She had been narrowly missed by two torpedoes in an unsuccessful seaplane operation on 29 January, but returning from her next trip she hit a mine on 11 February just laid by one of the Flanders U-boats in the Gledway. The destroyers *Lightfoot* and then the *Loyal* tried to take her in tow, but she drifted on to the Cutler and broke her back, the explosion having been under the boilers. Despite prolonged efforts she could not be salved, although it was hoped at one time to fit her engines in a new cruiser! The loss of *Arethusa* was felt to be a national blow, and the cruiser's 18 months of active service certainly maintained the reputation of her name.

In March 1916 another daring attack on airship sheds was launched by the Harwich Force, during which *Undaunted* had her second collision, when she ran into the light cruiser *Cleopatra* after the latter had cut a German destroyer in two. Darkness and bad weather made the situation worse and *Undaunted* became separated from the rest of the force, and all this was only 120 miles NW by N from Heligoland. Eventually Captain St John was very relieved to see the 5th Battle Squadron come to his rescue.

The Lowestoft raid of 25 April 1916 brought *Penelope* into the limelight, as she was one of the three light cruisers with which Tyrwhitt attempted to drive off the German battlecruisers from their bombardment. The cruiser *Conquest* was hit by an 11in shell, though not disabled, and the action probably shortened the bombardment if nothing else. On the way back, however, *Penelope* was torpedoed by *UB 29* off the Norfolk coast, her steering gear was wrecked, and the whole stern distorted. She was towed into Chatham successfully.

JUTLAND AND AFTER

Apart from another raid, this time by the Grand Fleet cruisers, Jutland was the next important event. The *Arethusa*s did not come to the fore in this great action apart from the essential function of *Galatea* and *Phaeton* in being the first to sight the enemy at 1420 on 31 May, opening fire on two German destroyers at 1428. While the 1st LCS engaged their opposite numbers of the 2nd Scouting Group during the battlecruiser action, they lost touch afterwards. *Royalist* with the 4th LCS countered a German torpedo attack on the head of the British line at 1930, and about an hour later, together with *Caroline*, she fired torpedoes herself at the German 2nd Battle Squadron – a rare case of cruisers using their torpedo armament.

As a result of Jutland, further changes were made to the *Arethusa*s. A suggestion in 1915 that director-firing should be fitted to light cruisers had been turned down as none could be spared for a sufficient time. But in mid-1916, more cruisers were available and the equipment was becoming more necessary. Accordingly, a tripod mast was fitted to allow a larger top to

accommodate the layer and equipment. Of course, this extra weight, high up, caused anxiety over the stability, and some of the oil fuel tanks were fitted to take water ballast when they were empty. *Penelope*, repairing after Lowestoft, was the first to be fitted, and an inclining test was carried out on her at Chatham on 15 September 1916, with satisfactory results. Possibly as a result of *Royalist*'s experience at Jutland, it was decided to increase the torpedo armament of all light cruisers. Two additional twin sets were mounted in the *Arethusa*s on the quarterdeck abaft the third set of 4in, with suitable precautions to prevent the crews being affected by the

A fine view of the forepart of *Phaeton* in 1917–18 with a Sopwith Pup on a flying off platform above her 6in gun. Also well shown are her capstan, cable holders and the numerous voice pipes from the foretop (beside the range clock).
NMM/Royal Naval Air Service

blast of the after 6in firing forward of the beam. *Royalist* was the first so treated, trials being made in February 1917.

About the same time, it was pointed out by the discerning that the heavy conning towers were death traps if hit, but that in fact no-one used them, the ships always being conned from the upper bridge. The Director of Naval Construction gladly took the

TABLE 1: CLASS OUTLINE

Name	Laid down	Launched	Completed	Built/engined
Arethusa	28.10.1912	25.10.1913	11.8.1914	Chatham DY/Fairfield
Undaunted	21.12.1912	28.4.1914	29.8.1914	Fairfield
Aurora	24.10.1912	30.9.1913	5.9.1914	Devonport DY/Parsons
Penelope	1.2.1913	25.8.1913	10.12.1914	Vickers, Barrow
Galatea	9.1.1913	14.5.1913	12.1914	Beardmore
Inconstant	3.4.1913	6.7.1914	27.1.1915	Beardmore
Phaeton	12.3.1913	21.10.1914	2.1915	Vickers, Barrow
Royalist	3.6.1913	14.1.1915	3.1915	Beardmore

Three fine views of *Aurora* in September 1915 at speed in the North Sea showing her forecastle, open bridge and midships. *NMM*

opportunity of removing them, this being about the only gain in weight to be recorded.

Minelaying became important in 1916, and all the *Arethusa*s were fitted to do so, although they had to land the new torpedo tubes when required to lay mines. The fittings were therefore only shipped when laying was actually required. By 1918, however, the use of light cruisers for this purpose had ceased. About 70 mines could be carried, varying slightly according to the mark. Again, *Royalist* was the first, and was the only one to lay mines on any scale. The Harwich ships were also fitted with two 2pdrs against torpedo craft.

THE 1918 REARMAMENT

The last major alteration made to the class was the rearmament. By 1917, the *Arethusa*s had been followed by a series of light cruisers developed from them, the six *Caroline*s and two *Calliope*s, then the four *Cambrian*s, all of which had mixed armament, and then the two *Centaur*s introduced an all 6in centreline armament, which was followed by the later 'Cs' and 'Ds'. It was naturally suggested that the earlier cruisers should be altered to extend the advantages. Topweight, however, once again made difficulties, and, at first, the proposal was rejected. The earlier 'Cs' were eventually altered late in 1917, and the *Arethusa*s were reconsidered late that year with the experience of the action of 17 November very much in mind. Two proposals were made. Both included a second 6in aft where the AA gun was, but differed in that one proposed a 6in either side of the bridge, whereas the other suggested a superfiring 6in on a bandstand just before the bridge. Beatty and Tyrwhitt both preferred the second plan, although it required some alterations to the bridge, and also prevented the fitting of an aeroplane platform which had recently been authorised. The aeroplane was, however, not felt to be indispensable, although in fact the platforms were fitted, as none of the ships ever received the second 6in.

Royalist was taken in hand at Rosyth in April 1918, but it was reported that there was not time to make the alterations forward, and authority was given to ship the after 6in only, thus giving her three 6in and four 4in, which was done. The resiting of the displaced HA gun had its comic elements, as the position ordered, just forward of the after control, was found by the yard actually to be occupied by that structure, and they wired asking what they should do. It appeared that, when the SL towers were enlarged, this was done with no official sanction or even knowledge, and, while the Harwich ships seem to have had them in the original place, the Grand Fleet vessels had them moved forward. It was only pointed out, as a result of this episode, that the position ordered was not a good one in any case, as the gun could not fire aft where it was often most needed,

nor had it a very good arc to fire starshell, one of its other functions. The solution was to fit two 3in HA instead on the small structures abaft the original torpedo tubes, without any change of weights. The rearming also involved moving the additional torpedo tubes forward of the original set, to give the new 6in a clear field of fire. Five of the class were rearmed thus during 1918, but *Undaunted* and *Aurora* were never so treated, as the war ended before they went into the dockyard.

There is relatively little to record of action during 1917 and 1918. The 1st LCS were principal participants in the chase action of 17 November 1917, where the value of 6in guns was clearly shown, as well as the disadvantages of not having superfiring guns forward. In February 1918 the three Harwich ships went to the Grand Fleet as the 7th LCS (with *Carysfort*). *Phaeton* led in the German light cruisers in the surrender of 20 November 1918.

POSTWAR CAREERS

The war was over – what was the future? The Grand Fleet and the Harwich Force remained in being until the spring of 1919, when reductions began in earnest. *Aurora*, *Penelope* and *Undaunted* all paid off at this

Aurora in dock at Hull in July 1917.
NMM

Galatea returning to Portsmouth from the Black Sea in April 1919. The St Andrew's Cross attests her service with the White Russians.
NMM

time, shortly followed by *Inconstant*, which had had a short spell in the Baltic. The other three of the class, however, all spent much of 1919 in that sea. *Galatea* took out General Sir Hubert Gough, leader of the British Military Mission to the Baltic Provinces, and conveyed him on his various tasks. Additionally she was present at the action off Seskar on 30 March 1919, and later joined the force at Biorko with *Phaeton*. All three also spent time at the troubled port of Libau. They paid off early in 1920.

Meanwhile, the future of the whole class darkened as postwar retrenchment set in. The first proposals for the postwar fleet, early in 1919, envisaged three *Arethusa*s on the East Indies Station. This scheme was so lavish that it soon gave way under successive cold douches of economy, but it did bring out a deficiency of all the war-built cruisers, – lack of any refrigerating space, without which tropical service was obviously impossible. However, reductions in the proposals eliminated the *Arethusa*s as candidates for such service, and indeed, soon they were the oldest light cruisers on the Navy List, except for the later 'Town' groups, which were, however, much favoured for foreign service. In October 1919 *Inconstant* recommissioned for the only full postwar commission served by one of the class, as the ship of the Captain S/M of the 1st Submarine Flotilla (the K-boats), paying off in February 1922. In July 1920 *Aurora*, *Galatea* and *Royalist* were briefly commissioned in a test mobilisation at Portland. Soon afterwards, *Aurora* with the destroyers *Patriot* and *Patrician*, was transferred to become the nucleus of the Royal Canadian Navy, and made the only transatlantic voyage of any of the class. *Undaunted* made a trooping trip to the Mediterranean in the spring of 1921, but as pressure for reduction in the Service Estimates became greater and greater, so did the breaker's yard come nearer and nearer. The crucial years were 1921 and 1922. In October 1921 *Galatea* was sold, and by the middle of 1922 all the others (except *Aurora*) were on the Sale List. But Canada was finding even her small navy too much, and *Aurora*, as the biggest ship, offered greatest scope for economy. So she was paid off, and after lingering as a hulk for some years, was sold in 1927, last of them all. Hard war service, their relative age, their mixed armament and political necessity brought the *Arethusa*s to a premature end.

SUMMARY

In conclusion, an assessment of the design as a whole might be made, as it does point some useful morals. They were clearly good ships that could have been better. They were obviously a vast improvement on the *Active*s on which they were based, as their contrasting wartime careers show. Admitting that any ship has to be a compromise, there were some obvious faults, but the basic trouble was that they were slightly too small for what was required, so that there was no spare space, no margin of weight, nor, as time went on, much margin of stability. Thus they were rather too heavy and could not make the hoped-for 30 knots, and it became difficult to incorporate later improvements. Nevertheless, the idea

TABLE 2: PARTICULARS

Displacement:	3512 tons (nominal), 3945 tons (average normal condition), 4410 tons (average deep load)
Dimensions:	436ft (oa) 410ft (pp) × 39ft × 13ft 6in (mean), 15ft 6in (max)
Guns:	(as completed) 2–6in BL MK III (2×1), 94 rounds per gun, 6–4in QF Mk V (6×1), 200rpg, 1–3pdr AA gun (differed in some ships)
	(as rearmed) 3–6in (3×1), 4–4in (4×1), 2–3in AA (2×1)
Torpedo tubes:	4–21in (2×2), increased to 8–21in (4×2)
Protection:	3in belt amidships, 2½–1in deck, 6in CT
Machinery:	4-shaft Parsons impulse-reaction steam turbines (Brown-Curtis in *Arethusa* and *Undaunted*), 40,000shp = 29 knots (max); eight Yarrow boilers
Complement:	276 rising to 318 by 1919
Fuel:	810 tons oil, but normally only 429 tons carried
Endurance:	5000 miles at 16 knots

Note: The anti-aircraft armament differed in some cases from the official outfit; eg *Arethusa*'s plans show a 13pdr (ex-Royal Horse Artillery) gun, and a 4in later became standard. This gun was mounted on the centreline aft, and was replaced by 3in guns (winged out) in 1918.

TABLE 3: MODIFICATIONS AND IDENTIFICATION

Principal External Modifications to the Arethusa *Class in chronological order*
Addition of AA gun.
Aircraft carried in Harwich ships, later removed.
Tripod mast for director control; range clocks.
Additional torpedo tubes on quarterdeck.
Minelaying equipment (later removed).
Searchlight platform removed.
After searchlight and control tower enlarged.
Mizen masts fitted.
Conning towers removed.
Aircraft platforms again fitted.
Rearmament with three 6in and altered AA armament.

Variations in rig and number of boats carried were numerous.

Distinguishing features of individual ships

Arethusa	1	Never had a mizzen mast of any kind.
	2	Scuttles on forecastle on same level.
Aurora	1	Originally had hull ensign staff on after SL platform.
	2	As *Arethusa*.
	3	Later, SL tower right aft.
Undaunted	1	No searchlight platform on foremast.
	2	Two windows in charthouse only.
	3	Scuttles at after end of forecastle raised.
	4	Later, SL tower right aft.
Galatea	1	Small windows in charthouse.
	2	Raised forecastle scuttles.
Penelope	1	Projecting flag lockers on bridge front.
	2	Scuttles on forecastle as *Undaunted*.
	3	Later, SL tower right aft.
Phaeton	1 2	} As *Penelope*.
Inconstant	1	Forecastle scuttles on same level.
Royalist	1	Raised scuttles.

of the 'light armoured cruiser' was sound. They were well able to operate with and support destroyers, and the 6in guns gave a very useful superiority in actions between light forces. They manifestly stood up well to shellfire, torpedoes and collisions, and they could stay

TABLE 4: MINELAYING 1917–18

Ship	Fitted	Mine capacity	Operations	Mines laid
Royalist	Feb 1917	74	16	1183
Undaunted	Apr 1917	70	–	–
Aurora	May 1917	74	3	212
Phaeton	Aug 1917	74	5	358
Inconstant	Sep 1917	74	5	370
Penelope	Nov 1917	70	3	210
Galatea	Nov 1917	74	3	220

All minelaying gear was ordered to be removed in December 1918.

Inconstant with a rare display of awnings during her long 1919–1922 commission as flagship of the Captain of 1st Submarine Flotilla.　　　　　　　　*NMM*

A rather melancholy picture of *Undaunted* and *Penelope* in reserve, funnels covered, at the Nore (1919 or 1920). They were sold to the breakers in April 1923 and October 1924 respectively.　　　　　　　　*NMM*

out in any weather, wet though they might be.

Many of the obvious faults were remedied in the *Caroline*s which had 10ft more length; the forward beam 4in guns, which were so wet in the *Arethusa*s, raised on to the forecastle – this was a lesson which might have been learnt from the *Bristol*s; an extended superstructure aft which gave a super-firing 6in and some extra accommodation, which, with the abolition of the peace tanks, made them much roomier; and a magazine between the engine and boiler rooms for the midship guns. But even here, the old broadside armament still bedevilled design, and there were still several further stages to go through before the emergence of *Carlisle* brought the immediate development of the design to its culmination – five well arranged 6in on the centreline, eight torpedo tubes, geared turbines, trawler bows, bridge well aft, all within an extra 15ft yet with much greater fighting power and radius of action.

SOURCES

Steamships of England 1914–18 (Official)
Light Cruisers 1912–20 (Official)
Ships Covers (National Maritime Museum)
Ships' Plans (NMM)
Warship recognition notes by Richard Perkins (NMM)
British Warships 1914–1919 by Dittmar & Colledge (London, 1972)
Marine News and *M N Warship Supplements* with particular reference to the *Arethusa* class notes by John Dominy.
Photographs from the Imperial War Museum, P A Vicary and NMM collections, particularly the Gunn Collection.

The author thanks his colleagues at the National Maritime Museum for their help, particularly the late George Osbon, and John Roberts for providing photographs from his own collection.

HMS *Savage* was a World War II destroyer used as a trials ship for new propeller designs. Glass windows were fitted above the propellers so that their performance could be seen.

Stealth & HMS Savage

by D K Brown RCNC

'The underwater war is a silent war, too much noise and the hunter becomes the hunted.'
Admiralty Experiment Works Centenary Film

The development of the reduced noise propellers by Admiralty research laboratories in the late 1940s and early 1950s gave the Royal Navy a long lead in this silent war. This work has been published in technical terms by E P Lover, RCNC, himself a pioneer (Ref 1) and, mainly in terms of personalities (Ref 2).

A ship moving through the sea will generate noise over a wide range of frequencies from its machinery and from the flow of water over the hull and propellers.

TABLE 1: MAIN SOURCES OF UNDERWATER NOISE (Ref 3)

Speed	Source	Frequency	Notes
Low	Machinery	Low	Easily Identified
Medium	Propeller cavitation	High	Broad band
High	Flow turbulence	High	broad band

The noise radiated by a warship can attract acoustic torpedoes or activate mines; it can enable an enemy submarine to detect and identify a hunting vessel and noise can interfere with the effective use of the ship's own sonar. All these problems became apparent during World War II and by 1944 it was clear that the next generation of escort vessels would have to be much quieter. As a first step, the rotational speed of the propellers was reduced considerably in the new designs (Type 12 and 14 frigates) compared with those of the traditional destroyer machinery.

CAVITATION

One of the major noise sources was, and still is, cavitation in the flow of water over a propeller. If the pressure is dropped sufficiently water will change to vapour – 'boil' – even at normal sea temperatures, forming vapour filled cavities. Propeller blades generate thrust both from increased pressure on the face of the blade and from suction on the back. As speed increases more

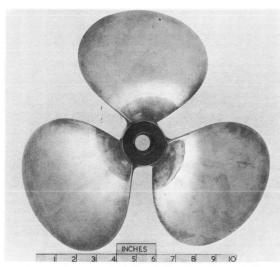

Set A propellers were those fitted when the ship was built. They had 3 blades, constant pitch and segmented sections.

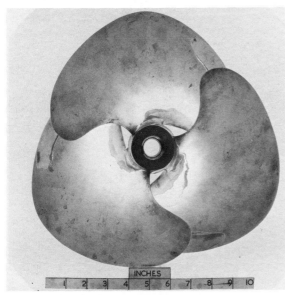

Set J were designed by Dr Lerbs, using new theoretical methods, to delay the onset of cavitation. Their very large blade area (BAR 1.1) contributed to this but also led to a very low efficiency.

thrust is developed and, sooner or later, cavitation will develop on the back of the blade.

Water will also be drawn across the tip of the blade from the high pressure side to the suction area generating a tip vortex like those that can be seen on high flying aircraft. If the water in a vortex spins fast enough, the pressure will drop at the core, eventually causing cavitation. A somewhat similar process can be seen in the vortex formed when bath water runs out.

When vapour bubbles pass out of the suction area they will collapse rapidly, generating loud, high frequency (over 300 Hz) noise. In a typical World War II destroyer

such cavitation noise would begin at about 8 knots or even earlier if the propeller blades were damaged.

At high speeds, from about 22 knots upwards, cavitation will begin to affect the thrust produced by the propeller and its efficiency. This effect would cause about a knot loss of speed in a typical destroyer. Under such conditions the cavitation bubbles collapse with immense force and will cause large pits to form in the hard metal of the propeller. Pressures of up to 100 tons/psi are known to occur leading to pits up to $\frac{1}{2}$in deep in a few hours' high speed running if the design is less than perfect.

HMS HELMSDALE

Pre-war naval architects were included to use the word 'cavitation' rather loosely to mean the loss of efficiency and erosion that occurred at high speed. Some were a little surprised when the noise at 8 knots or so was also found to be due to cavitation.

The clearest of proof was soon provided. In 1948 scientists at the Under Water Detection Establishment (UDE, now part of AUWE) at Portland, under Dr Fisher, fitted glass ports in the bottom of the 'River' class frigate HMS *Helmsdale* through which cavitation could be seen and photographed.

The procedure used then, and only slightly modified today, involved using high voltage lights, worked from contacts on the propeller shaft so that there was a flash each time a particular blade passed the viewing port. This stroboscopic lighting made the blade appear stationary. Controls were provided so that different blades could be examined or the same blade seen in different positions.

Viewing trials are held at night to give better contrast and areas of clear water, away from the muddy outfall of rivers, must be found. The viewing ports are usually small and in inconvenient boxes of structure under the steering gear making the trial one for dedicated men with strong stomachs.

EARLY TRIALS

It was generally realised that a radically new approach to propeller design was needed but, while the necessary theoretical work was in hand, a series of trials was carried out with modified, conventional propellers. Virtually all British World War II propellers had a 'face' (the pressure side, towards the stern of the ship) which was a section of a constant pitch, helocoidal surface (like the thread of a bolt). On this surface, the sections were formed by an arc of a circle. Such propellers were easy and hence cheap to manufacture, suffered little from erosion and thrust loss at high speed and were predictable in performance.

Nine propeller designs suitable for the new large destroyer HMS *Diamond* were tested as models in the cavitation tunnel at the Admiralty Experiment Works, Haslar (AEW, now part of AMTE) with variations in thickness, blade section shape, blade area and in numbers of blades. A further seven designs for the older destroyer HMS *Savage* were also tested in model form. These included two intended to run at much lower rotational speed.

Of these standard design propellers six sets were tested full size on *Savage* and two more on *Diamond*. Not one of these propellers was any improvement over the basic design and some were worse. A great deal was learnt from these trials and, in particular, they confirmed the findings of the *Helmsdale* trial, that the then current method of estimating the cavitation performance of ship propellers from model tests was very inaccurate.

A NEW DESIGN METHOD

In the meantime, naval constructors and scientists at AEW had been developing an entirely new design method (Ref 2). This was based on the work of Dr Lerbs who had come to Haslar from Germany after World War II. It became possible to produce a mathematical representation of the flow round a propeller and so match the geometry of the flow and the propeller more precisely. The section at each radius was given an individual pitch so that water would flow onto the leading edge with the least disturbance. The sections were then curved (cambered) to give a fairly uniform pressure and suction distribution over the chord length avoiding peak suctions which wold give early cavitation.

In addition the thrust loading was considerably reduced towards the tip of the blade to reduce the strength of the tip vortex.

In 1946, the mathematical theory was incomplete and a number of approximations had to be made in order to make the mathematics correspond to reality. By about 1948 models had been designed which showed a real promise of improvement over the standard propeller.

In those days, before computers, the mathematical design of a propeller meant some two or three weeks of tiresome arithmetic. It then took three or five months to make a model to the required accuracy and at least a fortnight to carry out model tests. If these were successful, another year or so would elapse before ship trials were carried out. Incorporating the lessons of a trial into a new design was necessarily a slow business. It is also no coincidence that one of the first computers to be purchased by the Admiralty was installed at Haslar in the early 1950s.

The stern of a destroyer model is seen from underneath with a standard propeller on one shaft cavitating severely while a modern design at the same loading on the other shaft is free of cavitation.

STRENGTH

Most of these new designs had thinner blades than the older propellers and a separate research programme, led by J E Conolly, was needed to ensure that the new shapes were strong enough. Models were loaded and the stresses measured in order to confirm theoretical estimates. Two conventional propellers were made, one 20 per cent and the other 40 per cent thinner than normal and were tried at sea. The thinnest set eventually broke at speed, as was expected.

Another full size propeller was fitted with strain gauges so that the stress on the propeller at sea could be compared with estimates. This was an extremely difficult trial with the equipment then available but it was successful.

MORE TRIALS

By 1950 the new propellers for *Diamond* had been made and tried incorporating different distributions of thrust loading and these broadly confirmed expectations. A more radical design was tested and built for *Savage*.

This had a much greater blade area and very lightly loaded tips. The surface area of the blades was 1.1 times the area of a circle of the same diameter as the propeller. This overlapping of the blades made manufacture expensive. Trials showed a 3–4 knot improvement in quiet speed but at the expense of a 5 per cent drop in efficiency at cruising speed The designs also failed to produce the correct thrust at the intended speed and rpm.

A standard design with the same very large blade area was also made to see if this was the principal reason for the delay in cavitation onset. It was no more successful than other standard designs.

During the early 1950s, 14 model propellers were designed for *Savage* of which four were tried on full scale (five sets counting considerable modification to one set after first trial). Initially, these designs covered variations in blade area and in section shape. The proportion of thrust developed from angle of attack and from curvature (camber) of the section was altered systematically. As a result of these tests, AEW gained a complete understanding of the way in which propeller geometry could be matched to the ship's characteristics and her machinery.

Towards the end of this period of development, *Savage* paid off and the last trials were carried out on her sister ship HMS *Teazer*. By this time it had been realised that spreading the thrust over an increased number of blades would reduce the strength of each tip vortex and further. increase the quiet speed. Model tests were carried out on 7, 9 and 11 bladed propellers as well but the improvement has to be balanced against the extra cost involved. Some of these propellers can be seen in the accompanying photographs.

THE DIFFERENCE BETWEEN MODEL AND SHIP

The laws of model testing are such that if the flow pattern is geometrically the same in model and ship, then the cavitation number

$$\frac{Local\ pressure}{\frac{1}{2} - density \times (velocity)^2}$$

will be the same when the model and ship propeller are advancing at the same speed. There are some other conditions which must also be satisfied relating to viscosity, number and size of air bubbles in the flow, pressure gradient, etc.

The importance of these conditions were recognised right from the beginning of the development programme but it took many years of hard and difficult work to reach a satisfactory outcome. For a start, the original cavitation tunnel at Haslar was small and could only test propellers by themselves, without a ship ahead to modify the flow pattern. It was possible to run experiments with the shaft line at an angle to the flow but the arrangements were not entirely satisfactory and only occasional tests could be run in this way. As a result, some quite elaborate geometrical corrections had to be developed to correct for the different flow in model and ship.

The other conditions can never be fully and simultaneously satisfied. Long series of tests of models were tried with different air buble contents, and at different water speeds and rotational speeds. Matching these results to theory, itself inadequate in some areas, enabled correction factors to be produced by about 1960 which seemed to relate correctly all the model tests and ship trials up to that time – with the exception of vortex cavitation at the tip.

No complete theory has been produced even now but, by 1960, enough trials had been run to enable a further correction to be made to the model tests, based on average blade width. Many further trials since then have shown that this correction is necessary and soundly based in experiment even though a physical explanation is still awaited.

The table below shows how the various corrections made alter the estimated speed at which cavitation will first occur on a ship.

TABLE 2: CAVITATION ONSET

	Speed (kts)
Model tests, without correction	25
Corrected for flow geometry	20
– and air bubble effect	18
– and for vortex effect	12

By the time the full set of corrective factors had been obtained the first production sets of noise reduced propellers were being made. Predictions of their performance were made from model tests and results from viewing trials on the ships were eagerly awaited. Lover (Ref 1) quotes a typical result as follows.

Type of cavitation	Estimate from model (kts)	Ship Trial (kts)
Flashes of cavitation at the tip	15.5	16
Continuous vortex at the tip	16.5	17
On the back of the blade	18	20
On the face of the blade	None	23

While all this work had been going on for frigates, similar developments had been taking place on submarines. The new design principles had been applied and models tested. Initially, it was not possible to look at

submarine propellers and estimates of success at the ship were based on sound measurements only. More recently, some full scale observations have been made on submarines using remote controlled cameras and these results have broadly confirmed the results from surface ships.

By 1960, a much larger cavitation tunnel had been opened at Haslar that could accept an almost complete model of the underwater hull of a frigate together with shafts, shaft brackets, propellers and rudders. This improved understanding of the complex flow around hull and propeller and led to improved accuracy in estimating cavitation onset speed.

PRODUCTION SETS IN THE 1960s
About 1957 a series of 18 model propellers was designed and tested to meet the flow characteristics of the frigate HMS *Whitby*. The distribution of thrust along the blade was varied as was the balance of pitch to camber. From this work, a full size ship propeller was developed and tried in HMS *Whitby*. This gave a much higher quiet speed, reduced noise levels at speeds above cavitation onset and also the vibration at the stern of the ship was very considerably reduced. For the first time, the stokers in the after mess deck could keep cups on the tables. Propellers generally similar to this design were introduced throughout the Fleet in the early 1960s.

In parallel with the development of the propeller itself, the Admiralty Under Water Weapons Establishment (AUWE), Portland, had developed a system for reducing cavitation noise by injecting low pressure air into the areas of the flow where cavitation was likely. The air compressor was in the engine room and air was passed down the hollow shaft, into the propeller and ejected through holes along both sides of the leading edge of the propeller blades. Propellers so fitted had to have thicker leading edges in order to accommodate the air channel. Some difficulty was experienced in realising the system, particularly with controllable pitch propellers.

It was also difficult to ensure that air reached the very localised areas of cavitation on the face of the blade. A series of model propellers was tried in which the pitch was increased, and camber reduced, to ensure that cavitation would only occur on the back of the blade. Ship trials were carried out in the frigate HMS *Penelope* about 1970 and as a result this modified design was adopted. developments continue but much work cannot yet be considered.

REFERENCES
1 E P Lover RCNC and C B Wills
Cavitation Tunnel Testing for the Royal Navy (Newcastle University Conference 1979).
2 D K Brown RCNC *A Century of Naval Construction* (Conway Maritime Press 1983).
3 D J Andrews RCNC and D K Brown RCNC 'Cheap Warships are not Simple' (SNAME New York 1982).

My thanks are due to the Chief Superintendant, Admiralty Marine Technology Establishment, Haslar for permission to use the illustrations.

S-boats at War 1939-40
by Pierre Hervieux

The 1st Flotilla S-boat tender *Carl Peters* with a 115-ton *S 18* type boat in Bergen (Norway) soon after the invasion in April 1940. Two 2900-ton (standard) *Adolf Lüderitz* class S-boat tenders had been launched in February 1939. They measured 374ft wl and 4 MAN double-acting 4-stroke diesels gave 12,400bhp = 23kts. Armament was 2–105mm (2×1) and 6–37mm/83 C 33 (3×2) with a crew of 225. *Carl Peters* was commissioned as 1st Flotilla tender on 6 January 1940.

ECP Armées

When World War II broke out on 1 September 1939, at 0445, the German Navy only had 18 motor torpedo boats *(Schnellboote)* in service. *S 6* to *S 23*, forming two flotillas. The 1st Flotilla, under the command of Kapitänleutnant Sturm, came back to the North Sea in October 1939 with its depot ship *Tsingtau* with *S 18–S 21* and *S 23*. *S 24*, which had just ended her sea trials, joined the Flotilla. It must be recalled that *S 1* to *S 5* had been sold to the Spanish Nationalists. During operations in Baltic, against Polish forces, except for a small Polish pilot boat, the *Lloyd Bydgoski* (80 tons), sunk by gunfire from *S 23*, in position 54°35′N/19°08′E, there were no encounters with the enemy. Those shots were the first ones fired by an MTB in World War II. Not a single torpedo was launched during the Polish campaign.

The 2nd Flotilla (Kapitänleutnant Petersen) operated in the North Sea from 3 September 1939, based at Heligoland. It was composed of *S 10–S 13* and *S 15–S 17*. During the first sortie, on 3 September, *S 17* was badly damaged by rough weather. This last and the hard early winter prevented the two flotillas from taking any important offensive action against British forces. So on 29 November, the 1st Flotilla returned to Kiel where on 1 December, Kapitänleutnant Birnbacher took command of it. Meanwhile, *S 1* (ex-requisitioned Bulgarian *F 5*), *S 25*, *S 30* and *S 31* were commissioned before the end of the year.

INVASION OF NORWAY

It was during the invasion of Norway and Denmark (Operation *Weserübung*) that the *Schnellboote* were more active. The 1st Flotilla, with five boats (*S 19*, *S 21–S 24*) and the depot ship *Tsingtau*, received orders to support Naval Group 4 in capturing Kristiansand and Arendal. On the evening of 8 April 1940, *S 19* and *S 21* collided because of fog and *S 19* which was completely put out of action had to get help from the torpedo-boat *Wolf*. The *Schnellboote* were creeping into the fjords and landed small contingents, particularly in Bergen where *S 24* was the first German ship to come alongside. After the success of the landing in Norway, the *Schnellboote* were employed on reconnaissance duties within the numerous fjords. On 18 April 1940, two S-boats of the 1st Flotilla so severely damaged the small Norwegian torpedo-boats *Sael* (1901, 84 tons), in the Hardanger Fiord (SE of Bergen), that she was beached and later sank. On 25 April, when boats of 1st Flotilla were boarding merchant ships, they were caught in a violent machine gun fire, off Ubrik. All the boats were hit and several men wounded, the flotilla leader included. The *Schnellboote* also took part in the capture of several Norwegian ships, for instance on 9 April, the old minelayer *Uller* (1876, 250 tons) in Bergen.

The first sinking accomplished by a German S-boat in the North Sea was the Dutch trawler *Bep* (151 tons), on 22 April off Terschelling, it was probably a mistake, for the Netherlands were not yet at war. During the night of 9/10 May, a British naval force composed of the light cruiser HMS *Birmingham* and seven destroyers made a sortie into the Skagerrak looking for eventual German minelayers. That force was attacked by four boats of the 2nd Flotilla, *S 30, S 31, S 32* and *S 33*. *S 31* (Oberleutnant Opdenhoff) succeeded in hitting the destroyer HMS *kelly* (1938, 1760 tons), amidships, with a torpedo. Heavily damaged and very low in the water she was towed by the destroyer HMS *Bulldog* and brought to Newcastle with difficulty after 91 hours! The Germans believed she had been sunk. *Kelly* was under the command of Lord Louis Mountbatten.

The British did not yet realise the danger they were running from those 'little sea greyhounds' that were the *Schnellboote*. And so several years after the war, they were still thinking that the mine destructor vessel HMS *Corburn* (1936, 3060 tons) had been sunk on a mine, during the night of 20/21 May 1940, off Le Havre, when in fact *S 32* was responsible! For indeed, in mid-May, the *Kriegsmarine* had restored its flotillas at Borkum, the

1 S-boats in 1940. The outer craft is a new *S 26* type and the inner one an earlier flush-decked type.
ECP Armées

2 Loading a 21in torpedo on board an S-boat.
ECP Armées

3 An *Adolf Lüderitz* class S-boat tender with a flush-decked and an *S 26* type boat (inner) alongside.
ECP Armées

4 A camouflaged *S 32* on her way to a successful ambush off Le Havre on 20 May 1940.
Koehlers card

great island on the German-Dutch border. The S-boats were very low in the water, mere whitish and fleeting shadows; by night it was very difficult to see them. Their light paint made them even less little visible, even to boats of their own flotilla while commanding officers only had radio telephone to keep in contact. At that time their anti-aircraft armament only comprised two single 20mm guns, nevertheless *S 34* succeeded in shooting down a two-engine bomber, on 25 May, in the western North Sea. Some of the boats were also covered with a camouflage paint scheme.

OPERATIONS OFF DUNKIRK

On 23 May at 0030, *S 21* (Oberleutnant von Mirbach) and *S 23* (Oberleutnant Christiansen) were put on the alert by the German Western Group's HQ whose radio listening-post had decoded French naval signals. The two boats laid an ambush in the Western Channel off Dunkirk and torpedoed the big French destroyer *Jaguar* (1923, 2126 tons), under the command of *Capitaine de Frégate* Adam, who later became Rear-Admiral. After half an hour, trimming by the head, listing heavily to starboard and unable to stem the tide, she was towed and grounded on the beach of Malo les Bains where the wreck was finished off by the *Luftwaffe*, a few days later. Thirteen of her crew were killed and 23 wounded. On 26 May, off the Belgian coast, the Dutch submarine *O 13* and the British destroyer HMS *Vega* were attacked by S-boats who mistakenly claimed to have sunk both of them. But on 28 May *S 34* sank the British cargo ship *Abukir* (694tons, 51°20′N/02°16′E). On 29 May, off Nieuport, *S 30* (Oberleutnant Zimmermann) sank the British destroyer HMS *Wakeful* (1917, 1100 tons) which was broken in two and disappeared in 15 seconds. On 31 May, at 0100, on a very dark night, starry sky, no moon, calm and very phosphorescent sea, the French destroyer *Sirocco* (1925, 1319 tons), evacuating troops, skilfully avoided two torpedoes heading for her bow, but almost at once was hit by two others in her starboard quarter. Two minutes later, *Sirocco* suddenly capsized on to her starboard side. In addition to her crew, there were 750 soldiers on board. Only 270 men survived. The attacking S-boats were *S 23* and *S 26* (Oberleutnant Fimmen). The *S 23*'s torpedoes sank the destroyer. That very same night, *S 24* (Oberleutnant Detlefsen) torpedoed the French destroyer *Cyclone* (1925, 1319 tons). With her bow blow off right to the first 130mm gun, she nevertheless succeeded in reaching Brest, being scuttled on 18 June before being captured by the Germans. On 1 June *S 34* scored a double off Dunkirk, in sinking the British armed trawlers HMS *Argyllshire* (1938, 540 tons) and HMS *Stella Dorado* (1935, 550 tons).

FIRST SOUTH COAST OPERATIONS

The first sortie bringing a success to S-boats, off the English coast, took place during the night of 19/20 June 1940. Shortly past midnight, *S 19* and *S 26* sank the British cargo ship *Roseburn* (3103 tons) with torpedo and 20mm gunfire, off Dungeness. *S 19* was under the command of Oberleutnant Töniges. The first lost S-boat

was *S 32* (commissioned on 22 March 1940), she hit a mine in the Channel, south of Dungeness, on 21 June 1940. The officer in command and 6 crew-members perished with her, the survivors being rescued by *S 31* and *S 35*. During the night of 23/24 June S-boats operated again off Dungeness. Two British merchant vessels were sunk, the cargo ship *Albuera* (3477 ons) by *S 36* (Oberleutnant Babbel), 2 miles SW of Lydd light float, and the small coaster *Kingfisher* (276 tons), 50°30′N/00°28′E, by *S 19*. On 4 July, the British convoy OA 178, already roughly handled by Stukas, was also attacked by *S 19*, *S 20*, *S 24* and *S 26* of the 1st Flotilla now based at Cherbourg. *S 19* sank the cargo ship *Elmcrest* (4343 tons), 13 miles south of Portland, while *S 20* and *S 26* torpedoed and damaged the tanker *British Corporal* (6972 tons, 50°13′N/02°35′W) and the cargo ship *Hartlepool* (5500 tons), 16 miles SSW of Portland light. In the meantime, on 30 June, the British cargo ship *Clan Ogilvy* (979 tons) had been damaged by a torpedo and gunfire from an S-boat off St Catherine's Point (Isle of Wight). In addition to attacks with torpedoes, S-boats also laid many mines on coastal convoy routes. The first mines (8 mines could be carried on the after deck) were laid on 6 June 1940. The German MTBs were now split between their new bases at Ostend, Calais, Boulogne and Cherbourg.

On 8 July the armed trawler HMS *Cayton Wyke* (1932, 550 tons) was sunk off Dover by an unidentified S-boat, perhaps *S 36*. When it was possible the Germans planned combined air-sea attacks against British convoys in the Channel. For example, on 26 July, convoy CW8, which on the previous day had already lost five merchant ships sunk by Stukas, was attacked by *S 19*, *S 20* and *S 27* of the 1st Flotilla (Kapitänleutnant Birnbacher). They sank three other vessels, all of them British and coasters: the *Lulonga* (821 tons), 10 miles south of Shoreham, the *Broadhurst* (1013 tons), 14 miles SW of Shoreham, and the *London Trader* (646 tons), 13 miles SW of the same harbour. The day before CW 8 was attacked, south of Portland, a tragedy took place. The French passenger ship *Meknès* (6127 tons), sailing independently and carrying 1100 French sailors repatriated from England to Marseilles, was torpedoed and sunk by *S 27* (Oberleutnant Klug). Nearly 400 men were lost. The ship's movements had not been notified to the German High Command. On 12 July, the 1st Flotilla had lost *S 23*, on a mine, north of Calais. It also must be mentioned that the day before, the small British cargo ship *Mallard* (352 tons) had been torpedoed and sunk by an S-boat, between St Catherine's Point and Beachy Head. On 8 August, the 1st Flotilla of S-boats under the command of Korvetten kapitän Birnbacher, with *S 20*, *S 21*, *S 25* and *S 27*, attacked convoy CW 9 off Newhaven. *S 21* and *S 27* sank the British coasters *Holme Force* (1216 tons) and *Fife Coast* (367 tons), the latter ship about 12 miles west of Beachy Head. The attack took place by night and the convoy, composed of 25 ships, was thrown into confusion. A third vessel, the cargo ship *Ouse* (1004 tons), collided with the minesweeper HMS *Rye* avoiding a torpedo from an S-boat, and sank. Two other cargo ships were damaged

S 21 (113ft long, 115 tons deep load and 39.5kts) which helped destroy the big French destroyer *Jaguar* as well as sinking the British merchant ships *Corbrook* and *New Lambton* during 1940.

Drüppel

by German gunfire, the *Polly M* (380 tons), 15 miles from Newhaven and the *John M* (500 tons), 10 miles south of the Needles. Some men on *S 21* and *S 27* were wounded by British gunfire.

EAST COAST OPERATIONS

From September, S-boats operating off the South Coast of England numbered 10–15. Added to the ships sunk and damaged by their torpedoes, were also those, much more numerous, sunk and damaged by their mines and also the mines laid by R-boats, destroyers, torpedo boats as well as auxiliary minelayers. These minelayings were carried out by night between two escort missions, for the Germans had also to dispatch convoys along the French coasts and had to protect them. On 4 September the 1st Flotilla sailed again to attack a British convoy, NE of Great Yarmouth. *S 21* (Oberleutnant Klug) sank two cargo ships, the *Corbrook* (1729 tons) and the *New Lambton* (2709 tons). *S 18* (Oberleutnant Christiansen) sank two cargo ships too, the British *Joseph Swan* (1571 tons) and the Dutch *Nieuwland* (1075 tons). The *S 22* (Oberleutnant Grund) torpedoed and sank the British

cargo ship *Fulham* (1572 tons) on which she also fired with her 20mm guns. Another cargo ship, the *Ewell* (1350 tons) was damaged by gunfire from *S 54*. The position of the 4 September attack was 52°50'N/02°09'E. On 7 September the British convoy FS 273 was attacked by *S 33* and *S 36*. The Dutch cargo ship *Stad Almaer* (5750 tons) being sunk by *S 33* (Oberleutnant Popp), east of Lowestoft. On 24 September an unidentified S-boat sank the British *Continental Coaster* (555 tons, 52°59'N/02°10'E). On 12 October the 2nd Flotilla lost *S 37* on a mine, east of Orfordness. On 17 October, an operation took place off the East Coast; *S 18* torpedoed the cargo ship *Hauxley* (1595 tons), 6 miles NNW of Smith's Knoll. That ship sank the following day. *S 24* and *S 27* torpedoed and damaged the British cargo ships *PLM 14* (ex-French, 3754 tons) and *Gasfire* (2972 tons, 52°52'N/02°06'E). On the night of 19/20 November, in the Thames estuary, 3 S-boats of the 3rd Flotilla were engaged by the

S 33 at speed. This 107ft, 100-ton boat (36kts) sank the Dutch cargo ship *Stad Almaer* on 7 September 1940.

Drüppel

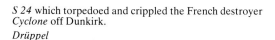

S 24 which torpedoed and crippled the French destroyer *Cyclone* off Dunkirk.

Drüppel

Flush-decked S-boats under way. At least half the lead boat's crew of 21 are on deck.

ECP Armées

destroyers HMS *Campbell* and *HMS Garth* which sank *S 38, S 54* and *S 57* escaping; 18 of the *S 38*'s crew of 23 were picked up by the destroyers.

From the summer of 1940 a total of 3 S-boat flotillas operated in the West, a 3rd Flotilla having been formed at Kiel on 15 May 1940. Its first Commanding Officer had been Oberleutnant Töniges, who was replaced at the end of May by Kapitänleutnant Kemnade. As new boats were commissioned, 22 in 1940 (*S 26–29, S 32–38, S 54–60, S 101–102, S 201–202* (ex-Dutch TM 52/53), making a total of 27 boats since the war began, it became possible to withdraw the old boats which had a tendency to breakdown, and to use them for training. On 1 October 1940, new S-boats being available, a 4th Flotilla was formed under the command of Kapitänleutnant Bätge. But it was not before 1941 that the boats were fully operational. On 24 November, the British motor trawler *Lent Lily* (44 tons), 6 miles ESE of Wolf Rock, was attacked and damaged by gunfire from an S-boat, probably estimating she was too small to warrant a torpedo! On 15 December, a more important quarry, the Danish cargo ship *N C Monberg* (2301 tons) was torpedoed and sunk, in a British

convoy, by *S 58* (Leutnant Geiger), east of Yarmouth, 52°40′N/02°10′E. On 24 December, the British convoy FN 366 was sailing off the East Coast when 7 S-boats of the 1st Flotilla attacked it. *S 59* (Leutnant Müller) sank the large Dutch cargo ship *Stad Maastricht* (6552 tons) and *S 28* (Leutnant Klug) sank the armed trawler HMS *Pelton* (1925, 358 tons), off Yarmouth. The other boats taking part were *S 26, S 29, S 34, S 56* and *S 58*.

BALANCE SHEET

Between April and December 1940, excluding Poland and Norway, the *Schnellboote* torpedoed and sank in the North Sea and the Channel:

  3 destroyers (2 French, 1 British)
  1 British mine destructor vessel
  4 British armed trawlers
  24 merchant ships of different nationalities, most of them British, these merchant ships totalling 48,989 tons.

These figures do not include ships damaged by torpedoes and guns from S-boats. An even greater tonnage was sunk and damaged by mines. In British waters, 509,889 tons, representing 201 ships, were sunk by mines (including those laid by U-boats and aircraft) during 1940. About 10 per cent of that tonnage can be credited to the mines laid by *Schnellboote*. All this damage was inflicted for the loss of only 4 boats: *S 23, S 32, S 37* by mines and *S 38* by destroyers.

To be continued

Of Ships & Money

The Rising Cost of Naval Power

By P E Pugh

By the time she was commissioned in May 1975 the nuclear-powered aircraft carrier USS *Nimitz* had cost $1881 million. The money paid for this single ship was equal to Britain's entire expenditure on new defence equipment (RN, Army & RAF) between April of the year of her commissioning and the end of February in the following year. Alternatively, the same sum would have paid for the entire upkeep of the RN general purpose forces for about 14 months – covering pay, fuel, repairs, maintenance, refits etc. as well as new construction. On a more modest scale, a single Type 22 frigate cost £85 million in 1979 and each new frigate is costing about 3 times as much as the vessels it replaces. Even after allowing for inflation, two *Lion* class dreadnought battlecruisers of 1914 cost less than a single Type 22 frigate and the comparatively 'cheap' and simple Type 21 frigate cost £29 million in 1974 or, in terms of contemporary purchasing power, about the same as an entire squadron of three pre-war 'County' class cruisers or somewhat less than the *Hood*. Such escalation of unit costs has an obvious impact upon the size of navy that can be afforded and, in common with similar escalation of other defence equipment, has been termed 'the road to absurdity'. This article outlines the history of warship costs and analyses the causes for their rapid (and continuing) growth.

MONEY MATTERS

Since Themistocles persuaded the ancient Athenians to forego a general share out and, instead, to spend the proceeds of the silver mines at Laurium upon 200 triremes, the cost of naval vessels has been a matter for public debate. The cost of building even one capital ship has always been large enough to require evident sacrifice of immediate civilian benefits and they are clearly suited only to the waste of war. It is little wonder that from Athenian galleys through the *Great Harry, Sovereign of the Seas, Royal George, Warrior, Dreadnought* to *Nimitz* and *Ohio* the cost and capabilities of major naval units have attracted contemporary attention and discussion far beyond those persons immediately concerned with their construction and use. Conversely, cost has always been a determining factor in their design and of the numbers procured; thence, of naval strengths and tactics and so of the outcome of battles and the fate of empires.

While naval historians generally acknowledge the significance of cost, it has by no means attracted the close analysis accorded to even the finest of technical details. What is possible technically, what is required tactically and what may be afforded are so symbiotically interlinked that our understanding of the history of the warship is only partial if it excludes the last aspect – however deep our study of the other two.

It is hardly possible even to begin to rectify this imbalance within the compass of a brief essay. Instead, I hope to stimulate interest in the topic and to set out the broadest survey of the evolution of warship costs over the last century or so. I begin with some thoughts as to how costs incurred during different eras may best be compared and then touch upon factors causing economic competition to be particularly fierce in military equipment.

FUNNY MONEY

Units of technical measurement change only infrequently. From one decade to the next they remain fixed. A speed of, say, 10 knots is the same in 1984 as it was in 1884. Even if a range of 6000 yards is now described as 5486 metres, the conversion factor is well known, precise and universal. With costs we are on much less certain ground. Inflation has made everyone painfully aware that £1 in 1984 is very different from £1 in 1974 – let alone in 1884. The units of measurement are changing constantly and by factors that are uncertain and fluctuating. How, then, are we to effect meaningful comparisons between costs in different eras? The most obvious method is to split a cost into its various elements – so much for labour, for steel, for fittings, etc – and to recalculate the total using current prices for each element. This implicitly assumes that the methods (and efficiency) of construction remain the same and that the only variation is in the prices of the various inputs. While valid over a period of a few years and, hence, useful when updating an estimate from one year to the next; this assumption is clearly nonsensical when set against the technical changes of, say, the last century. Many of these changes have been prompted by radical changes in the relative costs of the inputs to production and, in turn have caused machinery to be substituted for labour, affected the supply of various materials, etc. The 400 loads of oak that went into a 74-gun ship or the ton upon ton of wrought iron consumed by an ironclad are not to be had today at any price.

In brief, the way costs are updated depends upon the purpose for which the results are needed. The cost today of building an exact replica of *Warrior* or of a full-sized

FIGURE 1:
GROWTH IN SIZE FROM ANCIENT TIMES

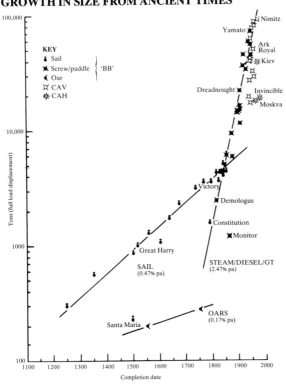

MILITARY COMPETITION

Economic competition generally takes place between producers striving to meet the needs of potential purchasers. By selecting from a range of competing goods the consumer influences changes in the type of goods produced towards those that most nearly meet his needs. The type of goods on offer will also be influenced by the way in which technical possibilities, investment in plant machinery, etc bear upon the manufacturer's opportunity to make profits. What is eventually made will depend upon the extent to which the producer's and the consumer's interests converge or diverge and their relative market power (ranging from free competition to unfettered monopoly).

Such factors influence both military and civilian goods; but military goods are subject to competition in another way too – that between users. One person's choice of television sets, refrigerators, meals and the like are little influenced by the choices others may make – apart from some element of 'keeping up with the Jones'. In military matters 'keeping up with the Jones' is everything. Equipment is 'good' or 'bad' only in relation to the equipment of a potential adversary. There are no other standards. The benefits of improved armament are largely those of devaluing existing equipment – such as that possessed by the potential adversary. He sees this as a reduction in his security which he must remedy by re-equipping his forces to a yet higher standard. Such is the major driving force behind the competition of attack and defence, continual technical innovation and increasing costs.

We may suppose that each new generation of equipment seeks to improve over its predecessor's in some proportion and, thus, we may expect unit costs to increase, upon average, by a given percentage with each year that passes. With this in mind the accompanying graphs are plotted on semi-logarithmic paper so that the expected exponential (compound interest) growth of costs appear as straight line variations with date.

Within the constraints of a given defence budget, naval staffs must strive to allocate resources between different classes of vessel so as to maximise the Fleet's overall capability. Those perceived as having the greatest cost/effectiveness will attract the greatest share of available money. Nations will promote advances whenever they feel that these will redirect competition along avenues where they have some special advantage. For example, the promotion of the torpedo boat and submarine by the French *'jeune école'* eventually denied resort to the traditional British strategy of close blockade while Fisher's advocacy of the 'Dreadnought' drew upon a belief that Britain could readily outbuild any rival and, hence, competition in building fleets anew would be to her advantage. Conversely, earlier Admiralty opposition to the steamship and the submarine must be seen in the context of a less advantageous position *vis à vis* the building capacities of rivals and the British sailing fleet's established superiority leading to a logical inclination to preserve the status quo for as long as possible.

Cost growth cannot go on for ever in the face of

'working model' in modern materials or of providing the same fighting capacity are different both one from another and from the impact of its construction upon the economy of 1860.

The most significant aspect of cost is that it measures the extent to which resources are diverted from other desirable ends. Are taxes to be raised or lowered? Is defence or social welfare to benefit from government spending? Is capital to be invested in armaments or in hospitals, bridges and roads? Guns or butter? Legions or bread and circuses? Such are the questions that confront policy makers throughout all ages and which are the constants linking Themistocles to the present day. Cast in economic terms this suggests the use of retail price indices or GNP deflators for updating costs since the object is to measure the extent to which other (civilian) benefits were foregone in order to purchase warships for defence. There still remain numerous subtle problems that economists could debate forever, but the preceding discussion suffices to justify my approach of using contemporary exchange rates coupled with UK retail price inflation. Where warships were long in construction I have used indices averaged over the period from laying the keel to first commissioning. Throughout this essay all costs have been thus adjusted to price levels at September 1980 – a date of no special significance beyond being when I began these studies.

constant (or slowly growing) budgets. Higher unit costs mean fewer ships. It is true that naval staffs have long been acquainted with the problems of small numbers of major vessels. Only five British 1st rates with 100 or more guns were built during the period of almost continuous naval warfare between 1750 and 1790. However, the concentration of naval power into very few hulls must always place severe inhibitions on its use. There will be an inevitable reluctance to employ a navy to the full when so large a fraction of total strength can be suddenly lost to a single navigational hazard or accident of war. Contrasting British 'close blockade' and French 'fleet in being' philosophies of the Napoleonic Wars is a classic example while the difference between British and German deployment of their capital ships during World War II is a more recent instance.

As the cost of a particular class of ship grows, the time may come when a nation can no longer afford even one of them. It can then no longer discharge those missions for which such ships were necessary. There must be readjustments in strategy and, perhaps, consequences for foreign policy and influence. In such fashion military competition can alter the history of nations without a shot being fired in anger.

FROM ANCIENT TIMES TO THE PRESENT

Costs are especially difficult to trace for ancient and mediaeval times. However, cost must be associated with size so that the evolution of displacement provides some clues. Over so long a period even measures of as fundamental a quantity as size have varied but there are sufficient examples of overlap between usages for the relationships between these to be estimated and, hence, for a consistent series to be developed. Fig 1 shows the results. The expectation of exponential (compound interest) growth is clearly justified. Even the mediaeval

period appears to have been one of steady advance leading into, and continuing through, the great age of fighting sail. This result contradicts the common belief that these were ages of excessive conservatism – indeed stagnation. Progress may have been slow but it was continuous. However, the growth in size was sufficiently slow for it to be offset by improved productivity and greater economy in decoration etc. From the very sparse evidence, costs of 1st rates seem to have been constant, or even declined, between the Dutch and the Napoleonic wars.

The pace greatly quickened with the advent of the steamship as a child of the Industrial Revolution. By 1850 it had surpassed the sailing vessel and continued to grow at a pace that shows no sign of slackening – except in so far that less wealthy nations are unable to afford the largest classes of ship. The aircraft carrier grew especially rapidly before superseding the battleship as the capital ship of major navies.

CAPITAL SHIPS

The most obvious form of military competition is that between capital ships designed to slug it out with hostile counterparts – whether in line of battle or by dispatching air strikes over the horizon. The evolution of their costs from the Victorian era to the present is shown in Fig 2.

Early battleships competed with ships of the same class and, assuming adequate protection by their escorts against torpedo attack, this 'like against like' competition was their sole function. This exactly corresponds to the simple model discussed earlier and, so, it is no surprise to find a trend of steady exponential growth in cost over several decades. No distinction has been drawn between battleships and battlecruisers for their costs were very similar – as, indeed, were those of the large armoured cruisers that preceded the latter. Presumably, this reflects some equality of importance attached to the protection (or interdiction) of commerce on the one hand and hopes of a decisive fleet action on the other. Certainly, individual armoured cruisers were built to counter specific foreign ships just as battleships were. The Battles of Coronel, Falklands and Dogger Bank exemplify the type of actions for which such ships were designed and demonstrate the overwhelming importance of technical superiority – the struggle for which drives up cost.

World War I saw the emergence of a new threat in the aircraft whose rapid development had two effects. First, escort vessels, while useful, could not unfailingly protect capital ships against the bomber. Anti-aircraft armament did not contribute to the ship v ship battle so that its provision conflicted with the battleship's primary role. Driven by the need to cope with this rapidly growing new threat (in addition to continuing competition with its own kind), it appears that the cost of the few battleships built between the wars grew at a considerably faster rate than before. The second effect was that the growing usefulness of aircraft justified greater expenditure upon the means of taking them to sea. Thus, aircraft carrier costs rose very steeply on average but with exceptionally large scatter of costs

FIGURE 2: CAPITAL SHIPS

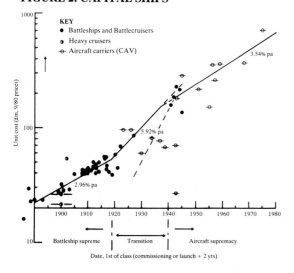

KEY
● Battleships and Battlecruisers
◐ Heavy cruisers
⟲ Aircraft carriers (CAV)

3.54% pa

5.92% pa

2.96% pa

Unit cost (£m, 9/80 prices)

1900 1910 1920 1930 1940 1950 1960 1970 1980

Battleship supreme | Transition | Aircraft supremacy

Date, 1st of class (commissioning or launch + 2 yrs)

about the trend – reflecting widely differing views of their role and utility.

Eventually, the effectiveness of aircraft grew so great that they became the primary means of striking the enemy. Thus, foreshadowed by Taranto and Pearl Harbor, the aircraft carrier emerged as the new form of capital ship at Coral Sea, Midway and the subsequent major Pacific Ocean battles of World War II. The sinking of *Yamato* demonstrated that the aircraft carrier now had little to fear from the battleship. The sole threat came from the aircraft of an opponent so that the situation reverted to the simple competition of like with like. Thus, it may not be entirely coincidental that since the aircraft carrier supplanted the battleship as capital ship the rate of cost growth has reverted to around the value it had during the hey-day of the dreadnought.

The growth in cost of the most powerful aircraft carriers has now reached the stage where they can be afforded only by the USA. If major units are possessed by only one nation competition will cease (save with land-based aircraft). One might expect costs to then cease to grow – at least until the other super power develops a fully-fledged naval air capability. It could be that the 15-year long debate over the number of *Nimitz* class carriers to be built marks the beginning of an end to the rapid growth in the cost of capital ships that began over 130 years ago.

ESCORTS AND THEIR ADVERSARIES

The sight of so much power (and money) invested within the hull of a capital ship has always been both a source of pride to her owners and a tantalising temptation to their opponents. To nullify its military value by some cheap means would upset the whole balance of power and, hence, has always been the fervent wish of nations with maritime interests but relatively weak navies.

Technical innovations of this type have always been the special province of economically weaker nations who can see no possibility of ultimate victory in continuing competition along established lines – with unit costs spiralling upwards. But measure begets countermeasure so that the usual result is only to redirect competition along new lines. Once the game has settled down to its new rules the poorer nation is as badly placed as before in terms of the probable long-term outcome. Its transient advantage having evaporated, it must seek yet another innovation. In this fashion, the success of the US Navy in the War of 1812 prompted a major British effort in building similar large frigates and the French introduction of the ironclad was promptly countered by the *Warrior, Black Prince* and their successors so that the French turned to the torpedo boat and submarine. Likewise, the introduction of large armoured cruisers for commerce raiding caused a revitalisation of the British cruiser force during the late Victorian era while we are, at present, in the middle of competition between close-in defence systems and the missile-armed fast patrol boat. By contrast, the emerging and rapidly growing economic power of Imperial Germany found its primary expression in the High Seas Fleet and the resulting competition in dreadnought construction rather than in the U-boat to whose unfettered use against commerce they came reluctantly and late (in the aftermath of Jutland).

The multiplication of threats to the capital ship had led to the development of classes of vessel specifically intended for its escort. Whereas Nelson's 'wooden walls' could roam the oceans as an expression of sea power complete in themselves, the modern capital ship is encompassed about by numerous protective escorts. Fig 3 shows the evolution of the unit costs of destroyers and postwar frigates such as might escort ocean-going capital ships together with costs of submarines – one of their main antagonists.

Destroyers were developed to counter torpedo boats but soon took the torpedo on board themselves. Competition was then between destroyer and destroyer who were expected to fight their own kind between the opposing battle-lines – with the victor then able to deliver a torpedo attack upon the enemy capital ships.

The potential of the submarine to evade the escorts and cripple capital ships prompted efforts to give it an ocean-going capability extending, in a few cases, to the development of submarines intended to operate as an integral part of the fleet. These efforts lead to rapidly growing size and cost.

The addition of anti-submarine duties to the destroyer's role lead, as we would now expect, to an acceleration in the growth of its cost. The threat of aircraft attack must also have contributed to this acceleration, but these events were too close in time for their effects to be discerned individually within the available data. Competition between destroyer and (fleet) submarine has continued for over half a century with the unit costs of each rising broadly in step. There is no obvious evidence of either type forcing the other to more rapid cost growth as might be expected had either gained a decisive advantage. The fact that the submarine can choose the time and place of its attack is offset by its being two or three times more expensive so that fewer submarines than escorts can be afforded given the same expenditure on each. This rate of growth in costs cannot be sustained for much longer for, at this rate, both destroyer and fleet submarine will soon cease to be affordable for most navies. Failing some eleventh hour technical innovation this will be a competition with no winners.

Whatever the outcome of that issue there will still be shipping to be protected from submarine attack. Where the threat was wholly from the submarine it has been possible to dispense with the destroyer's other roles and to simplify and cheapen designs by concentrating upon specialised anti-submarine functions. Hence, the war-time corvettes and many post-war frigates – the costs of a few of which are shown (Fig 3) to illustrate the large reduction thus achieved.

The increasing capability of helicopters for anti-submarine work has meant that a helicopter carrier (CAH) can dispose its detection and attack resources over a wide area. In effect, it can be in several places at once which must go far to nullify the traditional advantages of the attacker (choice of time and place).

Such vessels are the successors of wartime escort carriers and the little data available seems to show that their cost is growing much less rapidly than that of submarines or destroyers. If so, it implies that these are an effective answer to the submarine and, by remaining affordable while submarine costs escalate beyond reach, they could turn out to be the ultimate answer to almost a century of submarine threat.

Some would argue on contrary lines and suggest that submarine costs have ceased to grow since the advent of nuclear power. Whatever has been the case over the last decade or so, a plateau in submarine costs (if it exists) cannot last. The hunter-killer submarine is accepted to be a potent anti-submarine weapon in its own right. As we have seen, such like-with-like competition must engender an upward trend in unit cost which will be accelerated by the other threats to which submarines are subject from surface vessels and from the air.

In all, we are clearly in a complex period of evolution in equipment whose outcome is far from obvious. However, a study of costs illuminates the tendency for medium-sized navies to be organised around helicopter carriers (or older small aircraft carriers used in similar roles) and frigates while there is some reason to question whether the submarine will ever become the omnipotent capital ship of the future as its proponents would argue.

CONCLUSION

This essay has attempted to show how studies of unit cost can supplement analyses of tactics and technical performance. The histories of the costs of capital ships and of submarines and escort vessels has been presented and interpreted. No doubt some of these interpretations will provoke debate. If so, the author's purpose will have been satisfied.

SOURCES AND ACKNOWLEDGEMENTS

Costs are scattered through the published literature but nowhere presented systematically. Those presented here are taken from the author's notes accumulated over some years through gleaning standard references such as *Jane's, Brassey's,* *Warship*, etc. The author particularly wishes to acknowledge his debt to his friend and colleague Dr D L I Kirkpatrick who freely lent of the fruits of his own researches into the cost of battleships.

FIGURE 3: SUBMARINES AND ESCORTS

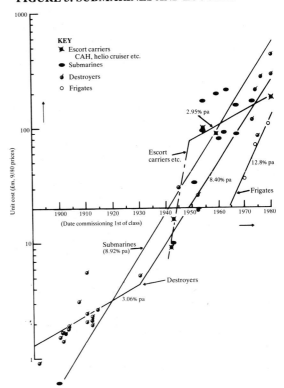

BOOK REVIEWS

THE SHIP OF THE LINE, VOLUME 2
Design, Construction and Fittings
by Brian Lavery
Published by Conway Maritime Press, April 1984
191pp (30cm × 25cm) 170 illustrations and diagrams,
index.
ISBN 0 85177 287 0. £20

THEY BUILT SHIPS OF THE LINE
'Take it all in all a Ship of the Line is the most
honourable thing that man, as a gregarious animal,
has ever produced.'
John Ruskin – *Harbours of England* (1856)

'They' built some 900 of these honourable ships
between 1640 and 1845 and the two volumes of Brian
Lavery's book *Ship of the Line* do full justice to the
builders. The publication of Volume II, which deals
with specific features of the ship, is a suitable occasion
on which to consider the whole work and to extend the
brief review of Volume I in Issue 30.

There has been no previous book on the subject
which has been able to use the full, official records. The
author points out that the Navy Board questionnaire on
sailing qualities, while still subjective, forced captains
to be specific about these aspects of the ship which were
good and those which were not. He also tries to put the
ship of the line into perspective showing what national
resources were available to the Navy in the form of
skilled men, money and scarce materials. The
Admiralty, then as now, had to make a balance
between the quantity and quality of its ships.

No single answer is given to the old question 'Were
British ships better or worse than those of our
enemies?' and indeed the careful reader will soon learn
that such a question is meaningless. However, Brian
Lavery shows that British ships were usually well fitted
to protect Great Britain from invasion, make the seas
fairly safe for British ships and deny such use to the
enemy. Volume I has 13 chapters:

The ship of the line was an unusual weapon system in
that its firepower could only be directed effectively at
right angles to its line of advance. It was this aspect of
the broadside armed ships which led to the concept of
fighting with the fleet in line ahead. This concept of the
line of battle was only fully established in 1653 and one
may well consider that this was the true birthday of the
line of battleship.

The introductory chapter sets the scene and describes
the early purpose-built fighting ships from the Armada
to the introduction of the battleline during the Dutch
Wars. Many of the British admirals had made their
name as generals in the New Model Army and were
accustomed to well-disciplined units moving in pre-
scribed formations. To such men the battleline was an
obvious step. The design of the ships was gradually
modified to concentrate heavy guns on the broadside
rather than arrange many lighter guns in a fore castle
and after castle, useful only in hand-to-hand boarding.

Under Charles II, considerable freedom was allowed
to the builder and many ships completed with greater
dimensions than planned – partly since payment was
based on tonnage completed. There was still conflict
between King and Parliament in the early years of the
Restoration and neither the number of ships nor their
quality could be sufficient because of lack of decision
and lack of money. The King and Pepys were finally
able to persuade Parliament in 1677 that the Royal
Navy was in a poor state and obtained funds for 30 new
ships. Conditions were imposed on the maximum
tonnage of each class which were unduly restrictive.
These restrictions had some logic as there was a
considerable shortage of suitable timber, a shortage
exacerbated by the need to rebuild London after the
Great Fire.

The growth of the French Navy led to another
building programme in 1690. Though the permitted
size of each class was increased, Parliament imposed

Title	Dates	Number of Ships
Galleons and the Great Ship	1588–1642	32
Frigates and the Line of Battle	1642–1660	60
Expansion and Enlargement	1660–1677	34
The First Great Shipbuilding Programme	1677–1688	40
The Wrong Turning	1688–1697	87
Stagnation sets in	1697–1714	142
The Age of the Establishments	1714–1739	83
The Impact of War	1739–1755	83
The Breakthrough	1755–1763	76
Stability and Defeat	1763–1783	107
The French Influence	1783–1801	74
The Limits of Technology	1801–1815	55
Last of the Line	1815–1845	37

further conditions on armament etc. The Royal Dockyards were busy with repair work and much of the new construction had to be put out to commercial yards, then inexperienced in warship work. This led to the Surveyor, Edward Dummer, imposing tighter control on the builders and insisting on rigid obedience to the specification. In Dummer's progressive hands this control was beneficial but it was to have unfortunate effects later.

During the late seventeenth and early eighteenth centuries stagnation set in. Politicians lost interest in the Navy, surveyors were selected who would not make risky innovation and, indeed, maintained that further improvement in the ships was impossible. It is unfortunate that the only previous history of the sailing warship, by John Charnock, concentrates on this period and even more unfortunate that all too many superficial works quote his criticisms, out of context, as referring to the Napoleonic War period.

By 1745 a new Board of Admiralty, of which Anson was the most effective member, was taking steps to remedy the situation. A committee was set up to consider proposals for the new 'Establishments' or list of approved dimensions. They recommended a considerable increase in size though falling well short of that suggested by Anson and his fellow reformers. Unfortunately, proposals for two-deck 74s were rejected in favour of more of the unsatisfactory three-deck 80s. A few 74s were built or converted by subterfuge and the capture of the French 74, *Invincible*, in 1747 led to further development of this class of ship.

The two-decker 74-gun ship was arguably the most effective wooden sailing ship. It could carry its lower guns sufficiently high above the water to be effective in bad weather without the excessive freeboard of the three-decker which made handling difficult in high winds. The gradually increasing length of the 74 gave them better speed, better seakeeping and, more important, greater space between guns which made them easier and faster to work.

The appointment of Sir Thomas Slade as Surveyor in 1755 led to a further improvement in designs. Though famous for his three-decker, *Victory*, it was for the design of big two-deckers that he most deserves credit. By 1757, when he designed the *Bellona*, 74, he had brought these ships to near perfection and many later designers were less successful. The 74-gun ship and other classes continued to increase in size as clearly shown in Brian Lavery's beautifully clear diagrams.

By the end of the eighteenth century, the extreme formality of the line of battle had been discredited and the Royal Navy was winning by breaking the line and forcing close action. The carronade, a close-range, lightweight gun firing a heavy ball, was the ideal weapon for such fighting and carronades were fitted from 1779 to the forecastle and quarterdecks of many ships. There were other technical innovations such as the copper sheathing that protected the bottom against the teredo worm so giving longer life while at the same time delaying and reducing the extent of fouling. Fouling could reduce the speed of a ship by one or two

knots (sometimes more) and the tactical advantage of a coppered fleet over one not so protected was considerable. This development is discussed in Volume II but its significance is perhaps undervalued. There is no mention of the improvements in ventilation at the end of the eighteenth century which did much to improve the health of the ship's timber as well as that of the crew.

The Royal Navy entered the long wars with Revolutionary France in good shape. Its ships of the same gunpower were somewhat smaller than those of its enemies and there were more ships in the smaller classes. This emphasis on large numbers of smaller ships is inevitable for a navy which seeks to control the sea with limited resources. The French Navy, seeking to deny or interrupt our use of the sea, could afford to build few, bigger ships. The French view of British ships is rarely quoted but seems to have been generally favourable. In particular, the French accounts frequently state that ships of their own design, captured by the Royal Navy, performed better in British hands due to greater skill in adjusting trim, rigging, etc.

It is perhaps unfortunate that Chapter 12 (1801–1815) should be titled 'The Limits of Technology' as the developments after 1815 led to a very great increase in the size of ships and an even greater increase in their fighting capacity.

The years 1815 to 1845 were an era of great feuds over warship design and it is hard to be impartial. As a naval architect I regard the closing of the School of Naval Architecture and the dismissal of Sir Robert Seppings in 1832 as disasters. The ultimate success of the School was demonstrated by mid-century when its great graduates such as Isaac Watts and Thomas Lloyd were designing the ships of the navy and graduates of only slightly lesser ability were the new style Master Shipwrights responsible for building them.

Seppings' work is discussed at length in Volume II, but I still feel is not given sufficient credit. He had a view of the unity of ship design embracing strength, stability, seakeeping and long life which was unique amongst his predecessors and contemporaries. Incidentally, he was a great supporter of the School of Naval Architecture and their rivalry in design was on a friendly basis.

Sir William Symonds had considerable skill as a yacht designer and the favour he won from yacht owning politicians led to him becoming the first non-technical Surveyor in 1832. In some degree he used his political connections wisely and to the benefit of the Navy. He was able to win approval for a further increase in size of each class of ship and he implemented a longstanding proposal from the School to standardise the spars of all classes so that a big ship's smaller spars were interchangeable with the bigger items of small ships. He also gave his ships more beam which together with the high metacentre of his 'peg tapped' form gave them sufficient stability to reduce the weight of ballast required. However, depending as he did on revelation rather than calculation, Symonds overdid his stability.

His designs were notorious for rapid, heavy rolling

which is a sign of excess stability, not the reverse as suggested in Volume II. As well as making them a poor gun platform this rolling led to rapid wear in the rigging. Symonds himself only claimed credit for the proportions and form of his ships and the actual design was in the hands of a former master shipwright, John Edye, who is not mentioned in the book. Edye was an extremely competent but uninspired designer who was able to extend Seppings' work on iron diagonals in frigates to the battlefleet. It seems reasonable caution on Seppings' part to introduce this novel feature in frigates while using well-tried materials in the biggest ships.

Volume II deals specifically with hull design and construction, decoration, masts, sails and rigging and with fittings, accommodation and armament. Hull design was an unscientific process throughout the era and discussion was mainly centred on various geometrical constructions to produce a fair form. In later years, experience led to the development of forms which met the requirements well. The designers of the period believed that the shape of the midship section affected the sailing performance of the ship and this view is supported by the author. In fact, midship section shape as opposed to area has virtually no effect on resistance though it would have had some effect on course keeping under sail.

The description of hull construction is clear and generally comprehensive though one would have wished for more on nineteenth century changes. In particular there is no mention of the virtual replacement of beam knees by shelf pieces. The changing style of decoration is important to the modern student as it is the best clue to the date of an unknown painting or model. It is interesting that warship decoration became almost non-existent in Victorian times when decoration work ashore was increasing.

The development of masts, yards, sails and rigging go well together and the changes are clarified by further simple diagrams. The making of ropes and sails is explained and the way in which the whole complicated sail plan was assembled is discussed. Another chapter deals with anchors and capstans, rudders and their gear pumps and boats. The boats were an important part of the armament of a ship being used for cutting out and landing parties. Well chosen illustrations show how several hundred men were packed into the lower deck of a battleship. The officers were better off but even the most aristocratic junior officer would have little more than a dog kennel in which to sleep and a very small part of a dingy and ill-furnished wardroom in which to eat.

The author has not set out to write a treatise on armament but the chapter on this subject is clear and comprehensive.

Like Volume I, the second book concludes with the reproduction of a number of important and fascinating documents which add verisimilitude to the lengthy list of references. There is a little less entirely novel material in Volume II than in its predecessor but nowhere else can such a full account be found in a single volume. Together the two books cover the history of the British line-of-battleship as no other book has ever tried to do.

D K Brown

OTHER BOOKS RECEIVED

Operations of the Fremantle Submarine Base 1942—1945 by David Creed (The Naval Historical Society of Australia, May 1984), 64pp, 26 photographs, ISBN 0 909153 09 4, 5½in × 8½in paperback. A compact booklet this, devoting individual chapters to the US Navy operations in the years 1942–45 as well as chapters detailing British and Dutch submarine activity at Fremantle. The human element is not neglected in this concise account.

The Flying 400, Canada's Hydrofoil Project by Thomas G Lynch (Nimbus Publishing Limited, June 1984) 128pp, 25 photographs, 12 line drawings, appendices, index, ISBN 0 920852 22 X, 10in × 8in paperback. An explorative account of the experimental *Bras d'Or* hydrofoil developed by the Canadians. Much technical data backs up the more human story of endeavour and perseverance which went into this ship's building. And all to no purpose: the ship was decommissioned in 1972, became a museum exhibit and is now the source of much controversy.

The Pollen Papers: The Privately Circulated Printed Works of Arthur Hungerford Pollen 1901–1916, edited by Jon Tetsuro Sumida (George Allen & Unwin/Navy Records Society Vol 124, June 1984) 405pp, index £6.50/£17.50, ISBN 0 04942 182 4, 6in × 9¼in. A technical account, by any standards, of the designs and ideas behind the fire control systems developed by Pollen (1866–1937). Naval gunnery in general is also touched on giving comprehensive coverage of this complicated subject.

Aircraft Carriers of the World, 1914 to the Present: an Illustrated Encyclopaedia by Roger Chesneau (Arms & Armour Press, June 1984) 288pp, over 400 photographs and line drawings, index, £19.95, ISBN 0 85368 636 X, 9¾in × 10in. Perhaps one of the most substantial offerings of recent months, this book can rightly claim to be a 'first' in that *every* carrier ever built is listed and illustrated. The information is presented in two sections; the first is more general covering development, design and rôle and contains photographs of early seaplane carriers as well as some well-presented statistics. The majority of pages are taken up by a gazetteer of the carriers listed alphabetically by country commencing with the brief Argentinian entry and the ill-starred *25 de Mayo* and rounding off with the 82pp US section.

HMS Thunderer, The Story of the Royal Naval Engineering College Keyham and Manadon by Geoffrey Penn (Kenneth Mason, May 1984) 208pp, 41 photographs, bibliography, index, £12.95, ISBN 0 85837 321 5, 5½in × 9¾in. An historical account back to the coming of steam, drawing on numerous quotations – many very amusing – from former students and portraying life both inside and outside teaching hours. The ways in which the college has had to adapt over the years are well documented and there is a forward-looking final chapter surveying Manadon's future role.

Fleet Command by Paul Beaver (Ian Allan, June 1984) 48pp, 85 photographs, £2.95, ISBN 0 71101 387 0, 8¼in × 11¼in paperback. Second in a series covering Britain's armed forces, this brief and straightforward survey contains four well-illustrated chapters: Organisation, Warships, Weapons and In Action. If you want to know the facts without ploughing through too much text, this is the place to find them.

Vom Kanal zum Kaukasus: Die 3.R-Flotille, Feuerwehr an allen Fronten by Gerd-Dietrick Schneider (Koehler, 1982), 292pp, 66 photographs, tables, diagrams, maps, DM 39.80, ISBN 3 7822 0260 0, 6¼in × 9¾in. A well-produced book devoted to a fairly neglected topic – minesweeper operations during the Second World War. The author, himself a member of the 3rd Minesweeping Flotilla, details operations in Norway (1940), transport of boats overland to the Black Sea and the many operations which took place there. Helpful maps and diagrams augment the text.

Modern Combat Ships 1: 'Leander Class' by Cdr C J Meyer OBE, RN (Ian Allan, July 1984), 112pp, 162 photographs, 6 line illustrations, appendices, no index, £6.95, ISBN 0 7110 1385 3, 6½in × 9½in. A valuable survey by a serving submarine officer of the highly successful frigate design that still forms half the RN strength in that category, nor are the 18 *Leander*s serving India, Australasia, the Netherlands and Chile neglected. There are chapters on 1960s, 1970s, and 1980s operations as well as the class's technical evolution. The appendices give their predecessors, battle honours and associations as well as weapon/data handling systems, helicopters and a class list.

A's & A's

6IN HOWITZER (*Warship* 30, photograph p141) from N J M Campbell, Ryde, Isle of Wight.

The photograph of a 6in howitzer from Ian Sturton is most interesting. Altogether 5 were mounted afloat in the earlier part of the Dardanelles campaign, one on each turret of *Majestic* and *Prince George* and another on one of the turrets in *Canopus*. The ammunition returns show that the following shells were fired.

		Common	HE
Majestic	1.3.1915	26	8
	6.3.1915	61	5
	10.3.1915	6	10
Prince George	9.3.1915	69	nil
Canopus	3/7.3.1915	5	1
	13/16.3.1915	13	nil

The type of howitzer was the 6in/30cwt of 14 calibres firing a 100lb shell at 857fs with a max range of *c*7000yds. The mounting is hidden by the improvised shield but was probably the standard high elevation 70° version. In this the wheels of the 35° field mounting were removed, the trail lowered on to a pivot plate and an upper carriage added to raise the cradle trunnions. The howitzer was of obsolete design but was all that was in service at the time apart from the 12 calibre 6in/25cwt special to India. This had the same performance and was similar or identical to Elswick Pattern A. The 12.2 calibre 19¾cwt 6in Pattern B, firing a 100lb shell at 1000fs, was mounted in the Argentine gunboats *Parana* and *Rosario*. Vickers Mark A of 15.75 calibres and 18¾cwt was of more modern type with MV 1150fs when firing a 100lb shell. One was mounted in the submarine *E 20* for Dardanelles service, and it was suggested that the old name carronade be revived as the special mounting only allowed 22° instead of the usual high angle for howitzers. *E 20* was however lost before this could be implemented.

THE PERFORMANCE OF SAILING WARSHIPS
(*Warship 30 The Ship of the Line* book review p139) from Brian Lavery, London NW10.

Almost all the precise evidence available on the speed and sailing qualities of warships in the age of sail is to be found in the Sailing Reports which were made out on printed forms by the captains of the ships, and sent to the Navy Board in London. Hundreds of these can now be found in the Adm 95 series in the Public Record Office at Kew. They are not indexed, and are only crudely sorted into chronological and alphabetical order, so to find a report on an individual ship may involve searching through several volumes. While preparing *Ship of the Line* I searched all the volumes which were available (some were withdrawn for rather long periods for repair) and made notes on all the ships of the line. There is evidence that captains were expected to complete some form of sailing report by the third quarter of the seventeenth century, but the earliest ones in the PRO collection date from 1742. A few isolated examples are to be found in other collections, such as the National Maritime Museum.

The printed questionnaire is too long to reproduce here, but can be found on page 209 of *The Ship of the Line*, and on pages 174–5 of R F Johnson's *The Royal George*. Regarding the maximum speeds obtained, the important questions are no 3 – 'How she proves in sailing through all varieties of the wind, from being a point or two abaft the beam, to its veering forward upon the bowline in every strength of gale, especially in a stiff gale, and a head sea; and how many knots she runs in each circumstances; and how she carries her helm.' – and in question 4 – 'The most knots she runs before the wind, and how she rolls in the trough of the sea'. In the case of *Invincible*, the answer to question 3 was 'I have gone 13 knots large (*ie* with the wind on the beam or astern) and 8 by the wind, and would have went more could I have made proper sail. Carries her helm generally half a turn a-weather'. It is surprising how often the maximum speed is found to be with the wind directly astern. It is generally believed that sailing ships performed best with the wind on the quarter, for with the wind astern one sail was often masked by another. Another surprise is the speed of some ships. The *Royal Oak* of 1769, for example, was said to be capable of 14kts. I have not examined any reports on frigates or smaller vessels, and it is possible that some of them were even faster.

Such speeds, of course, could only be attained on the very rare occasions when wind and sea conditions were perfect, and were often largely irrelevant to the more useful qualities of a ship of the line, such as stability and seakeeping. Most ships would spend their days in blockade service or as part of a fleet, and would never have the opportunity to test their best speed. Those ships which already had a reputation for speed would be chosen for individual tasks and for pursuits, and would thus be given an opportunity to enhance their reputation. Another surprising feature of the sailing reports is that, though they give the captain full opportunity to boast about the maximum speeds attained, they ask nothing about performance in light winds, or about how close a ship could sail to the wind.

The sailing report was generally compiled at the end of a commission, perhaps after three years, and would therefore not be affected by the cleanness of a ship's bottom, for she would have entered drydock several times during that period. Thus, for example, a report was compiled on *Bellona* on 28 May 1783, as she waited to pay off after the American War. Her captain, Richard Onslow, had been in command since February 1780, and since then the ship had been docked twice.

The measurement of a ship's speed was very crude, by any standards. A piece of wood (the log) was thrown over the side, at the same time as an hour glass was turned over. Attached to the wood was a line with knots tied in it at fixed intervals, and the line was allowed to run out until the glass emptied, when the line was stopped – hence the expression 'how many knots she runs'. Obviously a captain who was impressed with his ship would tend to round up the figures slightly, while another would not even try to reach maximum speed, even it he was given the opportunity.

But, apart from adding a few extra questions to the sailing reports, it is difficult to see how the naval administrators of the times could have done any more to assess the performance of their ships on actual operational service. The documents in the PRO give us a record of the real performance of sailing ships which is probably unique in the world.

SPEED AND RESISTANCE (*Warship* 30 *The Ship of the Line* book review p139) from D K Brown RCNC

A very interesting letter has been received from Mr P G Pugh CEng, MRAeS of Bedford disagreeing with my comments in the review of Volume I, on the speed of the *Invincible* (1747). First, I must confess to an elementary error in equating power to resistance. The resistance of a floating body at low speeds increases approximately as the square of the speed and the power as the cube. Such a law applies exactly if the engineers' conditions of dynamic similarity are satisfied. Under these conditions 13 knots would require a propulsion force 40 per cent greater than 11 knots or 65 per cent more power.

At higher speeds the effects of wave making lead to a more rapid increase in resistance. Fig 1 shows the resistance curve of HMS *Victory* from model tests carried out by G S Baker at the National Physical Laboratory. It will be seen that the square law is followed quite closely up to 10 knots and that above that speed resistance beings to increase more rapidly. Comparison of resistance when wave making is important can be made at equal values of speed/√Length (V/√L). On this basis one would expect the resistance of *Invincible* to depart from the square law at a speed of about 9½ knots and increase more rapidly than (speed)².

The driving power required to drive *Invincible* at 13 knots would be more than 40 per cent greater than that for a similar ship at 11 knots.

Mr Pugh then suggests that *Invincible* had a better shape than contemporary British ships and could carry more sail, giving her a greater driving force. Both these suggestions are likely to be right but it is very difficult to say what their effect on speed would be.

Resistance per ton of displacement would be reduced by increased length. However the length of *Invincible* compared with that of *Chichester* (1745 establishment) has increased by 7 per cent while her beam is 10 per cent more. The critical parameter is immersed volume/(length)³ and even if they had the same draught (unlikely) the displacement would go up by 17.7 per cent and L³ by 22 per cent, a very small change in volume /L³. This rough analysis assumes that waterline length varied in the same proportion as length on the gun deck and, more important, that the lines of the hulls were similar.

The resistance of a modern warship can be regarded, approximately, as made up of two components only, the friction of the water past the side and the pressure forces associated with wave making. This simple division omits what is known as viscous pressure resistance due to the separation of eddies etc. This force can be neglected in modern ships but was quite large in eighteenth century vessels, perhaps a quarter of the total.

The evidence seems clear that *Invincible* had a good form which probably implied that eddy making was less than usual. However, even if eddy making were eliminated entirely, which is inconceivable in a vessel of *Invincible*'s proportions, the reduction of drag would only add 1 knot to her speed. It seems likely that the benefits of form are unlikely to account for more than half this amount and probably much less.

Perhaps more important is the power to carry sail. By the late nineteenth century the 'power to carry sail' was defined as

$$\frac{\text{Displacement} \times \text{metacentric height}}{\text{Sail area} \times \text{height of centre of effort of sails above half draught}}$$

In the mid-eighteenth century the concept of the metacentre was unknown in England and probably not used in design in France. However, generations of experience had probably arrived at rules of thumb with similar results. Now, the extra beam of *Invincible* would probably have given her a greater metacentric height, roughly in proportion to the increase in beam. One might expect sail area to increase in the ratio of displacements times the ratio of beams, say 1.12 × 1.1 = 1.23 ie 23 per cent more sail. However, the larger sails had to propel a bigger ship. The relevant parameter is the ratio of sail area to wetted area of the hull so that the effective driving force (corrected for difference in hull size) was roughly proportional to

$$\frac{\text{sail area}}{(\text{displacement})^{2/3}}$$

and would increase by about 14 per cent. This would

HMS VICTORY – RESISTANCE
(based on G S Baker's Model Tests)

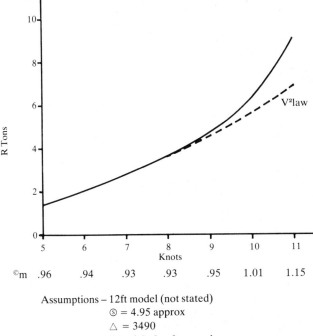

Assumptions – 12ft model (not stated)
ⓢ = 4.95 approx
△ = 3490
Froude's ○ values apply

Ref: G S Baker 6th Andrew Laing Lecture NEC I

give an increase in speed of less than 7 per cent or just over half a knot.

Thus compared with a British 70-gun ship of the 1745 establishment one would expect *Invincible* to gain (a) less than half a knot from form and (b) about half a knot from increased sail area. Following an interesting correspondence, Mr Pugh has reached virtually identical results from a slightly different approach.

In the mid-eighteenth century ships were not copper sheathed and would foul very quickly. It does not take many months in these conditions for the resistance of a ship to double or even more. Fouling is also very variable in its rate of increase depending much on the temperature of the water the ship has experienced in previous months, the locality and the amount of salt in the water. (Fresh water will kill many types of fouling.)

When copper sheathing was introduced to the Royal Navy in the late 1770s, such British ships soon began to show a marked speed advantage over the unsheathed French ship. Knight (ref 1) quotes several examples, including Rodney's action off Gibraltar in 1780, which suggest a speed advantage to the British fleet of at least a knot. A rather tentative analysis of the speed trials of early wooden steam battleships again suggests 1–1½knots as a likely effect of fouling for even copper will foul after about a year in sea water.

The claimed speed of 13 knots for *Invincible* comes

from Navy Board questionnaires filled in by every commanding officer and explained in an accompanying note by Brian Lavery. There are many records showing British ships of the 1745 establishment to have a best speed of about 12 knots with 11 more common. *Invincible* was clearly better as he knows but enthusiasm for what was clearly a fine ship may have lead to exaggeration. The measurements were made using the best instrument available, the log, but it was very crude and errors all too likely. After 1755 there was a noticeable improvement in the speed of British 74s.

To sum up, I accept that *Invincible* was noticeably better than contemporary British designs. However, the difference in hull form and sail area are unlikely to have been the cause of more than 1 knot in speed and most probably less. Fouling is certainly capable of reducing the speed of any one ship by much more than a knot and the differences between ships can be great. While the brevity of my comment in the earlier review may have overstated the case, I do not believe that I was significantly wrong.

Ref 1 'The Introduction of Copper Sheathing into the RN 1770–1786' by R J B Knight, *The Mariner's Mirror* 1979.

BATTLESHIPS IN TRANSITION

The Creation of the Steam Battlefleet 1815–1860

Andrew Lambert

The period between 1815 and 1860 is the great neglected area of naval history, due to the historical obsession with both extremities of the period – the Napoleonic Wars overshadow any subsequent naval conflicts, while there is a misguided belief that the introduction of the ironclad around 1860 is the only technical development worthy of note. In fact, between these dates the construction, hull design, armament, propulsion and tactics of the battlefleet changed beyond recognition. Of these factors, the introduction of steam power and the screw propeller and the shell gun had the most significant impact – and this is the first book to study the influence of these advances on ship design, and international politics (for the wooden steam-driven ship of the line became a political scare weapon – the Cruise missile of the 1840s – and provoked the first ever 'Arms Race' between the Great Powers). This book serves therefore as well as a technical history of a fascinating period and a study of a neglected area of naval history (including the Crimean War) as a salutary reminder that one generation's super weapon is often forgotten by the next.

240 × 184mm (9½″ × 7¼″), 160 pages, 120 illustrations. ISBN 0 85177 215 X. **£11.95** (plus £1.50 post and packing)

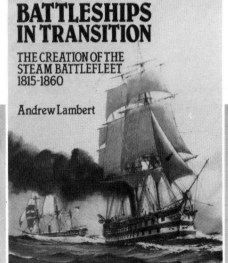

From your local bookseller or from

Conway Maritime Press Ltd,
24 Bride Lane, London EC4Y 8DR.